D1064254

TRENDS IN
BEHAVIOR THERAPY

TRENDS IN BEHAVIOR THERAPY

Edited by

PER-OLOW SJÖDÉN

Department of Psychology
University of Uppsala
Uppsala, Sweden

SANDRA BATES

Østmarka Hospital
Institute of Psychiatry
University of Trondheim
Trondheim, Norway

WILLIAM S. DOCKENS, III

Department of Psychology
University of Uppsala
Uppsala, Sweden

With a Foreword by B. F. Skinner

ACADEMIC PRESS   New York   San Francisco   London   1979

A Subsidiary of Harcourt Brace Jovanovich, Publishers

COPYRIGHT © 1979, BY ACADEMIC PRESS, INC.
ALL RIGHTS RESERVED.
NO PART OF THIS PUBLICATION MAY BE REPRODUCED OR
TRANSMITTED IN ANY FORM OR BY ANY MEANS, ELECTRONIC
OR MECHANICAL, INCLUDING PHOTOCOPY, RECORDING, OR ANY
INFORMATION STORAGE AND RETRIEVAL SYSTEM, WITHOUT
PERMISSION IN WRITING FROM THE PUBLISHER.

ACADEMIC PRESS, INC.
111 Fifth Avenue, New York, New York 10003

United Kingdom Edition published by
ACADEMIC PRESS, INC. (LONDON) LTD.
24/28 Oval Road, London NW1 7DX

Library of Congress Cataloging in Publication Data

Main entry under title:

Trends in behavior therapy.

    Includes bibliographies and index.
    1. Behavior therapy. I. Sjoden, Per—Olow.
II. Bates, Sandra. [DNLM: 1. Behavior therapy.
WM425 T794]
RC489.B4T73   616.8'914   79—6959
ISBN 0—12—647450—8

PRINTED IN THE UNITED STATES OF AMERICA

79 80 81 82   9 8 7 6 5 4 3 2 1

Contents

I   CONCEPTUAL ISSUES

1   The Present State and Future Trends of Behavior Therapy   3

NATHAN H. AZRIN

2   Treating the Real, Not the Concept   13

LEONARD P. ULLMANN

List of Contributors

Numbers in parentheses indicate the pages on which the authors' contributions begin.

LYN Y. ABRAMSON (69), Department of Psychology, State University of New York at Stony Brook, Stony Brook, New York 11794

TEODORO AYLLON (353), Department of Psychology, Georgia State University, Atlanta, Georgia 30303

NATHAN H. AZRIN (3), Anna Mental Health and Development Center, Anna, Illinois 62906

BRIAN W. BAUSKE (331), Oregon Social Learning Center, Eugene, Oregon 97401

CHARLES B. FERSTER (23), Department of Psychology, American University, Washington, D.C. 20016

RANDALL P. GRANT (135), Department of Psychiatry, University of Pennsylvania, Philadelphia, Pennsylvania 19104

IVER HAND (269), University Hospital, Department of Psychiatry, Behavior Therapy Outpatient Unit, D-2000 Hamburg 20, West Germany

HENRY KANDEL (353), Department of Psychology, Georgia State University, Atlanta, Georgia 30303

KATHLEEN KELLY (353), Foothills Area Mental Health/Mental Retardation Program, Marion, North Carolina 28752

ROBERT PAUL LIBERMAN (249, 369), Department of Psychiatry, University of California, Camarillo State Hospital, Camarillo, California 93010

MELVIN LYON (153), Department of Psychology, University of Copenhagen and Central Laboratory, E., Sct. Hans Hospital, Roskilde, Denmark

MICHAEL J. MAHONEY (39), Department of Psychology, Pennsylvania State University, University Park, Pennsylvania 16802

DONALD MEICHENBAUM (55), Department of Psychology, University of Waterloo, Waterloo, Ontario, Canada

SUZANNE M. MILLER (135), Department of Psychiatry, University of Pennsylvania, Philadelphia, Pennsylvania 19104

ARNE ÖHMAN (107), Institute of Psychology, University of Bergen, Bergen, Norway

GERALD R. PATTERSON (331), Oregon Social Learning Center, Eugene, Oregon 97401

R. W. RAMSAY (217), Department of Psychology, University of Amsterdam, Amsterdam, The Netherlands

STEN RÖNNBERG (181), Department of Education, University of Stockholm, Stockholm, Sweden

BRENDA L. ROPER (299), Marriage and Family Counseling Bureau, University of Utah, Salt Lake City, Utah 84112

MARTIN E. P. SELIGMAN (69), Department of Psychology, University of Pennsylvania, Philadelphia, Pennsylvania 19104

RICHARD B. STUART (299), Marriage and Family Counseling Bureau, University of Utah, Salt Lake City, Utah 84112

JOHN D. TEASDALE (69), Department of Psychiatry, University of Oxford, The Warneford Hospital, Oxford OX3 7JX, England

JAMES TEIGEN (249), Tri-Counties Regional Center for Developmental Disabilities, San Luis Obispo, California 93401

MARLEN TICHATZKY (269), University Hospital, Department of Psychiatry, Behavior Therapy Outpatient Unit, D-2000 Hamburg 20, West Germany

LEONARD P. ULLMANN (13), Department of Psychology, University of Hawaii, Honolulu, Hawaii 96822

MARK R. WEINROTT (331), Evaluation Research Group, Eugene, Oregon 97401

G. TERENCE WILSON (199), Graduate School of Applied and Professional Psychology, Rutgers University, Piscataway, New Jersey 08854

Foreword

Behavior therapy is only one part of what the public has come to know as behavior modification, or what is more precisely defined as the application of an experimental analysis of behavior. The papers in this volume therefore testify all the more eloquently to the explosive nature of the movement as a whole. Historians would seem to have every reason to speak of a great, liberating idea. In doing so, however, they would violate the very principle upon which the movement rests.

Behaviorism, as an active philosophy of a science of human behavior, is a product of the twentieth century. A few practical consequences were soon glimpsed, but a related technology did not appear before the third quarter of the century—after the central position had been solidly established in the laboratory. The crucial issue in both the science and the technology concerns the location of the "causes" of behavior.

We all have parts of the universe within our skin, and these private worlds are unquestionably important to us. The things we "feel" are much closer to us than the public world, and it is not surprising that for more than 2000 years they were put first in explaining behavior. People acted, it was said, because they *willed* to act, according to their *beliefs* or *expectations*, with *purposes* or *intentions*, as they *perceived* the world around them rather than as the world really was, with the help of acquired *knowledge*, recalling stored *memories*, expressing *ideas*, exhibiting traits of *character*, and so on. Psychoanalysis was a brilliant, perhaps a culminating, systematic organization of supposed internal causes of behavior of that sort.

The behavioristic explanations of facts that are said to demonstrate the existence of so-called mental states or processes would use genetic and personal histories. For example, evidence that is said to show that a person has an idea is related to past or present circumstances. That can be done without mentioning the idea. Fragmentary introspective data are dismissed as merely collateral to the central fact.

The liberating effect of this practice (not of "this idea!") is not surprising. The private world of the behaving individual has always been hard to reach. States and processes within the skin are not even well known by the person whose skin it is (that is why we have had so many systems of psychology). Mere inferences about a private world do not satisfactorily explain supposed public manifestations. The procedure of psychoanalysis testifies to these difficulties; it would be hard to prove that psychoanalysis does not solve problems by changing a mental apparatus, but it can easily be shown that it changes the patient's world—is, indeed, for a time an important part of that world—and may have its demonstrated effects for that reason.

Unlike the "depths of the mind" (a phrase that appeals because it suggests profundity), the environmental variables of which behavior is a function can be identified, changed, and supplemented. The behavioristic shift in emphasis from internal to external causes quite naturally led to a flood of practical applications. An early stimulus–response formula was too simple and seriously misleading, but once the role of the causal environment was properly understood, a flourishing technology was inevitable. The papers in this volume show some of the consequences.

B. F. SKINNER

Preface

Trends in Behavior Therapy is an up-to-date presentation of the state of the art by contributors from both sides of the Atlantic. The continual evaluation the publication of this treatise represents allows us to take stock of the field of behavior therapy. The book does not confine itself to an examination of the theoretical foundations of behavior therapy, nor to a presentation of effective methods of treatment. Rather, it seeks to give equal weight both to conceptual issues and to applications.

The original impetus for this book came during the International Congress of Behaviour Therapy held in Uppsala, Sweden in August, 1977, at which researchers and clinicians gathered to exchange ideas and results from a vast variety of fields and interests. In order to allow others to share the fruits of this congress, the contributions dealing with its major themes were combined with solicited articles to yield the volume you now hold in your hands.

Part I covers conceptual issues dealing with the flow of ideas and methods from the laboratory to the clinic and back again, and with the topical concern of the place of cognition in behavior modification. In Part II, the theme of laboratory–clinic interchange is developed further by presenting experimental models of such central clinical problems as depression, phobias, neurotic anxiety, and drug addiction. Part III is concerned with applications of behavior therapy in selected problem areas and presents a veritable smörgåsbord of innovative and multifarious approaches to a wide range of problems. In addition to contributions to more conventional clinical areas such as alcoholism, obesity, and obsessive–compulsive behaviors, there are chapters dealing with areas that have received comparatively little clinical and research attention from behavior therapists, namely pathological grief and marital problems. Part IV deals with another seldom-discussed complex of issues: that of the various obstacles of a political and organizational nature that hinder the development of treatment programs.

The clinician may find this book valuable for its explicit descriptions and empirical studies of treatment methods as well as for the elucidation of the theoretical underpinnings of behavior therapy. Furthermore, the extensive presentations of laboratory models of clinically relevant problems provide a rich soil for the development of novel treatment approaches. Researchers interested in the development of constructs and the testing of ideas in the laboratory will find discussions of laboratory–clinic interchange in the first two sections of the book. Students familiar with the basic concepts of behavior therapy and the advanced student of psychology can use this book as an introduction to the central areas of discussion and research within behavior therapy, as well as to novel developments in the field.

The strength of this book lies in its combination of discussions of central issues and reports of the development of treatment methods based on these issues. Behavior therapy has often been called a collection of methods. Not only do we believe this to be a false assertion, as attested to by Part I of this book, but we believe that behavior therapy possesses methods that work more effectively in most areas than methods derived from other theoretical backgrounds.

The Executive Committee of the International Congress of Behaviour Therapy, including Professor K. Gunnar Götestam and Dr. Lennart Melin, have generously given of their time and energy in the first draft of several chapters of this book. To them we extend our sincere thanks. We are indebted to Rosemari Finn, who typed the final copy of several chapters. The three remaining members of the executive committee, the co-editors of *Trends in Behavior Therapy*, have continued the editing process, and share final responsibility for the end product, together with the individual authors. It has been an enriching experience to have been part of the sifting and winnowing of material for this book, and we feel that it provides a valid sample of trends in the growth of behavior therapy.

TRENDS IN
BEHAVIOR THERAPY

I
CONCEPTUAL ISSUES

1

The Present State and Future Trends of Behavior Therapy

NATHAN H. AZRIN

All too often we discuss the present and future of behavior therapy and neglect any discussion of the past. Not only do we avoid getting entangled in long discussions of our patients' childhoods, but we also tend to overlook the beginnings of our own profession. But as we have often been reminded, those who ignore their history are doomed to repeat it.

From my own perspective, I would relish a return to the past, to those days when keeping abreast of the field was a simple task. The first journal in operant conditioning, the *Journal of the Experimental Analysis of Behavior*, was begun in 1958, when a small group of individuals felt that the existing journals were not suitable for this new field. From that journal, which dealt primarily with animal learning, arose an interest in the application of operant principles to practical problems and a need for other journals. But, whereas the animal operant conditioning field today continues to be a "one-journal" field, with that first journal containing almost all of the new findings of importance, behavior therapy has expanded greatly. The concepts of behaviorism, determinism, and conditioning, which seemed so radical and implausible at first, now seem to be part of a popular movement. The acceptance of these concepts by so many has caused some of us to pause and wonder whether these views could have been so profound if they met with such ready acceptance. Somehow it seems easier to believe one's work is important when everyone else is in opposition to it.

3

Copyright © 1979 by Academic Press, Inc.
All rights of reproduction in any form reserved.
ISBN 0-12-647450-8

A distinctive feature of behavior therapy today is that it has no identifiable father figure—no Sigmund Freud. We do have Pavlov, Skinner,
Eysenck, Wolpe, Bijou, and other princes, but there is no king whose
pronouncements can be quoted to establish truth in the face of conflicting
facts. And since most of these princes are still alive, it is difficult to assign
mystical wisdom to their early utterances. Lacking this ultimate authority,
the field must rely on its evidence to establish the truth of its statements:
"Let the data speak for themselves."

GROWTH OF THE FIELD

The Increase in the Number of Behavior Therapists

In the beginning of behavior therapy, almost all of the operant con-
ditioners were located in the eastern United States and belonged to professional psychologist organizations. Thus we could conveniently meet to
discuss new findings at the annual conventions each year. Now behavior
therapists are to be found in a host of professions ranging from the medical
practitioners to business consultants and city planners. The number of
conventions held could keep any behavior therapist globe-trotting for
every week of the year. The children of the early behavior therapists are
part of a population explosion that shows itself in sheer numbers.

At the moment, three separate national organizations of behaviorists
exist in the United States alone: the Division of the Experimental Analysis
of Behavior of the American Psychological Association, the Association for
the Advancement of Behavior Therapy, and the most recently formed, the
Midwestern Association of Behavior Analysis. Outside the United States
there are over 20 national organizations, primarily in Europe, but even
Australia and New Zealand are represented. In addition, there are dozens
of regional and local associations of behaviorists. To meet the demand for
information about behavior therapy, workshops are given regularly, not
only by the professional organizations, but also by local institutions. Thus,
behavior therapy is no longer a highly specialized field that is of interest
only to a small number of highly trained individuals.

We have not only grown in sheer numbers, but also in the variety of
directions taken. The evidence of the growth of behavior therapy has
shown itself in a number of ways, many of them surprising because they
seem contrary to some of the presumed identifying characteristics of the
field.

The Diversity of Behavior Therapy Journals

Given the extensive geographical distribution, the increase in the
number of individuals and the diversity of fields, it is not surprising to find

that another indicator of the growth of behavior therapy has been the increased number of journals specifically devoted to behavioral topics. Dr. Goldiamond recently pointed out to me that there are now 13 new journals that deal exclusively with behavior therapy. The number of subscribers to most of these journals can be measured in the thousands. In fact, the largest journal, which is the *Journal of Applied Behavior Analysis*, has more subscribers than most of the general psychology journals. These numbers may be taken as evidence of the field's growing popularity, but of even greater interest is the diversity of titles found among the journals.

Behavior therapy arose in part out of a strong emphasis on empirical and experimental evaluation rather than on speculation and philosophizing. Traditional therapists engaged in lengthy discussions of whether or not it was morally right to treat a particular patient or whether an aggressive outburst was an indication of transference or insufficient sublimation. Behavior therapists were most interested in producing measurable change through clearly designed treatment procedures that could be replicated by others. Now, surprisingly, we find a journal dealing specifically with the philosophy of behavior studies—the journal *Behaviorism*.

Behavior therapy has long been in opposition to the once so prevalent medical model of psychological problems, as evidenced by Ullmann and Krasner's (1975) formulation. This model (see Ullmann, Chapter 2 of this volume), with its emphasis on traditional diagnostic procedures, seeks to discover the internal pathological defects behind the visible symptomatic behavior problems. Thus, it tends to foster the concept of a passive patient who should be taken care of. However, we now have a new journal called *Behavioral Medicine*.

Skinner's early writings (1938) gave voice to behavior therapy's protest against traditional concepts of mentalism, cognitions, and inner psychic causes. These were concepts that had been cherished by various psychological schools for decades, concepts that were easy to discuss but difficult to measure. In those days it was unusual to trust "mere" self-report. Now, a new journal called *Cognitive Therapy and Research* has been founded.

Behavior therapy early protested the dominance of analysis, especially psychoanalysis. Preoccupation with the past, an enterprise that was immune to verification or invalidation, was deemed unprofitable for study. Instead, behavior therapy turned its attention toward the future and concentrated on prediction and control of future behavior. Despite this point of view, the most widely read journal seems to substitute body for mind or behavior for psyche, so that we have the *Journal of the Experimental Analysis of Behavior*.

Although we were fervent opponents of the disease model of behavior, believing that behavior is not cured by subjecting it to *therapy*, we now find at least three journals with just that term—behavior therapy—in their titles. As still another example, the behaviorists were among the first to be challenged by legal questions (Wexler, 1973) concerning the use of procedures that modified or controlled people. Few of these early encounters with the law could be considered pleasant events and one might have anticipated avoidance behavior. But how did behaviorists react? The correct response, of course, was to start a journal called *Law and Behavior.*

One might draw several conclusions from this pattern. Naturally, as a behaviorist, I should perhaps collect more data and conduct a finer analysis, but I think it is safe to reach the following conclusions. We might conclude that many behaviorists read journals. But, perhaps it is just that every behaviorist who reads a journal wants to found a journal. Or, perhaps, behaviorists seldom remain at odds with fields of study that oppose them; instead the behaviorists form a partnership with them. A final possible conclusion I would prefer not to have to draw, yet a remotely possible explanation, is that behaviorists are much better at developing new treatments than they are at naming new journals.

APPARENT CONTRADICTIONS IN BEHAVIOR THERAPY

The diversity of new journals, however, is only one example of the apparent contradictions in almost every facet of this new field. A closer examination of recent theory and research reveals a number of other aspects that stand in surprising contrast to one another.

Consider the question of specification of the independent variable. In laboratory studies of operant conditioning, one universal rule was to introduce one variable at a time to make possible a correct identification of the factor producing the change. This is a logically reasonable and empirically sound position. Yet now we have many exponents of the view that treatment programs must be broad spectrum or multimodal, as Lazarus (1976) and others have advocated. Proponents of this view argue that one should use the full range of the therapeutic arsenal, with whatever variables produce the desired results (Azrin, 1977). This sounds quite reasonable as well as clinically ethical. The only problem is that it stands in direct contradiction to the first position.

If one examines the question of individual differences, one finds equally confusing contradictions. The early operant position was strictly idiographic, using the individual subject design with a limited number of subjects. In this way, individual differences could be excluded from the examination and evaluation of the learning variables and their effects. Reasonable as this position may seem to be, there have recently been many cries for studies that utilize hundreds of subjects in order to achieve population generality and convincing demonstrations of efficacy. How can one argue with that view? Yet it is antithetical to our beginnings in single-subject research.

Another example of contradictions in the area of experimental design is the early emphasis on ABA designs as the preferred method for demonstrating causality. The ABA design dictates that you take measurements during baseline (A) before treatment, introduce the treatment variable and measure the change in the desired behavior (B), and then remove the treatment variable (A). If the benefit disappears, then you have definitely proved that the treatment variable caused the effects. Although this conclusion may seem logically sound, it leaves one open to the valid criticism that treatment can hardly be considered beneficial if the effects simply vanish when therapy is terminated. One of the hallmarks of behavior therapy has been the quest for producing long-lasting effects. What is correct in these two opposing views?

The apparent contradictions described in the preceding paragraphs go beyond questions of experimental design and directly concern the nature of professional practice. One view that seems both obvious and valid is that the techniques of behavior therapy are becoming so numerous that special precautions are needed to ensure professional competence. One needs supervised internships, specialized instruction, and licensing laws to certify the competence of practitioners so that consumers will be protected from both mercenary charlatans and inept or inexperienced therapists. How can one argue with this noble desire to protect the public interest? Yet many behaviorists do. From another point of view, one of the characteristics of behavior therapy has been that the treatments developed have been so rigorously specified and standardized, and have so involved readily available personal and environmental variables, that the layperson can easily perform them without the need for professional assistance. Therapy is thus no longer limited by the rate at which highly qualified specialists can be educated and trained. Instead, personnel on all levels can be active participants in therapy. We seem faced by another apparent contradiction. On the one hand, popular books dealing with a host of problems are becoming readily accessible to the average person, while on the other hand the number of specialized internships and certification programs is steadily increasing. Which perspective is correct?

Let me briefly note other examples of opposites at work in this field. Many behaviorists deplore the growing popularity of behavior therapy, feeling that increased exposure and attention puts it into the same category as a number of other faddish therapies. At the same time, others are happy to see behavior therapy come to the attention of the general public but are most upset about the bad press created by extreme caricatures, such as the "Clockwork Orange" image. Some consider the principal mechanism of learning that occurs in treatment to be based on Pavlovian associationism (Wolpe, 1958), a solid, fundamental concept that has been with us from the beginning. Others are more convinced that the Skinnerian principles of operant contingencies are the most efficacious guidelines for therapy and change (Skinner, 1953). Still other voices are now being raised in support of the notion that the problems are in fact located in the mind and that thinking something really does make it so (Meichenbaum, 1977).

Many recent studies have been criticized for being too complex, encompassing too many variables, and manipulating too many factors. The critics urge a return to the laboratory where experimental control is much more rigorous and nearly all the factors can be neatly varied. At the very least, such critics suggest that our knowledge is too limited to conduct more complicated research than simple analogue studies. In stark contrast to these views, the cry has been sounded that it is time for behavior therapy to deal with the larger issues of society, to demonstrate the effectiveness of our methods with relevant problems that are of pressing urgency for large numbers of citizens. The advocates of this view promote the fields of community psychology and active field work. In their view, the more complex the problem, the better equipped they are to structure the problem through learning principles. These social behavior therapists criticize opposing views as simplistic and lacking in overall social impact.

One type of behavior therapist believes that therapy should be provided for exactly 1 hour—no more and no less. Therapy is conducted decorously in the office with a desk and chair and certainly not a couch. According to this type of therapist, the effective means of treatment is desensitization, relaxation, and assertive training. Another type of behaviorist, however, insists that learning as well as treatment must take place in the natural situation in which the problem occurs. So the treatment room is dispensed with and therapy is conducted within the framework of the classroom, the large mental institutions, and the schools for the retarded. Not content with treating the individual in the environment, the therapist often restructures the immediate environment to enhance learning effects. Rather than talking to the alcoholic about how to behave in a barroom, the therapist builds a reasonable facsimile and conducts treatment there. If one is to toilet train the individual, it is reasoned, what better place to practice than in the toilet?

EXPERIMENTAL EVALUATION:
NOT LAISSEX FAIRE ECLECTICISM

What are we to make of all these differences? Are they indeed a symptom of an underlying lack of information and identity in the field? I prefer to think of these apparent contradictions in a different light. From my perspective they are indications of a healthy, robust, and growing field in which all assumptions are challenged. When the ideal state of affairs that one avidly desires is confronted with the complications of clinical reality, compromises emerge that force us to attack different problems with different approaches. When we acknowledge reality for what it is, dogma is often forced to take a back seat to facts. I see the field as defined within the boundaries of learning theory based on reinforcement, but capable of including not only classical and operant definitions, but also learning by imitation, by cognitions, by instruction, or by whatever type of mechanism that is yet to be formulated. The rules of experimental design should be continuously altered to accommodate the therapeutic objectives we set up for ourselves. If we allow the debate to center solely on the correctness of dogma, we are doomed to repeat the errors of our predecessors.

The guiding principle must be that experimental evaluation will be the ultimate criterion of usefulness, but that all contenders for the truth will be welcomed to enter the arena. Since behavior therapy aspires to scientific status, apparent conflicts will have to be resolved by the experimental method, by the slow but sure accumulation of evidence that gives weight to theoretical claims. The diversity of views at any given moment is not an indication of eclecticism superceding behaviorism, but rather it is a reflection of our confidence that rigorous experimental evaluations will ultimately prevail.

Does this view of the field suggest that all points of view and all methodological orientations are equally valid? Such a perspective can be an invitation to eclectic anarchy. The ultimate objective of behavior therapy is to help patients solve behavior problems and, as a consequence of that goal, the ultimate test of treatment is the outcome study that evaluates the extent to which we have achieved a cure. As behavioral scientists we must insist that such outcome evaluations be based on general scientific research principles and that the experimental evidence be collected with the help of reliable measures and stringent control conditions. As behaviorists we must insist that the behavioral measures be taken from direct observations of relevant categories of responses. In summary, the final test of usefulness is the large-scale outcome evaluation including experimental control conditions, reliability and validity measurements of direct observations of behavior, and a firm conceptual foundation in general principles of learning. These central criteria will ensure that treatment is effective and that our conclusions are scientifically based.

Given this centrality of the scientific outcome study, a diversity of research strategies would seem to be compatible with the realization of this ultimate goal. We cannot afford to put all our money on one horse. Laboratory studies of both animals and people are still necessary to firmly establish the general principles of learning. In the light of findings from other lines of research, we can go back to the laboratory paradigms to further refine the concepts as they are presently formulated. Analogue studies have their function in isolating specific variables in clinically relevant but carefully controlled settings. Single-variable treatments are necessary to determine the role of each treatment factor in order to streamline the therapeutic strategies now in use. Package treatment programs are valuable for combining consequences in the most optimal fashion. For the hard-working clinician, this combination of treatment methods offers a workable synthesis that can maximize efficacy. All these lines of research are worthy of good research efforts. Learning by operant consequences, by classical conditioning, or by imitation of models have all been offered as explanatory mechanisms. More recently the usefulness of instructions and cognitive routes have been acclaimed. It is both logically feasible and empirically quite probable that these various mechanisms are complementary rather than mutually exclusive. But by seeking to demonstrate the truth of one mechanism, we risk neglecting several other effective tools. Similarly, treatment in the office and treatment in the natural environment do not necessarily preclude each other. Given the multitude of positions and the many faces of reality, it can hardly be expected that all therapy can be conducted from a particular point of departure. As long as the scientific behavioral outcome test is accepted as the final basis, all of these strategies are to be welcomed.

THE FUTURE OF BEHAVIOR THERAPY

What then is the future of behavior therapy? Given our fondness for prediction, our best guess should derive from a survey of the field's current accomplishments. We have successfully demonstrated effective methods in a number of fields—for the mildly and severely retarded, there is no other method that works. For severely disturbed autistic children, a number of workers have made progress previously considered unlikely, if not impossible. Parents and teachers have learned how to achieve the goals they strive for with the help of concrete procedures and general strategies of change. For fears and phobias, as well as anxiety, behavior therapy has developed specific procedures to replace maladaptive responses. For obesity and alcoholism, we have at least achieved better results than previous attempts to alleviate the problem behaviors. Sexual difficulties, marital problems, unemployment, aggressions, nervous habits, and many other complaints have been the target of concentrated efforts to produce positive behavioral outcomes. The list of new treatments and new problems tackled has been increasing at an impressive rate. Not only can we take pride in the accomplishments thus far achieved, but we can also confidently predict that this progress will continue. But even more important than developing new treatments is the behaviorist's insistence on saying "I don't know" when the experimental evidence is insufficient, and his or her willingness to ask "Are you sure?" in the face of "There's nothing to be done about it."

Even more valuable is the behaviorists' mania for criticizing and dissecting their own results until the evidence is compelling and the new treatment is perfected. Constructive criticism from interested peers has provided the impetus for the reworking and continued improvement of many of the best known methods. Lacking a father figure as the fountain of truth, we must instead pursue improved outcomes as our golden fleece.

What are the implications of this analysis for the future? If experimental evaluation is the ultimate criterion, one must find a method of communicating the findings. Communication is best accomplished by the active reading, listening, and digestion of information. We can rest assured that behaviorists will continue to organize conferences to provide communication about new findings in this rapidly growing field, that they will found more journals and contribute more articles. Most certainly, we can count on continued collections such as this book to trace the trends of behavior therapy.

REFERENCES

Azrin, N. H. A strategy for applied research: Learning based but outcome oriented. *American Psychologist*, 1977, *32*, 140–150.

Lazarus, A. A. *Multimodal behavior therapy*. New York: Springer, 1976.

Meichenbaum, D. *Cognitive-behavior modification. An integrative approach*. New York: Plenum Press, 1977.

Skinner, B. F. *The behavior of organisms*. New York: Appleton-Century-Crofts, 1938.

Skinner, B. F. *Science and human behavior*. New York: Macmillan, 1953.

Ullmann, L. P., & Krasner, L. *A psychological approach to abnormal behavior* (2nd ed.). Englewood Cliffs, N.J.: Prentice-Hall, 1975.

Wexler, D. G. Token and taboo: Behavior modification, token economies and the law. *California Law Review*, 1973, *61*, 81–109.

Wolpe, J. *Psychotherapy by reciprocal inhibition*. Stanford, Calif.: Stanford University Press, 1958.

2

Treating the Real, Not the Concept
LEONARD P. ULLMANN

The very definition of the behavioral approach indicates positions on some of the most important pivotal issues of psychotherapy. While there are significant variations among behaviorists themselves (Bandura, 1969; Bellack & Hersen, 1977; Craighead, Kazdin, & Mahoney, 1976; Eysenck, 1960; Kanfer & Phillips, 1970; Leitenberg, 1976; O'Leary & Wilson, 1975; Rimm & Masters, 1974; Schwitzgebel & Kolb, 1974; Staats, 1975; Thomas, 1974; Ullmann & Krasner, 1965; Watson & Tharp, 1977; Wolpe, 1958), there is a core of agreement among them that transcends the differences in emphasis, stemming from differences in intellectual background and varying experiences with clients and settings.

UNIFYING THEMES IN BEHAVIOR THERAPY

The first major unifying concept is that *behavior is real*. This may seem obvious, but the pivotal issue is whether behavior is to be the target and measure of therapeutic intervention or whether, as in psychoanalysis, overt behavior is taken to be symptomatic and symbolic of an underlying, intrapsychic deviation from normality. According to the latter approach, overt behavior that brings the client to treatment is, by definition, not the

13

Copyright © 1979 by Academic Press, Inc.
All rights of reproduction in any form reserved.
ISBN 0-12-647450-8

target for intervention. In fact, given the symptom substitution hypothesis, overt behavior that brings the client to therapy is one of the last things to be dealt with in psychoanalysis and presumably, the troublesome behavior will alter by itself once the true intrapsychic problem has been ameliorated.

The crux of the matter, then, is the manner in which the overt behavior that brings the client to therapy is formulated and treated by the therapist. If the behavior is considered real rather than symptomatic, the therapist is on his or her way to becoming a behaviorist. The reality and importance of overt behavior leads to other pivotal aspects of the behavioral approach.

If the target behavior is real rather than symptomatic, then intervention can and should *directly* influence that behavior or its incompatible alternatives. This is in contrast to the idea that treatment should be aimed at changing hypothesized intrapsychic variables prior to changing behavior. The behavioral approach generally sides with Festinger, who holds that behavior change precedes rather than follows attitude change. It sides with Sartre in the position that "Being precedes Essence."

Next, if the treatment is to be direct rather than indirect, then any process or procedure, whether organizational, economic, ecological, chemical, or interpersonal, that has been shown to have an impact in developing, maintaining, or altering behavior, may provide a form of behavioral intervention. The pivotal concept here is that principles are developed *empirically*. Further, the therapeutic situation is viewed as but one of many human interactions, all of which follow the same general rules. That is, therapy targets and relationships are not special—the scientific concepts of human behavior and relationships apply to them.

In short, *theory and procedure should be investigated and documented prior to clinical application rather than have them rationalized after the fact.* Further, both what occurs within treatment (process) and as a result of treatment (outcome) must be closely scrutinized. This leads to a number of further pivotal issues, such as the place of measurement in treatment.

One deduction is that there is an ethical and professional obligation to base one's efforts on publically verifiable knowledge rather than on feelings, testimonials, or chance. To "sell" services, especially to a public that is under stress and without training to evaluate what it is buying, places a great ethical burden on the therapist. The therapist needs to obtain informed consent from the client, and this cannot be done without the therapist having necessary evaluative information as to the appropriateness of a specific procedure for a particular client. Diplomas, registers, licenses, and titles present an image to the public, whereas substance can only be based on strict methodology. Where evaluative information is lacking, the therapist should be reluctant to sell service for fees. Instead he or she should openly identify the procedure as research with attendant modesty and reduction of fees. Research or organizational funds should then be used as the basis of support.

Related to the matter of professional service is a position on a pivotal issue: Therapeutic application should be *disciplined* and impersonal in terms of its being based on what the therapist knows as a professional rather than what is felt personally or intuitively. A client expects that the procedures of a professional are based on study, experience, and information that is specialized and not influenced by personal feelings or conflicts of interest. Service is impersonal in that all clients receive the best efforts of the professional, based on knowledge and aimed at the problem. Clients should be confident that they will not be used to meet the professional's personal, financial, or political needs in a manner that is not overt (i.e., informed consent) at the very start of the relationship. Documentable knowledge is an ethical necessity, not a luxury. Ethically and professionally, the therapist holds personal needs in abeyance and is at the service of the client. If this cannot be done, the conflict of interest is made manifest and the case is transferred. This is what I mean by discipline.

A behavioral focus leads to the solution of many problems that are now rising to a legal status (Martin, 1975). Aside from genuine informed consent, the position taken so far leads to a more direct relation between problem and treatment (process) and a clearer basis for accountability (outcome). While behaviorists are as irked as any other group of professionals over the intrusion of laypeople (lawyers) into their professional decisions, treatment is not considered a special creation or a relationship separate from other interactions. As such, when working within a given culture, the therapist is obligated to abide by the rules of that group (Ullmann, 1969a). An area where this is currently being debated is that of confidentiality; I can only say, without digressing too far afield, that confidentiality is not absolute and that the therapist tells the client, as part of informed consent, the limits imposed by society.

In short, from a behavioral viewpoint the therapist is *responsible*. This issue has a number of dimensions, that is, she or he is responsible to the profession and society as noted previously. It also has a clear differential impact as to who—client or therapist—is responsible for therapeutic movement. If the problem is intrapsychic and treatment is indirect, then the therapist may blame the client for lack of progress. In a psychodynamic approach, hypothesized concepts within the individual, such as resistance, are the cause of failure, not therapist incompetence. In the behavioral approach, the task of the therapist is to select, implement, evaluate, and—as events and evidence, both in and outside the therapy dictate— revise a plan of intervention. It is the therapist who is responsible for the intervention plan, and it is the therapist who bears the burden and is accountable for progress. It is expected that the therapist will recognize when the procedure is deficient, and if the alternatives are exhausted, will so admit to the client and transfer the case rather than blame the client and add to the person's feelings of ineffectiveness and worthlessness.

THE THERAPEUTIC RELATIONSHIP

This leads to a client–therapist relationship, notably what has been called transference and countertransference phenomena. The client and therapist regard each other as *student and teacher rather than as patient and physician*. This stems from the formulation of targets for intervention being behavior rather than diseases, labels, or abstractions. To the extent that the purpose of the treatment process is one of providing useful experiences, therapy is a teaching and learning process.

The behavior therapist sees the client the same way as a teacher views a student: as a person with the capacity to use new experiences to deal more effectively with a world that is not necessarily identical to that of the teacher. If students have problems with mathematics, we do not label them as mathematically defective, nor do we say that the problem stems from the individual's personality, or that treatment should be directed at the personality problem rather than at the mathematical deficiency. Rather, we are likely to collect data to determine if the conditions necessary, but not sufficient for mathematical skills, have been met—that is, we use tests of abstract thinking, tests of prerequisites of content, and measures of the student's studying procedures and test-taking behavior. We will take into account the student's history of success or failure with mathematics and be alert to circumstances under which there may have been poor learning experiences (missing school, having a punitive instructor, and the like). Frequently, people appear "stupid" or "boorish" when they do not possess what everyone presumes to be general knowledge. Rather than a trait, much less a symptom of an underlying intrapsychic conflict or disease, we simply describe the problem as a skill that is lacking. While a person may indeed have experienced aversive stimuli either paired with or as a consequence of mathematics, and while the individual may have avoided the situation ever since, it is a far better strategy to teach the lacking skill rather than to "work through" the previous circumstances. When reconditioning of surplus emotional responses is required—and such systematic desensitization is done only after we are assured that the skills are present—it is more effective to make use of hierarchies of coping behavior in present and future situations than to focus on situations in the past. Remediation of the deficit is the first and necessary step. Sometimes it is sufficient in itself and makes possible the rewards of progress that have been blocked; sometimes, however, one must strive for further changes that may be required as a result of the change in the target behavior. Incidentally, I see the latter as a major aspect, too often overlooked, in situations of a dyadic nature, such as in assertive training and marital counseling. A change in the client's behavior, even if it is toward goals that therapists and clients consider "good," must be evaluated in terms of the client's significant others. This touches on a pivotal issue: The behavioral position implies that behavior that is learned is preponderantly of a *social nature*. We must think of behavior as social and take situation and context into account, rather than focus solely on responses or regard them as responses only in the sense of symptoms within the individual. A most crucial feature of the behavioral approach is that we think of *reactions to situations* and *not of responses per se.*

There are two deductions: (*a*) that the prime areas for evaluation and treatment are situations leading to emission or failure of emission of the target behavior; and (*b*) that we must look at the consequences of behavior. Turning to the latter first, we look at both immediate and long-term consequences and note that immediate feedback may well be stronger and override long-term considerations. We may also note that what unifies behavior over time may well be cues that people themselves generate and use as discriminative stimuli or guiding fictions. In the example cited previously, mathematics was not chosen fortuitously, because there has been a wide interest in it recently. Women have the natural ability, but at present are underrepresented at college levels in curricula that have mathematical skills as a prerequisite—such as engineering, economics, the hard sciences, both social and biophysical. How so? In checking the short-term consequences for acts, we must do so both in terms of what follows an act and what does not follow.

Specifically, if an act avoids a (falsely) presumed unpleasant consequence, it will continue to be made in similar circumstances. Here, re-education by modeling, systematic desensitization, and gradual *in vivo* exposure are indicated to provide information that the situation is not as presumed by the client. If avoidance leads to sympathy and control over others, such as an invalid may have over those who are "well," the avoidance is followed by an immediate favorable event. Here, a frequent technique is finding alternative ways to obtain such pleasant experiences and enlisting the assistance of significant others, who are instructed to stop being pleasant when the person is avoiding but to be pleasant when the person makes the alternative and more favorable response. The cues provided by oneself may be approached through a variety of experiences: Some are implicit in the changing of behavior by the techniques noted previously, and some are of the semantic and cognitive nature that is one of the major interests in current behavioral work. I can only note here that "thoughts" are behaviors that are developed, maintained, and changed in the same way as more readily measured motor acts. That is, speech is an operant, and the procedures that have been used successfully to alter speech to others are applicable to the speech one emits to oneself.

To return to the relationship between therapist and client: By focusing on the task to be learned rather than on the person's "dynamics," the relationship becomes task oriented and a mutual respect is generated. The therapist has respect for the client as a learning, striving, and coping person who is not sick but who will benefit from guided experiences in dealing with particular and specified situations. The client may well view the therapist as an expert, but like all good students he or she is encouraged to learn actively, to question the teacher, to master the strategy and reason behind the experiences provided, rather than passively undergo those experiences and learn only the specific acts without generalizing them and the procedures to other, new situations. Just as we prepare students to apply both specific and general procedures to new situations, to see relationships and consequences, so behaviorists have as their ultimate goal making their clients their own therapists (Ullmann, 1969b). It is the ability to analyze situations and select appropriate reactions that leads to generalization to new situations.

Becoming a patient or a student is a well-defined cultural role. The very behavior that is considered changeworthy, and even the idea that behavior can be changed, is cultural in nature. To the extent that the student-teacher relationship is one of more active task orientation than the patient-physician one, and to the extent that analysis of situations in the future is taught, and most of all, to the extent that the person in treatment is considered a rational adult rather than a flawed personality, the student role is likely to avoid transference problems. Again, the therapist focuses on prior history only as relevant and not as routine.

A crucial pivotal issue enters into the nature of the relationship as well as the basis of the formulation of problems and treatment (direct versus indirect). This is so whether there is *a dynamic unconscious or not*. By dynamic unconscious we mean one that is ahistorical, one in which the needs and frustrations of today and of childhood are equally vivid and equally strong in pressure to gain expression and gratification. The behavioral position rejects this concept. While not denying that learning has a history, it centers on the current situations and behaviors to seek explanations and interventions. If one does have a dynamic unconscious in one's formulations, one will focus more on the individual's intrapsychic dynamics and, most germane to the present topic, on transference neurosis in which the client's relationship with the therapist is a major area of investigation. The very focus on the relationship in the therapy room may create problems. The therapist is indicating what is considered important and may shape, by interest and responsiveness, that is, by verbal operant conditioning, statements that are of a passive, distorted, transference nature. A task-oriented, student–teacher relationship does not foster either such dependency or new problems that are not necessarily related to the person's striving and success in the extratherapy social world.

GENERALIZATION OF TREATMENT EFFECTS

Related to transference are issues of *generalization* and *termination*. Taking the latter first, when is treatment complete? The behavioral approach steadily gathers material on the person's activity in the extratreatment situation and provides a source of feedback. When the person is being successful and has abilities and strategies that will help in dealing with new situations, the teaching experience is complete. The ongoing stream of behavior with the person's significant others is the source of maintenance of new behaviors, and it is from this reality feedback that feelings of worth and effectiveness are gleaned. Termination is as with students: The person may indeed wish to come back for additional courses as these are relevant, and hopefully, students think well and feel kindly toward those teachers who have been helpful and relevant. The major point is that a focus on behavior provides feedback for termination in the same ways that it provides feedback for intervention plans during the course of treatment. Our goal is to teach clients to do for themselves what therapists did for them.

For the behaviorist, generalization from the treatment situation to the extratherapy environment is fostered by discussion of strategies and discriminative stimuli ("cognitions" or "guiding fictions") as well as actual experiences and changes in clients and significant others. *Generalization is not automatic*; the conditions fostering generalization are the subject of programming and work. At the token economy level (with children, hospitalized psychotics, retardates, etc.), very overtly, acts that receive reinforcement are increased in complexity, paired with social reinforcement, and placed on more complex schedules and under finer discriminative stimulus control so that what was terminal becomes instrumental and part of a larger unit of social behavior. An example is reading as an act that early in life is rewarded in and of itself, but that in adult life is continued not because of the praise or kindness of the school teacher, but because it makes possible communication and hence a more rewarding adjustment to the current environment. To be even more explicit, I am writing this article not because of the effects of that lovely person, Ms. Beck, who taught me how to read and write, but because such reading and writing is part of my social role as psychologist, professor, and behaviorist.

I will not belabor the alternative, psychoanalytic model in terms of bases of generalization or improvement. However, I would like to point out a paradox: Nonbehaviorists are very likely to have a more uncritical view of learning concepts than behaviorists. For example, many dynamic therapists conceive of single incidents as traumas to which the person reacts even 40 years later. Such "one-trial" conditioning is rare, and in fact, respondent conditioning, in my experience and opinion, is quite weak, unstable, and leads to higher order conditioning only under special circumstances. In similar fashion, and in terms of behavior in the extratherapy situation, generalization is very far from automatic. To say that what has been learned in terms of relating to the therapist will be applied to people in the extratherapy environment, that what has been achieved with one person has been achieved with all, seems to place more faith in generalization than I think proper. Rather, both for generalization itself and for effective social action, one must learn when to generalize and when not to. In short, discrimination training is necessary. Changing one's intrapsychic structure or one's way of talking to a therapist does not automatically lead to reentry into avoided situations or the successful emission of social acts that one has not practiced. Insight does not automatically lead to behavior change, and most clients discriminate between their therapists and their significant others. Those who act toward their significant others in the way they act toward their therapists are likely to find that there are people, times, and places where such behavior is a problem rather than a solution. Unlike the professional, significant others are likely to wish to satisfy their own needs and do not always show the unconditional positive regard, warmth, empathy, genuineness, and appropriate feedback or confrontation of therapists. Again, generalization requires conditions among which a crucial one is discrimination; without this, the generalized behavior will meet an extinguishing rather than a supportive reception. I consider it to be the therapist's obligation to teach the client to recognize the proper social situation for a specific act. This kind of discrimination training must not be relied on to be automatic.

BEHAVIORISM: A WAY OF THINKING ABOUT PEOPLE

The most crucial issue in treatment is that of *formulation*. We have touched on it in our discussion of the issue of direct or indirect intervention. I wish here only to reiterate that behavior is real rather than symptomatic and that this leads to a number of stands on pivotal issues. The first is that *each person is different*. While this seems to be obvious, it leads to a difference in procedure. The same overt behavior may have different antecedents, and different antecedents may lead to different overt behaviors depending on the culture. In short, and as noted earlier, one must deal with reactions to situations and not reactions only. One effect is that traditional categorizations obscure the actualities of the case. Behaviorists avoid labels or a designation of treatment in terms of such labels (Ullmann & Krasner, 1965, 1975).

Associated with and underlying the avoidance of labels is a major aspect of the behavioral approach. This is that behaviorism is an approach and *a way of formulating and thinking about people* and *not a set of techniques* such as contingency contracting or systematic desensitization. The focus is on specifying and measuring overt actions in response to situations. A person is no more a behaviorist because he or she uses a particular technique than a person is a psychoanalyst because he or she uses free association or owns a couch. The focus on behavior leads to the relationship with the client as described previously; it also leads to a demand that all labels, whether of feelings, diagnoses, or therapy processes, be operationally defined. Another way of describing this difference is to say that rather than asking "why" questions, behaviorists ask "what" questions. We ask what behavior leads some person (the client, spouse, parent, child, teacher, or physician) to wish a change? We do not treat "schizophrenia" but rather behaviors that make it difficult for the person to get along in the general social milieu and that lead others to use that label. Such behaviors usually are of low rate: The majority of patients in psychiatric hospitals are able to care for themselves and do socially useful work. Similarly, a person is not simply anxious in the abstract, but rather is anxious in response to certain stimuli. Rather than use the label "neurotic," we ask, what are the situations that are avoided or the ones that give rise to changeworthy behavior? We do not say a person is a sexual deviate, but one who, under certain circumstances, emits behavior of a sexual nature that differs from some cultural norm. We must always look to specific situations, to what would be possible and appropriate responses, and to actual immediate and long-term consequences. Not only do we not label the person, we demand that our treatments be explicable and specifiable in terms of overt actions. I personally believe that words such as "reinforcement" are so badly overused that they may obscure rather than communicate meaning. We need to ask what pleasant or unpleasant event is increased or decreased contingent on the client's behavior. The focus on behavior applies as much to the therapist as it does to the client.

Such specification leads to a number of positions on pivotal issues as outlined earlier. At this point, I do wish to stress that measurement is a crucial ongoing activity throughout treatment. Whether we deal with biofeedback, operants, complex social roles, or self-instruction, the test of our efforts is the overt, measurable, and measured behavior of our clients. The measures may be by physiological apparatus, client self-reports, or the records of significant others, such as teachers and parents. What is crucial is that there be a focus on relevant (validated) behavior and that this focus lead to gathering information that is related to the intervention.

To come full circle, the reality of behavior leads to positions on pivotal issues such as formulation of clients' problems, selection of targets for treatment, evaluation procedures, intervention procedures, professional role, termination of treatment, confidentiality, and case formulation. A consistent focus on clients' behavior in social situations rather than on abstractions held by the therapist leads to an improved stance in legal and ethical matters and increases the quality of communication, research, and accountability. But above all, a consistent focus on behavior leads to a more dignified role for the client as a person coping.

REFERENCES

Bandura, A. *Principles of behavior modification*. New York: Holt, Rinehart, & Winston, 1969.

Bellack, A., & Hersen, M. *Behavior modification: An introductory textbook*. Baltimore: Williams & Wilkins, 1977.

Craighead, W. E., Kazdin, A. E., & Mahoney, M. J. (Eds.). *Behavior modification: Principles, issues, and applications.* Boston: Houghton Mifflin, 1976.

Eysenck, H. J. (Ed.). *Behaviour therapy and the neuroses.* Oxford: Pergamon Press, 1960.

Kanfer, F. H., & Phillips, J. S. *Learning foundations of behavior therapy.* New York: Wiley, 1970.

Leitenberg, H. (Ed.). *Handbook of behavior modification and behavior therapy.* Englewood Cliffs, N.J.: Prentice-Hall, 1976.

Martin, R. *Legal challenges to behavior modification.* Champaign, Ill.: Research Press, 1975.

O'Leary, K. D., & Wilson, G. T. *Behavior therapy: Application and outcome.* Englewood Cliffs, N.J.: Prentice-Hall, 1975.

Rimm, D. C., & Masters, J. C. *Behavior therapy: Techniques and empirical findings.* New York: Academic Press, 1974.

Schwitzgebel, R. K., & Kolb, D. A. *Changing human behavior: Principles of planned intervention.* New York: McGraw-Hill, 1974.

Staats, A. W. *Social behaviorism.* Homewood, Ill.: Dorsey Press, 1975.

Thomas, E. J. (Ed.). *Behavior modification procedure: A sourcebook.* Chicago: Aldine, 1974.

Ullmann, L. P. Behavior therapy as social movement. In C. M. Franks (Ed.), *Behavior therapy: Appraisal and status.* New York: McGraw-Hill, 1969. Pp. 495–523. (a)

Ullmann, L. P. Making use of modeling in the therapeutic interview. In R. D. Rubin, & C. M. Franks (Eds.), *Advances in behavior therapy, 1968.* New York: Academic Press, 1969. Pp. 175–182. (b)

Ullmann, L. P., & Krasner, L. (Eds.). *Case studies in behavior modification.* New York: Holt, Rinehart, & Winston, 1965.

Ullmann, L. P., & Krasner, L. *A psychological approach to abnormal behavior* (2nd ed.). Englewood Cliffs, N.J.: Prentice-Hall, 1975.

Watson, D. L., & Tharp, R. G. *Self-directed behavior: Self-modification for personal adjustment* (2nd ed.). Monterey, Calif.: Brooks/Cole, 1977.

Wolpe, J. *Psychotherapy by reciprocal inhibition.* Stanford, Calif.: Stanford University Press, 1958.

3

A Laboratory Model of Psychotherapy: The Boundary between Clinical Practice and Experimental Psychology

CHARLES B. FERSTER

Experimental psychology can be regarded as a complement to clinical practice. This view is at variance with the conventional role of the operant conditioner–behaviorist as one who develops clinical methods out of laboratory work (Ferster, 1967b, 1972a, 1972b, 1973, 1974), and it implies that there is a boundary between the two disciplines. Both may be concerned with the same items of conduct but with different purposes. The practitioner is obligated to engage in whatever problem the patient brings. His or her primary task is to ameliorate distress. Practitioners involve themselves totally and usually cannot be responsible for proving what has been accomplished. On the other hand, experimental psychologists choose their own ground, being required only to look objectively and with conceptual clarity and to communicate in the terms of natural science. They are the kinds of doctors who know more and more about less and less and who do not do anyone any good. The complementarity of behavioral analysis and application was recently stressed by Azrin (1977), who described how clinical treatments he had developed were shaped by interactions with patients rather than deduced logically.

I will attempt to use the basic concepts of the functional analysis of operant behavior, particularly Skinner's concept of the generic nature of the response, and that of arbitrary and natural reinforcement, to show: (a) the difficulties of literal extensions of laboratory procedures; and (b) the

23

TRENDS IN BEHAVIOR THERAPY

Copyright © 1979 by Academic Press, Inc.
All rights of reproduction in any form reserved.
ISBN 0-12-647450-8

advantages that accrue when direct encounters between patient and therapist are used as opportunities to uncover the content of human nature.

THE GENERIC DEFINITION OF THE FREE OPERANT

Whether performances reinforced in the natural environment by one reinforcer could be developed equally well by any other is a crucial question for those who try to apply operant conditioning procedures to practical problems in everyday life. A strict, technical analysis of behavioral principles applied to complex phenomena in the natural environment leads to the conclusion that performances reinforced arbitrarily are *not* equivalent to similar topographies of action in the natural environment. The theoretical basis of the definition of the operant emerged from Skinner's discussion of the generic nature of the response in *The Behavior of Organisms* (1938), where bar presses were defined as a generic class, each press functionally equivalent to the other, despite the variations in topography from instance to instance.

Findley (1962) and Kelleher (1966) took the concept one step further in experiments with second-order schedules of reinforcement in which larger units of behaviors functioned like a simpler operant because of the programmed connection to a conditioned reinforcer. A thoroughgoing view of the operant as a functional unit is even more radical, since it views the operant as an integral unit that can be defined equivalently by the performance or by the reinforcer. Thus, the key peck is either the movement that closes the switch behind the key, or the mechanical characteristics of the way the key is connected to the switch that increases the frequency of those movements that move the armature of the key sufficiently to operate the switch. It is the light and sound of the feeder mechanism that is the generic definition of the key peck rather than the food that follows distantly. The generic quality comes from the mechanical connection between the movements of the bird's head and beak and the switch behind the key. One could describe the activity of a rat pressing a lever—the free operant that heralded so much of operant conditioning—as walking to the bar, standing up on the hind legs, lowering until one or both paws touch it, and then pressing the bar far enough to actuate the switch, which in turn operates the solenoid and drops a pellet into the food tray, accompanied by a loud click. We could just as easily describe a bar press as an act that moves the bar sufficiently to close the switch and produce the click of the food mechanism, or we could describe it by giving an account of the actual complex acts. The physical properties of the bar and its connection to the switch that operates and sounds the food dispenser are a reinforcer that has a natural and exact relation to the movements that are required. In the technical sense of how the reinforcer functions, it is the click that determines the behavior. The food, although necessary for the process, is the reinforcer for grasping the pellet and eating it, itself another complex chain of behaviors. However, the food does not have the precise, natural connection to the bar press that exists with the click.

The concept of the performance and the reinforcer as a functional unit needs to be elaborated in some detail because it is the vehicle that allows crossing back and forth between clinical practice and experimental psychology. The generic definition of the operant also parallels the distinction between arbitrary and natural reinforcement. There are practical and technical implications of noting that it is the click and not the food that reinforces bar pressing. Only with such a natural and precisely guaranteed connection between the animal's activity and the reinforcer, can a stable operant be maintained. If the importance of the precision that occurs so naturally with the click (as opposed to the food that comes later) seems exaggerated, the practical implications become clearer with more complicated activities, such as a seal balancing a ball or a person riding a bicycle, activities considerably short of human social interactions.

Teaching a seal to balance a ball on its nose is an instructive case because the discrepancy between food and the reinforcer generic to balancing the ball is greater than with simpler acts, such as bar pressing. Although the fish thrown to the seal is an important, perhaps even necessary factor, the pressure of the ball on the seal's nose is the stimulus that actually differentially reinforces the repertoire. There is an exquisitely fine interplay between the movements of the seal's head, the action of gravity on the ball, and its position on the seal's nose. It seems virtually unthinkable to synthesize this dynamic tension, which results naturally from the physical system, with a reinforcer such as food that has an arbitrary connection to the balancing. Despite the natural relation between the seal's movements and the position of the ball, the events are nonetheless definite and objective if they are observed carefully enough.

To deliberately reinforce the component activities of riding a bicycle, for example with food, would be even more difficult than reinforcing the seal for balancing its ball. Riding a bicycle requires precise, subtle shifts in posture coordinated with the inertial forces, the movement of the pedals, and the balance with gravity. All of this is accomplished with precision by the physical properties of the system as they are expressed by the upright position of the bicycle. Of course, we still need to account for why balancing the bicycle is a reinforcer. Food, or other consequences that have no intrinsic or generic connection to balancing, obviously may be an important, even necessary influence, but it is the natural precision between the component performances and their generically related reinforcers that allows the application of behavioral principles.

THE GENERIC DEFINITION OF VERBAL BEHAVIOR

Generic or natural reinforcement is even more crucial to social and verbal behavior and psychotherapy than to complex motor activities such as balancing. It is important because the topographies of speech, listening, and personal interactions are so complex, and because most of the activities of psychotherapy involve two people talking to each other. If a science of behavior is to understand and describe the events of psychotherapy, it will need to be clear about the reinforcers for these verbal and interpersonal behaviors. The topographies of verbal behavior, intrinsically, muscle movements of the mouth, lips, diaphragm and tongue, seem capable of objective description as, for example, by the phoneticist. Yet, the total phenomenon, as it operates socially, appears hopelessly complex when one observes the continuous ebb and flow of an actual speech episode. The reaction of the listener is the generic or natural counterpart of speaking, a reinforcer that is capable of the complex and delicate shaping that clearly happens between them. The reinforcer for speaking, parallel to the example of the rat pressing a bar and the seal balancing a ball, is the influence that speaking has on a listener—including the speaker as his or her own listener. Were it not for the listener, speaking would be just warm, moist, vibrating air. The speaker as his or her own listener is the bridge between the complex activities of speaking and a reinforcer that is capable of shaping the fine grain that occurs so naturally in balancing a ball or a bicycle. This refined definition of verbal behavior (Skinner, 1957, pp. 224–226), appeals to the speaker's influence on the listener as the reinforcer. Conversationally, we say that someone speaks to influence or to make the listener understand. The reality, behaviorally, is reversed. The reaction of the listener, as the generic counterpart of the speaker, is the reinforcer that determines the speaker's behavior. It is mainly for this reason that the major part of Skinner's analysis of verbal behavior (1957) deals with the listener.

Developing an Autistic Child's Speech

The verbal development of a child is an illustration of how the understanding by another person creates the reinforcement for speaking. Parents frequently give a running account of their activities as they minister to a preverbal baby as, for example, when they prepare its bottle, change its diaper, or, less practically, announce the arrival of one person or another. Because the parents' speech consistently sets the occasions for the components of these important actions, it also takes discriminative control, in the sense that we say the child understands what the parents say. More technically, a fine-grain control emerges in which there is point-to-point correspondence between elements of the parents' speech and the behaviors for which they set the occasion. Once the child can understand what its parent is saying, it can, as well, attend to its own developing speech.

The reaction of the child to its own emerging speech patterns is an exquisitely prescribed reinforcer and a bridge between what it says and what it hears from parents and others. First, the reinforcer derives from standard verbal practices that the parent shares with the rest of the verbal community. Second, it is an instantaneous consequence of speaking; as his or her own listener, the child carries a replica, continuously available to him or herself, of the community that shaped him. And third, it is a stable reaction that reinforces closer and closer approximations to standard verbal practices. It is a common observation that children's speech erupts in substantial form without overt evidence of successive approximations. Obviously, in these cases, the approximations must have occurred intraverbally, reinforced by the child as listener.

The natural reinforcement of speech development makes it clear why it is so difficult to teach a mute, autistic child to speak by the use of food or some other reinforcer that has an arbitrary, rather than a generic or natural, connection to speaking (Ferster, 1967a, 1972a). For a mute, autistic child to learn to speak, the first requirement is that he or she is inclined to influence or be influenced by another person. Otherwise, there is no basis for development as a listener, a necessary prerequisite for generic verbal reinforcement. The therapist or parent who says to a child "Give me the ball" (as opposed to the box, also present) assumes the child is inclined to hand over one or the other objects; otherwise, there is no way that speaking to the child can influence which object is picked. Such language development is a stable, natural product of the verbal community that has influenced the parent. It is also a by-product of the practical events in the child's life rather than a result of reinforcing it directly. Practical events, such as food, tokens, or the release from threats have the same relation to the child's verbal activity as the fish thrown to the seal has to the balance of the ball on its nose. Attempts to reinforce speech arbitrarily with events like food and tokens, which do not have a generic, natural relation to speaking, face the same practical difficulties as would occur in arbitrary ways of reinforcing the balancing of the ball on the seal's nose. On the other hand, once a child is inclined to deal with persons who have stable verbal and social patterns of conduct, their natural reactions are fine-grain differential reinforcers, generically related to speaking so that the reinforcement of speech occurs without conscious or deliberate intervention (Ferster, 1972a).

Arbitrary and Natural Reinforcement in Learning a
New Language

Learning a new language is another useful sphere for illustrating generic or natural reinforcement of verbal behavior. The difference between speaking a language in a natural as opposed to an educational situation comes from the reason for speaking—the reinforcer responsible for its frequency. The classroom student speaks largely because grades depend on speaking, because speaking leads to the approval of the teacher, and because the student may wish to get the reaction of other students. The correspondence, in the sense of a generic connection, between these reinforcers and speaking a language is much less consistent, much less fine grained, and much less reactive than the instant give-and-take that occurs when the student speaker has an extended life in a community where speaking is the main form of social and practical commerce (Ferster & Culbertson, 1974). Although the natural community lacks the careful approximation to the student's existing repertoire that can be arranged in the classroom, it has the advantage of the fine grain of a generic reinforcer that produces the instant give-and-take between performance and consequence (here speaker and listener) that is the quintessence of reinforcement. The effect of classroom reinforcement, essentially arbitrary, pales before the changes that speaking can make in another person's understanding. Such effects are also powerful because they mediate the daily commerce with members of a larger community, who all speak the same language that mediates the many transactions of one's life.

Conditioning Verbal Behavior in Animals

The difficulties that have been encountered in attempts to teach animals verbal behavior, even when it is not vocal, highlights the fact that speech is a by-product of social control in which one person is the instrument of another's reinforcement. Those experiments in the nature of *tours de force*, that have met some success, have essentially synthesized a verbal community that mediated a variety of reinforcers (Kellog & Kellog, 1933/1967; Premack, 1976). Abstract language—such as arithmetic, the vocabulary of which can consist of lights to be turned on or off—overcomes the limitations of the animal's vocal apparatus but lacks the essential verbal quality that comes from a generic and socially stable connection to a listener who already speaks (Ferster, 1964).

THE APPLICATIONS OF BEHAVIORAL PRINCIPLES TO PSYCHOTHERAPY ACCENTS ITS VERBAL NATURE

I have stressed the qualities of natural or generic reinforcement because they are so important for the reinforcement of verbal behavior and because psychotherapy, behavioral or otherwise, is so predominately verbal. The objective events are two people (usually) talking together, sometimes about the immediate interaction of the therapy and sometimes about occurrences elsewhere. The behaviors that occur in therapy are predominately the muscle movements of the vocal apparatus, producing moist, warm, vibrating air, whatever the circumstances in the patient's daily life that are talked about and however behaviorally they are discussed. Although counseling and behavioral therapies purport to set up objectives for the patient in his or her daily life as practical, definable goals, and although they attempt to help the patient achieve this repertoire in successive approximations, the actual events that occur in most of these therapies are people talking together *about* the procedures and *about* the events. It is hard to imagine how it could be otherwise, since it would not be possible, in practice, for a therapist to observe a significant portion of these events firsthand.

Confusion between Events and What Is Said about Them

The speech and collateral events occurring between the patient and therapist are behaviors that are observable and potentially objective. The events talked *about*, those of the patient's life elsewhere, are inferences subject to distortion and incomplete descriptions, no matter how objective the terms. If the description of ordinary events is subject to distortion, then the patient's account of why he or she acts is even more in doubt. There is often the loosest of correspondence, for example, between a patient's description of what led him or her to miss an appointment or the reason why certain topics are overlooked and the independent variable that may eventually be uncovered. The failure to differentiate what is being talked about from the talk itself is a serious technical difficulty that may occur in any verbal therapy; but it is more visible in behavioral therapies than in others because behavioral language makes the discrepancy clearer.

One reason for confusion between the events of the patient's life and the talking that occurs in psychotherapy is that the verbal reinforcers are arbitrary with respect to the behaviors talked about in the patient's daily life and vice versa. The generic counterpart of the patient's behavior in therapy is the influence on the therapist who is listening and on the patient as his or her own listener. The generic counterparts of the ongoing events of the patient's daily life are the day-to-day occurrences there. Obviously, what is said about the patient's life influences what he or she might do subsequently, but the connection is a repertoire that needs to be examined separately.

The Correspondence between the Patient's Speech and the Events They Purport to Describe Is the Subject of a Behavioral Analysis

Despite the complexity and uncertainty, and however distorted and profoundly influenced they may be by many collateral variables, the correspondence between the patient's speech and the events he or she is talking about is one of the most important aspects of the therapy task. When a patient can accurately describe his or her own conduct, the conduct of those who influence him or her, and the connection between the two, the remaining remedies that might be required can occur naturally or by simple educational supports. We would expect that when a patient is capable of utilizing specific suggestions and instructions, there would have been a change in the kinds of verbal activities that predominate in psychotherapy. Until the high frequency of complaints and demands gives way to tacts and intraverbal behaviors that correspond to and amplify the patient's current conduct and the variables of which it is a function, it may be predicted that little use could be made of instructional prompts.

THE KINDS OF REINFORCERS AND BEHAVIORAL CHANGES THAT CAN OCCUR IN A VERBAL INTERACTION

Even though the ultimate task of a behavioral analysis is to discover how to influence the practical events of the patient's life, the first approximation to this task is the analysis of the kinds of repertoires and reinforcers that can emerge from an essentially verbal interaction.

Initial Control of the Patient's Speech

When we say that a patient "talks to the therapist" the implication is that the patient's speech is sustained by the way it influences the therapist. When we say that the therapist "listens to the patient," the immediate events are the control of the therapist by the patient. Yet, to begin with, neither party has a history of being controlled by the other. Clearly, the control over the patient is not, at first, entirely specific to that particular therapist. Otherwise, it would not be likely that a patient would talk at length, frequently with little comment by the therapist, during the first interview. Functionally, this behavior appears to be *a magic mand,* such as "I wish it would stop raining," "My kingdom for a horse" or "Gosh, I'm hungry," all generalized complaints that are extensions beyond the circumstances where there might be any realistic expectation that a normal listener could comply with relief (Skinner, 1957, Chapter 3). These generalized complaints have a connection to past circumstances where similar succor has been forthcoming. The therapy situation, as well as the examples of magical mands that were mentioned previously, are different from the usual situation where negatively reinforced operants occur. In these cases, the level of deprivation of the speaker–patient has exceeded the normal history of audience control so as to cause the emission of the complaint or request for relief, despite the lack of history with this particular therapist. It is for this reason that first interviews are technically so difficult in psychotherapy. The initial repertoire out of which the connection between the two parties is to emerge is a fantasy to which a listener could not conceivably comply with relief. Yet, it is this repertoire, the initial one, from which further behavioral development needs to emerge.

Reinforcement of Verbal Behavior by the Therapist–Listener

The change from generalized complaints to performances reinforced by their generic effect on the listener–therapist is, in itself, an exercise in the analysis of generic reinforcement. Even though complaints and requests for relief may require the participation of the therapist–listener, they function differently than the verbal interactions that can occur later in therapy when the immediate interaction with the therapist begins to sustain the patient's speech. The initial repertoire of the patient is relatively insensitive to the reaction of the therapist largely because it is a negatively reinforced operant, a mand in verbal jargon, largely under the control of the patient's deprivation and aversive stimulation.

In the final line of *Portnoy's Complaint*, Philip Roth's novel about psychoanalysis, the therapist says, "Now we can begin." This statement is made after virtually an entire novel of a soliloquy of complaints and illustrates the same shift in the functional control over the patient's speech to the therapist's repertoire. The change of the patient's behavior from generalized complaints to performances mediated by the therapist is an example of the refined definition of verbal behavior discussed earlier, in which the form and characteristics of the speaker's (patient's) behavior are determined by the uniquely verbal reactivity of the listener (therapist). The analogy, from the example of the seal balancing the ball, is to the pressure on the nose as the reinforcer rather than the food. The refined definition of verbal behavior involves the immediate effect of the interaction between the two persons such as occurs in the flash of an eye, the turning of the head, and how the content of a reply corresponds to the variables that control the patient's statement. The same process occurs, of course, with even more immediacy and fine grain when the speaker listens to him or herself. The speaker as his or her own listener, is an extension of interactions with other persons and hence is a special case of an external listener.

The Verbal Repertoire that Emerges under the Control of the Immediate Events of the Psychotherapeutic Interaction

The uniquely verbal aspect of the therapist's capacity to reinforce the patient's speech in a highly differentiated way is a by-product of his or her role as a trained listener. The therapist does not react equally to everything the patient says. For example, if a patient becomes annoyed at the sound of someone playing a piano in a nearby room, the therapist can comment on any one of several aspects of the patient's reaction. One particular therapist, at a particular time, may note how important music is for the patient and direct a comment to that. Other dimensions could have been dealt with equally, such as the interruption of the primary task, criticism of the therapist for having an office with such distractions, the low involvement in what was being said that such a mild intrusion would be diverting, or that the patient would waste money listening to music rather than get on with the work of the therapy. Almost any event that occurs during therapy is likely to have multiple determinants, and the therapist as the listener whose attention is the generic counterpart to what the patient is saying, has the capacity to differentially reinforce one or the other of the operants, depending on which aspect he or she reacts to. The therapist can therefore bring the patient's attention to one aspect of behavior rather than another. The control of the patient by the therapist is that of a generically defined performance, including the reinforcer of which it is a function, rather than the content, topography, or surface meaning of what the patient says.

Once the therapeutic pair is a dyad in which the reactivity of one reinforces the activity of the other, one outcome is an increased verbal repertoire under the control of the immediate events that are occurring in therapy. The important controlling events include the patient's behavior, the therapist's behavior, private events within the patient's repertoire, and the functional control between all of them. Possibly, the most important function of the verbal development is to make it possible for the patient to describe the variables of which his or her behavior is a function, many of which operate covertly. Prolonged silences, conflicts over appointment or fee schedules, discrepancies between the patient's demands and a practical view of what kinds of help are possible, arriving late or missing appointments, for example, frequently occur because some of the current events are too aversive to talk about. Once the therapist becomes a listener whose attention is generically connected to the patient's speech, there is the possibility of a verbal repertoire that can bring the variables controlling the lateness or the silence from the covert to the overt. The process appears analogous to the control by an aversive stimulus when it is preceded by a stimulus (a preaversive stimulus) and when, in the absence of a preceding stimulus, there is an explicit reinforcer for terminating or avoiding the aversive situation.

The differential reaction of the therapist can reinforce descriptions of current happenings, talk about private events within the patient's own person that she or he may be unaware of, the external variable of which such private events are a function, and the behaviors of others who interact in the process. Although it is customary, colloquially, to talk about how patients notice their own behavior, the reality, behaviorally, is the reverse, because it is the differential reaction of the therapist that reinforces verbal behavior under the control of the previously covert actions and influences. The new verbal repertoire increases the patient's observations of the variable controlling his or her behavior, overt behavior, and private events. Once such verbal behavior begins to develop, it would be expected to continue to grow autocatalytically. Desensitization of aversive control is another product of the patient's verbal activity that occurs when conditioned aversive reflexes are evoked in the natural context of therapy. While it is uncertain exactly how such desensitization can influence events elsewhere practically, the process surely contributes increased amounts of verbal activity that otherwise would be suppressed. The impact of such desensitization, of course, depends on the practical usefulness of the verbal activity that is facilitated, a topic that will be taken up next.

In summary, the increased verbal activity that occurs during psychotherapy emerges as *tacts* and *intraverbal* behavior under the control of (i.e., describing) the interactions between patient and therapist as they deal with the immediate events that accrue from their common task.

HOW TALKING ABOUT PAST AND PRESENT EVENTS TO A TRAINED LISTENER CAN INFLUENCE THE PATIENT'S LIFE ELSEWHERE

Since the behaviors that occur in therapy are different from the activities that occur elsewhere, a crucial task of a behavioral analysis is to describe the process by which the two repertoires influence each other. If there was no large discrepancy between what actually happened to a patient in daily living, and his or her report of what happened, there would not, in most cases, be a problem of the sort that required therapy.

Interpersonal Control with the Therapist

The interaction between the two parties is in itself an increase in repertoire and a model, for better or worse, of what may happen between any two people. To the extent that the patient learns to influence the therapist, there are elements of a repertoire that can influence other persons elsewhere. To the extent that the patient can observe the details of the therapist's conduct, how he or she has influenced it, and the reverse process, the patient has made progress toward the ability to make the same observations elsewhere. If a patient observes his or her own drowsiness or boredom and learns to search for provocative antecedents for this evidence of anxiety, there is a likelihood that he or she may be able to do a similar search when these symptoms occur elsewhere. The therapist as a trained observer, who is constantly making a functional analysis of the current transactions in therapy, is in the position analogous to the violin teacher, who can help the student hear nuances of pitch that are at first audible to the teacher and not to the student. The necessary condition, however, is that there is a significant disposition to play the violin so that notes are played that can be scrutinized.

The Verbal Repertoire from Psychotherapy Enhances Observation Elsewhere

The patient's ability to observe events in life is intimately connected to the ability to talk about them, just as touching something point-to-point with the forefinger, as the beginning reader touches the print on a page, brings behavior under a finer-grain control of the component details than if the only movement was that of the eyeball and its focus. An educational advantage of a verbal repertoire, tacts and intraverbals, is that it allows discrete, point-to-point correspondence with the details of what is observed. An art student, for example, has a vocabulary that touches nuances of a picture that otherwise go unnoticed. Having words for different colors provides tension, through the verbal community whose reactivity created the distinctions, to notice the differences. The psychotherapist, as the trained listener, provides the equivalent community for an analogous language that is in point-to-point correspondence with the interpersonal items that emerge in the therapy situation. Such descriptions, if they can be extended from psychotherapy to daily life, will move the functional control of the patient's behavior there from the covert to the overt forms.

A Verbal Repertoire Increases the Frequency of Positive Reinforcement and Decreases the Frequency of Aversive Control

There are large practical consequences of the presence or absence of a verbal repertoire that corresponds to one's own behavior, that of others, and the way that they control each other. Without such a repertoire, there is little possibility of reducing either the amount of aversive control or the amount of intermittent reinforcement and extinction. The process is analogous to the occurrence of *ad libitum* shocks in animal experiments as compared with a preshock stimulus; or it is analogous to an uncertain occurrence of a positive reinforcer as compared with clear events that set the occasion when a performance can be reinforced and when it goes unreinforced. A verbal repertoire that corresponds closely to the conditions of reinforcement and punishment is an orderly, predictable view of events that maximizes the frequency of positive reinforcement and minimizes aversive control. When such a repertoire is absent, a corollary is the emotional by-products, related to extinction and intermittent reinforcement, that are described colloquially as loss, isolation, pain, abandonment, hopelessness, and despair. Which one is described depends on which reinforcers and aversive events are involved. In general, pain, for example, alludes to aversive control, whether by a noxious stimulus or by the withdrawal of positive reinforcement, whereas hopelessness indicates a level of nonreinforcement approaching extinction. The contrast between a daily life amplified by verbal behavior about it and an absence of such verbal amplification is like the difference between a world that is orderly and predictable and one that is capricious (Beck, 1967).

It is commonly observed, for example, that a patient interrupted during therapy by frequent telephone calls may not be able to talk about his or her complaints, either overtly or intraverbally. The persistence and magnitude of the annoyance may be so large, however, as to preempt almost all other kinds of interaction with the therapist, and the patient will talk about being bored, about having nothing to say, or about quitting therapy; the patient may even be late or forget an appointment. If the patient can talk about this reaction and its connection to the therapist's telephone activity, there is some possibility of seeing them clearly and of actively influencing the important events—the interruptions of the therapy session or the anger about the interruptions. The alternative is a confused mixture of three corners of a triangle: the patient's observation of the interruption, the annoyance or anger at it, and a view of the therapist as the person who is responsible.

Desensitization and Self-Control

The desensitization that occurs as a corollary of the descriptive repertoire that the patient acquires about the events of therapy supports the development of self-control. So long as talk about difficult matters evokes substantial aversive control, the result will be some kind of overt activity that will reduce, by negative reinforcement, the aversive events. In other words, the patient will act overtly in some way to be removed from the provocative situation. Such overt activity, automatically reinforced by any incipient anxiousness, is the antithesis of self-control. It is significant that most prescriptions for self-control are verbal and involve titrating, to manageable levels, the aversiveness of the activity that is to be controlled.

THE DIFFERENCE BETWEEN PSYCHOTHERAPY AND EDUCATION

Some of the confusion between behavior modification techniques and the functional analysis of behavior can be clarified by distinguishing between educational and therapeutic methods. The generic relation between speaker and listener that has been described as the core process of psychotherapy is the crux of the distinction. Psychotherapeutic modes of behavior change make no assumptions about the patient's initial repertoire, except that it is assumed that there is a basis for some kind of generic connection between the patient's conduct and its influence on the therapist. Successive approximations from the patient's initial repertoire occur by interaction with the therapist that is equivalent to differential reinforcement of the one person by the other. The conversation may be about current events or after the fact, but the actual shaping of each other's conduct as they interact is the crucial factor on which all else rests.

Educational techniques, on the other hand, involve the rearrangement of an existing repertoire, aptly characterized by Goethe in the aphorism that you can only teach a student what he already knows. The behavioral changes are typically intraverbal and the reinforcers are predominately generalized, often arbitrary or aversive. Although educational changes optimally start with the student's existing repertoire, the progressive developments are more accurately seen as occurring with collateral sources of control and supplementary stimuli than with successive approximations. Controlling stimuli are faded and collateral variables are progressively withdrawn, in contrast to the successive approximation of discrete behaviors by specific reinforcers that occurs in psychotherapy. The psychotherapy behaviors are the specific items of conduct of each person as that conduct is reinforced by its direct effect on the other. Despite the importance of distinguishing between these two ways of altering behavior, there clearly are important instructional components in psychotherapy, and the immediate personal interactions between student and teacher control substantial amounts of behavior in educational situations. The distinction is based on which task is primary.

Interpretations of the kind that occur in psychodynamic therapy are an intermediate case. Interpretations are instructional because they prompt and recombine elements of an existing repertoire. A successful interpretation evokes thoughts that the patient is very close to saying unaided. On the other hand, interpretations are therapeutic to the extent that the interpretation is *about* behavioral interactions that occurred between patient and therapist that both of them observed. Practical advice given in therapy is also instructional because it functions to direct the patient's existing competence. However, it also serves as a pivotal tension in therapy when the therapist needs to react to unrealistic or impractical demands for advice, which may fail the patient because he or she distorts the advice that is given, or which the patient does not have the requisite repertoire to follow. Even more serious, the patient may not ask for advice at all and may not follow advice, even if it is given. In that event, the development of a connection between patient and therapist that allows educational interaction between them becomes an important objective of the therapy.

Even though the primary task is educational, the immediate interactions between teacher and student are influenced by the same processes that occur in psychotherapy. Initially, the student presents him or herself to the teacher as helpless and passive, demanding overtly or covertly that he or she be taught. Like the patient who spends the initial interviews in a long litany of complaints, the student begins the encounter with the professor as if knowledge were a liquid to be physically infused in a passive process. The student is often incapable of using instructional advice and spends considerable energy avoiding the teacher's competence.

Thus, the target repertoire of psychotherapy is the conduct that occurs as people influence each other with particular emphasis on explicit descriptions of how the individual controls and is controlled by other persons. Inevitably, there is an emphasis on bringing to overt states the kinds of control that were initially covert. Educational repertoires, largely intraverbal, are in the nature of added stimuli that can amplify observations and actions elsewhere or serve in verbal play between people. The mixture of educational and therapeutic procedures that occurs in almost any kind of therapy adds a special complexity to the generic nature of performances. Therapies that lean on instructional modes risk failure especially because there may not be a reinforcer to maintain the verbal development in the patient's daily life. The very nature of psychopathology suggests a repertoire with inertial qualities that resists change by advice, instruction, or experience. An example has already been given to suggest the complex development that has to occur before a patient can take advantage of any advice that a therapist may be able to give. Instruction, as a largely intraverbal event, has an arbitrary relation to the practical parts of life that are instructed about. Although there are clearly some circumstances when talking to someone in an office about life at home with spouse and children can influence those affairs, the influences can hardly be by direct reinforcement.

SUMMARY

It seems natural that an analysis of psychotherapy would give priority to the treatment practices that are shaped by interactions between patient and therapist. The immediate events of psychotherapy are the contingencies of reinforcement analogous to those of the experimental laboratory, where reinforcement is defined practically and theoretically as the instant and immediate consequence of a performance.

Many applications of behavioral analysis to practical situations have used reinforcers without a generic connection to the behavioral objectives. Technically, the utilization of reinforcement, as the immediate consequence of a performance, requires careful observation of the target behavior in the natural environment in order to identify the generically related reinforcers. A strict, technical analysis of behavioral principles applied to complex phenomena in the natural environment leads to the conclusion that performances reinforced arbitrarily are *not* equivalent to similar topographies of action maintained by other reinforcers that occur in the everyday situations where the behavior normally occurs. The emphasis on the fine grain of the performance and its reinforcer has led to powerful techniques of control in the animal laboratory and to the discovery of many new behavioral phenomena, as well as a language and a conceptual framework for communicating these. The analogous approach in psychotherapy emphasizes the priority of the fine-grain interaction between therapist and patient, the practical discoveries of control that have emerged from experience, and the concepts of a functional analysis of behavior that are applicable to the moment-to-moment objective events.

REFERENCES

Azrin, N. H. A strategy for applied research: Learning based but outcome oriented. *American Psychologist, 1977, 32,* 140–149.

Beck, A. *Depression.* Philadelphia: University of Pennsylvania Press, 1967.

Ferster, C. B. Arithmetic behavior in chimpanzees. *Scientific American, 1964, 210,* 98–106.

Ferster, C. B. Arbitrary and natural reinforcement. *Psychological Record, 1967, 17,* 341–347. (a)

Ferster, C. B. Transition from animal laboratory to clinic. *Psychological Record, 1967, 17,* 145–150. (b)

Ferster, C. B. Clinical reinforcement. *Seminars in Psychiatry, 1972, 4,* 101–111. (a)

Ferster, C. B. An experimental analysis of clinical phenomena. *Psychological Record, 1972, 22,* 1–16. (b)

Ferster, C. B. Behavioral language. *International Journal of Psychiatry, 1973, 11,* 189–195.

Ferster, C. B. The difference between behavioral and conventional psychology. *Journal of Nervous and Mental Disease, 1974, 159,* 153–157.

Ferster, C. B., & Culbertson, S. A psychology learning center. *Psychological Record, 1974, 24,* 33–46.

Findley, J. D. An experimental outline for building and exploring multi-operant behavior repertoires. *Journal of the Experimental Analysis of Behavior, 1962, 5,* 113–166.

Kelleher, R. T. Chaining and conditioned reinforcement. In W. K. Honig (Ed.), *Operant behavior: Areas of research and application.* New York: Appleton-Century-Crofts, 1966. Pp. 160–212.

Kellog, W. N., & Kellog, L. A. *The ape and the child: A study of environmental influences upon early behavior.* New York: Hatner, 1967. (Originally published, 1933.)

Premack, D. *Intelligence in ape and man.* Hillsdale, N.J.: Lawrence Erlbaum, 1976.

Skinner, B. F. *The behavior of organisms.* New York: Appleton-Century-Crofts, 1938.

Skinner, B. F. *Verbal behavior.* New York: Appleton-Century-Crofts, 1957.

4

Cognitive and Noncognitive Views in Behavior Modification

MICHAEL J. MAHONEY

The invitation to expound my views on cognition and behavior modification left me both flattered and eager to see what could be said. As the deadline drew closer, however, I wondered what new gleanings could be harvested—at least in print. For a moment I feared a contentless monologue, and I was bewildered as to how I could fill the space available without repeating previous remarks. In the absence of content, of course, my Irish genes would have me turn to humor—and I must admit I spent a few enjoyable moments fantasizing the friendly pokes that might be taken. As a token mentalist, for example, I thought about the fact that extreme experimentalists are sometimes described as both "hard-nosed" and "tight-assed." Now these adjectives conjure up some vivid acrobatic contortions with which one might have some metaphorical fun. My colleagues, on the other hand, might equally enjoy stretching the metaphor of "soft-headed" and point out the lyric similarities between "inference" and "imbecile." They might also endorse the saying recently attributed to television actor Robert Blake, star of "Baretta," who allegedly has a wall plaque that reads "Thinking Sucks."

But after enjoying these brief moments of fantasized jest, I realized that we may not yet be ready for such good-natured sparring. I have become very concerned of late about some of the animosity—both real and imagined—that has been evidenced between traditional behavior modifiers

39

Copyright © 1979 by Academic Press, Inc.
All rights of reproduction in any form reserved.
ISBN 0-12-647450-8

and the more recent cognitive mutants. Of course, there have been welcome exceptions, and I have been personally fortunate enough to enjoy simultaneous friendship and disagreement with several respected representatives of nonmediational views. On the other hand, I have also witnessed some lively animosities and even personal attacks emanating from both quarters. An implicit polarity has developed, and its extremes have been clearly visible in recent arguments for and against a cognitive division within the Association for the Advancement of Behavior Therapy (AABT). Rumors have multiplied about "separatist" plans—that the mentalists would march off and form their own group if they were not adequately represented. Some of the nonmediational people welcomed these rumors with comments of "good riddance," while others said that if the cognitivists were given representation then they would strike out to form their own nonmediational grouping.

Needless to say, all of this is very disconcerting—especially if one believes, as I do, that science progresses more efficiently through critical dialogue than through isolationism and polarities. There are important ideological differences that seem to divide our opinions, but I hope they need not also divide our commitment to a humane science—or blind us to the vast commonalities that we share. For example, I like to think of myself as an experimentalist who suffers occasional fits of conjecture. Experimentation and inference are, however, only prerequisites to the common task to which we have all committed ourselves—namely, helping people change.

Churchman once said that there are two kinds of people in the world—those who believe that there are two kinds of people and those who do not. It has long been my belief that there are few real dichotomies in science—or, indeed, in life—and that we are often better served by the idea of continua. If that notion is correct, then it would suggest that some of the polarities that seem to be thriving on the "cognitivism" issue may be receiving unwarranted nourishment. There are differences of opinion, to be sure, but I doubt that their extent or their epistemological centrality are as dire as some have painted them up to be. But these, of course, are conjectures, and at some point we must pay the piper with data.

AN EXPLORATORY SURVEY

For that reason, I decided to embark on an exploration of the ideological differences and commonalities that characterize contemporary representatives of the various perspectives. I constructed a questionnaire (see the appendix to this chapter) of 75 Likert-type questions dealing with the following topics: (a) environmentalism; (b) cognitive influence; (c) interactionism; (d) learning as conditioning; (e) determinism; (f) materialistic monism; (g) justificationism and factual relativity; (h) the role of theory; (i) single-subject versus group research methodology; (j) statistical inference; (k) parsimony and inference: (l) isolationism; (m) confirmatory bias; (n) satisfaction with paradigm; and (o) dogmatism. These topics obviously span a wide range of ontological, cosmological, and epistemological issues.[1]

After the questionnaire was completed, I struggled with the task of making some artificial but defensible groupings of persons believed to hold different professional opinions. After considerable deliberation, I came up with two relatively distinct groups—those who eschew cognitive variables and those who endorse what are called cognitive social learning perspectives. These categories are obviously arbitrary, and their margins are somewhat vague—a point consistent with my earlier hunch—but I think that they can be at least considered as loose groupings of divergence. Placing representatives within each grouping was also difficult in that there are so many productive and respected persons in each. There are also a few who span both categories or who would demand a separate grouping. Thus, I had trouble classifying Alan Kazdin and had considered a special category for him (such as hyperkinesis in remission). To make a short story boring, I originally considered restricting myself to 12 persons in each group (the "dirty dozen," I guess) but became concerned about attrition and ended up sending the questionnaires to 25 persons in each category.

Survey Results

Those who responded are shown in Table 4.1. They are, I think, a respected group of representatives, and I am indebted to them for their willingness to interrupt their busy schedules for a lengthy questionnaire. If it seems that an obvious participant was overlooked, please assume that the person was among the nonresponding subjects. The tongue-in-cheek remarks of one respondent who shall remain nameless may convey some flavor of one response style. In apologizing for the delay in his response, he wrote: "I can only hope that my delay won't preclude your making some use of my views. This is especially desirable inasmuch as my views are the correct views, and I assume that's why you asked me to respond— as an anchor point for the erroneous views of my colleagues." Comments such as this are often intermittent treasures in otherwise heady research. As the questionnaires were returned, I also found myself enjoying the realization that there are at least a few colleagues out there who may be just as confused as I am.

It would take more space than I have at my disposal to report all the data on their responses—although the details might be as interesting as the conclusions drawn from them. Needless to say, the conclusions drawn

[1] I am indebted to Walt Weimer for helping me refine some of the questions and for assuring me that he would deny any knowledge whatsoever of my endeavors. Todd Rogers and Diane Arnkoff were also responsible for reinforcing some of my efforts.

TABLE 4.1
Survey Participants

Noncognitive respondents	Cognitive respondents
Abel	Bandura
Agras	Beck
Azrin, N.H.	Bem, D.J.
Baer	Davison
Barlow	Ellis
Bijou	Frank
Brady	Gelfand, D.
Cautela	Goldfried, M.R.
Ferster	Kanfer
Franks, C.M.	Lazarus, A.A.
Kazdin	Lazarus, R.S.
Krasner	Mahoney, M.J.
Leitenberg	Marlatt
Liberman	Meichenbaum
O'Leary, K.D.	Phares
Paul	Rimm
Ullmann	Rotter
Wolpe	Sarason, I.G.
	Seligman
	Singer, J.L.
	Spivack
	Strickland
	Thoresen
	Wilson

from this survey are subject to the usual limitations imposed by sampling, response bias, and so on. Likewise, because of the large number of questions, I used a significance level of .01 (two-tailed) to provide a more conservative test of differences. Behrens–Fisher t tests were employed in all comparisons.

ENVIRONMENTALISM

One set of statements dealt with respondents' views on the role of environment in behavior control. A representative statement here read, "In the final analysis, almost all behavior is a function of environment." There were seven questions in this cluster—ranging from genetic influence to the role of nutrition and biochemistry. Although there was a trend toward greater environmentalism among noncognitive respondents, there was considerable variance and the group difference did not reach the selected significance level ($p < .02$). Analyses of responses to each of the seven questions similarly revealed a lack of dissension. The two groups were in basic agreement on six of the questions. Their only dissension took the form of cognitive respondents disagreeing with the contention that "reinforcement or punishment are necessary factors in most human learning" ($p < .001$).

COGNITIVE INFLUENCE

One might expect that the single most distinguishing topic between these two groups would be their attribution of causal influence to cognitive processes. Seven questions were directed to this issue. Interestingly, the summary comparison did not reveal a significant group difference ($p < .03$). On individual questions, both groups felt that awareness is an important variable in learning and that expectancy is a powerful factor in some behavior therapy techniques. They also agreed that relationship factors "are significant elements in the effectiveness of behavior therapy." Their only clear disagreement was on the promise and power of private events and thought patterns as influential factors in adjustment ($p < .01$). Needless to say, this finding is an interesting one in terms of the polarity presumed to exist on the dimension of cognitive influence.

INTERACTIONISM

Three questions were addressed to the issues of interactionism and reciprocal determinism. Overall, the two groups showed a wide range of opinions and could not be said to be in general disagreement on the topic. For example, both cognitive and noncognitive respondents strongly agreed that "an adequate model of human behavior must acknowledge interactionism or reciprocal determinism." On the other hand, persons classified as noncognitive were less satisfied with the term "self-control" and were more likely to assert that "all control begins with the environment" ($p < .001$).

LEARNING AS CONDITIONING

The first topic on which there was clear disagreement was the question of whether learning is a conditioning process. Four questions were devoted to this topic. A representative statement asserted that "the basic process in clinical behavior change is conditioning." The two groups disagreed on all four statements, both individually and combined ($p < .001$). Noncognitive respondents were very strong in their endorsement of the assertion that "conditioning models offer the most adequate contemporary perspective on human learning" ($p < .001$). It seems clear, then, that the processes of learning may be a differentiating issue between cognitive and noncognitive adherents.

DETERMINISM

Four questions were devoted to the topics of determinism and causation. There were no significant disagreements between the two groups on any of the four. Both cognitive and noncognitive persons were determinists in the sense of seeing all events as having a cause and (in principle) being predictable. Likewise, both groups were skeptical about the existence of free will.

MATERIALISTIC MONISM

Given the frequency with which cognitive theorists are accused of being mentalists (Skinner, 1974), one might expect to find a group difference on the metaphysical issue of "mind." This was not the case, however. The two groups were indistinguishable on the existence of a nonphysical entity called the mind. This was also true of their opinions on physical reductionism and the wisdom of emulating the physical sciences in our research. It should be noted, however, that this lack of overall disagreement was partially owing to the wide dispersion of opinions within each group.

JUSTIFICATIONISM AND FACTUAL RELATIVITY

Justificationism and factual relativity are very relevant topics in terms of contemporary views of science (Mahoney, 1976; Weimer, 1979). Briefly, justificationism refers to philosophies that make at least one irrational leap of faith to an absolute authority (e.g., data or logic). They are "justificational" in the sense that they presume that their rationality is "justified" on the basis of some indisputable criterion. As noted by Bartley (1962), however, all such philosophies are inherently irrational by virtue of self-contradiction. That is, they demand that a perspective be able to defend or justify its rationality, but they then invoke an unjustifiable criterion for their own rationality. The perplexity and implications of this predicament are discussed at length elsewhere (Mahoney, 1976; Weimer, 1979).

Factual relativity refers to the assumption that facts are not immutable pieces of truth but, rather, are relative to the paradigm from which they are viewed. Contemporary philosophers seem to generally concede the relativity of evidence and have rejected the notion that science progresses by simply accumulating facts. Six questions were devoted to these two issues. Interestingly, there were no group differences on any of the six questions, although the noncognitive group seemed to tend toward justificationism and factual fixedness when the questions were pooled ($p < .01$). There was again tremendous variance within groups. It is worth noting, however, that both groups objected strongly to the assertion that "data never lie" and both agreed that "facts are not fixed pieces of truth."

Factual relativism and a rejection of justificational philosophies need not, incidentally, threaten the importance of data in science. While our evidence may be relative rather than absolute in its authority, it is still an integral component of empiricism. With regard to the relative emphasis placed on data by cognitive and noncognitive persons, it would appear that both groups were heavily data oriented. As mentioned earlier, there was a tendency for noncognitive respondents to place more absolute authority in experimental evidence, but this should not be interpreted as suggesting that cognitive respondents placed little emphasis on evidence. Data figured as an important arbiter for both groups. Likewise, given the frequency with which the label "cognitive" is associated with connotations of being non-rigorous, it is noteworthy that the two groups were strong and identical in their endorsement of quantitative assessment as "a critically important component in successful therapy."

ROLE OF THEORY

Four questions were addressed to the role and value of theory in scientific research. There were no intergroup differences on any of these questions, either individually or in combination. Interestingly—and, I think, reassuringly—members of both groups strongly agreed that "theories or hypotheses significantly influence how and what a scientist will observe." This is obviously a reflection of some of my own biases in philosophy of science, but they are at least biases that are shared by a number of contemporary metatheorists (Kuhn, 1962; Weimer, 1979). It is, I think, commendable that behavior therapists in general appear to be aware of the impact of their theories on their perception and interpretation of reality.

SINGLE-SUBJECT VERSUS GROUP RESEARCH

Three questions were aimed at the relative strengths of single-subject and group designs. Cognitive and noncognitive respondents differed on only one of these—namely, that "single-subject experimental designs are adequate and sufficient for demonstrating the effects of a particular variable" ($p < .001$). There was a tendency, however, for cognitive respondents to rate the internal and external validity of group designs as superior to that of $N = 1$ research ($p < .04$). Neither of the groups felt that replication was substantially more important in one kind of research than in the other.

STATISTICAL INFERENCE

Data interpretation is another area that is presumed to differentiate the groups under study. Four questions dealt with the issues of statistical inference and experimental results. There was a tendency for cognitive respondents to view inferential statistics as more invaluable in the interpretation of data ($p < .02$). On the other hand, both groups strongly agreed that "even when statistical procedures are appropriately applied, they can sometimes be quite misleading." Although there was considerable variance, the two groups were also in general agreement that good experiments do not necessarily yield clear "yes or no" results.

PARSIMONY AND INFERENCE

Even though Skinner and others have acknowledged the possible role of private events in human behavior, they have also rendered a clear recommendation to uphold parsimony and minimize inference. This viewpoint was reflected in the eight questionnaire items devoted to these issues. There was an overall group difference that reflected greater faith in parsimony and more concern about inference on the part of noncognitive respondents ($p < .001$). It is noteworthy that both groups showed a strong consensus on the value of operationism. On the other hand, noncognitive persons tended to more strongly believe that "one cannot be a scientist without being a behaviorist" ($p < .01$). They were likewise less tolerant of the notion that unobservable events are legitimate variables in behavioral science ($p < .002$). Finally, noncognitive respondents tended to be more supportive of the assertion that "unless they can be operationalized, feelings are of little use in a scientific analysis of human behavior" ($p < .025$).

ISOLATIONISM

Krantz (1971) has noted the isolationism of operant researchers and the influence of this factor in scientific progress is clearly discernible (Kuhn, 1962; Mahoney, 1976). Although periods and degrees of isolationism may be beneficial at various stages of paradigm development, isolationism appears to function more as an impediment than as an impetus to scientific progress. It was therefore somewhat sobering to find that the noncognitive respondents in this survey appeared to have read more of the cognitive literature relative to the cognitive people having read recent operant literature ($p < .01$). More reassuring was the strong consensus that we need "a continuing interchange between traditional and cognitive behavior modifiers." Noncognitive persons were, however, less optimistic about whether "cognitive psychology has much to offer the behavior therapist" ($p < .001$). They were also more inclined to view "the recent interest in cognition among behavior modifiers [as] an unfortunate and counter-productive development" ($p < .001$). Neither group was particularly impressed with the potential promise of existentialism and phenomenological approaches. The wide range of respondents' opinions is worthy of note, however.

CONFIRMATORY BIAS AND INDUCTIONISM

Confirmatory bias refers to a scientist's views on the role of positive versus negative results in theory evaluation (Mahoney, 1976). It is basically a tendency to emphasize and elaborate data that are congruent with one's beliefs and, at the same time, to ignore, disqualify, or otherwise deemphasize disconfirmatory data. The philosophical and psychological aspects of this pattern are, I think, among the most significant in the whole of science.

In the present study, the two groups were indistinguishable in their views on positive and negative results. A wide range of opinions yielded means that were midrange—that is, neither supportive nor critical of the importance of negative results. One clear assertion—and there was again strong consensus on this—was that "a hypothesis merits greater confidence the more it is supported by replication." Likewise it was reassuring to find that both groups were consistent in rejecting the notion that our confidence in a hypothesis should reflect a simple ratio of positive to negative results. Given the significance of anomalies in paradigm development, however, one might wish that there were more consensual appreciation of negative results by members of both categories.

SATISFACTION WITH PARADIGM

One of the clearest signs of scientific revolution is dissatisfaction with one's paradigm. Since we do not have data on past satisfaction, however, it is impossible to determine whether the respondents were in the process of changing their confidence. It was noteworthy, however, that persons in the present study were generally dissatisfied with their current understanding of human behavior. On a 7-point scale, noncognitive respondents rated their satisfaction at a mean of 2.06 as compared with 1.83 on the part of cognitive respondents. This difference was not statistically significant. Unfortunately, the question itself may have been poorly phrased in that one can be very satisfied with one's paradigm and still frustrated with one's understanding of human behavior. It would be interesting to study changes in our own beliefs over a decade to get a better idea of our development as a paradigm (see Kuhn, 1962).

DOGMATISM

The final topic addressed by the questionnaire was that of dogmatism, which is here meant to be synonymous with strength and fixedness of belief. Interestingly, both groups felt strongly that they could think of "an experiment or set of experiments whose results would persuade me to abandon my current views." There were individuals in both groups who could not conceive of such experiments, but they were in the minority. A supplementary analysis was performed to see whether persons classified as cognitive or noncognitive were differentially inclined toward "extreme" views—that is, using the polarized ends of the Likert scale rather than its middle. There was no significant group difference in strength of opinion. Once again, individuals within each group ranged from adamant to noncommital in their opinions, and this was often evident *within* respondents *across* issues.

The questionnaire concluded with a brief section that asked respondents to rate 14 individuals on a cognitive–noncognitive dimension of 1 to 10. Of the individuals rated, there were no significant group differences—

partly because of the extreme variability in responding. There was a trend toward dissension in the rating of four individuals (Brady, Cautela, Ullmann, and myself), with noncognitive respondents always seeing these persons as more cognitive than did their mediational peers. The list of names was intentionally comprised of past AABT presidents and the two 1978 presidential candidates. This allowed me to graph (after the 1978 election) the perceived "cognitiveness" of the AABT president from its beginnings until now. Figure 4.1 shows that no consistent trend can be discerned.

DISCUSSION AND CONCLUSION

Depending on whether these results are congruent with our personal beliefs, we may either welcome or reject their implications. For those who would reject them, there are ample points for attack: Did I choose a representative sample? Was my assignment to groups objective? Were my questions unambiguous and relevant? While I do not harbor any delusions about the possible shortcomings of my methodology, I am reluctant to simply dismiss the results as uninformative. Within the constraints of the sample and design, I think there are some interesting conjectures that are warranted by the present data.

First, there is monumental variance in opinion—both within groups and in a given individual across topics. This is illustrated in Figure 4.2, which shows the range of responses on selected questions. Note that it was not uncommon for individuals in both groups to span the entire range from strong agreement to strong disagreement. This variability is something worth bearing in mind (or wherever one bears such things) as we classify ourselves and our colleagues. It would appear that our dichotomous stereotypes do not hold up very well. As George Kelly once pointed out,

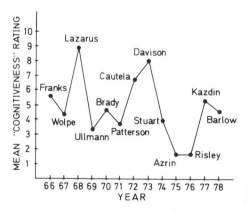

FIGURE 4.1. *Mean "cognitiveness" ratings of presidents of the Association for the Advancement of Behavior Therapy.*

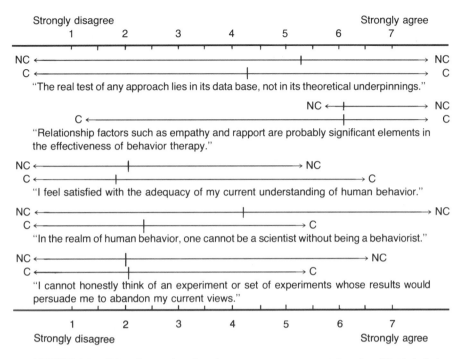

FIGURE 4.2. *Selected examples of variance on responses to questionnaire. (Vertical slashes indicate means; horizontal lines indicate range. NC = noncognitive; C = cognitive.)*

we may need to be careful to avoid the insidious disease that he called "hardening of the categories." As I reviewed the data, I began to wonder whether I should not have classified the respondents as "more cognitive" versus "less cognitive." It would perhaps be more accurate not to classify them at all. We must bear in mind that our human tendency to classify is one that necessarily distorts and disregards individual variance.

This leads to the second general implication of the present data—namely, that we are mistaken if we assume that cognitive and noncognitive behavior therapists are necessarily polarized in all of their views. Out of the 15 topics addressed, there were only a handful on which the two groups displayed strong and consistent divergence of opinion. The general consensus on the value of operationism, assessment, and replication is particularly noteworthy. To highlight points of disagreement is to overlook the more extensive points on which there seems to be consensus. I do not mean to imply by this that the differences may be nominal—they involve critical issues that merit our continuing appraisal. It is my concern, however, that we appreciate our commonalities and the value of ongoing dialectical exchange. The data suggesting a shared endorsement of such an exchange were, to me at least, encouraging. Less reassuring was the finding that cognitive people seem to be isolating themselves from the conditioning literature, while noncognitive persons seem to view cognitive behavior modification as an unfortunate and counterproductive development in the field.

We are now, I think, at an important crossroad in terms of the future interaction of cognitive and noncognitive perspectives. At the one extreme we face the possibility of increasing polarization and all that comes with it—personal animosity, misunderstandings, and (I think worst of all) isolationism and stagnation. The history of science shows clearly that lively exchange and critical dialogues tend to nurture knowledge, not retard it. Thus, I hope that we will turn toward a path of continuing and even expanded intercourse, with thoughtful exploration of our differences, reflective appreciation of our commonalities, and mutual respect for our integrity in pursuing a science that is truly humane in its achievements.

APPENDIX: ASSUMPTIONS AND PRINCIPLES QUESTIONNAIRE

		Strongly Disagree					Strongly Agree
1.	Human learning is basically governed by principles of operant and classical conditioning.	1 2 3 4 5 6 7
2.	Single subject experimental designs are adequate and sufficient for demonstrating the effects of a particular variable.	1 2 3 4 5 6 7
3.	Physiology usually has little to offer in terms of relevant information for behavior change.	1 2 3 4 5 6 7
4.	Experimenters tend to "find" what they expect to find.	1 2 3 4 5 6 7
5.	Operationism is a valid and valuable component of behavioral research.	1 2 3 4 5 6 7
6.	Human behavior is predominantly determined by principles of learning (as contrasted with genetic influence).	1 2 3 4 5 6 7
7.	Behavioral science should emulate the rigor and philosophy of the physical sciences.	1 2 3 4 5 6 7
8.	In the realm of human behavior, one cannot be a scientist without being a behaviorist.	1 2 3 4 5 6 7
9.	Awareness of contingencies is a very powerful factor in human learning.	1 2 3 4 5 6 7
10.	Animal research on punishment and schedules of reinforcement is very relevant to the goals of the clinical behavior therapist.	1 2 3 4 5 6 7
11.	Determinism is true; all events have a cause and are (in principle) predictable.	1 2 3 4 5 6 7
12.	Reinforcement or punishment are necessary factors in most human learning.	1 2 3 4 5 6 7
13.	Behaviors influence environments and vice-versa, so that an adequate model of human behavior must acknowledge "interactionism" or "reciprocal" determinism.	1 2 3 4 5 6 7

	Strongly Disagree					Strongly Agree

14. Events which cannot be directly observed have no place in behavioral science.
   1 2 3 4 5 6 7

15. Genetics probably play a minimal role in the determination of human behavior.
   1 2 3 4 5 6 7

16. Inferential statistics are an invaluable aid in interpreting the results of an experiment.
   1 2 3 4 5 6 7

17. Expectancy, demand characteristics, and similar "non-specific" variables probably play an important role in the effectiveness of some behavior therapy techniques.
   1 2 3 4 5 6 7

18. Theories or hypotheses always precede observation.
   1 2 3 4 5 6 7

19. Science progresses by accumulating facts (or data) from which knowledge is eventually distilled.
   1 2 3 4 5 6 7

20. At present, there is considerable evidence to suggest that private events (e.g., patterns of thought) may be very influential factors in human adjustment.
   1 2 3 4 5 6 7

21. In terms of internal and external validity, group experimental designs are superior to single subject designs.
   1 2 3 4 5 6 7

22. There is no such thing as a non-physical entity called the "mind."
   1 2 3 4 5 6 7

23. Logical induction is the cornerstone of scientific progress.
   1 2 3 4 5 6 7

24. Data never lie.
   1 2 3 4 5 6 7

25. The principles which govern observable behaviors also govern the "private events" which are sometimes termed "cognition."
   1 2 3 4 5 6 7

26. There is nothing in the world which is not, in final analysis, reducible to physical properties.
   1 2 3 4 5 6 7

27. For any hypothesis which has yielded both "positive" (successful) and "negative" (unsuccessful) predictions, our confidence in its truth status should be a simple ratio of "positive" to "positive plus negative." For example, if 100 methodogically sound experiments have yielded 70 successes and 30 failures, we are logically warranted in being about 70% confident in the truth of the hypothesis.
   1 2 3 4 5 6 7

28. Causality can never be demonstrated.
   1 2 3 4 5 6 7

29. I have extensively read the past and current literatures on traditional (operant and respondent) behavior modification.
   1 2 3 4 5 6 7

30. I would favor a continuing interchange between "traditional" and "cognitive" behavior modifiers in the interest of stimulation and growth.
   1 2 3 4 5 6 7

31. The real test of any approach lies in its data base, not its theoretical underpinnings.
   1 2 3 4 5 6 7

32. Parsimony is a valid and valuable guideline in theory evaluation.
   1 2 3 4 5 6 7

33. At some level of analysis, all human behavior can be conceptualized in terms of stimuli and responses.
   1 2 3 4 5 6 7

	Strongly Disagree	Strongly Agree

34. Data play a relatively minor role in the evaluation of theoretical models.   1 2 3 4 5 6 7

35. Thoughts and mental images are probably conditioned mediating responses which act as stimuli for subsequent behavior.   1 2 3 4 5 6 7

36. A truly empirical philosophy requires that one's inferences be kept to a minimum.   1 2 3 4 5 6 7

37. Unconscious processes probably play a minor role (if any) in human behavior.   1 2 3 4 5 6 7

38. A person's perception of a contingency can override the effects of the actual contingency.   1 2 3 4 5 6 7

39. The term "self-control" is an enigma in that all control begins with the environment.   1 2 3 4 5 6 7

40. Human beings possess "free will"--i.e., they are capable of consciously overriding their current stimulation and past learning history.   1 2 3 4 5 6 7

41. "Relationship" factors such as "empathy" and "rapport" are probably significant elements in the effectiveness of behavior therapy.   1 2 3 4 5 6 7

42. The only difference between prediction, description, and explanation is timing--all three are technically descriptions which either precede, parallel, or follow the event in question.   1 2 3 4 5 6 7

43. A person's choices are completely determined by his learning history and the current stimulation.   1 2 3 4 5 6 7

44. Observational (or vicarious) learning is probably based on generalized (conditioned) imitation.   1 2 3 4 5 6 7

45. When the behaviorist begins to infer private events from observable performances, he has abandoned behaviorism.   1 2 3 4 5 6 7

46. I have extensively read the recent literature on cognitive and social learning models.   1 2 3 4 5 6 7

47. Negative results are very informative and should be published as readily as positive results.   1 2 3 4 5 6 7

48. In the final analysis, almost all behavior is a function of environment.   1 2 3 4 5 6 7

49. I feel satisfied with the adequacy of my current understanding of human behavior.   1 2 3 4 5 6 7

50. The advancement of a model or theory is dramatically influenced by the personalities and rhetorical skills of its proponents.   1 2 3 4 5 6 7

51. I cannot honestly think of an experiment or set of experiments whose results would persuade me to abandon my current views.   1 2 3 4 5 6 7

52. Logical positivism is the current and most reasonable foundation of science.   1 2 3 4 5 6 7

53. Science is a demonstrably logical and rational endeavor.   1 2 3 4 5 6 7

	Strongly Disagree					Strongly Agree	

54. The proper or most efficient scientific sequence is: observation, hypothesis, experiment. 1 2 3 4 5 6 7

55. The "health" of a theory is solely determined by its congruence with available evidence. 1 2 3 4 5 6 7

56. Private events (thoughts, images, etc.) offer little promise in enhancing our understanding and control of human behavior. 1 2 3 4 5 6 7

57. Conditioning models offer the most adequate contemporary perspective on human learning. 1 2 3 4 5 6 7

58. Biological factors (such as nutrition and sleep patterns) probably play a relatively minor role in maladaptive human behavior. 1 2 3 4 5 6 7

59. Facts are not fixed pieces of truth but are relative to the observer's conceptual framework. 1 2 3 4 5 6 7

60. The best procedures for effecting behavior change rely primarily on changing the observable anetcedents and consequences of a behavior. 1 2 3 4 5 6 7

61. Cognitive psychology may have much to offer the behavior therapist. 1 2 3 4 5 6 7

62. Hypothetico-deductive method is superior to induction as an approach to knowledge. 1 2 3 4 5 6 7

63. Public debates and discussions of non-traditional views are generally a waste of time. 1 2 3 4 5 6 7

64. Data are the ultimate authority in science. 1 2 3 4 5 6 7

65. Theories or hypotheses significantly influence how and what a scientist will observe. 1 2 3 4 5 6 7

66. The recent interest in "cognition" among behavior modifiers is an unfortunate and counter-productive development. 1 2 3 4 5 6 7

67. Quantitative assessment is a critically important component in successful therapy. 1 2 3 4 5 6 7

68. The basic process in clinical behavior change is conditioning. 1 2 3 4 5 6 7

69. Existentialism and phenomenological approaches have little to offer the behavior therapist. 1 2 3 4 5 6 7

70. An hypothesis merits greater confidence the more it is supported by replication. 1 2 3 4 5 6 7

71. Even when statistical procedures are appropriately applied, they can sometimes be quite misleading. 1 2 3 4 5 6 7

72. An adequate psychology would not describe the organism and stimuli independently. 1 2 3 4 5 6 7

73. Good experiments yield clear "yes or no" results. 1 2 3 4 5 6 7

74. Unless they can be operationalized, "feelings" are of little use in a scientific analysis of human behavior. 1 2 3 4 5 6 7

75. Replication is more important in single subject than in group research. 1 2 3 4 5 6 7

Please rate each of the following persons on the hypothetical continuum
between cognitive and non-cognitive viewpoints. It is important that
you rate all 14 persons, even if you happen to be one of them.

	Very Non-Cognitive									Very Cognitive	
Nathan H. Azrin	0	1	2	3	4	5	6	7	8	9	10
John Paul Brady	0	1	2	3	4	5	6	7	8	9	10
Joseph R. Cautela	0	1	2	3	4	5	6	7	8	9	10
Gerald C. Davison	0	1	2	3	4	5	6	7	8	9	10
Cyril M. Franks	0	1	2	3	4	5	6	7	8	9	10
Alan E. Kazdin	0	1	2	3	4	5	6	7	8	9	10
Arnold A. Lazarus	0	1	2	3	4	5	6	7	8	9	10
Michael J. Mahoney	0	1	2	3	4	5	6	7	8	9	10
David H. Barlow	0	1	2	3	4	5	6	7	8	9	10
Gerald R. Patterson	0	1	2	3	4	5	6	7	8	9	10
Todd R. Risley	0	1	2	3	4	5	6	7	8	9	10
Richard B. Stuart	0	1	2	3	4	5	6	7	8	9	10
Leonard P. Ullmann	0	1	2	3	4	5	6	7	8	9	10
Joseph Wolpe	0	1	2	3	4	5	6	7	8	9	10

Thank you again for your time and cooperation. If you would like to see the
results of this study, please check the space below. My best wishes for a
pleasant summer.

Michael J. Mahoney

_____ Please send me a copy of the results.

REFERENCES

Bartley, W. W. *The retreat to commitment*. New York: Knopf, 1962.

Krantz, D. L. The separate worlds of operant and non-operant psychology. *Journal of Applied Behavior Analysis*, 1971, 4, 61–70.

Kuhn, T. S. *The structure of scientific revolutions*. Chicago: University of Chicago Press, 1962.

Mahoney, M. J. *Scientist as subject: The psychological imperative*. Cambridge, Mass.: Ballinger, 1976.

Skinner, B. F. *About behaviorism*. New York: Knopf, 1974.

Weimer, W. B. *Notes on the methodology of scientific research*. Hillsdale, N.J.: Lawrence Erlbaum, 1979.

5

Cognitive–Behavioral Modification: Future Directions

DONALD MEICHENBAUM

The mid-1970s have seen an increasing interest in the role of cognitive factors in behavior change. This interest is evident in publications by Beck (1976), Goldfried and Davison (1976), Mahoney (1974), and Meichenbaum (1977a), and in the appearance of a journal, *Cognitive Therapy and Research*. Before considering potential new directions of this approach, a number of observations should be offered about the state of the art in general.

COGNITIVE–BEHAVIORAL MODIFICATION

A Shotgun Wedding

The area of cognitive–behavioral modification (CBM) has evolved out of an attempt to wed the technology of behavior therapy with the clinical concerns of cognitive–semantic therapists. Could the behavior therapy techniques of desensitization, modeling, behavioral and imaginal rehearsal, and conditioning procedures be combined with the clinical concerns expressed by such therapists as Jerome Frank, George Kelley, Albert Ellis, Aaron Beck, and others? Out of this "shotgun wedding" has come a variety of new therapeutic procedures.

TRENDS IN BEHAVIOR THERAPY

Copyright © 1979 by Academic Press, Inc.
All rights of reproduction in any form reserved.
ISBN 0-12-647450-8

Collected Diversity

An important observation is that a "uniformity myth" should not be imposed upon CBM, for it includes a wide range of treatment procedures and different theoretical views about the role cognitions play in behavior pathology and behavior change. For example, Mahoney and Arnkoff (1978) list rational psychotherapies, coping skills therapies, self-instructional training, and problem-solving therapies all under the rubric of CBM. Each of these therapy procedures focus on different aspects of the client's cognitive processes, such as beliefs, attributions, expectations, and problem-solving strategies. Moreover, each CBM therapy provides different prescriptions about the best point of intervention in the chain of cognition–affect–behavior and environmental consequences. Some CBM therapies frontally attack beliefs, whereas others encourage clients to produce incompatible behaviors before focusing on expectations, beliefs, and so on. The CBM techniques differ in terms of relative emphasis placed on formal logical analysis (i.e., isolation and evaluation of premises), the degree of directness with which the therapeutic rationale and procedures are presented, and the relative reliance on adjunctive behavior therapy procedures.

Stated simply, there is *no* clearly agreed upon or commonly accepted definition of CBM. Interestingly, Wilson (1978) has drawn a similar conclusion with regard to the definition of behavior therapy. Given the present state of affairs, a precise definition of CBM could prove to be too restrictive.

Empirical Support

The third observation involves the efficacy of CBM procedures. At this point the enthusiasm for CBM procedures exceeds its empirical support. Although some initial promissory notes have been offered with regard to CBM (e.g., Di Guiseppe, Miller, & Trexler, 1977; Meichenbaum, 1977a, 1978; Rush, Beck, Kovacs, & Hollon, 1977) uncritical acceptance is clearly not indicated.

CBM's Predecessors

Finally it should be noted that CBM in fact has a past of sorts. Theorists and therapists (such as Dubois, 1905; Shaffer, 1947; and many others) have previously described procedures similar to current CBM techniques.

Now that I have observed that CBM cannot be explicitly defined and that its empirical basis is only promissory, I intend to speculate about future directions. Like most soothsayers, data need not restrict my prognostications. My speculations about the new directions will first examine work with children; I will then consider CBM treatment procedures with adults.

COGNITIVE–BEHAVIORAL MODIFICATION WITH CHILDREN

Treatment studies with children initially have focused on the problem of impulse control with hyperactive and aggressive children (e.g., Bornstein & Quevillon, 1976; Camp, Blom, Herbert, & van Doorninck, 1977; Douglas, Parry, Marton, & Garson, 1976; Meichenbaum & Goodman, 1971). These studies have indicated that self-control can be established in children by means of a self-instructional training program, which is composed of modeling, overt and covert rehearsal, prompts, feedback, and social reinforcement. In short, a multifaceted training format is employed in order to teach children to "think before they act." The Douglas *et al.* (1976) study nicely illustrates the general treatment approach. Hyperactive children were initially exposed to a model who verbalized cognitive strategies that the child rehearsed, first aloud and later covertly. The cognitive strategies included: (*a*) stopping to define a problem and the various steps within it; (*b*) considering and evaluating several possible solutions before acting on any one; (*c*) checking one's work throughout and calmly correcting any errors; (*d*) sticking with a problem until everything possible has been tried to solve it correctly; and (*e*) giving oneself a pat on the back for work well done. Elsewhere (Meichenbaum, 1977a), I have offered a number of clinical suggestions for conducting self-instructional training with children.

New Directions in Self-Instructional Training Procedures

A number of new directions can be identified with regard to self-instructional training procedures with children. These directions are discussed in the sections that follow.

COMPARATIVE OUTCOME STUDIES

In terms of outcome studies, the major research task will be a comparison of the relative efficacy of self-instructional training versus alternative treatment modes such as operant procedures and medication treatment (e.g., with disruptive children labeled hyperactive). The question of how self-instructional procedures can be combined with other techniques has recently received some attention by Kendall and Finch (1978), who found that the addition of an operant response cost system to the self-instructional package enhanced treatment efficacy.

DISMANTLING STUDIES

A second research strategy that will be employed is the dismantling procedure, whereby various components of the self-instructional training procedure will be systematically examined. Two types of dismantling pro-

cedures are likely to be considered. One strategy will be to compare treatment groups that receive interpersonal instructions alone, behavioral
modeling alone, verbal modeling alone, or overt and covert rehearsal alone.
As in the studies with desensitization, the treatment components will be
considered in various combinations. Some beginnings in this direction
have been offered by Bender (1976) and Wein and Nelson (1978).

A second dismantling research approach is to compare various elements of the modeled self-statements that the children, in turn, rehearse.
Such an approach has been followed by Alkus (1977) and Spates and
Kanfer (1977). Alkus found that children who employed coping self-
statements that focused on error-correcting strategies and normalizing
self-statements of a self-reinforcing nature improved more in academic
performance than did children who employed problem-solving self-
statements. Similarly, Spates and Kanfer found that criterion-setting self-
statements were most important in fostering children's academic performance.

What is intriguing about the latter dismantling strategy approach,
which focuses on specific self-statements, is that it raises basic theoretical
questions about the nature of rule-generative behavior. How are interpersonal instructions, modeled by a therapist, teacher, or parent, converted
into the child's own private speech and thought? Moreover, how does
private speech come to influence, on the one hand, the child's overt behavior, and on the other hand, his or her cognitive structures (i.e., beliefs,
attributions, and meanings)? Vygotsky (1962) observed in *Thought and Language* that the processes of "internalization" and "abbreviation" should not
be viewed merely as faded speech; instead the transformation from interpersonal speech to thought represents qualitative differences in structure.
The future research on self-instructional training must explain the basic
transformation process by which overt interpersonal speech alters covert
intrapersonal speech. The explication of these processes will have major
implications for the potential of self-instructional training.

In short, we will continue to examine a number of technological questions that involve comparative outcome studies and dismantling studies. In
addition, we must begin to examine the more basic theoretical questions
that are central to the self-instructional training regimen.

INDIVIDUAL DIFFERENCES

Another direction will be the examination of the role of individual
differences in response to self-instructional training. For example, Bugenthal, Whalen, and Henker (1977) have recently found an interaction between children's motivational style and the particular mode of treatment
intervention. Hyperactive boys were individually tutored for 2 months in a
classroom setting; half received self-instructional training and half participated in an operant social reinforcement program. Significant interactive

differences were found between the intervention approach and children's attributional style. Those boys who attributed their success to "luck" showed greater improvement following the reinforcement method, whereas those who attributed their progress to "effort" benefited from self-instructional training. The Bugenthal *et al.* (1977) study highlights the potential value of matching a child's attributional style with attributional assumptions in an intervention package. As we learn to analyze more adequately the nature of the deficit that underlies the children's problems (e.g., Camp, 1977; Meichenbaum, 1977a) we can begin to tailor our treatment intervention more effectively.

THE USE OF PLAY AND IMAGERY

The major focus thus far in the application of CBM procedures to children has been on the use of language as a useful medium for teaching problem-solving and decision-making skills that can lead to altered behavioral patterns. This focus on the use of language should not lead us to forget another powerful but often neglected medium for enhancing children's self-control, namely, play and the accompanying processes of imagery and fantasy. Elsewhere (Meichenbaum, 1978) I have reviewed the potential of play as a means of enhancing children's performance. In suggesting the viability of play for implementing behavior change I am not suggesting a return to traditional play therapy procedures but rather a structured play and imagery technique such as Schneider and Robin's (1976) "turtle technique" or Goodwin and Mahoney's (1975) "circle game." In the "turtle technique" the child is read a story about a turtle who copes by going into its shell and practicing relaxation and self-instructional problem-solving skills. The child is encouraged to "do turtle" by emulating the same ritual when frustrated. In the "circle game" aggressive children are placed around a circle and asked to taunt and tease the therapist, who is in the middle of the ring. The therapist acts as a cognitive coping model, emitting the behavior and self-statements by which he or she can handle the provocations. The children in turn rehearse similar coping skills by following the lead of the therapist.

Two remaining directions for work on self-instructional training include a concern with prevention and an extension of the procedures to the teaching of academic subject material.

PREVENTION STUDIES

The Zeitgeist is moving in the direction of prevention, especially with high-risk populations. CBM may provide a useful format for teaching interpersonal problem-solving and coping skills. One can look to the work of Allen, Chinsky, Larcen, Lochman, and Selinger (1976); Fagan, Long, and Stevens (1975); Russell and Thoresen (1976); Spivack and Shure (1974); and Stone, Hinds, and Schmidt (1975) for ways to develop a curriculum for teaching children competence and self-control. These many approaches share a common feature, namely, the view that competence and self-control should be viewed as a number of component skills, each of which is teachable. A multifaceted training approach to problem solving is adopted in order to teach children to identify the problems, generate alternatives, collect information, recognize personal values, make a decision, and then review that decision at a later time. In order to teach such skills, several teaching modes are used, including verbal and behavioral modeling and rehearsal, videotape, cartoon workbook, poster pictorial, and even flash card activities. These procedures suggest that another new direction, perhaps one that is in the somewhat distant future, will be the inclusion of such CBM techniques as part of an academic curriculum to be employed for preventive purposes.

ACADEMIC SKILLS

Recent studies (Asarnow & Meichenbaum, 1977; Meichenbaum, 1975; Wozniak & Neuchterlein, 1978) have indicated that self-instructional procedures can be employed to directly enhance memory recall, creative problem solving, and reading comprehension. The focus of these training procedures is to teach children *how* to think, *not what* to think. In short, component analyses of the skills to be taught are conducted (à la Gagné), then each of these components is translated into mediational strategies that can be modeled for and rehearsed by the child. In turn, the child is taught how to conduct task analyses or other metacognitive skills needed to perform in various academic subjects.

This new direction reflects the cross-fertilization of two areas. The developmental work on metacognitive development as illustrated in the work of Campione and Brown (1977) and Flavell (1977) will coalesce with CBM technology in order to teach children the "how to" elements of learning. The CBM technology will provide the means of achieving the goals outlined by Polya (1945) in his classic book *How to Solve It*.

One important distinction that needs to be highlighted and indeed carefully examined in the application of self-instructional training is the difference between acquisition and performance. Recent research (Higa, 1973; Robin, Armel, & O'Leary, 1975; Wein & Nelson, 1978) has suggested that self-instructional training may prove most valuable for children who already have skills within their repertoires but who tend to act impulsively. That is, such training may prove most valuable where problems of inhibition are evident. On the other hand when the child is attempting to develop skills, such as writing or arithmetic, the value of self-instructional modeling and rehearsal may be significantly less. In dealing with problems of acquisition more emphasis should be directed to the component analyses of subskills with accompanying concern for the development of graded task material. For example, I have discussed (Meichenbaum, 1977a) what self-statements an investigator should employ if negative results are obtained from a self-instructional training study.

COGNITIVE–BEHAVIORAL MODIFICATION WITH ADULTS

Parallel development will occur in CBM with adults. We will see a proliferation of comparative outcome studies of various CBM procedures. For example, comparisons between CBM as offered by Ellis versus Beck versus Goldfried–D'Zurilla versus Meichenbaum will be conducted, in order to determine the best way to include cognitions in behavior change processes. A second research approach will be to dismantle specific CBM procedures such as stress-inoculation training (e.g., Horan, Hackett, Buchanan, Stone, & Demchik-Stone, 1977) or cognitive-restructuring procedures (Thorpe, Amatu, Blakey, & Burns, 1976). I have some concern, however, about what we will learn from such multiple comparative studies and dismantling studies. In order to appreciate my concern, consider for a moment what we have learned from 10 years of studies on systematic desensitization, especially in the light of Kazdin and Wilcoxon's (1976) review. As you consider this question, keep in mind that we tend to do the same studies over and over again, only the techniques and researchers seem to change. In short, the internal dialogue or strategies of the investigators appear to remain constant. What, then, is the alternative?

Theories of Behavior Change

An important new direction will be the development of theories of behavior change. Attempts to identify the common mechanisms that contribute to change will increase, no matter which therapeutic approach is being considered. The highlighting of cognitive processes in behavior therapy has contributed to a "detente" between the various therapy approaches and a recognition that theories of change are needed. Some beginnings have been offered by Bandura (1977), Frank (1974), Meichenbaum (1977a), and others. Space does not permit a comparison of these various theories, but it is suggested that a framework for a metatheory of behavior change is possible (see Meichenbaum, 1977a).

A concern with theory represents a move away from a technological/eclectical view of therapy à la Arnold Lazarus (Lazarus, 1976; Meichenbaum, 1977b). Insofar as we can develop testable theories of behavior change, our field will progress. In order to illustrate the limitations of a technological/eclectic view of therapy, consider for a moment that there are over 20 different ways to use imagery in psychotherapy and that there are an equal number of ways to alter clients' cognitions, let alone the innumerable ways to directly influence behavior. The question then becomes, What do we stand to gain by conducting studies that compare imagery technique 1 versus imagery technique 2 with smokers, or CBM technique 1 versus CBM technique 2 with low assertives, and so forth? At present our journals are filled with just such comparisons, but such a "batting average approach" is scarcely the most productive way to progress. A new direction for CBM and for the field of psychotherapy will then be a greater concern with the mechanisms of change.

Deficits Analyses

Complementing the concern with theory will be an increasing interest in assessment of our clients' deficits (e.g., see the task analysis conducted by Schwartz & Gottman, 1976). Once again the desensitization literature illustrates the importance of a deficit analysis. Desensitization was employed in the treatment of test-anxious clients, not because it was particularly suited for the test-anxious client's deficit, but rather because such clients represented a readily available population. Studies by Sarason (1975) and Wine (1971) have implicated an attentional deficit as central to test-anxious individuals, that is, a preoccupation with task-irrelevant self-oriented ideation plays a major role in contributing to inadequate performance. An analysis of the test-anxious client's deficit revealed that a more appropriate and effective means of intervention would be one that focused on the highly test-anxious client's cognitive style rather than on the reduction of muscular tension by means of desensitization. In a recent review of treatment studies of test anxiety, Spielberger, Anton, and Bedell (1976) have found evidence that attentional cognitive interventions were more effective than an anxiety-reduction desensitization procedure. The point to be underscored is that the analysis of the client's deficit (in this case test-anxious clients) had specific treatment implications.

Thus, a new direction for therapy research, including CBM, will be to focus initially by means of a systematic set of studies on the nature of our clients' deficits. Only then should we focus our concern on the various modes of treatment intervention. Similar conclusions have been offered in an excellent work by Gottman and Markman (1978).

A by-product of this deficit research approach will be the study of matched "normal" controls. In our search for an understanding of our clients' deficits we are more likely to examine instances of maladaptive behavior in nonclinical populations. For example, we do not know how nonclinical populations cope with anxiety or depression or anger. In my own laboratory, we are trying to understand how non-child-abuse parents refrain from engaging in aggressive behavior toward their children, or phrased differently, why isn't the incidence of child abuse higher? The answers to these questions will illuminate the nature of the coping mechanisms nonclinical populations employ to deal with intensive affective states. Such research will have implications for preventive intervention programs (e.g., see Meichenbaum & Novaco, 1978). The potential use of CBM techniques for preventive purposes was nicely illustrated by Novaco (1977), who was able to teach policemen a set of intra- and interpersonal skills in order to control anger. Novaco's study is another illustration of a new direction for CBM.

In summary, the new directions for CBM will involve both comparative outcome and dismantling therapy studies. Such approaches seem endemic to the concern of behavior modification researchers. It has been proposed, however, that two other research strategies may prove more worthwhile. These strategies involve: (a) a concern with theories of change that explicate the common mechanisms that contribute to behavior change; and (b) a greater concern with programmatic studies of our clients' maladaptive behaviors and deficits. Another new direction for CBM will be an increasing concern with the development of preventive procedures. Headed in these directions, CBM has the potential of having a salutory effect on the field of behavior therapy.

REFERENCES

Alkus, S. *Self-regulation and children's task performance: A comparison of self-instruction, coping and attribution approaches.* Unpublished doctoral dissertation, University of California, Los Angeles, 1977.

Allen, G., Chinsky, J., Larcen, S., Lochman, J., & Selinger, W. *Community psychology and the schools: A behaviorally oriented multi-level preventive approach.* Hillsdale, N.J.: Lawrence Erlbaum, 1976.

Asarnow, J., & Meichenbaum, D. *Mediational training and serial recall in kindergartens.* Paper presented at meeting of the Canadian Psychological Association, Vancouver, 1977.

Bandura, A. Self-efficacy: Towards a unifying theory of behavior change. *Psychological Review,* 1977, *89,* 191–215.

Beck, A. *Cognitive therapy and emotional disorders.* New York: International Universities Press, 1976.

Bender, N. Self-verbalization versus tutor verbalization in modifying impulsivity. *Journal of Educational Psychology,* 1976, *68,* 347–354.

Bornstein, P., & Quevillon, R. The effects of a self-instructional package on overactive preschool boys. *Journal of Applied Behavior Analysis,* 1976, *9,* 176–188.

Bugenthal, D., Whalen, C., & Henker, B. Causal attributions of hyperactive children and motivational assumptions of two behavior-change approaches: Evidence for an interactionist position. *Child Development,* 1977, *48,* 874–884.

Camp, B. Verbal mediation in young aggressive boys. *Journal of Abnormal Psychology,* 1977, *86,* 145–153.

Camp, B., Blom, G., Hebert, F., & van Doorninck, W. "Think aloud": A program for developing self-control in young aggressive boys. *Journal of Abnormal Child Psychology,* 1977, *5,* 157–169.

Campione, J., & Brown, A. Memory and metamemory development in educable retarded children. In L. Kail & T. Hagens (Ed.), *Perspectives on the development of memory and cognition.* Hillsdale, N.J.: Lawrence Erlbaum, 1977.

Di Guiseppe, R., Miller, N., & Trexler, L. A review of rational-emotive psychotherapy: Outcome studies. *The Counseling Psychologist*, 1977, *7*, 64–72.

Douglas, V., Parry, P., Marton, P., & Garson, C. Assessment of a cognitive training program for hyperactive children. *Journal of Abnormal Child Psychology*, 1976, *4*, 389–410.

Dubois, P. *The psychic treatment of nervous disorders: The psychoneuroses and their moral treatment*. New York: Funk & Wagnalls, 1905.

Fagan, D., Long, I., & Stevens, R. *Teaching children self-control*. Columbus, Ohio: Charles E. Merrill, 1975.

Flavell, J. *Metacognitive development*. Paper presented at the NATO Advanced Study Institute on Structural Process Theories of Complex Behavior, Banff, Alberta, 1977.

Frank, J. *Persuasion and healing*. Baltimore: Johns Hopkins Press, 1974.

Goldfried, M., & Davison, G. *Clinical behavior therapy*. New York: Holt, Rinehart, & Winston, 1976.

Goodwin, S., & Mahoney, M. Modification of aggression via modeling: An experimental probe. *Journal of Behavior Therapy and Experimental Psychiatry*, 1975, *6*, 200–202.

Gottman, J., & Markman, H. J. Experimental designs in psychotherapy research. In S. L. Garfield & A. E. Bergin (Eds.), *Handbook of psychotherapy and behavior change* (2nd ed.). New York: Wiley, 1978. Pp. 23–62.

Higa, W. *Self-instructional versus direct training in modifying children's impulsive behavior*. Unpublished doctoral dissertation, University of Hawaii, 1973.

Horan, J., Hackett, G., Buchanan, J., Stone, C., & Demchik-Stone, D. Coping with pain: A component analysis of stress inoculation. *Cognitive Therapy and Research*, 1977, *3*, 211–222.

Kazdin, A., & Wilcoxon, L. Systematic desensitization and non-specific treatment effects: A methodological evaluation. *Psychological Bulletin*, 1976, *83*, 729–758.

Kendall, P. C., & Finch, A. J., Jr. A cognitive–behavioral treatment for impulsivity. A group comparison study. *Journal of Consulting and Clinical Psychology*, 1978, *46*, 110–118.

Lazarus, A. A. *Multi-modal behavior therapy*. New York: Springer, 1976.

Mahoney, M. J. *Cognition and behavior modification*. Cambridge, Mass.: Ballinger, 1974.

Mahoney, M., & Arnkoff, D. Cognitive and self-control therapies. In S. L. Garfield & A. E. Bergin (Eds.), *Handbook of psychotherapy and behavior change* (2nd ed.). New York: Wiley, 1978. Pp. 689–722.

Meichenbaum, D. Enhancing creativity by modifying what subjects say to themselves. *American Educational Research Journal*, 1975, *12*, 129–145.

Meichenbaum, D. *Cognitive–behavior modification: An integrative approach*. New York: Plenum Press, 1977. (a)

Meichenbaum, D. Acronym therapy: A real danger or sensible eclecticism. A book review of A. Lazarus's *Multimodal behavior therapy*. *Contemporary Psychology*, 1977, *22*, 200–201. (b)

Meichenbaum, D. Teaching children self-control. In B. Lahey & A. Kazdin (Eds.), *Advances in child clinical psychology* (Vol. 2). New York: Plenum Press, 1978. Pp. 317–330.

Meichenbaum, D., & Goodman, J. Training impulsive children to talk to themselves: A means of developing self-control. *Journal of Abnormal Psychology*, 1971, *77*, 115–126.

Meichenbaum, D., & Novaco, R. Stress-inoculation: A preventative approach. In C. Spielberger & I. Sarason (Eds.), *Stress and anxiety* (Vol. 5). New York: Halstead Press, 1978.

Novaco, R. A stress-inoculation approach to anger management in the training of law enforcement officers. *American Journal of Community Psychology*, 1977, *5*, 327–346.

Polya, G. *How to solve it*. Princeton, N.J.: Princeton University Press, 1945.

Robin, A., Armel, S., & O'Leary, D. The effects of self-instruction on writing deficiencies. *Behavior Therapy*, 1975, *6*, 178–187.

Rush, A., Beck, A., Kovacs, M., & Hollon, S. Comparative efficacy of cognitive therapy and pharmacotherapy in the treatment of depressed outpatients. *Cognitive Therapy and Research*, 1977, *1*, 17–38.

Russell, M., & Thoresen, C. Teaching decision-making skills to children. In J. Krumboltz & C. Thoresen (Eds.), *Counseling methods*. New York: Holt, Rinehart, & Winston, 1976. Pp. 377–383.

Sarason, I. Anxiety and self-preoccupation. In I. Sarason & C. Spielberger (Eds.), *Stress and anxiety* (Vol. 2). Washington, D.C.: Hemisphere Publishing Corp., 1975.

Schneider, M., & Robin, A. The turtle technique: A method for the self-control of impulsive behavior. In J. Krumboltz & C. Thoresen (Eds.), *Counseling methods.* New York: Holt, Rinehart, & Winston, 1976. Pp. 157–163.

Schwartz, R., & Gottman, J. Toward a task analysis of assertive behavior. *Journal of Consulting and Clinical Psychology,* 1976, *7,* 285–288.

Shaffer, L. The problem of psychotherapy. *American Psychologist,* 1947, *2,* 459–467.

Spates, C., & Kanfer, F. Self-monitoring, self-evaluation and self-reinforcement in children's learning: A test of a multistage self-regulation model. *Behavior Therapy,* 1977, *8,* 9–16.

Spielberger, C. D., Anton, W. D., & Bedell, J. The nature and treatment of test anxiety. In M. Zuckerman & C. Spielberger (Eds.), *Emotions and anxiety: New concepts, methods, and applications.* New York: Wiley, 1976. Pp. 317–345.

Spivack, G., & Shure, M. *Social adjustment of young children: A cognitive approach to solving real life problems.* San Francisco: Jossey Bass, 1974.

Stone, G., Hinds, W., & Schmidt, G. Teaching mental health behaviors to elementary school children. *Professional Psychology,* 1975, *6,* 34–40.

Thorpe, G., Amatu, H., Blakey, R., & Burns, L. Contributions of overt instructional rehearsal and "specific insight" to the effectiveness of self-instruction training. A preliminary study. *Behavior Therapy,* 1976, *7,* 504–511.

Vygotsky, L. *Thought and language.* New York: Wiley, 1962.

Wein, K., & Nelson, R. *The effect of self-instructional training on arithmetic problem-solving skills.* Unpublished manuscript, University of North Carolina at Greensboro, 1978.

Wilson, T. Cognitive behavior therapy: Paradigm shift or passing phase. In J. Foreyt & D. Rathjen (Eds.), *Cognitive behavior therapy: Research and application.* New York: Plenum Press, 1978.

Wine, J. Test anxiety and direction of attention. *Psychological Bulletin,* 1971, *76,* 92–104.

Wozniak, R., & Neuchterlein, P. *Reading improvement through verbally self-guided looking and listening* (Summary report). Minneapolis: University of Minnesota, 1978.

II
EXPERIMENTAL MODELS

6

Learned Helplessness in Humans: Critique and Reformulation[1]

LYN Y. ABRAMSON, MARTIN E. P. SELIGMAN,
AND JOHN D. TEASDALE

Over the past 10 years a large number of experiments have shown that a variety of organisms exposed to uncontrollable events often exhibit subsequent disruption of behavior (see Maier & Seligman, 1976, for a review of the infrahuman literature). For example, whereas naive dogs efficiently learn to escape shock by jumping over a barrier in a shuttle box, dogs that first received shocks they could neither avoid nor escape show marked deficits in acquisition of a shuttle escape response (Overmier & Seligman, 1967; Seligman & Maier, 1967). Paralleling the experimental findings with dogs, the debilitating consequences of uncontrollable events have been demonstrated in cats (Masserman, 1971; Seward & Humphrey, 1967; Thomas & Dewald, 1977), in fish (Frumkin & Brookshire, 1969; Padilla, 1973; Padilla, Padilla, Ketterer, & Giacolone, 1970), and in rats (Maier, Albin, & Testa, 1973: Maier & Testa, 1975; Seligman & Beagley, 1975; Seligman, Rosellini, & Kozak, 1975). Finally, the effects of uncontrollable events have been examined in humans (Fosco & Geer, 1971; Gatchel &

[1]This work was supported by U.S. Public Health Service Grant MH-19604, National Science Foundation Grant SOC-74 12063, and a Guggenheim fellowship to Martin Seligman.

Ivan Miller (1978) had proposed an almost identical reformulation. We believe this work to have been done independently of ours, and it should be so treated.

This chapter is reprinted from the *Journal of Abnormal Psychology*, 1978, *87*, 49–74. Copyright 1978 by the American Psychological Association. Reprinted by permission.

Proctor, 1976; Glass & Singer, 1972; Hiroto, 1974; Hiroto & Seligman, 1975; Klein, Fencil-Morse, & Seligman, 1976; Klein & Seligman, 1976; Krantz, Glass, & Snyder, 1974; Miller & Seligman, 1975; Racinskas, 1971; Rodin, 1976; Roth, 1973; Roth & Bootzin, 1974; Roth & Kubal, 1975; Thornton & Jacobs, 1971; among others). Hiroto's experiment (1974) is representative and provides a human analogue to the animal studies. College student volunteers were assigned to one of three groups. In the controllable noise group, subjects received loud noise that they could terminate by pushing a button four times. Subjects assigned to the uncontrollable noise group received noise that terminated independently of subjects' responding. Finally, a third group received no noise. In the second phase of the experiment all groups were tested on a hand shuttle box. In the shuttle box, noise termination was controllable for all subjects; to turn off the noise, subjects merely had to move a lever from one side of the box to the other. The results of the test phase were strikingly similar to those obtained with animals. The group receiving prior controllable noise as well as the group receiving no noise readily learned to shuttle, but the typical subject in the group receiving prior uncontrollable noise failed to escape and listened passively to the noise.

Although a number of alternative hypotheses (see Maier & Seligman, 1976, for a review) have been proposed to account for the debilitating effects of experience with uncontrollability, only the learned helplessness hypothesis (Maier & Seligman, 1976; Maier, Seligman, & Solomon, 1969; Seligman, 1975; Seligman, Maier, & Solomon, 1971) provides a unified theoretical framework integrating the animal and human data. The cornerstone of the hypothesis is that learning that outcomes are uncontrollable results in three deficits: motivational, cognitive, and emotional. The hypothesis is "cognitive" in that it postulates that mere exposure to uncontrollability is not sufficient to render an organism helpless; rather, the organism must come to expect that outcomes are uncontrollable in order to exhibit helplessness. In brief, the motivational deficit consists of retarded initiation of voluntary responses and is seen as a consequence of the expectation that outcomes are uncontrollable. If the organism expects that its responses will not affect some outcome, then the likelihood of emitting such responses decreases. Second, the learned helplessness hypothesis argues that learning that an outcome is uncontrollable results in a cognitive deficit, since such learning makes it difficult to later learn that responses produce that outcome. Finally, the learned helplessness hypothesis claims that depressed affect is a consequence of learning that outcomes are uncontrollable.

Historically, the learned helplessness hypothesis was formulated before helplessness experiments were performed with human subjects. In the main, early studies of human helplessness attempted to reproduce the animal findings in humans and were rather less concerned with theory building. Recently, however, investigators of human helplessness (e.g., Blaney, 1977; Golin & Terrell, 1977; Roth & Kilpatrick-Tabak, 1977; Wortman & Brehm, 1975) have become increasingly disenchanted with the adequacy of theoretical constructs originating in animal helplessness for understanding helplessness in humans. And so have we. We now present an attributional framework that resolves several theoretical controversies about the effects of uncontrollability in humans. We do not know whether these considerations apply to infrahumans. In brief, we argue that when a person finds that he is helpless, he asks *why* he is helpless. The causal attribution he makes then determines the generality and chronicity of his helplessness deficits as well as his later self-esteem. In developing the attributional framework, we find it necessary to refine attribution theory (Heider, 1958; Weiner, 1972, 1974). Finally, we discuss the implications of the reformulation for the helplessness model of depression (Seligman, 1972, 1975; Seligman, Klein, & Miller, 1976).

PERSONAL HELPLESSNESS VERSUS UNIVERSAL HELPLESSNESS

Inadequacy 1 of the Old Theory

Several examples highlight a conceptual problem encountered by the existing learned helplessness hypothesis when applied to human helplessness. Consider a subject in Hiroto's experiment (1974) who is assigned to the group that received uncontrollable noise. The experimenter tells the subject there is something he can do to turn off the noise. Since the noise is actually uncontrollable, the subject is unable to find a way to turn off the noise. After repeated unsuccessful attempts, the subject may come to believe the problem is unsolvable; that is, neither he nor any other subject can control noise termination. Alternatively, the subject may believe that the problem is solvable but that he lacks the ability to solve it; that is, although he can't control noise termination, other subjects could successfully control the noise. The old helplessness hypothesis does not distinguish these two states, either of which could be engendered by the procedure of presenting uncontrollable outcomes.

In a recent publication, Bandura (1977) discussed a similar distinction:

> Theorizing and experimentation on learned helplessness might well consider the conceptual distinction between efficacy and outcome expectations. People can give up trying because they lack a sense of efficacy in achieving the required behavior, or they may be assured of their capabilities but give up trying because they expect their behavior to have no effect on an unresponsive environment or to be consistently punished. These two separable expectancy sources of futility have quite different antecedents and remedial implications. To alter efficacy-

based futility requires development of competencies and expectations of personal effectiveness. By contrast, to change outcome-based futility necessitates changes in prevailing environmental contingencies that restore the instrumental value of the competencies that people already possess [pp. 204–205].

A final way of illustrating this inadequacy concerns the relation between helplessness and external locus of control. Early perspectives of learned helplessness (Hiroto, 1974; Miller & Seligman, 1973; Seligman, Maier, & Geer, 1968) emphasized an apparent similarity between the helplessness concept of learning that outcomes are uncontrollable and Rotter's (1966) concept of external control. Rotter argued that people's beliefs about causality can be arrayed along the dimension of locus of control, with "internals" tending to believe outcomes are caused by their own responding and "externals" tending to believe outcomes are not caused by their own responding but by luck, chance, or fate. Support for this proposed conceptual similarity of externals and helpless individuals was provided by studies of verbalized expectancies for success in tasks of skill (Klein & Seligman, 1976; Miller & Seligman, 1975). Helpless subjects gave small expectancy changes, which suggests a belief in external control, whereas subjects not made helpless gave large expectancy changes, which suggests a belief in internal control. These findings indicated that helpless subjects perceived tasks of skill as if they were tasks of chance. A puzzling finding, however, was consistently obtained in these studies. On postexperimental questionnaires, helpless and nonhelpless subjects rated skill as playing the same large role in a person's performance on the skill task. Both helpless and nonhelpless subjects said they viewed the skill task as a skill task. Thus, the relation between the concepts of external control and uncontrollability may be more complex than implied by the old hypothesis.

Taken together, these examples point to one conceptual problem concerning the notions of uncontrollability and helplessness. Recall the distinction made by the old helplessness hypothesis between controllable and uncontrollable outcomes. An outcome is said to be uncontrollable for an individual when the occurrence of the outcome is not related to his responding. That is, if the probability of an outcome is the same whether or not a given response occurs, then the outcome is independent of that response. When this is true of all voluntary responses, the outcome is said to be uncontrollable for the individual (Seligman, 1975; Seligman et al., 1971). Conversely, if the probability of the outcome when some response is made is different from the probability of the outcome when the response is not made, then the outcome is dependent on that response: The outcome is controllable. The early definition, then, makes no distinction between cases in which an individual lacks requisite controlling responses that are available to other people and cases in which the individual as well as all other individuals do not possess controlling responses. These three examples all illustrate the same inadequacy. In the next section we outline a framework that resolves this inadequacy, and we discuss the implications of this framework.

Resolution of Inadequacy 1

Suppose a child contracts leukemia and the father bends all his resources to save the child's life. Nothing he does, however, improves the child's health. Eventually he comes to believe there is nothing he can do. Nor is there anything anyone else can do, since leukemia is incurable. He subsequently gives up trying to save the child's life and exhibits signs of behavioral helplessness as well as depressed affect. This example fits the specifications of the old learned helplessness hypothesis. The parent believed the course of the child's disease was independent of all of his responses as well as the responses of other people. We term this situation *universal helplessness.*

Suppose a person tries very hard in school. He studies endlessly, takes remedial courses, hires tutors. But he fails anyway. The person comes to believe he is stupid and gives up trying to pass. This is not a clear case of uncontrollability according to the old model, since the person believed there existed responses that would contingently produce passing grades, although he did not possess them. Regardless of any voluntary response the person made, however, the probability of his obtaining good grades was not altered. We term this situation *personal helplessness.*

Before discussing the distinction between universal and personal helplessness, it is useful to spell out the flow of events leading to symptoms of helplessness in both examples. First, the person perceived that all of his acts were noncontingently related to the desired outcome; regardless of what the father did, the child's illness did not improve, and the student continued to do poorly no matter how hard he tried. The person then made an attribution for the perceived noncontingency between his acts and the outcome; the father came to believe leukemia was incurable, and the student came to believe he was stupid. In each case, the attribution led to an expectancy of noncontingency between future acts of the individual and the outcome. Finally, the symptoms of helplessness were a consequence of the person's expectancy that his future responses would be futile in obtaining the outcome. The usual sequence of events leading from objective noncontingency to the helplessness is diagramed in Figure 6.1.

Both the old and reformulated hypotheses hold the expectation of noncontingency to be the crucial determinant of the symptoms of learned helplessness. Objective noncontingency is predicted to lead to symptoms

Objective noncontingency → *Perception* of present and past noncontingency → *Attribution* for present or past noncontingency → *Expectation* of future noncontingency → *Symptoms* of helplessness

FIGURE 6.1. *Flow of events leading to symptoms of helplessness.*

of helplessness only if the expectation of noncontingency is present (Seligman, 1975, pp. 47–48). The old model, however, was vague in specifying the conditions under which a perception that events are non-contingent (past or present oriented) was transformed into an expectation that events will be noncontingent (future oriented). Our reformulation regards the attribution the individual makes for noncontingency between his acts and outcomes in the here and now as a determinant of his sub-sequent expectations for future noncontingency. These expectations, in turn, determine the generality, chronicity, and type of his helplessness symptoms. In the context of this general account of the role of attribution in the production of symptoms, the distinction between universal and per-sonal helplessness can now be clarified.

Table 6.1 explicates the distinction between universal helplessness and personal helplessness and ultimately serves to define our usage of the attributional dimension of internality. We take the self–other dichotomy as the criterion of internality. When people believe that outcomes are more likely or less likely to happen to themselves than to relevant others, they attribute these outcomes to internal factors. Alternatively, persons make external attributions for outcomes that they believe are as likely to happen to themselves as to relevant others.

In Table 6.1, the x axis represents the person's expectations about the relation between the desired outcome and the responses in his repertoire.[2] The person expects the outcome either to be contingent on some response in his repertoire or not to be contingent on any response in his repertoire. The y axis represents his expectations about the relation between the de-sired outcome and the responses in the repertoires of relevant others. The person expects the outcome to be either contingent on at least one response in at least one relevant other's repertoire or not contingent on any response in any relevant other's repertoire. Cell 4 in Table 6.1 represents the univer-sal helplessness case and includes the leukemia example, and Cell 3 repre-sents the personal helplessness case and includes the school failure exam-ple. Because the person does not believe he is helpless in Cells 1 and 2, these cells are not relevant here and are not discussed. It should be pointed out, however, that a person in Cell 2 would be more likely to make an internal attribution for his perceived control than would a person in Cell 1.

In Table 6.1, the y axis represents the person's expectations about

<hr>

[2]For the purpose of exposition, dichotomies rather than continua are used. The person expects that the controlling response is or is not available to him and that the controlling response is or is not available to others. These two dichotomies allow for four possible belief states. Strictly speaking, however, the x axis is a continuum. At the far right, the person expects there is a zero probability that the desired outcome is contingent on any response in his repertoire. Conversely, on the far left he expects there is a probability of one that the desired outcome is contingent on a response in his repertoire. Similar considerations apply to the y axis as a continuum.

whether someone else, a relevant other, had the controlling response in his repertoire. The following example makes it clear why we use a "relevant other" rather than a "random other" or "any other"; it is of no solace to a floundering graduate student in mathematics that "random others" are unable to do topological transformations. Crucial to the student's self-evaluation is his belief that his peers, "relevant others," have a high probability of being able to do topological transformations. Nor is it self-esteem damaging for a grade school student to fail to solve mathematical problems that only professional mathematicians can solve, although he may have low self-esteem if his peers can solve them. Therefore, the y axis is best viewed as representing the person's expectations about the relation between the desired outcome and the responses in the repertoires of relevant others.[3]

Implications

The distinction between universal and personal helplessness resolves the set of inadequacies with which we began the article. Situations in which subjects believe they cannot solve solvable problems are instances of personal helplessness according to the reformulated hypothesis. Alternatively, situations in which subjects believe that neither they nor relevant others can solve the problem are instances of universal helplessness. Similarly, Bandura's (1977) conceptual distinction between efficacy and out-

---

[3]Our formulation of "internal" and "external" attributions resembles other attributional frameworks. Heider (1958), who is generally considered the founder of attribution theory, made a basic distinction between "factors within the person" and "factors within the environment" as perceived determinants of outcomes. Similarly, in the locus of control literature, Rotter (1966) distinguished between outcomes that subjects perceive as causally related to their own responses and personal characteristics and outcomes that subjects perceive as caused by external forces such as fate. Unlike these previous formulations that ask whether a factor resides "within the skin" or "outside the skin" to determine whether it is internal or external, we define the self–other dichotomy as the criterion of internality. Although these two formulations may appear to be at odds, analysis reveals strong similarities. For example, Heider (1958) argued that in making a causal attribution, individuals hold a condition responsible for an outcome if that condition is present when the outcome is present and absent when the outcome is absent. Likewise, Kelley (1967) suggested that the procedure individuals use in determining the cause of events is similar to an analysis of variance procedure employed by scientists. The factor that consistently covaries with an outcome is considered to be its cause.

Let us examine the leukemic child and the school failure examples from the perspective of Kelley and Heider. The response of "no person" are consistently associated with improvement of the leukemic child's disease. If the father performed Kelley or Heider's causal analysis, he would conclude that his failure was due to some external factor (e.g., leukemia is incurable). Alternatively, in the school example, failing is consistently associated with the student and not associated with his peers. Here, the student would conclude that some internal factor (e.g., stupidity) was the cause of his failure. Thus, Heider and Kelley also rely on social comparison as a major determinant of internality.

TABLE 6.1
Personal Helplessness and Universal Helplessness

Other	Self	
	The person expects the outcome is contingent on a response in his repertoire	The person expects the outcome is not contingent on any response in his repertoire
The person expects the outcome is contingent on a response in the repertoire of a relevant other	1	personal helplessness 3 (internal attribution)
The person expects the outcome is not contingent on a response in the repertoire of any relevant other	2	universal helplessness 4 (external attribution)

come expectancies relates to the reformulation in the following way: Personal helplessness entails a low efficacy expectation coupled with a high outcome expectation (the response producing the outcome is unavailable to the person), whereas universal helplessness entails a low outcome expectation (no response produces the outcome). Finally, the reformulation regards "external locus of control" and "helplessness" as orthogonal. One can be either internally or externally helpless. Universally helpless individuals make external attributions for failures, whereas personally helpless individuals make internal attributions. The experimental finding that helpless individuals view skill tasks as skill tasks, not as chance, is no longer puzzling. The task is one of skill (relevant others can solve it), but they do not have the relevant skill. These subjects view themselves as personally rather than universally helpless.

The distinction between universal helplessness and personal helplessness also clarifies the relation of uncontrollability to failure. In the literature these two terms have often been used synonymously. Tennen (1977), arguing from an attributional stance, suggested that the terms are redundant and that we abandon the concept of uncontrollability for the simpler concept of failure. We believe this suggestion is misguided both from the point of view of attribution theory and from common usage of the term *failure*.

In current attribution theories (e.g., Weiner, 1972) success and failure refer to outcomes. Success refers to obtaining a desired outcome and failure to not obtaining a desired outcome. According to this framework, then, the term *failure* does not embrace all cases of uncontrollability. Thus, from a strict attributional point of view, failure and uncontrollability are not synonymous: Failure is a subset of uncontrollability involving bad outcomes. Early theoretical accounts of helplessness suggested that good things received independently of responding should lead to helplessness deficits. Recent evidence bears this out: Uncontrollable positive events produce the motivational and cognitive deficits in animals (Goodkin, 1976; Welker, 1976) and in humans (Eisenberger, Mauriello, Carlson, Frank, & Park, 1976; Griffiths, 1977; Hirsch, 1976; Nugent, n.d.; but see Benson & Kennelly, 1976, for contrary evidence) but probably do not produce sad affect. Similarly, Cohen, Rothbart, and Phillips (1976) produced helplessness effects in the absence of perceived failure. In the future, such studies should measure perception of noncontingency as well as performance, since Alloy and Abramson (1977) found that noncontingency is more difficult to perceive when one is winning than when one is loosing. So the notion of uncontrollability means more than just failure, and it makes predictions concerning both failure and noncontingent success.

In ordinary language, failure means more than merely the occurrence of a bad outcome. People say they have failed when they have tried unsuccessfully to reach a goal and attribute this to some internal factor. Obtaining poor grades in school is considered failure, but being caught in a flash flood is generally considered misfortune. The concepts of trying and personal helplessness are both necessary to analyze failure in the ordinary language sense. According to the reformulated model, then, failure, seen from the individual's point of view, means the subset of personal helplessness involving unsuccessful trying.

The final ramification of the distinction between universal and personal helplessness is that it deduces a fourth deficit of human helplessness—low self-esteem. A major determinant of attitudes toward the self is comparison with others (Clark & Clark, 1939; Festinger, 1954; Morse & Gergen, 1970; Rosenberg, 1965). Our analysis suggests that individuals who believe that desired outcomes are not contingent on acts in their repertoires but are contingent on acts in the repertoires of relevant others, will show lower self-esteem than individuals who believe that desired outcomes are neither contingent on acts in their repertoires nor contingent on acts in the repertoires of relevant others. That is, an unintelligent student who fails an exam his peers pass will have lower self-esteem than a student who fails an exam that all of his peers fail as well.

The dichotomy between universal and personal helplessness determines cases of helplessness (and depression, discussed later) with and without low self-esteem. But it is neutral with regard to the cognitive and motivational deficits in helplessness. It is important to emphasize that the cognitive and motivational deficits occur in both personal and universal helplessness. According to both the old and the new hypotheses, the expectation that outcomes are noncontingently related to one's own responses is a sufficient condition for motivational and cognitive deficits.

We now turn to the second set of inadequacies. The old hypothesis was vague about when helplessness would be general across situations and when specific, and when it would be chronic and when acute. We now formulate this inadequacy and develop an attributional framework that resolves it.

GENERALITY AND CHRONICITY OF HELPLESSNESS

Inadequacy 2 of the Old Theory

A second set of examples points to the other inadequacy of the old helplessness hypothesis. Consider debriefing in a typical human helplessness study: The subject is presented with an unsolvable problem, tested on a second solvable task, and finally debriefed. The subject is told that the first problem was actually unsolvable and therefore no one could have solved it. Experimenters in human helplessness studies seem to believe that telling a subject that no one could solve the problem will cause helplessness deficits to go away. The prior discussion suggests that convincing a subject that his helplessness is universal rather than personal will remove self-esteem deficits suffered in the experiment. Neither the old nor the new hypothesis, as it is developed to this point, however, predicts that such debriefing will remove the cognitive and motivational deficits. What does debriefing undo and why?

A second way of illustrating this inadequacy is the following: A number of investigators (Hanusa & Schulz, 1977; Tennen & Eller, 1977; Wortman & Brehm, 1975) have emphasized those cases of learned helplessness in which a person inappropriately generalizes the expectation of noncontingency to a new, controllable situation. It is important to point out that the old hypothesis does not require an inappropriate generalization for helplessness. Helplessness exists when a person shows motivational and cognitive deficits as a consequence of an expectation of uncontrollability. The veridicality of the belief and the range of situations over which it occurs are irrelevant to demonstrating helplessness. But the old hypothesis does not specify where and when a person who expects outcomes to be uncontrollable will show deficits. In keeping with the resolution of the first inadequacy, an attributional framework is now presented to resolve the second inadequacy by explaining the generality and chronicity of deficits associated with helplessness.

A Resolution: The Attributional Dimensions of Stability and Generality

Helplessness deficits are sometimes highly general and sometimes quite specific. An accountant, fired from his job, may function poorly in a broad range of situations: He cannot get started on his income tax; he fails to look for a new job; he becomes impotent; he neglects his children; and he avoids social gatherings. In contrast, his helplessness may be situation specific: He does not do his income tax and fails to look for a new job, but he remains an adequate lover, father, and party goer. When helplessness deficits occur in a broad range of situations, we call them *global*; when the deficits occur in a narrow range of situations, we call them *specific*.

The time course of helplessness (and depression, discussed later) also varies from individual to individual. Some helplessness deficits may last only minutes and others may last years. Helplessness is called *chronic* when it is either long lived or recurrent and *transient* when short lived and nonrecurrent.

The old hypothesis was vague about generality and chronicity. The helpless person had learned in a particular situation that certain responses and outcomes were independent. The deficits resulting could crop up in new situations if either the responses called for or the outcomes desired were similar to the responses and outcomes about which original learning had occurred. Helplessness was general when it depressed responses highly dissimilar to those about which original learning had occurred or when it extended to stimuli highly dissimilar to those about which original learning had occurred. No account was given about why helplessness was sometimes specific and sometimes general.

When helplessness dissipated in time, forgetting produced by interference from prior or later learning was invoked (e.g., Seligman, 1975, pp. 67–68). Forgetting of helplessness could be caused either by earlier mastery learning or by subsequent mastery learning. Again, the explanation was largely *post hoc*. Helplessness that dissipated rapidly was assumed to have strong proactive or retroactive interference; that that persisted was not.

The reformulated hypothesis makes a major new set of predictions about this topic: The helpless individual first finds out that certain outcomes and responses are independent, then he makes an attribution about the cause. This attribution affects his expectations about future response–outcome relations and thereby determines, as we shall see, the chronicity, generality, and to some degree, the intensity of the deficits. Some attributions have global, others only specific, implications. Some attributions have chronic, others transient, implications. Consider an example: You submit a paper to a journal and it is scathingly rejected by a consulting editor. Consider two possible attributions you might make: "I am stupid" and "The consulting editor is stupid." The first, "I am stupid," has much more disastrous implications for your future paper submitting than the second. If "I am stupid" is true, future papers are likely to be rejected as well. If "The editor is stupid" is true, future papers stand a better chance of being accepted as long as you do not happen on the same consulting editor. Since "I" is something I have to carry around with me, attributing the cause of helplessness internally often, but not always (discussed later), implies a grimmer future than attributing the cause externally, since external circumstances are usually but not always in greater flux than internal factors.

Recent attribution theorists have refined the possible attribution for outcomes by suggesting that the dimension "stable–unstable" is orthogonal to "internal–external" (Weiner, 1974; Weiner, Frieze, Kukla, Reed, Rest, & Rosenbaum, 1971). Stable factors are thought of as long lived or recurrent, whereas unstable factors are short lived or intermittent. When a bad outcome occurs, an individual can attribute it to: (a) lack of ability (an internal–stable factor); (b) lack of effort (an internal–unstable factor); (c) the task's being too difficult (an external–stable factor); or (d) lack of luck (an external–unstable factor).

While we applaud this refinement, we believe that further refinement is necessary to specify the attributions that are made when an individual finds himself helpless. In particular, we suggest that there is a third dimension—"global–specific"—orthogonal to internality and stability, that characterizes the attributions of people. Global factors affect a wide variety of outcomes, but specific factors do not.[4] A global attribution implies that helplessness will occur across situations, whereas a specific attribution implies helplessness only in the original situation. This dimension (like those of stability and internality) is a continuum, not a dichotomy; for the sake of simplicity, however, we treat it here as a dichotomy.

Consider a student taking graduate record examinations (GREs) measuring mathematical and verbal skills. He just took the math test and believes he did very poorly. Within the three dimensions, there are eight kinds of attribution he can make about the cause of his low score (internal–external × global–specific × stable–unstable). These attributions have strikingly different implications for how he believes he will perform in the next hour on the verbal test (generality of the helplessness deficit across situations) and for how he believes he will do on future math tests when he retakes the GREs some months hence (chronicity of the deficit over time in the same situation). Table 6.2 describes the formal characteristics of the attributions and exemplifies them. Table 6.1 relates to Table 6.2 in the following way: Table 6.2 uses the attributional dimensions of stability and generality to further subdivide the cases of personal helplessness (Cell 3—internal attribution) and universal helplessness (Cell 4—external attribution) in Table 6.1.

---

[4]In principle, there are a large number of dimensions on which attributions can be specified. Weiner (1977) suggested that the criterion for a dimension, as opposed to a mere property, of attribution be that we can sensibly ask, Does it apply to all the causes that we assign to behavior? So stable–unstable is a dimension because we can sensibly ask, Is ability a factor that persists stably over time? Is patience a factor that persists stably? and so on. Similarly, global–specific qualifies as a dimension since we can ask sensibly, Is ability a factor that affects many situations or only few? Is patience a factor that affects many situations? and so on.

TABLE 6.2
Formal Characteristics of Attribution and Some Examples

Dimension	Internal		External	
	Stable	Unstable	Stable	Unstable
Global Failing student	Lack of intelligence (Laziness)	Exhaustion (Having a cold, which makes me stupid)	ETS gives unfair tests (People are usually unlucky on the GREs)	Today is Friday the 13th (ETS give experimental tests this time that were too hard for everyone)
Rejected women	I'm unattractive to men	My conversation sometimes bores men	Men are overly competitive with intelligent women	Men get into rejecting moods
Specific Failing student	Lack of mathematical ability (Math always bores me)	Fed up with math problems (I have a cold, which ruins my arithmetic)	ETS gives unfair math tests (People are usually unlucky on math tests)	The math test was form No. 13 (Everyone's copy of the math test was blurred)
Rejected woman	I'm unattractive to him	My conversation bores him	He's overly competitive with women	He was in a rejecting mood

According to the reformulated hypothesis, if the individual makes any of the four global attributions for a low math score, the deficits observed will be far-reaching: Global attributions imply to the individual that when he confronts new situations the outcome will again be independent of his responses. So, if he decides that his poor score was caused by his lack of intelligence (internal, stable, global) or his exhausted condition (internal, unstable, global) or that the Educational Testing Service (ETS; the creator of GREs) gives unfair tests (external, stable, global) or that it is an unlucky day (external, unstable, global), when he confronts the verbal test in a few minutes, he will expect that here, as well, outcomes will be independent of his response, and the helplessness deficits will ensue. If the individual makes any of the four specific attributions for a low math score, helplessness deficits will not necessarily appear during the verbal test: that is, lack of mathematical ability (internal, stable, specific) or being fed up with math problems (internal, unstable, specific) or that ETS asks unfair math questions (external, stable, specific) or being unlucky on that particular math test (external, unstable, specific).

In a parallel manner, chronicity of the deficits follows from the stability dimension. Chronic deficits (he will be helpless on the next math GRE when he retakes it at a later time) will ensue if the attribution is to stable factors: lack of intelligence, lack of mathematical ability, ETS gives unfair tests, ETS gives unfair math tests. Attribution to stable factors leads to chronic deficits because they imply to the individual that he will lack the controlling response in the future as well as now. If the attribution is to an unstable factor—exhaustion, fed up with the math problems, unlucky day, or unlucky on the math tests—he will not necessarily be helpless on the next math GRE. If he makes any of the internal attributions—lack of intelligence, lack of math ability, exhaustion, or fed up with math problems—the self-esteem deficits will occur. In contrast, none of the external attributions will produce self-esteem deficits.[5]

Because so much real-life helplessness stems from social inadequacy and rejection, Table 6.2 illustrates a social example. Here a woman is rejected by a man she loves. Her attribution for failure will determine whether she shows deficits in situations involving most other men (global)

[5]A critical remark is in order on the adequacy of ability, effort, task difficulty, and luck as embodying, respectively, internal–stable, internal–unstable, external–stable, external–unstable attributions (Weiner *et al.*, 1971). While we find the orthogonality of internality and stability dimensions useful and important, we do not believe that the ability–effort/task difficulty–luck distinctions map into these dimensions. Table 6.2 presents (in parentheses) attributions that systematically violate the mapping. An internal–stable attribution for helplessness need not be to lack of ability; it can be to lack of effort: laziness (global), math always bore me (specific). An internal–unstable attribution need not be to lack of effort, it can be to (temporary) inabilities: I have a cold, which makes me stupid (global); I have a cold, which ruins my arithmetic ability (specific). An external–stable attribution need not be to task difficulty; it can be to lack of luck: Some people are always unlucky on tests (global); people

and whether she shows deficits in the future with this particular man or with other men (chronic). She might select any of four types of global attributions: I'm unattractive to men (internal, stable, global); my conversation sometimes bores men (internal, unstable, global); men are overly competitive with intelligent women (external, stable, global); men get into rejecting moods (external, unstable, global). All four of these attributions will produce helplessness deficits in new situations with most other men. The four specific attributions will produce deficits only with this particular man: I'm unattractive to him (internal, stable, specific); my conversation sometimes bores him (internal, unstable, specific); he is overly competitive with intelligent women (external, stable, specific); he was in a rejecting mood (external, unstable, specific). Any of the four stable attributions will produce chronic deficits either with that man (if specific) or with most men (if global); the four unstable attributions will produce transient deficits. The four internal attributions will produce self-esteem deficits; the four external attributions will not.

Having stated what we believe are the determinants of the chronicity and generality of helplessness deficits, a word about intensity or severity is in order. Severity is logically independent of chronicity and generality; it refers to how strong a given deficit is at any one time in a particular situation. We believe that the intensity of the motivational and cognitive deficits increases with the strength or certainty of the expectation of noncontingency. We speculate that intensity of self-esteem loss and affective changes (see the section on Implications of the Reformulated Model for the Helplessness Model of Depression later in this chapter) will increase with both certainty and importance of the event the person is helpless about. We also speculate that if the attribution is global or stable, the individual will expect to be helpless in the distant future (both across areas of his life and across time) as well as in the immediate future. The future will look black. This expectation will increase the intensity of the self-esteem and affective deficits. If the attribution is internal, this may also tend to make these deficits more severe, since internal attributions are often stable and global.

Attribution and Expectancy

In general, the properties of the attribution predict in what new situations and across what span of time the expectation of helplessness will be

---

are always unlucky on math tests (specific). An external–unstable attribution need not be to bad luck; it can be to task difficulty: ETS gave experimental tests this time that were difficult for everyone (global): everyone's copy of the math test was blurred (specific). So, ability and effort are logically orthogonal to internal–stable and internal–unstable attributions, and luck and task difficulty are orthogonal to external–stable and external–unstable attributions.

likely to recur. An attribution to global factors predicts that the expectation will recur even when the situation changes, whereas an attribution to specific factors predicts that the expectation need not recur when the situation changes. An attribution to stable factors predicts that the expectation will recur even after a lapse of time, whereas an attribution to unstable factors predicts that the expectation need not recur after a lapse of time. Whether or not the expectation recurs across situations and with elapsed time determines whether or not the helplessness deficits recur in the new situation or with elapsed time. Notice that the attribution merely *predicts* the recurrence of the expectations, but the expectation *determines* the occurrence of the helplessness deficits. New evidence may intervene between the initial selection of an attribution and the new and subsequent situation and change the expectation. So the person may find out by intervening successes that he was not as stupid as he thought, or he may gather evidence that everyone obtained low scores on the math GRE and so now ETS is under new management. In such cases, the expectation need not be present across situations and time. On the other hand, if the expectation is present, then helplessness deficits must occur (see Weiner, 1972, for a related discussion of achievement motivation).

Implications

The attributional account of the chronicity and generality of the symptoms of helplessness explains why debriefing ensures that deficits are not carried outside the laboratory. The debriefing presumably changes the attribution from a global (and potentially harmful outside the laboratory) and possibly internal one (e.g., I'm stupid) to a more specific and external one (e.g., psychologists are nasty; they give unsolvable problems to experimental subjects). Since the attribution for helplessness is to a specific factor, the expectation of uncontrollability will not recur outside the laboratory any more than it would have without the experimental evidence.

These attributional dimensions are also relevant to explaining when inappropriate, broad generalization of the expectation of noncontingency will occur. Broad transfer of helplessness will be observed when subjects attribute their helplessness in the training phase to very global and stable factors. Alternatively, attributing helplessness to very specific and unstable factors predicts very little transfer of helplessness.

A final question concerns the determinants of what particular attribution people make for their helplessness. Attribution theorists (e.g., Heider, 1958; Kelley, 1967; Weiner, 1974) have discussed situational factors that influence the sort of attribution people make. In addition, Heider and Kelley pointed to systematic biases and errors in the formation of attributions. Later, we discuss an "attributional style" that may characterize depressed people.

VALIDITY OF THE REFORMULATED MODEL

The validity of the new hypothesis must ultimately be assessed by its ability to generate novel predictions that survive attempts at experimental disconfirmation. As it is a new hypothesis, no results from such attempts are yet available. However, a minimum requirement is that this hypothesis should be consistent with the available experimental evidence. Although such consistency can lend only limited support to the hypothesis (as the available evidence has been one factor shaping the hypothesis), inconsistency might seriously embarrass the hypothesis.

Is the Reformulated Hypothesis Consistent with the Experimental Evidence on Learned Helplessness in Humans?

Three basic classes of evidence are covered: (*a*) deficits produced by learned helplessness; (*b*) attributional evidence; and (*c*) skill/chance evidence.

DEFICITS PRODUCED BY LEARNED HELPLESSNESS

Nondepressed students given inescapable noise or unsolvable discrimination problems fail to escape noise (Glass, Reim, & Singer, 1971; Hiroto & Seligman, 1975; Klein & Seligman, 1976; Miller & Seligman, 1976), fail to solve anagrams (Benson & Kennelly, 1976; Gatchel & Proctor, 1976; Hiroto & Seligman, 1975; Klein *et al.*, 1976), and fail to see patterns in anagrams (Hiroto & Seligman, 1975; Klein *et al.*, 1976). Escapable noise, solvable discrimination problems, or no treatment does not produce these deficits. Both the old and the reformulated hypotheses explain these deficits by stating that subjects expect that outcomes and responses are independent in the test situation. This expectation produces the motivational deficit (failure to escape noise and failure to solve anagrams) and the cognitive deficit (failure to see patterns). The reformulated hypothesis adds an explanation of why the expectation for the inescapability of the noise or the unsolvability of the discrimination problems must have been global enough to transfer across situations (e.g., I'm unintelligent; problems in this laboratory are impossible) and stable enough to survive the brief time interval between tests. The data are ambiguous about whether the global, stable attribution is internal (e.g., I'm stupid) or external (e.g., laboratory problems are impossible); self-esteem changes would have been relevant to this determination. Nondepressed students who escape noise, solve problems, or receive nothing as pretreatment do not perceive response–outcome independence and do not, of course, make any attribution about such independence.

For a control procedure, subjects have been told to listen to noise (which is inescapable) but not to try to do anything about it (Hiroto &

Seligman, 1975); similarly, subjects have been given a panic button that "will escape noise if pressed" but have been successfully discouraged from pressing ("I'd rather you didn't, but it's up to you"; Glass & Singer, 1972). These subjects do not become helpless. Both the old and reformulated hypotheses hold that these subjects do not perceive noncontingency (in this latter case, they perceive potential response–outcome contingency; in the first case, they have no relevant perception) and so do not form the relevant expectations and attributions.

A number of studies on human helplessness have obtained findings that are difficult to explain with the old helplessness hypothesis. Examination of these studies suggests that investigators may have tapped into the attributional dimensions of generality and stability. For example, Roth and Kubal (1975) tested helplessness across very different situations: Subjects signed up for two separate experiments that happened to be on the same day in the same building. They failed on the task in Experiment 1 (pretraining) and then wandered off to Experiment 2 (the test task). When subjects were told in Experiment 1 that they had failed a test that was a "really good predictor of grades in college" (important), they showed deficits on the cognitive problem of Experiment 2. When told that Experiment 1 was merely "an experiment in learning" (unimportant), they did better on Experiment 2. In the case of "good predictor of grades," subjects probably made a more global, internal, and possibly more stable attribution (e.g., I'm stupid enough to do badly on this, therefore on college exams as well). The expectation therefore recurred in the new situation, producing deficits. In the unimportant condition, subjects probably made a more specific and less stable attribution, so the expectation of failure was not present in Experiment 2. (See Cole & Coyne, 1977, for another way of inducing a specific, rather than a global, attribution for failure.)

Similarly, Douglas and Anisman (1975) found that failure on simple tasks produced later cognitive deficits but that failure on complex tasks did not. It seems reasonable that failure on simple tasks should produce a more global and internal attribution (e.g., I'm stupid) whereas failure on the complex tasks could be attributed to external and more specific factors (e.g., these problems are too difficult).

An important advantage of the reformulation is that it better explains the effects of therapy and immunization than does the old hypothesis. The key here is the attributional dimension of generality. Helplessness can be reversed and prevented by experience with success. Klein and Seligman (1976) gave nondepressed people inescapable noise and then did "therapy," using 4 or 12 cognitive problems, which the subjects solved. (Therapy was also performed on depressed people given no noise.) Therapy worked: The subjects (both depressed and nondepressed) escaped noise and showed normal expectancy changes after success and failure. Following inescapable noise, the subjects presumably made an attribution to a relatively global factor (e.g., I'm incompetent, or laboratory tasks are unsolvable), which was revised to a more specific one after success on the next task (e.g., I'm incompetent in only some laboratory situations, or only some laboratory tasks are difficult). The new test task, therefore, did not evoke the expectation of uncontrollability. Teasdale (1978) found that real success experiences and recalling similar past successes were equally effective in shifting attribution for initial failure from internal to external factors. Only real success, however, reversed helplessness performance deficits. This suggests success does not have its effect by shifting attribution along the internal–external dimension. Although the relevant data were not collected, it is likely that real, but not recalled, success modifies attribution along the global–specific dimension. Immunization (Dyck & Breen, 1976; Thornton & Powell, 1974) is explained similarly: Initial success experience should make the attribution for helplessness less global and therefore less likely to recur in the new test situation.

A number of human helplessness studies have actually shown facilitation in subjects exposed to uncontrollable events (Hanusa & Schulz, 1977; Roth & Kubal, 1975; Tennen & Eller, 1977; Wortman, Panciera, Shusterman, & Hibscher, 1976). While such facilitation is not well understood (see Roth & Kilpatrick-Tabak, 1977; Wortman & Brehm, 1975, for hypotheses), it seems reasonable that compensatory attempts to reassert control might follow helplessness experiences, once the person leaves the situations in which he believes himself helpless (see Solomon & Corbit, 1973, for a relevant rebound theory). Such compensatory rebound might be expected to dissipate in time and be less strong in situations very far removed from the original helplessness training. When the "facilitation" effect of helplessness is brought under replicable, experimental control, the compensatory rebound hypothesis can be tested. People may also show facilitation of performance in uncontrollable situations when they cannot find a controlling response but have not yet concluded that they are helpless.

The reformulated hypothesis accounts for the basic helplessness results better than does the old hypothesis. The explanations given by the reformulated hypothesis are necessarily *post hoc*, however. Relevant measures of the generality, stability, and internality of attribution were not made. Helplessness studies can, in principle, test the hypothesis either by measuring the attributions and correlating them with the deficits that occur or by inducing the attributions and predicting deficits. We now turn to the few studies of helplessness that have induced or measured attribution.

ATTRIBUTIONAL EVIDENCE

Dweck and her associates (Dweck, 1975; Dweck, Davidson, Nelson, & Enna, 1976; Dweck, Goetz, & Strauss, 1977; Dweck & Reppucci, 1973) have demonstrated the differential effects of attribution for failure to lack of ability versus lack of effort. When fourth-grade girls fail, they attribute their failure to lack of ability (consonant with their teachers' natural classroom criticism of girls) and perform badly on a subsequent cognitive test. Lack of ability is a global attribution (as well as internal and stable) and implies failure expectation for the new task. Fourth-grade boys, on the other hand, attribute failure to lack of effort or bad conduct (also consonant with the teachers' natural classroom criticisms of boys) and do well on the subsequent test. Lack of effort is unstable and probably more specific (but also internal). Boys, having failed and attributed failure to lack of effort, put out more effort on the test task and do adequately. Similarly, when students are told to attribute failure on math problems to not trying hard enough, they also do better than if they attribute it to lack of ability (Dweck, 1975).

Effort is not only "unstable," but it is readily controllable by the subject himself, unlike being bored, for example, which is also unstable, specific, and internal, or unlike lack of ability. It should be noted that the dimension of controllability is logically orthogonal to the internal × global × stable dimensions (although it is empirically more frequent in the internal and unstable attribution), and as such it is a candidate for a 2 × 2 × 2 × 2 table of attributions. While we do not detail such an analysis here, we note that the phenomena of self-blame, self-criticism, and guilt (a subclass of the self-esteem deficits) in helplessness (and depression) follow from attribution of failure to factors that are controllable. Lack of effort as the cause of failure probably produces more self-blame than does boredom, although both are internal and unstable attributions. Similarly, a failure caused by not speaking Spanish attributed to lack of ability to speak Spanish, which might have been corrected by taking a Berlitz course, probably causes more self-blame than a less correctable lack of ability, such as ineptitude for foreign languages, even though both are internal and stable.

According to the reformulation, performance deficits should occur in cases of both universal and personal helplessness. In both cases people expect that outcomes are independent of their responses. In addition, attribution of helplessness to specific or unstable factors should be less likely to lead to performance deficits than attribution to stable or global factors. To date, four studies have manipulated attribution for helplessness in adults. In line with the reformulation, Klein et al. (1976) found that relative to groups receiving solvable problems or no problems at all, nondepressed students did poorly on an anagrams task following experience with unsolvable discrimination problems regardless of whether they attributed their helplessness to internal factors (personal helplessness) or external factors (universal helplessness).

Tennen and Eller (1977) attempted to manipulate attribution by giving subjects unsolvable discrimination problems that were labeled either progressively "easier" or progressively "harder." The authors reasoned that failure on easy problems should produce attribution to lack of ability (internal, stable, and more global) whereas failure on hard problems should allow attribution to task difficulty (external, unstable, and more specific). Subjects then went to what they believed was a second, unrelated experiment (see Roth & Kubal, 1975) and tried to solve anagrams. In line with the reformulation, attribution to inability (easy problems) produced deficits. Attribution to task difficulty (hard problems) resulted in facilitation of anagram solving. The most likely explanation for lack of performance deficits in the task-difficulty group is that their attributions for helplessness were too specific to produce an expectation of noncontingency in the test task.

Finally, two studies (Hanusa & Schulz, 1977; Wortman et al., 1976) found that relative to a group exposed to contingent events, neither a group instructed to believe they were personally helpless nor a group instructed to believe they were universally helpless on a training task showed subsequent performance deficits on a test task. While the results appear contrary to the reformulation, they are difficult to interpret. The problem is that in both studies, the typical helplessness group (a group exposed to noncontingent events in the training task but given no explicit attribution) did not show performance deficits on the test task. Thus, the test task may not have been sensitive to helplessness deficits. (For a discussion of the relative sensitivity of tasks to helplessness in animals, see Maier & Seligman, 1976.) It is interesting that Wortman et al. (1976) found that personally helpless subjects showed more emotional distress than universally helpless subjects.

Overall, then, the few helplessness studies directly assessing and manipulating attribution provide some support for the reformulation. Because of the methodological problems in some of these studies, future research that manipulates attribution is necessary. Care must be taken to ensure that one attributional dimension is not confounded with another. Past studies, for example have confounded externality with specificity and internality with generality.

HELPLESS SUBJECTS SHOW DAMPENED
EXPECTANCY CHANGES IN SKILL TASKS

In skill tasks, expectancy for future success increases less following success and/or decreases less following failure for helpless subjects than for subjects not made helpless (Klein & Seligman, 1976; Miller & Seligman, 1976; Miller, Seligman, & Kurlander, 1975; see also Miller & Seligman, 1973, and Abramson, Garber, Edwards, & Seligman, 1978, for parallel evidence in depression). The old hypothesis interpreted these results as a general tendency of helpless subjects to perceive responding and outcomes on skill tasks as independent, and it was assumed that this index measured the central helplessness deficit directly. In other words, it had been suggested that such subjects perceive skill tasks as if they were chance tasks. The rationale for this interpretation was derived from the work of Rotter and his colleagues (James, 1957; James & Rotter, 1958; Phares, 1957; Rotter, Liverant, & Crowne, 1961). These investigators argued that reinforcements on previous trials have a greater effect on expectancies for future success when the subject perceives reinforcement as skill determined than when he perceives it as chance determined. According to this logic, subjects will show large expectancy changes when they believe outcomes are chance determined.

Recent developments in attribution theory suggest that expectancy changes are not a direct index of people's expectations about response–outcome contingencies. Weiner and his colleagues (1971) argued that the attributional dimension of stability rather than locus of control is the primary determinant of expectancy changes. According to Weiner (Weiner, 1974; Weiner et al., 1972) people give small expectancy changes when they attribute outcomes to unstable factors and large expectancy changes when they attribute outcomes to stable factors. The logic is that past outcomes are good predictors of future outcomes only when they are caused by stable factors.

In the absence of knowledge about individual attributions, the reformulated helplessness hypothesis cannot make clear-cut predictions about expectancy changes and helplessness, since belief in response–outcome dependence or independence is orthogonal to stable–unstable. For example, suppose a person makes an internal attribution to lack of ability for his helplessness, that is, he believes in response–outcome independence for himself. When confronted with the skill task, he may show very large expectancy changes after failure, since he believes he lacks the stable factor of ability for the task. Alternatively, when confronted with the 50% success rate typically used in helplessness studies, he may maintain his belief that he lacks the stable factor of ability but conclude that ability is not necessary for success on the task. After all, he succeeded sometimes in spite of his perceived lack of ability. Under such conditions, the person will believe outcomes are a matter of chance (unstable factor) for himself but not for others. Accordingly, he will give small expectancy changes. Moreover, a nonhelpless person (who perceives response–outcome dependency) may believe unstable factors, such as effort, cause his outcomes and show little expectancy change; alternatively, if he believes a stable factor is responsible for response–outcome dependence, he will show large shifts.

Rizley (1978) similarly argued that expectancy changes on chance and skill tasks do not directly test the learned helplessness model of depression. We agree. As argued in the previous paragraph, small expectancy changes need not imply belief in independence between responses and outcomes, and large expectancy changes need not imply belief in dependence between responses and outcomes. Nor does belief in response–outcome independence imply small expectancy changes, or belief in dependence imply large changes. The fact that depressives often show smaller expectancy changes than nondepressed people (Abramson *et al.*, 1978; Klein & Seligman, 1976; Miller & Seligman, 1973, 1976; Miller *et al.*, 1975) is intriguing but provides only limited support for the learned helplessness model. In order for expectancy changes to be used as a way of inferring perception of response–outcome independence, the particular attribution and its stability must also be known. None of the studies to date that measured expectancy shifts also measured the relevant attributions, so these studies do not tell us unambiguously that helpless (or depressed) people perceive response–outcome independence. They support the model only in so far as these two groups show the same pattern of shifts, but the pattern itself cannot be predicted in the absence of knowledge about the accompanying attribution.

To conclude this section, examination of expectancy changes on chance and skill tasks is not a direct way of testing helplessness, since such changes are sensitive to the attributional dimension of stability and not to expectations about response–outcome contingencies. Recent failures to obtain small expectancy changes in depressed people (McNitt & Thornton, 1978; Willis & Blaney, 1978) are disturbing empirically, but less so theoretically, since both depressed and helpless subjects show the same pattern, albeit a different pattern from the one usually found.

IMPLICATIONS OF THE REFORMULATED MODEL
FOR THE HELPLESSNESS MODEL OF DEPRESSION

This reformulation of human helplessness has direct implications for the helplessness model of depression. The cornerstone of previous statements of the learned helplessness model of depression is that learning that outcomes are uncontrollable results in the motivational, cognitive, and emotional components of depression (Seligman, 1975; Seligman *et al.*, 1976). The motivational deficit consists of retarded initiation of voluntary responses, and it is reflected in passivity, intellectual slowness, and social impairment in naturally occurring depression. According to the old model, deficits in voluntary responding follow directly from expectations of response–outcome independence. The cognitive deficit consists of difficulty in learning that responses produce outcomes and is also seen as a consequence of expecting response–outcome independence. In the clinic, "negative cognitive set" is displayed in depressives' beliefs that their actions are doomed to failure. Finally, the model asserts that depressed affect is a consequence of learning that outcomes are uncontrollable. It is important to emphasize that the model regards expectation of response–outcome independence as a sufficient, not a necessary, condition for depression. Thus, physiological states, postpartum conditions, hormonal states, loss of interest in reinforcers, chemical depletions, and so on may produce depression in the absence of the expectation of uncontrollability. According to the model, then, there exists a subset of depression—helplessness depressions—that is caused by expectation of response–outcome independence and displays the symptoms of passivity, negative cognitive set, and depressed affect.

We believe that the original formulation of the learned helplessness model of depression is inadequate on four different grounds:

1. Expectation of uncontrollability per se is not sufficient for depressed *affect* since there are many outcomes in life that are uncontrollable but do not sadden us. Rather, only those uncontrollable outcomes in which the estimated probability of the occurrence of a desired outcome is low or the estimated probability of the occurrence of an aversive outcome is high are sufficient for depressed affect.

2. Lowered self-esteem, as a symptom of the syndrome of depression, is not explained.

3. The tendency of depressed people to make internal attributions for failure is not explained.

4. Variations in generality, chronicity, and intensity of depression are not explained. All but the first of these shortcomings are directly remedied by the reformulation of human helplessness in an attributional framework.

*Inadequacy 1: Expectation of Uncontrollability Is Not
Sufficient for Depressed Affect*

We view depression, as a syndrome, to be made up of four classes of deficits: (a) motivational; (b) cognitive; (c) self-esteem; and (d) affective (but see Blaney, 1977, for a review that contends that only affective changes are relevant to depression). Whereas the first three deficits are the result of uncontrollability, we believe that affective changes result from the expectation that bad outcomes will occur, not from their expected uncontrollability.

Everyday observation suggests that an expectation that good events will occur with a high frequency but independently of one's responses is not a sufficient condition for depressed affect (see Seligman, 1975, p. 98; versus Maier & Seligman, 1976, p. 17, for previous inconsistent accounts). People do not become sad when they receive $1000 each month from a trust fund, even though the money comes regardless of what they do. In this case, people may learn they have no control over the money's arrival, become passive with respect to trying to stop the money from arriving (motivational deficit), have trouble relearning should the money actually become response contingent (cognitive deficit), but they do not show dysphoria. Thus, only those cases in which the expectation of response–outcome independence is about the loss of a highly desired outcome[6] or about the occurrence of a highly aversive outcome are sufficient for the emotional component of depression. It follows, then, that depressed affect may occur in cases of either universal or personal helplessness, since either can involve expectations of uncontrollable, important outcomes.

At least three factors determine the intensity of the emotional component of depression. Intensity of affect (and self-esteem deficits) increases with desirability of the unobtainable outcome or with the aversiveness of the unavoidable outcome, and with the strength or certainty of the expectation of uncontrollability. In addition, intensity of depressed affect may depend on whether the person views his helplessness as universal or personal. Weiner (1974) suggested that failure attributed to internal factors, such as lack of ability, produces greater negative affect than failure attributed to external factors, such as task difficulty. The intensity of cognitive and motivational components of depression, however, does not depend on whether helplessness is universal or personal, or, we speculate, on the importance of the event.

Perhaps the expectation that one is receiving positive events noncontingently contributes indirectly to vulnerability to depressed affect. Suppose a person has repeatedly learned that positive events arrive independently of his actions. If the perception or expectation of response–outcome independence in future situations involving loss is facilitated by such a set, then heightened vulnerability to depression will occur.

Inadequacy 2: Lowered Self-Esteem as a Symptom
of Depression

A number of theoretical perspectives (Beck, 1967, 1976; Bibring, 1953; Freud, 1917/1957) regard low self-esteem as a hallmark symptom of depres-

[6]One problem remains. It is a "highly desired" outcome for the authors of this chapter that the editors of this book give us each $1 million, and we believe this to have a very low probability and to be uncontrollable. Yet, we do not have depressed affect upon realizing this. Some notion, like Klinger's (1975) "current concerns," is needed to supplement our account. We feel depressed about the nonoccurrence of highly desired outcomes that we are helpless to obtain only when they are "on our mind," "in the realm of possibility," "troubling us now," and so on. Incidentally, the motivational and cognitive deficits do not need current concerns, only the affective deficit. We take this inadequacy to be general not only to the theory stated here, but also to much of the entire psychology of motivation, which focuses on behavior, and we do not attempt to remedy it here. We find Klinger's concept heuristic but in need of somewhat better definition. We, therefore, use the notion of "loss of a highly desired outcome" rather than "nonoccurrence." Loss implies that it will probably be a current concern. Since this is only part of a sufficiency condition, we do not deny that nonoccurrence can also produce depressed affect.

sion. Freud (1917/1957) has written "The melancholic displays something else besides which is lacking in mourning—an extraordinary diminution in his self-regard, an impoverishment of his ego on a grand scale [p. 246]." A major shortcoming of the old model of depression is that it does not explain the depressive's low opinion of himself. Our analysis of universal and personal helplessness suggests that depressed individuals who believe their helplessness is personal show lower self-esteem than individuals who believe their helplessness is universal. Suppose two individuals are depressed because they expect that regardless of how hard they try they will remain unemployed. The person who believes that his own incompetence is causing his failure to find work will feel low self-regard and worthlessness. The person who believes that nationwide economic crisis is causing his failure to find work will not think less of himself. Both depressions, however, will show passivity, negative cognitive set, and sadness, the other three depressive deficits, since both individuals expect that the probability of the desired outcome is very low and that it is not contingent on any responses in their repertoire.

It is interesting that psychoanalytic writers have argued that there are at least two types of depression, which differ clinically as well as theoretically (Bibring, 1953). Although both types of depression share motivational, cognitive, and affective characteristics, only the second involves low self-regard. Further paralleling our account of two types of depression is recent empirical work (Blatt, D'Afflitti, & Quinlan, 1976) suggesting that depression can be characterized in terms of two dimensions: dependency and feelings of deprivation, and low self-esteem and excessively high standards and morality.

Inadequacy 3: Depressives Believe They Cause Their Own Failures

Recently, Blaney (1977) and Rizley (1978) have construed the finding that depressives attribute their failures to internal factors, such as lack of ability, as disconfirming the learned helplessness model of depression. Similarly, aware that depressives often blame themselves for bad outcomes, Abramson and Sackeim (1977) asked how individuals can possibly blame themselves for outcomes about which they believe they can do nothing. Although the reformulation does not articulate the relation between blame or guilt and helplessness, it clearly removes any contradiction between being a cause and being helpless. Depressed individuals who believe they are personally helpless make internal attributions for failure, and depressed individuals who believe they are universally helpless make external attributions for failure. A personally helpless individual believes that the cause of the failure is internal (e.g., I'm stupid) but that he is helpless (No response I could make would help me pass the exam).

What are the naturally occurring attributions of depressives? Do they tend to attribute failure to internal, global, and stable factors, and success to external, specific, and unstable factors?[7]

Hammen and Krantz (1976) looked at cognitive distortion in depressed and nondepressed women. When responding to a story containing "being alone on a Friday night," depressed women selected more depressed–distorted cognitions ("upsets me and makes me start to imagine endless days and nights by myself"), and nondepressed women selected more nondepressed–nondistorted cognitions ("doesn't bother me because one Friday night alone isn't that important; probably everyone has spent nights alone"). Depressed people seem to make more global and stable attributions for negative events. When depressed women were exposed to failure on an interpersonal judgment task, they lowered their self-rating more than did nondepressed women. This indicates that the depressed women are systematically generating more internal as well as global and stable attributions for failure.[8]

Rizley (1978) caused depressed and nondepressed students to either succeed or fail on a cognitive task and then asked them to make attributions about the cause. Depressed students attributed failures to incompetence (internal, global, stable), whereas nondepressed students attributed their failures to task difficulty (external, specific, stable). Similarly, depressed students attributed success to the ease of the task (external, specific, stable), whereas nondepressed students attributed their success to ability (internal, global, stable). Although inconsistent with the old model, Rizley's results are highly consistent with the reformulation.

Klein *et al.* (1976) assessed the attribution depressed and nondepressed college students made for failure on discrimination problems. Whereas depressed students tended to attribute failure to internal factors, nondepressed students tended to attribute failure to external factors. These findings parallel those of Rizley on attribution in achievement settings.

---

[7]The literature on the relation between internal locus of control and depression might be expected to yield direct information about internal attribution in depression. It is, however, too conflicting at this stage to be very useful. Externality, as measured by the Rotter scale, correlates weakly (.25–.30) with depression (Abramowitz, 1969; Miller & Seligman, 1973), but the external items are also rated more dysphoric, and the correlation may be an artifact (Lamont, 1972).

[8]Alloy and Abramson (1977) also examined distortion, not in attributions but in perception of contingency between depressed and nondepressed students. The subjects were exposed to different relations between button pushing and the onset of a green light and were asked to judge the contingency between the outcome and the response. Depressed students judged both contingency and noncontingency accurately. In contrast, nondepressed students distorted: When the light was noncontingently related to responding but occurred with a high frequency, they believed they had control. So there was a net difference in perception of contingency by depressed and nondepressed subjects, but the distortion occurred in the nondepressed, who picked up noncontingency less readily (see also Jenkins & Ward, 1965).

Garber and Hollon (1977) asked depressed and nondepressed subjects to make predictions concerning their own future success as well as the success of another person in the skill/chance situation. The depressed subjects showed small expectancy changes in relation to their own skilled actions, however, when they predicted the results of the skilled actions of others, they showed large expectancy changes, like those of nondepressives rating themselves. These results suggest that depressives believe they lack the ability for the skill task but believe others possess the ability, the internal attribution of personal helplessness.

Taken together, the studies examining depressives' attributions for success and failure suggest that depressives often make internal, global, and stable attributions for failure and may make external, specific, and perhaps less stable attributions for their success. Future research that manipulates and measures attributions and attributional styles in depression and helplessness is necessary from the standpoint of our reformulated hypothesis.

Inadequacy 4: Generality and Chronicity of Depression

The time course of depression varies greatly from individual to individual. Some depressions last for hours and others last for years. "Normal" mourning lasts for days or weeks; many severe depressions last for months or years. Similarly, depressive deficits are sometimes highly general across situations and sometimes quite specific. The reformulated helplessness hypothesis suggests that the chronicity and generality of deficits in helplessness depressions follow from the stability and globality of the attribution a depressed person makes for his helplessness. The same logic we previously used to explain the chronicity and generality of helplessness deficits applies here.

The reformulation also sheds light on the continuity of miniature helplessness depressions created in the laboratory and of real-life depression. The attributions subjects make for helplessness in the laboratory are presumably less global and less stable than attributions made by depressed people for failure outside the laboratory. Thus, the laboratory-induced depressions are less chronic and less global and are capable of being reversed by debriefing, but, we hypothesize, they are not different in kind from naturally occurring helplessness depressions. They differ only quantitatively, not qualitatively, that is, they are "analogues" to real helplessness depressions.

Do depressive deficits occur in situations that have nothing to do with the expectation of noncontingency? After failing a math GRE, the student goes home, burns his dinner, cries, has depressive dreams, and feels suicidal. If this is so, there are two ways our reformulation might explain this: (a) he is still in the presence of the relevant cues and expectations, for even at home the expectation that he will not get into graduate school is on his mind; and (b) the expectation, present earlier but absent now, has set off endogenous processes (e.g., loss of interest in the world, catecholamine changes) that must run their course. Remember that expectations of helplessness are held to be sufficient, not necessary, conditions of depression.

Finally, does the attributional reformulation of helplessness make depression look too "rational"? The chronicity, generality, and intensity of depression follow inexorably, "rationally" from the attribution made and the importance of the outcome. But there is room elsewhere for the irrationality implicit in depression as a form of psychopathology. The particular attribution that depressed people choose for failure is probably irrationally distorted toward global, stable, and internal factors and, for success, possibly toward specific, unstable, and external factors. It is also possible that the distortion resides not in attributional styles but in readiness to perceive helplessness, as Alloy and Abramson (1977) have shown: Depressed people perceive noncontingency more readily than do nondepressed people.

In summary, here is an explicit statement of the reformulated model of depression:

1. Depression consists of four classes of deficits: motivational, cognitive, self-esteem, and affective.
2. When highly desired outcomes are believed improbable or highly aversive outcomes are believed probable, and the individual expects that no response in his repertoire will change their likelihood (helplessness), depression results.
3. The generality of depressive deficits will depend on the globality of the attribution for helplessness, the chronicity of the depression deficits will depend on the stability of the attribution for helplessness, and whether self-esteem is lowered will depend on the internality of the attribution for helplessness.
4. The intensity of the deficits depends on the strength, or certainty, of the expectation of uncontrollability and, in the case of the affective and self-esteem deficits, on the importance of the outcome.

We suggest that the attributional framework proposed to resolve the problems of human helplessness experiments also resolves some salient inadequacies of the helplessness model of depression.

VULNERABILITY, THERAPY, AND PREVENTION

Individual differences probably exist in attributional style. Those people who typically tend to attribute failure to global, stable, and internal factors should be most prone to general and chronic helplessness depressions with low self-esteem. By the reformulated hypothesis, such a style predisposes depression. Beck (1967) argued similarly that the premorbid depressive is an individual who makes logical errors in interpreting reality. For example, the depression-prone individual overgeneralizes; a student regards his poor performance in a single class on one particular day as final proof of his stupidity. We believe that our framework provides a systematic framework for approaching such overgeneralization: It is an attribution to a global, stable, and internal factor. Our model predicts that attributional style will produce depression proneness, perhaps the depressive personality. In light of the finding that women are from 2 to 10 times more likely than men to have depression (Radloff, 1976), it may be important that boys and girls have been found to differ in attributional styles (Dweck, 1976), with girls attributing helplessness to lack of ability (global, stable) and boys to lack of effort (specific, unstable).

The therapeutic implications of the reformulated hypothesis can now be schematized. Depression is most far-reaching when: (a) the estimated probability of a positive outcome is low or the estimated probability of an aversive outcome is high; (b) the outcome is highly positive or aversive; (c) the outcome is expected to be uncontrollable; and (d) the attribution for this uncontrollability is to a global, stable, internal factor. Each of these four aspects corresponds to four therapeutic strategies.

1. Change the estimated probability of the outcome. Change the environment by reducing the likelihood of aversive outcomes and increasing the likelihood of desired outcomes.

2. Make the highly preferred outcomes less preferred by reducing the aversiveness of unrelievable outcomes or the desirability of unobtainable outcomes.

3. Change the expectation from uncontrollability to controllability when the outcomes are attainable. When the responses are not yet in the individual's repertoire but can be, train the appropriate skills. When the responses are already in the individual's repertoire but cannot be made because of distorted expectation of response–outcome independence, modify the distorted expectation. When the outcomes are unattainable, Strategy 3 does not apply.

4. Change unrealistic attributions for failure toward external, unstable, specific factors, and change unrealistic attributions for success toward internal, stable, global factors. The model predicts that depression will be most far-reaching and produce the most symptoms when a failure is attributed to stable, global, and internal factors, since the patient now expects that many future outcomes will be noncontingently related to his responses. Getting the patient to make an external, unstable, and specific attribution for failure should reduce the depression in cases in which the original attribution is unrealistic. The logic, of course, is that an external

TABLE 6.3
Treatment Strategies and Tactics Implied by the Reformulated Hypothesis

I. Change the estimated probability of the relevant event's occurrence: Reduce estimated likelihood for aversive outcomes and increase estimated likelihood for desired outcomes.
   a. Environmental manipulation by social agencies to remove aversive outcomes or provide desired outcomes, for example, rehousing, job placement, financial assistance, provision of nursery care for children.
   b. Provision of better medical care to relieve pain, correct handicaps, for example, prescription of analgesics, provision of artificial limbs, and other prostheses.

II. Make the highly preferred outcomes less preferred.
   a. Reduce the aversiveness of highly aversive outcomes.
      1. Provide more realistic goals and norms. For example, failing to be top of your class is not the end of the world—you can still be a competent teacher and lead a satisfying life.
      2. Attentional training and/or reinterpretation to modify the significance of outcomes perceived as aversive. For example, you are not the most unattractive person in the world. "Consider the counterevidence" (Beck, 1976; Ellis, 1962).
      3. Assist acceptance and resignation.
   b. Reduce the desirability of highly desired outcomes.
      1. Assist the attainment of alternative available desired outcomes. For example, encourage the disappointed lover to find another boy or girl friend.
      2. Assist reevaluation of unattainable goals.
      3. Assist renunciation and relinquishment of unattainable goals.

III. Change the expectation from uncontrollability to controllability.
   a. When responses are not yet within the person's repertoire but can be, train the necessary skills, for example, social skills, child management skills, skills of resolving marital differences, problem-solving skills, and depression-management skills.
   b. When responses are within the person's repertoire, modify the distorted expectation that the responses will fail.
      1. Prompt performance of relevant, successful responses, for example, graded task assignment (Burgess, 1968).
      2. Generalized changes in response–outcome expectation resulting from successful performance of other responses, for example, prompt general increase in activity; teach more appropriate goal setting and self-reinforcement; help to find employment.
      3. Change attributions for failure from inadequate ability to inadequate effort (Dweck, 1975), causing more successful responding.
      4. Imaginal and miniaturized rehearsal of successful response–outcome sequences: assertive training, decision-making training, and role playing.

IV. Change unrealistic attributions for failure toward external, unstable, specific; change unrealistic attributions for success toward internal, stable, global.
   a. For failure—
      1. External: for example, "The system minimizes the opportunities of women. It is not that you are incompetent."
      2. Unstable: for example, "The system is changing. Opportunities that you can snatch are opening at a great rate."

(continued)

TABLE 6.3 (*continued*)

---

     3. Specific: for example, "Marketing jobs are still relatively closed to women, but publishing jobs are not" (correct overgeneralization).
  b. For success—
     1. Internal: for example, "He loves you because you are nurturant, not because he is insecure."
     2. Stable: for example, "Your nurturance is an enduring trait."
     3. Global: for example, "Your nurturance pervades much of what you do and is appreciated by everyone around you."

---

attribution for failure raises self-esteem, an unstable one cuts the deficits short, and a specific one makes the deficits less general. Table 6.3 schematizes these four treatment strategies.

Although not specifically designed to test the therapeutic implications of the reformulated model of depression, two studies have examined the effectiveness of therapies that appear to modify the depressive's cognitive style. One study found that forcing a depressive to modify his cognitive style was more effective in alleviating depressive symptoms than was antidepressant medication (Rush, Beck, Kovacs, & Hollon, 1977). A second study found cognitive modification more effective than behavior therapy, no treatment, or an attention-placebo therapy in reducing depressive symptomatology (Shaw, 1977). Future research that directly tests the therapeutic implications of the reformulation is necessary.

The reformulation has parallel preventive implications. Populations at high risk for depression—people who tend to make stable, global, and internal attributions for failure—may be identifiable before onset of depression. Preventive strategies that force the person to criticize and perhaps change his attributional style might be instituted. Other factors that produce vulnerability are situations in which highly aversive outcomes are highly probable and highly desirable outcomes unlikely; here environmental change to less pernicious circumstances would probably be necessary for more optimistic expectations. A third general factor producing vulnerability to depression is a tendency to exaggerate the aversiveness or desirability of outcomes. Reducing individuals' "catastrophizing" about uncontrollable outcomes might reduce the intensity of future depressions. Finally, a set to expect outcomes to be uncontrollable—learned helplessness—makes individuals more prone to depression. A life history that biases individuals to expect that they will be able to control the sources of suffering and nurturance in their lives should immunize against depression.

ACKNOWLEDGMENTS

We thank Lauren Alloy, Judy Garber, Suzanne Miller, Frank Irwin, S. J. Rachman, and Paul Eelen for their critical comments on earlier drafts of this paper.

REFERENCES

Abramowitz, S. I. Locus of control and self-reported depression among college students. *Psychological Reports*, 1969, *25*, 149–150.

Abramson, L. Y., Garber, J., Edwards, N. B., & Seligman, M. E. P. Expectancy changes in depression and schizophrenia. *Journal of Abnormal Psychology*, 1978, *87*, 102–109.

Abramson, L. Y., & Sackeim, H. A. A paradox in depression: Uncontrollability and self-blame. *Psychological Bulletin*, 1977, *84*, 838–851.

Alloy, L. B., & Abramson, L. Y. *Judgment of contingency in depressed and nondepressed students: A nondepressive distortion.* Unpublished manuscript, University of Pennsylvania, 1977.

Bandura, A. Self-efficacy: Toward a unifying theory of behavioral change. *Psychological Review*, 1977, *84*, 191–215.

Beck, A. T. *Depression: Clinical, experimental and theoretical aspects.* New York: Hoeber, 1967.

Beck, A. T. *Cognitive therapy and emotional disorders.* New York: International Universities Press, 1976.

Benson, J. S., & Kennelly, K. J. Learned helplessness: The result of uncontrollable reinforcements or uncontrollable aversive stimuli? *Journal of Personality and Social Psychology*, 1976, *34*, 138–145.

Bibring, E. The mechanism of depression. In P. Greenacre (Ed.), *Affective disorders: Psychoanalytic contributions to their study.* New York: International Universities Press, 1953. Pp. 13–48.

Blaney, P. H. Contemporary theories of depression: Critique and comparison. *Journal of Abnormal Psychology*, 1977, *86*, 203–223.

Blatt, S. J., D'Afflitti, J. P., & Quinlan, D. M. Experiences of depression in normal young adults. *Journal of Abnormal Psychology*, 1976, *85*, 383–389.

Burgess, E. P. The modification of depressive behaviors. In R. D. Rubin & C. M. Franks (Eds.), *Advances in behavior therapy.* New York: Academic Press, 1968. Pp. 193–199.

Clark, K. B., & Clark, M. P. The development of consciousness of self and the emergence of racial identification in Negro preschool children. *Journal of Social Psychology*, 1939, *10*, 591–599.

Cohen, S., Rothbart, M., & Phillips, S. Locus of control and the generality of learned helplessness in humans. *Journal of Personality and Social Psychology*, 1976, *34*, 1049–1056.

Cole, C. S., & Coyne, J. C. Situational specificity of laboratory-induced learned helplessness. *Journal of Abnormal Psychology*, 1977, *86*, 615–623.

Douglas, D., & Anisman, H. Helplessness or expectation incongruency: Effects of aversive stimulation on subsequent performance. *Journal of Experimental Psychology: Human Perception and Performance*, 1975, *1*, 411–417.

Dweck, C. S. The role of expectations and attributions in the alleviation of learned helplessness. *Journal of Personality and Social Psychology*, 1975, *31*, 674–685.

Dweck, C. S. Children's interpretation of evaluative feedback: The effect of social cues on learned helplessness. In C. S. Dweck, K. T. Hill, W. H. Reed, W. M. Steihman, & R. D. Parke (Eds.), The impact of social cues on children's behavior. *Merrill-Palmer Quarterly*, 1976, *22*, 83–123.

Dweck, C. S., Davidson, W., Nelson, S., & Enna, B. *Sex differences in learned helplessness: (II) The contingencies of evaluative feedback in the classroom and (III) An experimental analysis.* Unpublished manuscript, University of Illinois at Urbana-Champaign, 1976.

Dweck, C. S., Goetz, T., & Strauss, N. *Sex differences in learned helplessness: IV. An experimental and naturalistic study of failure generalization and its mediators.* Unpublished manuscript, University of Illinois at Urbana-Champaign, 1977.

Dweck, C. S., & Repucci, N. D. Learned helplessness and reinforcement responsibility in children. *Journal of Personality and Social Psychology*, 1973, *25*, 109–116.

Dyck, D. G., & Breen, L. J. *Learned helplessness, immunization, and task importance in humans.* Unpublished manuscript, University of Manitoba, 1976.

Eisenberger, R., Mauriello, J., Carlson, J., Frank, M., & Park, D. C. *Learned helplessness and industriousness produced by positive reinforcement.* Unpublished manuscript, State University of New York at Albany, 1976.

Ellis, A. *Reason and emotion in psychotherapy.* New York: Lyle Stuart, 1962.

Festinger, L. A theory of social comparison processes. *Human Relations,* 1954, *7,* 117–140.

Fosco, F., & Geer, J. H. Effects of gaining control over aversive stimuli after differing amounts of no control. *Psychological Reports,* 1971, *29,* 1153–1154.

Freud, S. Mourning and melancholia. In J. Strachey (Ed. and trans.), *Standard edition of the complete psychological works of Sigmund Freud* (Vol. 14). London: Hogarth Press, 1957. (Originally published, 1917.). Pp. 243–258.

Frumkin, K., & Brookshire, K. H. Conditioned fear training and later avoidance learning in goldfish. *Psychonomic Science,* 1969, *16,* 159–160.

Garber, J., & Hollon, S. *Depression and the expectancy of success for self and for others.* Unpublished manuscript, University of Minnesota, 1977.

Gatchel, R. J., & Proctor, J. D. Physiological correlates of learned helplessness in man. *Journal of Abnormal Psychology,* 1976, *85,* 27–34.

Glass, D. C., Reim, B., & Singer, J. R. Behavioral consequences of adaptation to controllable and uncontrollable noise. *Journal of Experimental Social Psychology,* 1971, *7,* 244–257.

Glass, D. C., & Singer, J. E. *Urban stress: Experiments on noise and social stressors.* New York: Academic Press, 1972.

Golin, S., & Terrell, F. Motivational and associative aspects of mild depression in skill and chance. *Journal of Abnormal Psychology,* 1977, *86,* 389–401.

Goodkin, F. Rats learn the relationship between responding and environmental events: An expansion of the learned helplessness hypothesis. *Learning and Motivation,* 1976, *7,* 382–393.

Griffiths, M. Effects of noncontingent success and failure on mood and performance. *Journal of Personality,* 1977, *45,* 442–457.

Hammen, C. L., & Krantz, S. Effect of success and failure on depressive cognitions. *Journal of Abnormal Psychology,* 1976, *85,* 577–586.

Hanusa, B. H., & Schulz, R. Attributional mediators of learned helplessness. *Journal of Personality and Social Psychology,* 1977, *35,* 602–611.

Heider, F. *The psychology of interpersonal relations.* New York: Wiley, 1958.

Hiroto, D. S. Locus of control and learned helplessness. *Journal of Experimental Psychology,* 1974, *102,* 187–193.

Hiroto, D. S., & Seligman, M. E. P. Generality of learned helplessness in man. *Journal of Personality and Social Psychology,* 1975, *31,* 311–327.

Hirsch, K. A. *An extension of the learned helpless phenomenon to potentially negatively punishing and potentially positively reinforcing stimuli non-contingent upon behavior.* Unpublished manuscript, 1976. (Available from K. A. Hirsch, Galesburg Mental Health Center, Galesburg, Ill.)

James. W. H. *Internal versus external control of reinforcement as a basic variable in learning theory.* Unpublished doctoral dissertation, Ohio State University, 1957.

James, W. H., & Rotter, J. B. Partial and one hundred percent reinforcement under chance and skill conditions. *Journal of Experimental Psychology,* 1958, *55,* 397–403.

Jenkins, H. M., & Ward, W. C. Judgment of contingency between responses and outcomes. *Psychological Monographs,* 1965, *79* (1, Whole no. 594).

Kelley, H. H. Attribution theory in social psychology. In D. Levine (Ed.), *Nebraska symposium on motivation* (Vol. 15). Lincoln: University of Nebraska Press, 1967. Pp. 192–238.

Klein, D. C., Fencil-Morse, E., & Seligman, M. E. P. Learned helplessness, depression, and the attribution of failure. *Journal of Personality and Social Psychology,* 1976, *33,* 508–516.

Klein, D. C., & Seligman, M. E. P. Reversal of performance deficits in learned helplessness and depression. *Journal of Abnormal Psychology,* 1976, *85,* 11–26.

Klinger, E. Consequences of commitment to and disengagement from incentives. *Psychological Review*, 1975, *82*, 1–25.

Krantz, D. S., Glass, D. C., & Snyder, M. L. Helplessness, stress level, and the coronary prone behavior pattern. *Journal of Experimental Social Psychology*, 1974, *10*, 284–300.

Lamont, J. Depression, locus of control, and mood response set. *Journal of Clinical Psychology*, 1972, *28*, 342–345.

Maier, S. F., Albin, R. W., & Testa, T. J. Failure to learn to escape in rats previously exposed to inescapable shock depends on nature of escape response. *Journal of Comparative and Physiological Psychology*, 1973, *85*, 581–592.

Maier, S. F., & Seligman, M. E. P. Learned helplessness: Theory and evidence. *Journal of Experimental Psychology: General*, 1976, *105*, 3–46.

Maier, S. F., Seligman, M. E. P., & Solomon, R. L. Pavlovian fear conditioning and learned helplessness. In B. A. Campbell & R. M. Church (Eds.), *Punishment*. New York: Appleton-Century-Crofts, 1969. Pp. 299–342.

Maier, S. F., & Testa, T. J. Failure to learn to escape by rats previously exposed to inescapable shock is partly produced by associative interference. *Journal of Comparative and Physiological Psychology*, 1975, *88*, 554–564.

Masserman, J. H. The principle of uncertainty in neurotigenesis. In H. D. Kimmel (Ed.), *Experimental psychopathology*. New York: Academic Press, 1971. Pp. 13–32.

McNitt, P. C., & Thornton, D. W. Depression and perceived reinforcement: A reconsideration. *Journal of Abnormal Psychology*, 1978, *87*, 137–140.

Miller, I. *Learned helplessness in humans: A review and attribution theory model*. Unpublished manuscript, Brown University, 1978.

Miller, W. R., & Seligman, M. E. P. Depression and the perception of reinforcement. *Journal of Abnormal Psychology*, 1973, *82*, 62–73.

Miller, W. R., & Seligman, M. E. P. Depression and learned helplessness in man. *Journal of Abnormal Psychology*, 1975, *84*, 228–238.

Miller, W. R., & Seligman, M. E. P. Learned helplessness, depression, and the perception of reinforcement. *Behaviour Research and Therapy*, 1976, *14*, 7–17.

Miller, W. R., Seligman, M. E. P., & Kurlander, H. M. Learned helplessness, depression, and anxiety. *Journal of Nervous and Mental Disease*, 1975, *161*, 347–357.

Morse, S., & Gergen, K. J. Social comparison, self-consistency, and the concept of self. *Journal of Personality and Social Psychology*, 1970, *16*, 148–156.

Nugent, J. *Variations in non-contingent experiences and test tasks in the generation of learned helplessness*. Unpublished manuscript, University of Massachusetts, n.d.

Overmier, J. B., & Seligman, M. E. P. Effects of inescapable shock upon subsequent escape and avoidance learning. *Journal of Comparative and Physiological Psychology*, 1967, *63*, 28–33.

Padilla, A. M. Effects of prior and interpolated shock exposures on subsequent avoidance learning by goldfish. *Psychological Reports*, 1973, *32*, 451–456.

Padilla, A. M., Padilla, C., Ketterer, T., & Giacolone, D. Inescapable shocks and subsequent avoidance conditioning in goldfish (*Carrasius auratus*). *Psychonomic Science*, 1970, *20*, 295–296.

Phares, E. J. Expectancy change in chance and skill situations. *Journal of Abnormal and Social Psychology*, 1957, *54*, 339–342.

Racinskas, J. R. *Maladaptive consequences of loss or lack of control over aversive events*. Unpublished doctoral dissertation, Waterloo University, Ontario, Canada, 1971.

Radloff, L. S. *Sex differences in helplessness—with implication for depression*. Unpublished manuscript, Center for Epidemiologic Studies, National Institute of Mental Health, 1976.

Rizley, R. Depression and distortion in the attribution of causality. *Journal of Abnormal Psychology*, 1978, *87*, 32–48.

Rodin, J. Density, perceived choice, and response to controllable and uncontrollable outcomes. *Journal of Experimental Social Psychology*, 1976, *12*, 564–578.

Rosenberg, M. *Society and the adolescent self-image*. Princeton, N.J.: Princeton University Press, 1965.

Roth, A., & Kilpatrick-Tabak, B. *Developments in the study of learned helplessness in humans: A critical review*. Unpublished manuscript, Duke University, 1977.

Roth, S. *The effects of experimentally induced expectancies of control: Facilitation of controlling behavior or learned helplessness?* Unpublished doctoral dissertation, Northwestern University, 1973.

Roth, S., & Bootzin, R. R. Effects of experimentally induced expectancies of external control: An investigation of learned helplessness. *Journal of Personality and Social Psychology*, 1974, *29*, 253–264.

Roth, S., & Kubal, L. Effects of noncontingent reinforcement on tasks of differing importance: Facilitation and learned helplessness. *Journal of Personality and Social Psychology*, 1975, *32*, 680–691.

Rotter, J. B. Generalized expectancies for internal versus external control of reinforcement. *Psychological Monographs*, 1966, *80* (1, Whole no. 609).

Rotter, J. B., Liverant, S., & Crowne, D. P. The growth and extinction of expectancies in chance controlled and skilled tasks. *Journal of Psychology*, 1961, *52*, 161–177.

Rush, A. J., Beck, A. T., Kovacs, M., & Hollon, S. Comparative efficacy of cognitive therapy and pharmacotherapy in the treatment of depressed outpatients. *Cognitive Therapy and Research*, 1977, *1*, 17–37.

Seligman, M. E. P. Learned helplessness. *Annual Review of Medicine*, 1972, *23*, 407–412.

Seligman, M. E. P. *Helplessness: On depression, development, and death*. San Francisco: Freeman, 1975.

Seligman, M. E. P., & Beagley, G. Learned helplessness in the rat. *Journal of Comparative and Physiological Psychology*, 1975, *88*, 534–541.

Seligman, M. E. P., Klein, D. C., & Miller, W. R. Depression. In H. Leitenberg (Ed.), *Handbook of behavior modification and behavior therapy*. Englewood Cliffs, N.J.: Prentice-Hall, 1976. Pp. 168–210.

Seligman, M. E. P., & Maier, S. F. Failure to escape traumatic shock. *Journal of Experimental Psychology*, 1967, *74*, 1–9.

Seligman, M. E. P., Maier, S. F., & Geer, J. The alleviation of learned helplessness in the dog. *Journal of Abnormal and Social Psychology*, 1968, *73*, 256–262.

Seligman, M. E. P., Maier, S. F., & Solomon, R. L. Unpredictable and uncontrollable aversive events. In F. R. Brush (Ed.), *Aversive conditioning and learning*. New York: Academic Press, 1971. Pp. 347–400.

Seligman, M. E. P., Rosellini, R. A., & Kozak, M. Learned helplessness in the rat: Reversibility, time course, and immunization. *Journal of Comparative and Physiological Psychology*, 1975, *88*, 542–547.

Seward, J. P., & Humphrey, G. L. Avoidance learning as a function of pretraining in the cat. *Journal of Comparative and Physiological Psychology*, 1967, *63*, 338–341.

Shaw, B. F. Comparison of cognitive therapy and behavior therapy in the treatment of depression. *Journal of Consulting and Clinical Psychology*, 1977, *45*, 543–551.

Solomon, R. L., & Corbit, J. D. An opponent-process theory of motivation: II. Cigarette addiction. *Journal of Abnormal Psychology*, 1973, *81*, 158–171.

Teasdale, J. D. Effects of real and recalled success on learned helplessness and depression. *Journal of Abnormal Psychology*, 1978, *87*, 155–164.

Tennen, H. A. *Learned helplessness and the perception of reinforcement in depression: A case of investigator misattribution*. Unpublished manuscript, State University of New York at Albany, 1977.

Tennen, H., & Eller, S. J. Attributional components of learned helplessness and facilitation. *Journal of Personality and Social Psychology*, 1977, *35*, 265–271.

Thomas, E., & Dewald, L. Experimental neurosis: Neuropsychological analysis. In J. D. Maser & M. E. P. Seligman (Eds.), *Psychopathology: Experimental models*. San Francisco: Freeman, 1977. Pp. 214–231.

Thornton, J. W., & Jacobs, P. D. Learned helplessness in human subjects. *Journal of Experimental Psychology*, 1971, *87*, 369–372.

Thornton, J. W., & Powell, G. D. Immunization and alleviation of learned helplessness in man. *American Journal of Psychology*, 1974, *87*, 351–367.

Weiner, B. *Theories of motivation: From mechanism to cognition*. Chicago: Rand McNally, 1972.

Weiner, B. (Ed.). *Achievement motivation and attribution theory*. Morristown, N.J.: General Learning Press, 1974.

Weiner, B. Personal communication to M. E. P. Seligman, 1977.

Weiner, B., Frieze, I., Kukla, A., Reed, L., Rest, S., & Rosenbaum, R. M. *Perceiving the causes of success and failure*. Morristown, N.J.: General Learning Press, 1971.

Weiner, B., Heckhausen, H., Meyer, W., & Cook, R. E. Causal ascriptions and achievement behavior: A conceptual analysis of locus of control. *Journal of Personality and Social Psychology*, 1972, *21*, 239–248.

Welker, R. L. Acquisition of a free operant appetitive response in pigeons as a function of prior experience with response-independent food. *Learning and Motivation*, 1976, *7*, 394–405.

Willis, M. H., & Blaney, P. H. Three tests of the learned helplessness model of depression. *Journal of Abnormal Psychology*, 1978, *87*, 131–136.

Wortman, C. B., & Brehm, J. W. Responses to uncontrollable outcomes: An integration of reactance theory and the learned helplessness model. In L. Berkowitz (Ed.), *Advances in experimental social psychology* (Vol. 8). New York: Academic Press, 1975. Pp. 227–336.

Wortman, C. B., Panciera, L., Shusterman, L., & Hibscher, J. Attributions of causality and reactions to uncontrollable outcomes. *Journal of Experimental Social Psychology*, 1976, *12*, 301–316.

7

Fear Relevance, Autonomic Conditioning, and Phobias: A Laboratory Model[1]

ARNE ÖHMAN

INTRODUCTION

The purpose of the present chapter is to outline a laboratory model of phobias that accounts for the characteristics of the disorder more adequately than the traditional learning models. In order to achieve this purpose, some general properties of laboratory models will be briefly discussed, before traditional learning models of phobias are considered. A conspicuous failure of such models is that they are unable to account for a central clinical observation, namely the selectivity of phobias. This problem, as well as a theoretical development that promises a solution—the preparedness theory of Seligman (1971)—are then described. Before proceeding to empirical data from our laboratory that elucidate this theory and the acquisition of phobias, the nature of human autonomic conditioning will be briefly considered. Finally, some problems and implications of the advocated approach will be discussed.

Laboratory Models in Behavior Therapy

Following the tradition from Pavlov's (1927) pioneering work on experimental neurosis, laboratory models of psychopathology have been an

[1]Preparation of this manuscript was facilitated by grants from the Swedish Council for Social Science Research and from the Norwegian Research Council for Science and the Humanities.

TRENDS IN BEHAVIOR THERAPY

Copyright © 1979 by Academic Press, Inc.
All rights of reproduction in any form reserved.
ISBN 0-12-647450-8

essential ingredient in the scientific approach of behavior therapists. For example, Wolpe (1958) based his development of perhaps the most widely known behavioral technique, systematic desensitization, on a model derived from studies of experimentally induced conflicts in cats.

There are some obvious advantages in bringing the equivalent of a psychopathological behavior within the realm of laboratory analysis. First, it allows a causal analysis of a sophistication that is unattainable within more traditional clinical approaches. Second, it provides for a substantial increase in the precision of the conceptual analysis. Whereas clinical descriptions often are loose and open ended, a laboratory model "clips the clinical concept off at the edges by imposing necessary features on it [Seligman, 1975, p. 81]." Third, because laboratory analysis allows the use of genuine experimental designs with randomized groups, it circumvents a number of the hazards involved in comparing selected clinical groups and supposedly matched controls (e.g., Fowles, 1975; Venables, 1975). However, a laboratory approach also faces problems of its own. By necessity, a laboratory analysis forces simplification of the complexities in real life, and hence there is always a question as to the representativity of the laboratory model for the clinical phenomenon it purports to illuminate. This problem, however, can be empirically approached.

As argued elsewhere (Öhman, 1976), the successful development of a laboratory model of psychopathology rests on two basic assumptions. First, it requires a behavioral emphasis with regard to the clinical phenomenon (Hebb, 1947). Second, it prescribes that the psychological phenomenon under study is analyzed in functional terms. That is to say, it must be analyzed as relations between behavior and environment, rather than as behavior topography and environmental structures (e.g., see Ferster, Chapter 3 of this volume; Skinner, 1969). Thus, the functional definitions of behavior provide a conceptual bridge between the laboratory and the clinic (Öhman, 1976). Given that these requirements are fulfilled, the validity of the model can be assessed by examining a series of criteria of equivalence between the laboratory and clinical phenomena. Seligman (1975) has suggested four such classes of criteria. The laboratory model should parallel the psychopathology in terms of behavioral characteristics (symptoms), in terms of causal factors (etiology), in the effects of various treatments, and in the effects of preventive actions. According to these criteria, there is a structured series of tests to which a laboratory model claiming to capture a clinical phenomenon should be subjected.

Learning Models of Phobias

Phobias were one of the first targets to be successfully modified by behavioral techniques. Because they seemed amenable to an analysis in simple stimulus–response terms, there was also a widespread belief that their characteristics could be reasonably accounted for by simple conditioning theory, thus implying that good laboratory models were readily available.

A phobia may be defined as an involuntary fear of a specific situation, which is "irrational" in the sense that it does not match the objective dangers involved and which leads to avoidance of the feared situation (Marks, 1969). Since in common psychological lore, classically conditioned fear responses are involuntary and noncognitive and may mediate avoidance responses, they seemed to serve admirably as laboratory models of phobias (Eysenck & Rachman, 1965). However, as this simple theory, known as the two-stage theory of avoidance (Mowrer, 1947), has occasioned more and more fatal objections as an explanation of the original phenomenon, avoidance conditioning in animals (Bolles, 1970; Herrnstein, 1969; Seligman & Johnston, 1973), the behavior therapists have been left in a curious dilemma. Thus, on the one hand, they have been in the possession of efficient treatment methods, which, on the other hand, have been allegedly based on the very conditioning principles that fail to account for the etiology of the disorder. The shortcomings of the conditioning theory as a model of phobias have been discussed by several authors (Costello, 1970; Hugdahl, 1977; Öhman, Fredrikson, & Hugdahl, 1978a; Seligman, 1971). In this chapter only one of the most conspicuous failures will be dealt with.

A Central Datum: The Selectivity of Phobias

Behavior therapists have long failed to recognize the theoretical relevance of a central clinical observation, namely, that phobias are selective in the sense that they do not occur in an arbitrary set of situations (Marks, 1969). Traditional learning theory entails that intense fear should be elicited by any stimulus that happens to temporally overlap a traumatic experience. In modern urban societies, therefore, one would expect frequent phobias for electrical outlets and equipment, and for motor vehicles, but few for snakes and spiders. However, in almost any population, fears of small animals are much more frequent than, for instance, fears of motor vehicles. This datum is difficult to accommodate in learning theory, because it indicates the importance of a completely neglected variable, stimulus content, in the development of phobias. This neglect, furthermore, is no accident; it stems from one of the basic assumptions behind the application of learning theory to clinical problems. As outlined previously, the successful use of laboratory models in behavior therapy requires functional definitions of behavior. However, it is alien to a functional perspective to consider stimulus content, because this variable pertains to the nature or structure of the stimulus rather than to relations between stimuli or relations between stimuli and behavior. According to a functional analysis, the nature of the conditioned stimulus (CS) is unimportant. What matters is that this stimulus is presented in conjunction with another event, the unconditioned stimulus (UCS). The fact that widely different types of stimuli have been in the focus of interest in the laboratory study of fear on the one hand, and in clinical investigations on the other, has been given little attention. It has been presumed that the simple tone or light stimuli studied in the laboratory have effects similar to the more complex stimulus situations of phobias. From a functional viewpoint, both types of stimuli were regarded as equivalent, because they were assumed to derive their fear-arousing properties from previous associations with other, more powerful stimuli. It is the thesis of this chapter that the functional emphasis in this particular context has led behavior therapists astray (Seligman & Hager, 1972). As will be shown in the review of empirical data, the content of the CS is a potent determinant of human autonomic conditioning. Thus, when the CS is "potentially phobic," the resulting conditioned responses (CRs) closely mimic the characteristics of phobic fear. However, when the CS content is "neutral" there is no obvious parallel.

The Preparedness Theory

Given that the nature of the phobic situation is acknowledged as an important variable in the acquisition of phobias, there is an immediate need to delineate this factor more closely. In an attempt at theoretical specification, Seligman (1971) suggested that typical phobic situations have in common that they are potentially dangerous, particularly so in the natural environment of pretechnological man. Thus, an evolutionary basis of phobias was implied (see also Marks, 1969). This suggestion was supported by de Silva, Rachman, and Seligman (1977). They developed a reliable rating scale for the biological relevance of phobias and found that in a sample of 69 phobics, 66 had phobic objects of clear evolutionary significance.

Combining these observations with a biologically oriented reassessment of general process learning theory (Seligman, 1970; Seligman & Hager, 1972), Seligman (1971) proposed that phobias are instances of prepared learning. According to this view, humans have a biologically derived readiness to easily associate intense fear with potentially dangerous situations. From the prototype of prepared learning, taste aversion in animals (e.g., Garcia, McGowan, & Green, 1972; Rozin & Kalat, 1971), it may be suggested that phobias should be: (*a*) selective with regard to situation; (*b*) very rapidly acquired; (*c*) very resistant to extinction; and (*d*) noncognitive in nature (Seligman & Hager, 1972). In other words, this theory accounts for a number of salient characteristics of phobias that have been resistant to an interpretation in terms of traditional learning theory (see Öhman et al., 1978a; Öhman, Fredrikson, Hugdahl, & Rimmö, 1976; Seligman, 1971).

Before proceeding to a review of empirical findings relevant to the preparedness theory, it is necessary to begin with a brief diversion into the realm of general human autonomic conditioning, because the data to be reviewed were collected in such paradigms.

HUMAN AUTONOMIC CONDITIONING

In this section, I will briefly discuss some problems with human autonomic conditioning that should be kept in mind when the data on the effects of CS content are evaluated. For more complete reviews of the field, the reader is referred to Prokasy and Kumpfer (1973), and Grings and Dawson (1973).

Ethical Considerations

Ethical considerations dictate that the degree of aversiveness should be minimal in aversive conditioning studies and that the subject should be given a high degree of control over the situation. Therefore, the intensity of the aversive UCS is typically decided by the subject, who is also most often given the right to withdraw from the experiment at any point in time. These restrictions make human autonomic "fear" responses much more fragile and elusive than real-life fears or animal conditioned fear responses (see Bandura, 1977).

Sensitization and Orienting

By their very nature, autonomic responses are extremely sensitive to threat, stress, and novelty. Hence, because of potential stress, aversiveness, and novelty in the experimental situation, there is often a conspicuous peak of autonomic activity early in a conditioning session. This activity pertains both to tonic background levels and to phasic responses, since the autonomic effectors are components of the orienting response (Sokolov, 1963). As the session proceeds, the initial high level of responding habituates. Consequently, conditioning effects have to be assessed against uniformly decreasing levels of tonic and phasic activity. Therefore, the classical, negatively accelerated growth function assumed to describe the course of learning is seldom encountered in the human autonomic conditioning laboratory.

Control Procedures

Because of sensitization and orienting, a primary problem in autonomic conditioning involves disentangling associative conditioning effects from effects due to these factors. Such separation may be achieved by comparing a conditioning group given paired CS–UCS presentations with a control group given uncorrelated CSs and UCSs (Rescorla, 1967). Alternatively, a within-subject assessment of conditioning may be accomplished in a differential conditioning paradigm (Prokasy, 1977). In such a paradigm, two stimuli originally not producing differential responding are selected. One of them is then consistently reinforced by the UCS (CS+), and the other is consistently nonreinforced (CS −). If the former cue reliably elicits more responding than the latter, conditioning effects are demonstrated, even if the overall level of responding declines over trials because of reduced sensitization and orienting. Furthermore, with a differential paradigm, conditioning effects can be compared across various classes of CSs (e.g., differing in "fear relevance") independently of differences in responding between the classes prior to training.

The Use of Long Interstimulus Intervals

Because autonomic responses typically are slow (latencies of 1–2 seconds), long interstimulus intervals (ISIs) are necessary in order to study anticipatory responses. With ISIs of 5–10 seconds, there usually are multiphasic responses to the CS–UCS complex. An example from one of the most studied autonomic effectors, skin conductance responses (SCRs) are shown in Figure 7.1. This figure shows that the UCS is anticipated by two distinct response components, known as first- and second-interval anticipatory responses (FARs and SARs, respectively) (see Prokasy & Kumpfer, 1973). There is evidence that these two components code different psychological processes (e.g., Lockhart, 1973; Öhman, 1971, 1972), and that they mix into a single response if the ISI is shortened (Öhman, 1974). Therefore, in order to keep the presumed underlying processes separate, an ISI of about 8 seconds is preferable. The data quite uniformly indicate that the effect of the CS content variable is most clearly manifested in the

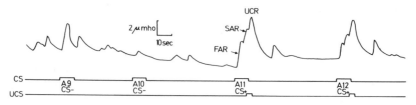

FIGURE 7.1. *Skin conductance tracing for a subject showing exceptionally large and distinct responses. A differential conditioning paradigm with pictures as reinforced and nonreinforced conditioned stimuli (CS+ and CS −, respectively) was used, and the unconditioned stimulus (UCS) was a 105 dB noise. The segment shows trials 9–12 of the acquisition phase (A9–A12). Note the occurrence of first- and second-interval anticipatory responses (FARs and SARs, respectively) to the CS+, and the unconditioned response (UCR) to the UCS. Note also that the responses are larger to CS+ than to CS −.*

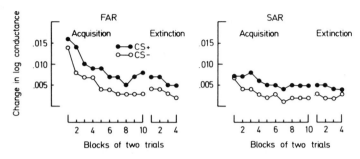

FIGURE 7.2. *Skin conductance responses from a differential conditioning experiment with different tones (200 and 3000 Hz) as reinforced and nonreinforced conditioned stimuli (CS + and CSs −, respectively), and an electric shock as the UCS. Data are shown separately for first- and second-interval anticipatory responses (FARs and SARs, respectively). (Data replotted from Öhman & Bohlin, 1973.)*

FAR, which may be taken to imply that variations of CS content accomplishes changes in the meaning of the CS rather than in the expectancy for the UCS (see Öhman, Fredrikson, Hugdahl, & Rimmö, 1976). Therefore, this review will be restricted to the FAR measure.

Figure 7.2 shows some typical FAR and SAR data from a skin conductance conditioning experiment, where 55 subjects were conditioned to an 80 dB tone of 200 or 3000 Hz with a shock UCS in a delayed differential conditioning paradigm with an ISI of 8 seconds (Öhman & Bohlin, 1973). Responding to the reinforced CS + and the nonreinforced CS − diverged as a function of training so that clear differential responding was achieved. Note, however, that the overall level of responding declined over trials, in spite of the administration of reinforcement during the acquisition period.

In sum, there are four salient points that should be kept in mind when the data in the next few sections are examined. First, ethical considerations force the use of "minimal" experimental situations. Thus, large magnitude changes should not be expected, and they should be much smaller than those observed in phobics confronting a feared situation. Second, the important dependent variable is always the differences in responding to the CS+ and the CS −. This difference reflects associative effects even if the asymptotic responding to the CS+ is below the initial level of responding. Third, there is good reason to use long, and so-called "nonoptimal" ISIs. Fourth, there is a complex of responses to the CS, and since various components reflect different processes, the choice of component may affect the conclusions drawn.

THE SELECTIVITY OF PHOBIAS

In previous sections, it was concluded that the nature of the CS may be an important determinant of human aversive conditioning, and that considerations of this variable may be instrumental in developing an adequate model of phobias. The effect of this variable will be considered in the next section.

General Method

In all experiments to be reported here, normal nonphobic college students were conditioned to visual CSs (slides) by means of aversive UCSs (mild electric shocks or loud noises), while autonomic activity such as skin conductance or vasomotor responses were monitored. Similar to the reference experiment in Figure 7.2, differential classical conditioning paradigms were used. Typically, one group of subjects was required to differentiate between two types of fear-relevant or potentially phobic stimuli (e.g., pictures of snakes and spiders) by having one of them followed by the UCS, while a control group differentiated between fear-irrelevant or neutral stimuli (e.g., flowers and mushrooms). Previous data indicate that there is no differential unconditioned responding to snakes and spiders, but that these stimuli tend to evoke more responses than the neutral stimuli (Öhman, Eriksson, Fredrikson, Hugdahl, & Olofsson, 1974). However, as discussed previously, this difference in initial responding between the phobic and neutral stimuli does not constitute a problem in differential conditioning designs, as long as the responses to the specific CS+ and CS − (e.g., snakes and spiders, respectively) do not differ before training. The particular stimuli serving as CS+ and CS − were counterbalanced within groups. The CS pictures were on for 8 seconds and were terminated by the UCS. The intertrial interval typically had a mean of about 30 seconds. Most often, there were three phases in an experiment: (*a*) habituation, where a few CSs were presented without the UCS; (*b*) acquisition, where 5–10 reinforced CSs+ were given intermixed with the same number of CSs −; and (*c*) extinction, involving up to 20 nonreinforced presentations of each stimulus. To control for irrelevant background features of the pictures, different subjects saw different pictures of snakes, spiders, etc. A more thorough review of the method and of strategical methodological decisions is given elsewhere (Öhman *et al.*, 1978a).

"Potentially Phobic" versus "Neutral" CSs

Some basic data on the effect of the CS content variable are given in Figure 7.3. In this experiment (Fredrikson & Öhman, 1979), one group of subjects was conditioned to pictures of snakes or spiders and another to flowers or mushrooms by help of a shock UCS. The dependent variables were probability of a FAR SCR and probability of digital vasomotor changes, measured as finger pulse-volume responses (FPVs). According to the SCR data in Figure 7.3, there was a divergence over acquisition trials for responses to the CS+ and CS − in both groups. During extinction,

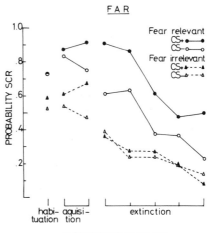

FIGURE 7.3. *Probability of a skin conductance response (SCR) for subjects trained with potentially phobic or neutral reinforced and nonreinforced conditioned stimuli (CSs+ and CSs −, respectively) with a shock UCS. (Copyright © 1979, The Society for Psychophysiological Research. Reprinted with permission of the publisher from "Cardiovascular and Electrodermal Responses during Conditioning to Phobic Stimuli," By M. Fredrikson & A. Öhman, Psychophysiology, 1979, 16, 1–7).*

however, the difference in response to CS+ and CS − remained for the fear-relevant stimuli, whereas it disappeared almost immediately for the fear-irrelevant stimuli. Thus, the effect of the stimulus content variable was particularly obvious during the extinction phase. This basic result has been replicated in a number of studies (Fredrikson, Hugdahl, & Öhman, 1976; Hugdahl, Fredrikson, & Öhman, 1977; Öhman, Eriksson, & Olofsson, 1975; Öhman, Erixon, & Löfberg, 1975; Öhman, Fredrikson, & Hugdahl, 1978b; Öhman, Fredrikson, Hugdahl, & Rimmö, 1976).

The SCR data were closely paralleled by the vasomotor responses. As is evident from Figure 7.4, this measure showed results very similar to those obtained with the skin conductance measures. Thus, the effect is evident in two sympathetically dominated effectors.

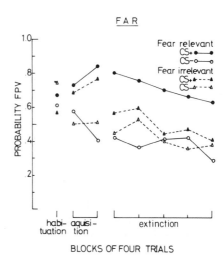

FIGURE 7.4. *Probability of a finger pulse-volume response (FPV) for subjects trained with potentially phobic or neutral reinforced and nonreinforced conditioned stimuli (CSs+ and CSs −, respectively) with a shock UCS. (Copyright © 1979, The Society for Psychophysiological Research. Reprinted with permission of the publisher from "Cardiovascular and Electrodermal Responses during Conditioning to Phobic Stimuli," by M. Fredrikson & A. Öhman, Psychophysiology, 1979, 16, 1–7).*

Facial Expressions as CSs

Another experiment (Öhman & Dimberg, 1978) examined an alternative set of stimuli, which has some interesting properties from a preparedness point of view. From Ekman's (1971) work on the manifestation of emotion in the human face, we know that both voluntary production and identification of emotional facial expressions are fairly independent of cultural context, thus implying a biological basis for human facial behavior. Furthermore, for some facial expressions of emotion, the evolutionary development can be fairly reasonably reconstructed (e.g., Hinde, 1974). Finally, faces, and especially eyes, are important stimulus factors in social phobias (Marks, 1969). From these considerations it should be apparent that converging lines of argument specify facial expressions as a biologically relevant stimulus category.

Facial expressions of emotion may be ordered on a continuum of probability of being associated with potential danger to pretechnological man. Thus, according to the scale of preparedness developed by de Silva *et al.* (1977), an expression of anger should be "probably dangerous to pretechnological man under not uncommon circumstances" (p. 67), whereas a happy expression should be "very unlikely to have ever been dangerous to pretechnological man" (p. 67). On the basis of Seligman's (1971) position, therefore, these two types of stimuli would be expected to differ widely in conditionability when the UCS is an aversive stimulus.

Utilizing the standard differential paradigm described earlier, three groups of subjects were exposed to angry, neutral, and happy faces, respectively. Each group differentiated between male and female faces expressing the same emotion, and the UCS was an electric shock. In order to randomize irrelevant features, different subjects saw different faces, and which face was reinforced was counterbalanced within groups.

Skin conductance data are given in Figure 7.5. All groups showed significant acquisition effects, with no between-group differences. During extinction, however, some clear differences emerged. Whereas responses extinguished rapidly in the neutral and happy groups, a significant difference between CS+ and CS − remained throughout the extinction sessions for the angry group, thus indicating superior resistance to extinction for this condition. If Figure 7.5 is compared with Figure 7.3, it will be apparent that the angry faces produced effects similar to those of more conventional phobic stimuli, whereas the neutral and happy faces were similar to the previously employed neutral stimuli.

"Ontogenetic" versus "Phylogenetic" Fear Relevance

The data presented so far indicate that fear-relevant stimuli that have been paired with an aversive UCS produce conditioned autonomic responses that are very hard to extinguish. Although the last of the described

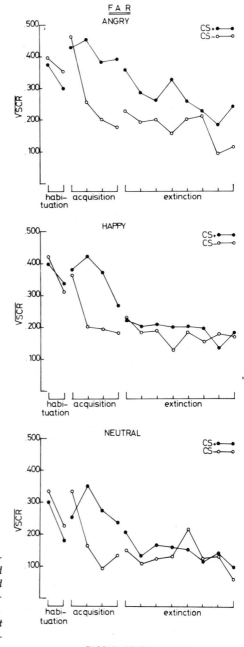

FIGURE 7.5. *Magnitude of skin conductance responses (SCR) for subjects trained with angry, neutral, or happy faces as reinforced and nonreinforced conditioned stimuli (CSs+ and CSs −, respectively) with a shock UCS. (From Öhman & Dimberg, 1978. Copyright 1978 by the American Psychological Association. Reprinted by permission.)*

experiments gives some substance to the more specific claims of the preparedness theory, the data are by no means conclusive. Thus, the basis for the effect might as well be previous learning as biological readiness. However, the inferential base could be improved if it were possible to find stimuli that are clearly dangerous to modern man, but were not dangerous to pretechnological man. In other words, we need stimuli that are "ontogenetically" but not "phylogenetically" fear relevant. Guns probably fall into one such category.

Three groups of American college students involved in a study (Hodes, Öhman, & Lang, 1977) differentiated, respectively, between: (*a*) fear-relevant and potentially phobic stimuli—snakes and spiders; (*b*) "nonevolutionary" fear-relevant stimuli—revolvers and rifles; and (*c*) neutral stimuli—household objects. The UCS was a loud complex noise, and the standard paradigm was used.

The results are shown in Figure 7.6. The preparedness theory predicts that the potentially phobic group should be superior to the other two groups. From an interpretation in terms of previous learning, however, one would expect no difference between the phobic and the gun group. As is obvious in Figure 7.6, there were significant acquisition effects, which did not differ as a function of stimulus content. The extinction results, however, were in line with the prediction from the preparedness theory. Thus, the potentially phobic group showed superior resistance to extinction to the other two groups. This result, then, indicates that there might be some evolutionary specificity to the effects observed with potentially phobic CSs.

Selectivity with Regard to Aversive UCSs

In concert, the data presented in the preceding sections clearly suggest that CS content is a strong and reliable determinant of resistance to extinction of conditioned autonomic responses. The nature and extent of this

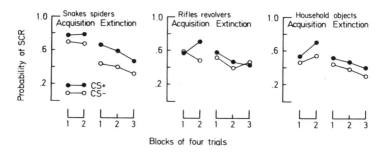

FIGURE 7.6. *Probability of a skin conductance response (SCR) for subjects trained with snakes and spiders, revolvers and rifles, and household objects as reinforced and nonreinforced conditioned stimuli (CSs+ and CSs −, respectively) with a loud noise as the UCS.*

selectivity, however, remains obscure. For example, it is unclear whether the effect is due to the specific content of the stimuli or to some general characteristic, such as salience or arousal value. One way of pursuing this question would be to explore whether the effect is a general one, or whether it is restricted to aversive UCSs, as would be required by the preparedness theory. Thus, potentially phobic and neutral stimuli could be compared when they signal aversive and nonaversive UCSs. If the effect is due to stimulus salience, one would expect superior conditioning to phobic stimuli, regardless of the UCS. However, if the effect is selective for associations between potentially phobic stimuli and fear, superior conditioning would be observed only with an aversive UCS.

It is not easy to find nonaversive UCSs that are effective in autonomic conditioning. However, there are some data showing that the imperative stimulus for a reaction-time (RT) task may be used as a UCS for electrodermal responses, and that it produces effects similar to those found with electric shock (e.g., Baer & Fuhrer, 1969). Consequently, we decided to compare conditioning to phobic (snakes and spiders) and neutral (flowers and mushrooms) stimuli with electric shock or an RT task as the UCS. Except for the variation of the UCS, the usual conditioning paradigm was used (Öhman, Fredrikson, Hugdahl, & Rimmö, 1976; Öhman *et al.*, 1978b).

The results are shown in Figure 7.7. Similar to previous findings, there was a markedly higher resistance to extinction with the potentially phobic CS as compared with the neutral CS when the UCS was aversive. However, with the nonaversive UCS, this picture was reversed. Thus, there was more resistance to extinction with the neutral CS, although, in contrast to the phobic CS with aversive UCS, the response extinguished over trials. This "double-dissociation" effect (Schwartz, 1974) effectively rules out any CS factor as the basis for the superior resistance to extinction of phobic stimuli, and it strongly suggests that the effect is restricted to aversive UCSs, as required by the preparedness theory.

PARAMETRIC CHARACTERISTICS OF PHOBIAS

Traditional learning theory faces problems with regard to two important parametric characteristics of phobias. Thus, from a learning perspective, phobias are too resistant to extinction and too rapidly acquired.

Resistance to Extinction

Laboratory-produced conditioned fear extinguishes readily, even if the UCS is of traumatic intensity (Annau & Kamin, 1961). This is also true for autonomic fear responses during avoidance conditioning, although the motor avoidance response may be very hard to extinguish (see Seligman &

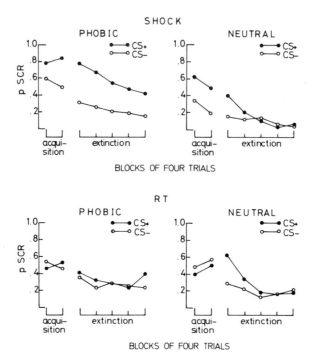

FIGURE 7.7. *Probability of a skin conductance response (SCR) for subjects trained with potentially phobic or neutral reinforced and nonreinforced conditioned stimuli (CSs+ and CSs −, respectively) either with a shock or a reaction-time (RT) UCS. (From Öhman, Fredrikson, & Hugdahl, 1978b. Copyright 1978 by the Society for Psychophysiological Research. Reprinted by permission.)*

Johnston, 1973). Phobias, on the other hand, are very persistent and do not seem to extinguish, even if the phobic is exposed to the feared object. As should be obvious from the data already presented, the outstanding characteristic of autonomic responses conditioned to phobic stimuli is that they show much higher resistance to extinction than responses to neutral stimuli. In fact, we have repeatedly failed to find any reliable evidence of extinction to phobic stimuli, in spite of relatively long extinction sessions. Thus, our data deviate from what would be expected from traditional learning theory and are similar to phobias in this respect.

One-Trial Learning

It always takes a number of trials to establish conditioned fear in the laboratory. Phobias, however, seem to be acquirable on a single pairing between the stimulus and a traumatic event. In the data that have been presented, the typical finding has been that potentially phobic and neutral stimuli do not differ during acquisition, but that responses seem to be as

TABLE 7.1

Magnitude of Skin Conductance Response (Micromho) during Extinction after One Acquisition Trial for Groups Submitted to Conditioning, Sensitization, and CS Alone Treatments with Phobic or Neutral Stimuli[a]

Groups	Phobic CS	Neutral CS
Conditioning	1.20	.42
Sensitization	.29	.32
CS alone	.16	.05

[a]Data are from Öhman, Eriksson, and Olofsson (1975).

readily and rapidly acquired to both types of stimuli. This, then, might provide an important discrepancy between our data and real phobias. However, in one experiment (Öhman, Eriksson, & Olofsson, 1975), we examined resistance to extinction as a function of the number of prior reinforcements. Specifically, phobic and neutral groups were given one or five reinforcements during the acquisition period. In this experiment, a between-subject assessment of conditioning was used so that the conditioning groups were compared to groups given the CS and the UCS explicitly unpaired (sensitization), or the CS only (CS alone). Mean magnitude of responses during extinction after one acquisition trial are given in Table 7.I.

The results indicated a markedly higher level of responding in the phobic conditioning group than in all other groups, which did not differ from each other. In other words, this experiment clearly demonstrated one-trial learning to phobic but not to neutral stimuli. Thus, similar to phobias, electrodermal responses to potentially phobic stimuli seem to be extremely rapidly acquired and to reach quite complete resistance to extinction after a single reinforcement.

THE "IRRATIONALITY" OF PHOBIAS

Phobias, by definition, involve situations that "the individual objectively recognizes should not be fear-provoking" (Leitenberg, 1976, p. 124), or a fear that is "out of proportion to the demands of the situation" (Marks, 1969, p. 3). Thus, phobias typically involve a dissociation between cognitions and fear responses, and rational arguments most often are completely inefficient in alleviating the fear. This provides an important example of a discrepancy between real-life fears and fear studied in the laboratory (Bandura, 1977). Human conditioned responses, both autonomic and somatic, characteristically are very sensitive to cognitive influences (Grant, 1973; Grings & Dawson, 1973), and there is a quite predictable relationship between cognitions and autonomic responses (e.g., Dawson & Furedy, 1976; Öhman, Ellström, & Björkstrand, 1976). In order for our situation to provide a good model of phobias, therefore, the responses conditioned to phobic stimuli should contrast sharply with responses conditioned to neutral stimuli in their sensitivity to cognitive factors.

This problem was addressed in an experiment where two groups of subjects were conditioned to phobic (snakes and spiders) or neutral (circles and triangles) stimuli, respectively (Hugdahl & Öhman, 1977). After the acquisition phase, half of the subjects in each group were informed that no more shock UCSs would be given, and the shock electrodes were removed. For the other half, the skin conductance electrodes were checked, and no comments were made regarding future trials. The ensuing extinction session was similar for all groups. After extinction, a questionnaire was administered, and subjects in the informed groups who indicated some suspicion concerning the instruction were replaced.

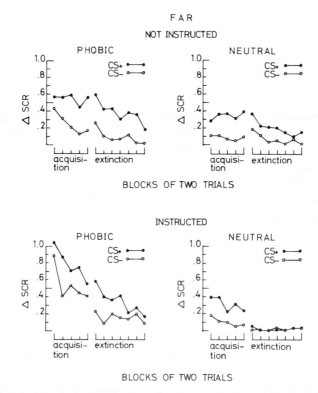

FIGURE 7.8. *Magnitude of skin conductance responses (SCR) for subjects trained with potentially phobic or neutral reinforced and nonreinforced conditioned stimuli (CSs+ and CSs −, respectively), and being instructed or not instructed about the omission of the UCS (shock) before extinction. (From Hugdahl & Öhman, 1977. Copyright 1977 by the American Psychological Association. Reprinted by permission.)*

Figure 7.8 shows the results. All four groups showed similar reliable acquisition effects. The subjects in the neutral groups showed a very clear instructed extinction effect. That is, information that no more UCSs were to be presented completely abolished responding, whereas differential responding was retained in the noninstructed group. In the phobic groups, on the other hand, there was no detectable effect of instruction even with statistical tests biased to discover differences. Thus, in agreement with previous less conclusive data (Öhman, Erixon, & Löfberg, 1975), the subjects exposed to phobic CSs continued to respond, although they were cognitively aware of the fact that no more shocks would be presented. In other words, there was a dissociation between cogitions and autonomic responding, thus matching a central clinical observation of phobias. These data, then, provide an important link in the argument that autonomic responses aversively conditioned to potentially phobic stimuli provide a good model of phobic fear.

PHOBIAS WITHOUT EXPLICIT TRAUMAS

The data presented so far indicate that autonomic responses conditioned to phobic stimuli, similar to real-life phobias, are selective with regard to stimulus, do not extinguish, are acquired on a single trial, and are unaffected by instructions that no further aversive stimuli will follow. It would appear, therefore, that they provide a model of phobic fear far superior to traditional learning theory interpretations. However, our model still involves conditioning, and therefore it is open to one common criticism of conditioning theories. That is to say, conditioning interpretations require an explicit pairing of the phobic stimulus with some traumatic event, whereas many phobics are unable to recall an explicit trauma as the origin of their disorder (Lazarus, 1971). For example, Rimm, Janda, Lancaster, Nahl, and Dittmar (1977) examined the origin of fear in a sample of fearful college students. They found that about half of the subjects could recall an original traumatic experience, whereas the other half could not. Some subjects reported verbal threats as a factor behind the fear, and a few had social modeling experiences.

The Effects of Verbal Threats

One way of accounting for phobias without explicit traumas would be to suggest that conditioning can take place on a symbolic level (e.g., Bandura, 1977). Thus, fear responses to a stimulus could develop because of consistent warnings and threats of the potential danger of the stimulus. There are data showing that threat of electric shock is sufficient to enhance autonomic responses to the cues associated with the threat (e.g., Grings, 1973).

To examine this problem, two groups of subjects were repeatedly exposed to phobic and neutral stimuli, respectively, after having been threatened that a previously experienced shock could follow a defined cue during the experiment (Hugdahl & Öhman, 1977). The data showed that the threat was significantly more effective when it was associated with a phobic than with a neutral stimulus, thus indicating that threat may function similarly to the direct aversive stimuli used in the previous experiments.

However, it is unclear whether the threat-induced responses really parallel those acquired by direct aversive UCSs. A plausible alternative is that the threat-induced responses merely denoted a more intense expectancy of shock in the phobic than in the neutral group. To examine this question, Hugdahl (1978) compared the effects of instructed extinction on responses acquired through threat and through direct electric shock. Groups of subjects were "conditioned" to phobic or neutral stimuli either by means of an electric shock UCS or by means of the same type of threat as in the previous experiment. Before the extinction session, shock electrodes were removed, and all groups were instructed that no more shocks would be presented.

The results are shown in Figure 7.9. There was a significant acquisition effect that did not differ reliably between the four groups. Thus, threat appeared as effective as shock during this period. Independently of whether the responses were acquired through threat or through shock, instructed extinction removed responses to neutral stimuli immediately while leaving responses to the phobic stimuli intact. Thus, in both the shocked and the threatened phobic groups, the subjects continued to respond during the extinction period, and did not differ from each other. This result, then, indicates that even responses to phobic stimuli established without an explicit aversive UCS show the dissociation between cognition and fear responding, which is characteristic of phobias.

Social Modeling

An alternative way to explain phobias without explicit traumas is to suggest that phobias can develop through social modeling (Bandura, 1977; Marks, 1969). Witnessing another person's fear in a specific situation may function as a UCS to condition fear to environmental cues in the observer (Berger, 1962). For instance, children may acquire a fear of snakes by observing a parent being fearful in the presence of snakes. This possibility was empirically examined by Hygge and Öhman (1978). An observer and a confederate model watched pictures of phobic or neutral content together in the experimental chamber. In an interruption of the experiment, the model expressed excessive fear of a stimulus that was reliably preceded by a phobic stimulus for one group and by a neutral stimulus for another.

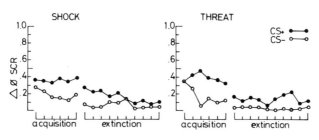

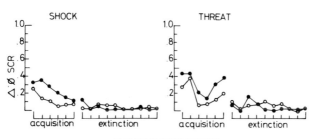

BLOCKS OF TWO TRIALS

FIGURE 7.9. *Magnitude of skin conductance responses (SCR) for subjects trained with potentially phobic or neutral reinforced and nonreinforced conditioned stimuli (CSs+ and CSs −, respectively) with either a shock UCS or through verbal threat of shock, and being instructed that the shock was omitted before extinction. (From Hugdahl, 1978. Copyright 1978 by Pergamon Press. Reprinted by permission.)*

Thus, the model's fear, in combination with the stimulus allegedly eliciting it, could be viewed as the UCS, and the preceding stimulus could be viewed as a CS+. Another stimulus of similar content (e.g., a spider if the CS+ was a snake) was presented independently of the model's fear response, thus completing a differential conditioning paradigm. After the interruption, a few trials were given that included the alleged fear-eliciting stimulus (acquisition), the experimenter then interrupted again to announce that the disturbing stimulus now would be omitted (instructed extinction), and finally a number of extinction trials followed.

The results from this experiment are shown in Figure 7.10. There were significant acquisition effects that did not differ between the phobic and neutral CSs. However, similar to the data from direct conditioning, the phobic CSs showed markedly more resistance to extinction than did the neutral ones. Thus, the responses to the phobic CS+ remained stable in spite of the instruction, whereas responses to the phobic CS − decreased to

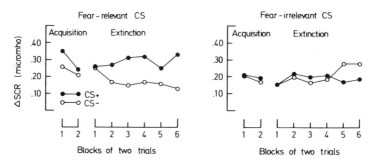

FIGURE 7.10. *Magnitude of skin conductance responses (SCR) for subjects vicariously conditioned through a fearful model to potentially phobic or neutral reinforced and nonreinforced conditioned stimuli (CSs+ and CSs −, respectively). (Data replotted from Hygge & Öhman, 1978.)*

the level of the neutral stimuli as the sensitization produced during acquisition decayed when the stimulus allegedly inducing fear in the model was omitted.

In summary, the data from this section show that responses to phobic stimuli mimicking phobic fear can be acquired symbolically or through vicarious conditioning. Therefore, the model of phobic fear provided by such responses can readily account for the fact that phobias often are acquired without explicit traumas.

PROBLEMS AND IMPLICATIONS

The data reviewed in this chapter indicate that conditioned autonomic responses to fear-relevant stimuli provide a good laboratory model of phobic fear, fulfilling two of the criteria proposed by Seligman (1975). First, they show some important characteristics of phobias such as selectivity with regard to stimulus, rapid acquisition, slow extinction, and resistance to cognitive arguments. Second, there are similarities in causal factors, that is, they can be developed on the basis of direct aversive stimulation, verbal threat, or social modeling (Rimm *et al.*, 1977).

The stability and consistency of the results across experiments, as well as the close similarity to phobias, are quite surprising in view of the limitations of autonomic conditioning discussed previously. Thus, the experimental situations we have used are indeed minimal ones. Pictures of snakes or spiders are clearly not dangerous in themselves, and the degree of aversiveness involved is modest. This consistency in spite of the minimal situation may indicate that we are dealing with quite a basic phenomenon, as suggested by the preparedness theory.

However, in spite of the compelling data, there are some limitations and shortcomings of the present model that must be discussed.

Phobic Fear and Phobic Behavior

In the clinic, phobias are defined in behavioral terms. The phobic characteristically avoids the feared situation. This avoidance response, however, does not in itself constitute a problem (Costello, 1970) unless there are also some approach contingencies at work (Hayes, 1976). As long as the phobic avoids successfully and has no reason to approach the feared situation, he or she behaves quite adaptively, and is unlikely to seek treatment. However, when a reason to approach the feared object is introduced, the irrationality of the fear becomes apparent and the fear may now be labeled as a "psychological problem" requiring some form of professional help. From these considerations, it is clear that intense fear provides a necessary but not a sufficient condition of phobias. Hence, a complete psychological analysis of phobias requires that the fear component is viewed in relation to the instrumental contingencies involved.

Although our data shed light on a necessary component of phobias, phobic fear, they have no specific implications for the instrumental contingencies. The two-stage theory of avoidance postulated a direct and simple relationship between fear and avoidance, but one of the most serious shortcomings of this theory is that this relationship has proven to be much more complicated than originally thought (e.g., Rachman, 1976). Thus, desynchronous relationships between fear and avoidance are often observed (Rachman & Hodgson, 1974). This has led to a reconceptualization of fear as involving three partially independent response systems: verbal reports, physiological responses, and overt behavior (Lang, 1968, 1971, 1978). Our data, then, pertain to only one of these systems, the physiological one, and complementary findings from the other two would be desirable.

There are some data indicating that effects of the conditioning procedure can be detected in verbal reports (Öhman, Eriksson, & Olofsson, 1975). Only subjects given paired presentations of phobic and aversive stimuli increased their fear ratings of the CS from before to after the conditioning session.

Behavioral data, however, are completely lacking. Furthermore, our experimental situation may not be suitable for an analysis of the interrelationships between the response systems, because the fear studied there is necessarily mild, and there is a general presumption that the desynchrony between response systems is particularly evident in mildly fear-producing situations (e.g., Hodgson & Rachman, 1974; Lang, 1971). Thus, an experimental analysis of response system interactions may have to move outside the restricted laboratory situation described in this chapter.

Origin and Maintenance of Phobias

A lesson to be learned from 20 years of practice of behavior therapy is the usefulness of a distinction between those factors originally giving rise to a behavior and those maintaining it. It is a common finding that behavioral interventions can be successfully directed at the current maintaining factors rather than at the factors responsible for the origin and development of a problem. The findings reviewed in this chapter elucidate the factors determining the onset of phobias. However, the data do not imply that these factors are the only ones responsible for their maintenance. For example, a person with a phobia is part of a social network that may provide various types of reinforcements and punishments for the phobic behavior. Furthermore, phobias may be maintained and augmented by cognitive factors such as self-instructions or "internal dialogues" (e.g., Rimm et al., 1977), and it may often be advantageous to direct treatment efforts toward these conditions (e.g., Meichenbaum, 1977, Chapter 5 of this volume). Our data provide some illumination of such factors. Thus, there is an asymmetrical effect of instruction-induced cognitions on autonomic responses conditioned to phobic stimuli. Cognitions are ineffective in attenuating responding (Hugdahl & Öhman, 1977; Öhman, Erixon, & Löfberg, 1975; see Figure 7.8), but are quite effective in enhancing responding (Hugdahl, 1978; Hugdahl & Öhman, 1977). These data, then, indicate that self-instructions should be more effective in augmenting than in reducing phobic fear.

Implications for Treatment

The data reviewed in this chapter are important for an understanding of the factors governing the development of phobias. However, while it is desirable to be able to account for the etiology of a disorder in a frame of reference consistent with the one used to derive treatment, such understanding does not guarantee increases in the precision and efficacy of the intervention. Thus, our results have no necessary implications for the treatment of phobias. One promise inherent in the results is that they may allow the development of a laboratory analogue of the treatment situation, where the effects of various factors thought to be effective in therapy could be investigated. The resistance both to extinction and to the influence of cognitive factors shown by these responses make them handy tools for assessing the relative importance of, for example, stimulus exposure, counterconditioning, and relaxation. One direction that such studies could take is indicated by the work of Grings and colleagues (Grings & Schandler, 1977; Grings & Uno, 1968), who have demonstrated that SCRs conditioned to neutral stimuli can be counterconditioned by relaxation induced through progressive relaxation training or biofeedback.

The clinical usefulness of the preparedness construct was discredited by some data reported by de Silva et al. (1977). In a retrospective study, these authors consistently failed to find relationships between the rated preparedness of the phobic object and clinical variables such as severity of the disorder, suddenness of onset, and therapeutic outcome. The results of this study may serve as a caveat, but they are by no means conclusive. Due to the limitations of the retrospective approach, the conditions for testing a theory were nonoptimal, and definitive conclusions should await proper prospective investigations.

A Biologically-Based Functional Analysis?

In the introduction to this chapter, it was argued that an important reason for the behavior therapists' neglect of the stimulus content variable is their commitment to a functional analysis of behavior. In view of the general success of behavior therapy, this commitment has clearly been warranted. However, the data presented in this chapter provide material for a discussion of the generality of an unrestricted functional approach to behavior. Although the data are not conclusive with regard to the biological basis of phobias, they nevertheless strongly suggest that the nature of the CS is an important determinant of conditioning. The role of biological factors in learning provides one of the most heated controversies in current learning theory (e.g., Krane & Wagner, 1975; Revusky, 1977; Rozin & Kalat, 1971; Shettleworth, 1972). This debate centers on whether it is possible to formulate general laws of learning without considering the nature of the stimuli, responses, and reinforcers involved, and thus it has far-reaching implications for the validity of a functional approach to behavior. Our data, as well as other considerations (e.g., Wilson & Davison, 1968) may be taken as suggesting that this discussion should be taken seriously by behavior therapists, and that limitations of the functional analysis of behavior ultimately must be considered.

ACKNOWLEDGMENTS

I am indebted to Ulf Dimberg, Mats Fredrikson, Kenneth Hugdahl, and Staffan Hygge, who not only collected most of the data, but also contributed ideas, suggestions, and enthusiasm at all stages of the research. Gunilla Bohlin's constructive comments on the manuscript are gratefully acknowledged.

REFERENCES

Annau, Z., & Kamin, L. J. The conditioned emotional response as a function of intensity of the US. *Journal of Comparative and Physiological Psychology*, 1961, *54*, 428–434.

Baer, P. E., & Fuhrer, M. J. Cognitive factors in the differential conditioning of the GSR: Use of a reaction-time task as the UCS with normal and schizophrenic subjects. *Journal of Abnormal Psychology*, 1969, *74*, 544–552.

Bandura, A. *Social learning theory*. Englewood Cliffs, N.J.: Prentice-Hall, 1977.

Berger, S. M. Conditioning through vicarious instigation. *Psychological Review*, 1962, *69*, 450–466.

Bolles, R. C. Species-specific defense reactions and avoidance learning. *Psychological Review,* 1970, *77,* 32–48.

Costello, C. G. Dissimilarities between conditioned avoidance responses and phobias. *Psychological Review,* 1970, *77,* 250–254.

Dawson, M. E., & Furedy, J. J. The role of awareness in human differential autonomic classical conditioning: The necessary-gate hypothesis. *Psychophysiology,* 1976, *13,* 50–53.

de Silva, P., Rachman, S., & Seligman, M. E. P. Prepared phobias and obsessions: Therapeutic outcome. *Behaviour Research and Therapy,* 1977, *15,* 65–77.

Ekman, P. Universals and cultural differences in facial expressions of emotion. In J. K. Cole (Ed.), *Nebraska Symposium on Motivation* (Vol. 19). Lincoln: University of Nebraska Press, 1971. Pp. 207–283.

Eysenck, H. J., & Rachman, S. *The causes and cures of neurosis.* London: Routledge & Kegan Paul, 1965.

Fowles, D. C. Theoretical approaches and methodological problems in clinical research. In D. C. Fowles (Ed.), *Clinical applications of psychophysiology.* New York: Columbia University Press, 1975. Pp. 192–224.

Fredrikson, M., Hugdahl, K., & Öhman, A. Electrodermal conditioning to potentially phobic stimuli in male and female subjects. *Biological Psychology,* 1976, *4,* 305–314.

Fredrikson, M., & Öhman, A. Cardiovascular and electrodermal responses during conditioning to phobic stimuli. *Psychophysiology,* 1979, *6,* 1–7.

Garcia, J., McGowan, B. K., & Green, K. F. Biological constraints on conditioning. In A. H. Black & W. F. Prokasy (Eds.), *Classical conditioning II: Current research and theory.* New York: Appleton-Century-Crofts, 1972. Pp. 3–27.

Grant, D. A. Cognitive factors in eye-lid conditioning. *Psychophysiology,* 1973, *10,* 75–81.

Grings, W. W. Cognitive factors in electrodermal conditioning. *Psychological Bulletin,* 1973, *79,* 200–210.

Grings, W. W., & Dawson, M. E. Complex variables in conditioning. In W. F. Prokasy & D. C. Raskin (Eds.), *Electrodermal activity in psychological research.* New York: Academic Press, 1973. Pp. 203–254.

Grings, W. W., & Schandler, S. L. Interaction of learned relaxation and aversion. *Psychophysiology,* 1977, *14,* 275–280.

Grings, W. W., & Uno, T. Counterconditioning: Fear and relaxation. *Psychophysiology,* 1968, *4,* 479–485.

Hayes, S. C. The role of approach contingencies in phobic behavior. *Behavior Therapy,* 1976, *7,* 28–36.

Hebb, D. O. Spontaneous neurosis in chimpanzees. Theoretical relations with clinical and experimental phenomena. *Psychosomatic Medicine,* 1947, *9,* 3–16.

Herrnstein, R. J. Method and theory in the study of avoidance. *Psychological Review,* 1969, *76,* 49–69.

Hinde, R. A. *Biological bases of human social behavior.* New York: McGraw-Hill, 1974.

Hodes, R., Öhman, A., & Lang, P. J. "Ontogenetic" and "phylogenetic" fear-relevance of the conditioned stimulus in electrodermal and heart-rate conditioning. Unpublished data, 1977.

Hodgson, R., & Rachman, S. II. Desynchrony in measures of fear. *Behaviour Research and Therapy,* 1974, *12,* 319–326.

Hugdahl, K. Conditioning, stimulus relevance, and cognitive factors in phobic fear. *Acta Universitatis Upsalienses: Abstracts of Uppsala Dissertations from the Faculty of Social Science,* No. 16, 1977.

Hugdahl, K. Electrodermal conditioning to potentially phobic stimuli: Effects of instructed extinction. *Behaviour Research and Therapy,* 1978, *16,* 315–321.

Hugdahl, K., Fredrikson, M., & Öhman, A. "Preparedness" and "arousability" as determinants of electrodermal conditioning. *Behaviour Research and Therapy,* 1977, *15,* 345–353.

Hugdahl, K., & Öhman, A. Effects of instruction on acquisition and extinction of electrodermal responses to fear-relevant stimuli. *Journal of Experimental Psychology: Human Learning and Memory*, 1977, *3*, 608–618.

Hygge, S., & Öhman, A. Modeling processes in the acquisition of fears: Vicarious electrodermal conditioning to fear-relevant stimuli. *Journal of Personality and Social Psychology*, 1978, *36*, 271–279.

Krane, R. V., & Wagner, A. R. Taste aversion learning with a delayed shock US: Implication for the "generality of the laws of learning." *Journal of Comparative and Physiological Psychology*, 1975, *88*, 882–889.

Lang, P. J. Fear reduction and fear behavior: Problems in treating a construct. In J. M. Shlien (Ed.), *Research in psychotherapy* (Vol. 3). Washington, D.C.: American Psychological Association, 1968. Pp. 90–102.

Lang, P. J. The application of psychophysiological methods to the study of psychotherapy and behavior modification. In A. E. Bergin & S. L. Garfield (Eds.), *Handbook of psychotherapy and behavior change: An empirical analysis*. New York: Wiley, 1971. Pp. 75–125.

Lang, P. J. Anxiety: Toward a psychophysiological definition. In H. S. Akiskal & W. L. Webb (Eds.), *Psychiatric disorders: Exploration of biological predictors*. Jamaica: Spectrum, 1978. Pp. 365–390.

Lazarus, A. A. *Behavior therapy and beyond*. New York: McGraw-Hill, 1971.

Leitenberg, H. Behavioral approaches to treatment of neurosis. In H. Leitenberg (Ed.), *Handbook of behavior modification and behavior therapy*. Englewood Cliffs, N.J.: Prentice-Hall, 1976. Pp. 124–167.

Lockhart, R. A. Cognitive processes and the multiple response phenomenon. *Psychophysiology*, 1973, *10*, 112–118.

Marks, I. M. *Fears and phobias*. London: Heinemann, 1969.

Meichenbaum, D. H. *Cognitive-behavior modification. An integrative approach*. New York: Plenum, 1977.

Mowrer, O. H. On the dual nature of learning: A reinterpretation of "conditioning" and "problem-solving." *Harvard Educational Review*, 1947, *17*, 102–148.

Öhman, A. Differentiation of conditioned and orienting response components in electrodermal conditioning. *Psychophysiology*, 1971, *8*, 7–22.

Öhman, A. Factor analytically derived components of orienting, defensive, and conditioned behavior in electrodermal conditioning. *Psychophysiology*, 1972, *9*, 199–209.

Öhman, A. Orienting reactions, expectancy learning, and conditioned responses in electrodermal conditioning with different interstimulus intervals. *Biological Psychology*, 1974, *1*, 189–200.

Öhman, A. Towards experimental models of "mental disease". In S. G. R. Nordström (Ed.), *Faculty of social science at Uppsala university. Uppsala university 500 years* (Vol. 7). Uppsala: Acta Universitatis Upsaliensis, 1976. Pp. 119–145.

Öhman, A. & Bohlin, G. The relationship between spontaneous and stimulus-correlated electrodermal responses in simple and discriminative conditioning paradigms. *Psychophysiology*, 1973, *10*, 589–600.

Öhman, A., & Dimberg, U. Facial expressions as conditioned stimuli for electrodermal responses: A case of "preparedness"? *Journal of Personality and Social Psychology*, 1978, *36*, 1251–1258.

Öhman, A., Ellström, P.-E., & Björkstrand, P.-Å. Electrodermal responses and subjective estimates of UCS probability in a long interstimulus interval conditioning paradigm. *Psychophysiology*, 1976, *13*, 121–128.

Öhman, A., Eriksson, A., Fredrikson, M., Hugdahl, K., & Olofsson, C. Habituation of the electrodermal orienting reaction to potentially phobic and supposedly neutral stimuli in normal human subjects. *Biological Psychology*, 1974, *2*, 85–93.

Öhman, A., Eriksson, A., & Olofsson, C. One-trial learning and superior resistance to extinction of autonomic responses conditioned to potentially phobic stimuli. *Journal of Comparative and Physiological Psychology*, 1975, *88*, 619–627.

Öhman, A., Erixon, G., & Löfberg, I. Phobias and preparedness: Phobic versus neutral pictures as conditioned stimuli for human autonomic responses. *Journal of Abnormal Psychology*, 1975, *84*, 41–45.

Öhman, A., Fredrikson, M., & Hugdahl, K. Towards an experimental model of simple phobic reactions. *Behaviour Analysis and Modification*, 1978, *2*, 97–114. (a)

Öhman, A., Fredrikson, M., & Hugdahl, K. Orienting and defensive responding in the electrodermal system: Palmar-dorsal differences and recovery-rate during conditioning to potentially phobic stimuli. *Psychophysiology*, 1978, *15*, 93–101. (b)

Öhman, A., Fredrikson, M., Hugdahl, K., & Rimmö, P.-A. The premise of equipotentiality in human classical conditioning: Conditioned electrodermal responses to potentially phobic stimuli. *Journal of Experimental Psychology: General*, 1976, *105*, 313–337.

Pavlov, I. P. *Conditioned reflexes*. London: Oxford University Press, 1927.

Prokasy, W. F. First interval skin conductance responses: Conditioned or orienting response? *Psychophysiology*, 1977, *14*, 360–367.

Prokasy, W. F., & Kumpfer, K. L. Classical conditioning. In W. F. Prokasy & D. C. Raskin (Eds.), *Electrodermal activity in psychological research*. New York: Academic Press, 1973. Pp. 157–202.

Rachman, S. The passing of the two-stage theory of fear and avoidance: Fresh possibilities. *Behaviour Research and Therapy*, 1976, *14*, 125–131.

Rachman, S., & Hodgson, R. I. Synchrony and desynchrony in fear and avoidance. *Behaviour Research and Therapy*, 1974, *12*, 311–318.

Rescorla, R. A. Pavlovian conditioning and its proper control procedures. *Psychological Review*, 1967, *74*, 71–80.

Revusky, S. Learning as a general process with an emphasis on data from feeding experiments. In N. W. Milgram, L. Krames, & T. M. Alloway (Eds.), *Food aversion learning*. New York: Plenum, 1977. Pp. 1–51.

Rimm, D. C., Janda, L. H., Lancaster, D. W., Nahl, M., & Dittmar, K. An exploratory investigation of the origin and maintenance of phobias. *Behaviour Research and Therapy*, 1977, *15*, 231–238.

Rozin, R., & Kalat, J. W. Specific hungers and poison avoidance as adaptive specializations of learning. *Psychological Review*, 1971, *78*, 459–486.

Schwartz, B. On going back to nature: A review of Seligman and Hager's *Biological boundaries of learning*. *Journal of the Experimental Analysis of Behavior*, 1974, *21*, 183–198.

Seligman, M. E. P. On the generality of the laws of learning. *Psychological Review*, 1970, *77*, 406–418.

Seligman, M. E. P. Phobias and preparedness. *Behavior Therapy*, 1971, *2*, 307–321.

Seligman, M. E. P. *Helplessness. On depression, development, and death*. San Francisco: Freeman, 1975.

Seligman, M. E. P., & Hager, J. E. (Eds.). *Biological boundaries of learning*. New York: Appleton-Century-Crofts, 1972.

Seligman, M. E. P., & Johnston, J. C. A cognitive theory of avoidance learning. In F. J. McGuigan & D. B. Lumsden (Eds.), *Contemporary approaches to conditioning and learning*. Washington: Winston, 1973. Pp. 69–110.

Shettleworth, S. J. Constraints on learning. In D. S. Lehrman, R. A. Hinde, & E. Shaw (Eds.), *Advances in the study of behavior* (Vol. 4). New York: Academic Press, 1972. Pp. 1–68.

Skinner, B. F. *Contingencies of reinforcement. A theoretical analysis*. New York: Appleton-Century-Crofts, 1969.

Sokolov, Ye. N. *Perception and the conditioned reflex*. Oxford: Pergamon, 1963.

Venables, P. H. Psychophysiological studies of schizophrenic pathology. In P. H. Venables & M. J. Christie (Eds.), *Research in psychophysiology*. New York: Wiley, 1975. Pp. 282–324.
Wilson, G. T., & Davison, G. C. Aversion techniques in behavior therapy: Some theoretical and metatheoretical considerations. *Journal of Consulting and Clinical Psychology*, 1968, *33*, 327–329.
Wolpe, J. *Psychotherapy by reciprocal inhibition*. Stanford: Stanford University Press, 1958.

8

The Blunting Hypothesis: A View of Predictability and Human Stress[1]

SUZANNE M. MILLER AND RANDALL P. GRANT

Individuals are continually faced with the prospect of aversive events, such as failing an exam, losing a job, or undergoing a surgical operation. Most theorists have assumed that when such events are predictable, the level of accompanying stress and anxiety is lowered (Berlyne, 1960; Perkins, 1955; Seligman, 1968). Indeed, unpredictability (or uncertainty) is often considered to be the hallmark of clinical anxiety (Epstein, 1972). While considerable data from the animal literature support this view, the human data are by no means clear-cut. That is, predictability sometimes decreases, and sometimes increases, stress and anxiety. None of the existing theories can account for these inconsistencies. We therefore propose a new hypothesis, the "blunting hypothesis," which integrates the literature by specifying the conditions under which predictability has stress-reducing effects and when it does not. The present chapter is organized in the following way. We begin by defining the terms "predictability" and "stress." Then we discuss the blunting hypothesis and its predictions in some detail. This constitutes the major part of the chapter. We also briefly review the other three major theories of predictability. Then we present the experimental evidence and contrast it with the predictions of each of the

[1]Research for this chapter was supported by U.S. PHS Grant MH 19604-07 from the National Institute of Mental Health and Grant RR-09069 from the National Institute of Health.

Copyright © 1979 by Academic Press, Inc.
All rights of reproduction in any form reserved.
ISBN 0-12-647450-8

theories. We find the blunting hypothesis to be most consistent with the evidence. Finally, we address some of the clinical implications of the blunting hypothesis.

A DEFINITION OF PREDICTABILITY

Three main classes of predictability have been manipulated in the literature. These classes have been loosely referred to as: temporal (or time) predictability; event predictability; and what-kind-of-event predictability (e.g., Epstein, 1973; Grings, 1973). We have recently undertaken a more fine-grained analysis of the predictability concept and have found the first two of these classes to be neither exclusive nor exhaustive. In order to circumvent these inadequacies, we have presented a reformulated classification schema, based on the following three dimensions: contingency predictability; stimulus-bound predictability; and what-kind-of-event predictability. It is not possible to present an in-depth discussion of this issue within the confines of this chapter (see Miller & Grant, 1978, for a detailed account). However, these definitions allow for a more precise quantification of each class of predictability. At the same time, they are more exhaustive than the traditional formulations, and are therefore able to encompass all the diverse procedures for manipulating predictability that have been used in the literature.

The first class of predictability is contingency predictability, which means that the individual knows something about the stimulus conditions under which the aversive event is most likely to occur. In contrast, lack of contingency predictability means that the individual does not know the stimulus conditions under which the aversive event is most likely to occur. That is, contingency predictability exists only when the individual knows that the aversive event (e.g., shock) has a greater probability of occurrence under one set of stimulus conditions (e.g., tone on) than under another set of stimulus conditions (e.g., tone off). This dimensions maps into the Pavlovian "conditioning space" of Rescorla (1967) and Seligman, Maier, and Solomon (1971), where the probability of the unconditioned stimulus (UCS) in the presence of the conditioned stimulus (CS) and the probability of the UCS in the absence of the CS are both specified. A UCS such as shock is predictable in the contingency sense if, and only if, its probability of occurrence is greater when the CS is present than it is when the CS is absent. Conversely, shock is unpredictable in the contingency sense when it has an equal probability of occurrence both in the signal's presence (i.e., during tone on) and in the signal's absence (i.e., during tone off). In this case, the presence of the tone provides the individual with no more information about shock occurrence than does the absence of the tone.

The bulk of laboratory research has focused on contingency predictability, and this is the class of predictability with which we shall be concerned in this chapter. Contingency predictability is most commonly operationalized in the laboratory by preceding the occurrence of the aversive event with some warning signal or CS. In contrast, under unpredictability, the CS is either presented randomly with respect to the UCS, or is withheld altogether (e.g., Averill & Rosenn, 1972; Furedy & Doob, 1972; Geer & Maisel, 1972; Miller, in press c; Price & Geer, 1972). Another manipulation involves presenting the event at regular intervals in the predictability condition and presenting it at irregular intervals in the unpredictability condition (e.g., Furedy & Chan, 1971; Glass, Singer, & Friedman, 1969; Lovibond, 1968). Finally, predictability can be operationalized by specifying in advance when the event will occur and providing the subject with a means of keeping track of the time. The unpredictability subject is simply told that the event can occur at any time (Bowers, 1971a; Gaebelein, Taylor, & Borden, 1974; Mansueto & Desiderato, 1971; Monat, Averill, & Lazarus, 1972).

Very briefly, the other two classes of predictability are (*a*) stimulus-bound predictability, which means that the individual knows how likely the event is to occur under a given set of stimulus conditions (e.g., tone on); and (*b*) what-kind-of-event predictability, which means that the individual knows exactly what the aversive event will be like and how it will affect him or her. The evidence and theory relating to these two classes will not be discussed here (see Miller & Grant, 1978, for a discussion).

It is important to point out that predictability has often been collapsed with controllability (Averill, 1973). According to Seligman (1975), an event is controllable if, and only if, some response in the individual's repertoire alters the probability of the event's occurrence. That is, when an individual can instrumentally control an aversive event by escape or avoidance, he or she can predict its occurrence or nonoccurrence. Thus controllability, by its very nature, increases contingency predictability. In contrast, merely being able to predict the occurrence of an event does not necessarily enable an individual to control or modify it. All of the studies relevant to the blunting hypothesis manipulate predictability while holding controllability constant, ideally by making the event uncontrollable. In a separate paper, Miller (in press a and in press b) has argued that the stress effects of controllability per se are readily distinguishable from those of predictability.

AN OPERATIONALIZATION OF "STRESS"

There are three ways in which "stress" reactions have been operationalized in predictability experiments. The first measure is to record what subjects choose when given an actual *choice* between a predictable and an unpredictable aversive event. Another means of assessing choice is to expose subjects to both predictable and unpredictable events and to obtain self-report ratings of preference for the alternatives.

The second measure is *anticipatory arousal*, that is, whether or not people are more aroused and anxious while waiting for a predictable or an unpredictable event. Anticipatory arousal has been assessed subjectively, via self-reported anxiety and tension, and physiologically. With respect to physiological indicators, tonic skin conductance level (SCL), phasic skin conductance responses (SCRs), and heart rate (HR) are the most popular measures. There is growing evidence that nonspecific (spontaneous) SCRs are closely linked to emotional arousal, while tonic SCL (Kilpatrick, 1972) and heart rate (Lacey, 1967) may reflect cognitive and attentional factors. When discussing anticipatory physiological arousal, we will therefore only consider evidence relating to nonspecific SCRs.

The third measure of stress is an *impact* measure, that is, whether or not a predictable aversive event hurts less than an unpredictable event. Impact responses have been assessed subjectively, by self-reports of pain and discomfort, and physiologically, by changes in skin conductance. It should be clear that no *one* measure can be viewed as representing the "stress" response per se. Rather, the convergence of evidence from all *three* measures provides an integrated index of overall level of "stress." In summarizing the predictability literature, then, we will take all of these measures into account.

AN EXPLICIT STATEMENT OF THE BLUNTING HYPOTHESIS

We now propose a statement of the blunting hypothesis, which extends Seligman's (1968) safety signal hypothesis to human beings. The safety signal theory says that when a signal reliably predicts danger, the absence of the signal reliably predicts safety. That is, if a tone (CS) predicts shock, then the absence of the tone ($\overline{CS}$) predicts no shock (or safety) and the individual can relax during silence. In contrast, if no one signal reliably predicts danger, then no one signal reliably predicts safety and the individual can never relax (all events equally predict danger). Thus, if given a choice, predictability should be chosen because the individual prefers to be exposed to acute periods of high danger (and long periods of safety and relaxation) rather than to chronic periods of moderate danger.

With human beings, however, it is important to realize that the danger signal must be both physically *and* psychologically present in order to produce arousal in the first place. There is no reason to expect, for example, that an individual will become aroused when medical results (CS) show that he or she requires surgery (UCS), but the patient does not yet know it. Arousal will be induced only when the danger signal becomes psychologically present, that is, when the doctor explains what the tests mean and the necessity to operate. Safety signal theory, like animal theories generally, fails to distinguish between the physical and the psychological presence of danger signals.

Moreover, once the individual has been faced with a physical (i.e., real or objective) danger signal and has been made psychologically aware of this danger signal, he or she can then adopt a variety of cognitive strategies that remove them from any further psychological awareness of it. The use of such strategies will, in turn, help to lower the level of arousal. In other words, having been told by the doctor that the tests signal the need for surgery, the individual can then use various cognitive strategies to become removed psychologically from this state of affairs, and so reduce arousal, even though the danger signal remains physically (objectively) present. We shall label those strategies that remove people psychologically from danger signals as "blunting" strategies, so-called because they help to blunt the psychological impact of physically present danger cues. Such strategies include distraction, self-relaxation, denial, detachment, intellectualization, and reinterpretation.

Table 8.1 specifies the relationships between the physical presence or absence of a danger signal and its psychological presence or absence. In cell A, the danger signal is both physically and psychologically present, and the result is realistic fear and heightened arousal. This is the case in which the individual's tests show that there is need for an operation, and the individual is attending to and scanning for the upcoming event. The more likely, imminent, and intense he or she *perceives* the UCS to be, the greater will be the level of arousal. On the other hand, in cell D, the danger signal is both physically and psychologically absent. This means that the indi-

TABLE 8.1

Relationships between the Physical and Psychological Presence and Absence of the Danger Signal

Psychological	Physical	
	Present	Absent
Present	**A** Attending to danger cues (realistic fear)	**C** Brooding, worrying, ruminating, rehearsing (unrealistic fear)
Absent	**B** Distraction—also, self-relaxation, denial, detachment, reinterpretation, intellectualization (unrealistic inhibition of fear)	**D** Attending to safety cues (realistic inhibition of fear)

vidual is attending to safety and is realistically inhibiting fear (i.e., the person is relaxed). Thus, the person is not faced with the prospect of surgery (physical danger signal) and is not thinking about or attending to the possibility of having to undergo surgery (psychological danger signal). When the danger signal is physically present but psychologically absent, as in cell B, the person is either unaware of the danger signal (the physician has not yet informed him or her about the test results) or, more interestingly, is engaging in a successful cognitive strategy that blunts the impact of the danger signal and reduces arousal. For example, the individual can be distracting him- or herself by thinking about other events; relaxing him- or herself by calming self-statements; reinterpreting the operation as a positive, beneficial experience; or intellectualizing about the situation. A person in cell C is not in any physical presence of a danger signal (the medical report shows a clean bill of health) but he or she is nonetheless in the psychological presence of the danger signal (i.e., he or she continues to think about the possibility that there may be a need for an operation). This individual can be said to be worrying, brooding, or ruminating about the danger signal, and should manifest heightened arousal. This cell, largely uninvestigated, has important implications for clinical anxiety and will be discussed later.

Distraction has been the most commonly investigated blunting strategy, since it is the most easily induced, measured, and operationalized. Therefore, the following discussion focuses on the use of distraction to accomplish psychological withdrawal from danger signals. Distraction can obviously occur spontaneously inside a subject's head, but it can also be induced by external means. For example, Averill and Rosenn (1972) and Miller (in press c) operationalized distraction by giving subjects a choice between listening for a signal that predicted shock (contingency predictability) or listening to music (distraction). Preference for distraction was indexed by the amount of time each subject spent listening to the music. Similarly, in an experiment by Rothbart and Mellinger (1972), subjects worked on an arithmetic task but could attend as often as they wished to a light that signaled shock onset. The less time spent looking at the light, the greater the preference for distraction.

Experiments such as these constitute a theoretically and practically important variant of studies on choice and arousal. In the more standard choice procedure, subjects can only choose between a predictable and an unpredictable aversive event, with no distraction available in the unpredictability condition. Typically, subjects are offered a choice between listening for a tone that signals shock or waiting passively for shock, with no warning signal. In real life, however, people have limitless opportunities for distraction in the face of unpredictable aversive events. To what extent, then, do people actually prefer and make use of such distractions?

Certain laboratory and real-life conditions should be more supportive of distraction than other conditions. First and foremost, it should be easier to distract oneself when the aversive event is unpredictable (in the contingency sense) than when it is predictable. Consider the case where a subject has been threatened with shock and is told that a tone will signal the occurrence of shock (contingency predictability). Here, the individual will be listening for the tone and hence will be in the psychological presence of the danger signal. Moreover, the danger signal itself is psychologically invasive and intrusive, even if the individual is trying to block it out. In contrast, when there is no explicit signal for the occurrence of shock (contingency unpredictability), the physical signals are more continuous and diluted. This makes the danger signal less invasive and intrusive on the psychological level. Similarly, when the event is controllable, or intense (i.e., high probability, high shock level, long duration, or imminent) distraction will be difficult or impossible. Conversely, under uncontrollable or low-intensity trauma, distraction will be relatively easy.

Finally, distraction is facilitated when external distractors are readily available or, in the laboratory, when subjects are explicitly told they are allowed to distract themselves. Indeed, there is a growing body of research that suggests that subjects are more likely to use distraction spontaneously under unpredictability and low intensity conditions than under predictability and high intensity conditions, and that this is associated with decreased anticipatory arousal (Averill & Rosenn, 1972; Monat, 1976; Monat et al., 1972). Moreover, providing external distractors during unpredictable trauma further reduces anticipatory arousal (Bloom, Houston, Holmes, & Burish, 1977). It has even been shown that tolerance for pain can be increased by providing external distractors, although the underlying mechanism has been disputed (Barber & Cooper, 1972; Chaves & Barber, 1974; Kanfer & Goldfoot, 1966; Kanfer & Seidner, 1973).

Here, then, are the main predictions that follow from the blunting hypothesis (see Table 8.2):

1. Predictable aversive events should be chosen over unpredictable aversive events, under invasive and intrusive conditions that make distraction difficult. This is because subjects can know at least when they are in safety and thereby relax.
2. In contrast, unpredictable aversive events should be chosen over predictable aversive events, under noninvasive conditions that facilitate distraction. This is because arousal is more effectively reduced by a blunting strategy, such as distraction, than by external safety signals.
3. The hypothesis predicts greater anticipatory arousal to the danger signal (CS) under predictability than during comparable periods for

TABLE 8.2

Summary of Experimental Evidence and Theoretical Predictions Concerning Contingency Predictability of Aversive Events[a]

Theory	Choice		Greater anticipatory arousal	Greater impact arousal
	No distraction	Distraction		
		Experimental evidence		
	P/N	UN/P	P	—
		Theoretical predictions		
Blunting	P/UN	UN/P	P	0
Information seeking	P/UN	P/UN	UN	UN
Preparatory response	P/UN	P/UN	0	UN
Safety signal	P/UN	P/UN	P	0

[a]P = predictability condition; UN = unpredictability condition; 0 = silent; — = no effect of predictability; P/UN = choice of predictability over unpredictability; UN/P = choice of unpredictability over predictability.

unpredictable aversive events. This effect should be particularly evident under noninvasive conditions that support distraction with unpredictability.

4. The blunting hypothesis makes no prediction about the effect of predictability on the impact of the aversive event. That is, it is silent on whether or not the UCS hurts less with predictability.

OTHER PREDICTABILITY THEORIES

There are three other major predictability theories, whose predictions will be briefly reviewed to contrast with the blunting hypothesis (see Table 8.2). The first theory is the information-seeking view (Berlyne, 1960), which says that people and animals seek information, and, when faced with uncertainty (unpredictability), they strive for certainty. This is because uncertainty causes conflict and therefore increases arousal. Another version of this theory (Sokolov, 1963) states that subjects can develop a "neuronal" model of the event under predictability, so that habituation proceeds more quickly. These theories predict: (*a*) choice of predictable over unpredictable aversive events, whether or not distraction is allowed; (*b*) higher anticipatory arousal with unpredictable aversive events, because the individual is in greater conflict; and (*c*) greater impact with unpredictable aversive events, because the UCS is more surprising.

The second theory is the preparatory response theory (Perkins, 1955, 1968), which states that when an aversive event is predictable, individuals can make an optimally timed response that makes the event hurt less. When faced with unpredictability, however, individuals are not able to make a well-timed response. The theory predicts: (*a*) choice of predictable over unpredictable aversive events, whether or not distraction is allowed; and (*b*) greater impact with unpredictable aversive events, since the UCS actually hurts more. The theory is silent about the effects of predictability on anticipatory arousal. On the one hand, unpredictability may lead to increased arousal, since the subjects are waiting for a more aversive UCS. However, predictability itself may lead to increased arousal, due to the act of engaging in a preparatory response.

The final theory, safety signal theory (Seligman, 1968), has been outlined previously. Briefly, it predicts: (*a*) choice of predictable over unpredictable aversive events, whether or not distraction is allowed; (*b*) greater anticipatory arousal with predictable aversive events when the danger signal is present. This is because the predictability subject is in high fear whereas the unpredictability subject is in moderate fear; and (*c*) the theory makes no prediction about impact.

THE EXPERIMENTAL EVIDENCE

A summary of the experimental evidence for contingency predictability on choice, anticipatory arousal, and impact is presented in Table 8.2. Beginning with the predictability data on choice, a review of seven studies shows that subjects clearly prefer predictability to unpredictability, even under uncontrollable aversive events (Badia, McBane, Suter, & Lewis, 1966; Badia, Suter, & Lewis, 1967; Elliott, 1969; Furedy & Klajner, 1972b; Jones, Bentler, & Petry, 1966; Maltzman & Wolff, 1970; Monat et al., 1972). Cook and Barnes (1964) and Furedy, Fainstat, Kulin, Lasko, and Nichols (1972) also reported a preference for predictability, while three studies by Furedy and Doob (1971a, 1971b, 1972) reported no such preference. However, these five studies suffer from various methodological and conceptual problems, which have been detailed elsewhere (Miller & Grant, 1978). We are therefore hesitant to draw any firm conclusions from this latter evidence.

As was mentioned earlier, the few studies that compare predictability with unpredictability plus distraction are more closely tied to real-life stress than the simple choice studies, and thus they provide a crucial test for the theories. The results from three studies show that the majority of people choose unpredictable aversive events when the option of distraction is explicitly provided (Averill & Rosenn, 1972; Miller, in press c; Rothbart & Mellinger, 1972). Of particular interest for the blunting hypothesis is that preference for distraction is most clearly observed under environmental conditions that should best support this strategy (i.e., under uncontrollability and under low-intensity trauma). As Table 8.2 shows, all of the proposed theories accurately predict choice of predictability over simple unpredictability. However, choice of unpredictability over predictability when distraction is provided is contrary to all the theories except the blunting hypothesis. Only the blunting hypothesis states that unpredictable aversive events are preferred when subjects can successfully distract themselves from danger signals.

Turning to anticipatory measures under contingency predictability, the physiological and subjective data generally show that predictable aversive events cause higher anticipatory arousal and anxiety than unpredictable aversive events. With respect to the physiological data, four out of five studies show that predictability leads to an increased frequency of nonspecific skin conductance responses (Miller, in press c; Monat, 1976; Monat et al., 1972, Experiments I and II). Geer and Maisel (1972) also reported fewer skin conductance responses with predictability, whereas Bowers reported no effect in one study (1971a) and the opposite result in a second study (1971b). However, the experimental designs employed in these three studies involved a confounding of contingency predictability with another class of predictability and should therefore be viewed with caution. Overall, then, the trend shows an increase in physiological arousal with predictable aversive events. For subjective measures, the trend is the same, with four out of six studies reporting increased ratings of anxiety with predictability (Miller, in press c; Monat, 1976; Monat et al., 1972, Experiments I and II). In contrast, one study found decreased ratings of anxiety with predictability (Klemp & Rodin, 1976), and one study found no differences (Averill & Rosenn, 1972).

The conflicting results may well be resolved by considering procedural differences affecting ease of distraction in the unpredictability condition. The two studies (Averill & Rosenn, 1972; Miller, in press c) that contrasted predictability to unpredictability with distraction are particularly informative in this regard. As was reported earlier, both studies found choice of unpredictability when distraction was explicitly provided. However, in the Miller study, use of distraction was associated with fewer nonspecific SCRs and lower self-reported anxiety. In contrast, Averill and Rosenn did not find that use of distraction reduced arousal and anxiety. However, since Averill and Rosenn actually shocked their subjects with moderate to intense UCS on each trial, their "distractors" may have performed less successfully than Miller's, who were only threatened with shock but never actually received a shock. In support of this notion, the "distractors" of the Miller study reported thinking less about shock during the experiment than subjects who listened for the warning signal. This was not the case for "distractors" in the Averill and Rosenn study.

The remaining studies that failed to find differences between predictability and unpredictability conditions all used extremely short anticipatory intervals (5 and 20 seconds in the Klemp and Rodin study, and 30 seconds in the Bowers studies). There is some correlational evidence showing that subjects find it hard to distract themselves during anticipatory intervals of less than 1 minute (Folkins, 1970). Moreover, Monat (1976) recently contrasted the effects of predictable versus unpredictable electric shock during 1-, 3-, or 12-minute anticipatory intervals. Although predictability generally increased physiological and subjective anxiety and number of shock related thoughts, this effect was greatest with the longer anticipatory intervals.

Taken together, the preceding evidence suggests that unpredictability leads to decreased anticipatory arousal, particularly under conditions that support distraction. These results are contrary to the information-seeking theory and to preparatory response theory. They are consistent with safety signal theory, which predicts greater anticipatory arousal with predictability when the danger signal is present. However, the variations with distractability cannot be accounted for by safety signal theory. The data are entirely consistent with the blunting hypothesis, which specifies that predictability is even more arousing than unpredictability under conditions that facilitate distraction (e.g., low-probability aversive events or events that are not very imminent).

With regard to the impact effects of predictable versus unpredictable aversive events, the available evidence is inconclusive. On the physiological level, impact is usually indexed by the emergence of a clearly discernible SCR. Such a response must exceed a given amplitude to be considered and should appear between 5 and 10 seconds after UCS onset. Despite such a standardized criterion, only 2 out of 5 unconfounded studies show decreased impact with predictability (Lovibond, 1968; Maltzman & Wolff, 1970); whereas 3 studies show no difference (Furedy & Chan, 1971; Furedy & Klajner, 1972a; Price & Geer, 1972). Among studies using confounded designs, Peeke and Grings (1968) found decreased impact with predictability, while Bowers (1971a; 1971b) and Geer and Maisel (1972) found no differences in impact. On the subjective level, the same inconsistencies obtain, with only 3 out of 11 studies showing that contingency predictability leads to decreased ratings of pain (D'Amato & Gumenik, 1960; Lovibond, 1968; Maltzman & Wolff, 1970). In contrast, 8 studies show no effect of predictability (Averill & Rosenn, 1972; Coles, Herzberger, Sperber, & Goetz, 1975; Furedy, 1973; Furedy & Chan, 1971; Furedy & Ginsberg, 1973; Furedy & Klajner, 1972a; Glass et al., 1969; Klemp & Rodin, 1976). There are 5 studies with confounded designs that also report no impact differences (Furedy, 1970; Furedy & Doob, 1971a, 1971b, 1972; Furedy et al., 1972); and 1 confounded study (Bowers, 1971a) that reports greater impact with predictability. On the whole, the data do not reveal any consistent effect of contingency predictability on impact. For the moment, then, it seems safest to conclude that this is because predictability has no effect. This is inconsistent with information-seeking theory and preparatory response theory, but it is consistent with safety signal theory and the blunting hypothesis, which are silent about impact.

In summarizing the fit of each of the theories to the data, it can be seen from Table 8.2 that only the blunting hypothesis fits the data well. Information-seeking theory and preparatory response theory are consistent only with the choice data under no distraction, and they are inconsistent with all other data. Safety signal theory is consistent with the choice data under no distraction and the anticipatory arousal and impact data. The blunting hypothesis, however, is consistent with all the choice data as well as the anticipatory arousal and impact data.

IMPLICATIONS FOR CLINICAL ANXIETY

The blunting hypothesis predicts that individuals vary in the extent to which they tend to seek information or use distraction in the face of aversive events. "Good blunters" should typically prefer to distract themselves from danger signals and will opt for distraction even when environmental conditions do not favor the use of distraction. Conversely, "poor blunters" should typically prefer to monitor for danger signals and will fail to distract even when environmental conditions support distraction. Miller (1978) has recently developed a questionnaire for identifying "monitors" and "blunters." This questionnaire has now been validated in both laboratory and naturally occurring stress situations. The results show that monitors (as defined by questionnaire results) choose predictability over distraction; whereas blunters opt for the reverse condition (see Miller, 1978; Miller, Mangan, Freed, & Burtnett, 1979). Furthermore, it is our belief that these individual differences in coping styles have implications for neurotic disorders. That is, where individuals chronically fall into the 2 × 2 table (Table 8.1) is relevant to the etiology of clinical anxiety and to the nature of therapeutic intervention.

Consider those individuals who do not have the ability to distract themselves from real danger signals (i.e., those who cannot enter cell B of Table 8.1 easily) and also continually find themselves in the psychological presence of potential danger signals, even when such signals are physically absent (cell C). We propose that these are the people who are usually diagnosed as anxiety neurotics. That is, in Beck's (1976) terms, they constantly monitor for danger signals, misinterpret neutral signals as danger signals, and ignore safety signals. This suggests that anxiety neurotics are deficient in the art of distraction—that is, they lack the strategies described in cell B that would remove them psychologically from danger signals. As the evidence shows, an emotional cost results from being in the psychological presence of danger signals. It may well be, then, that the lack of a distraction repertoire is one of the main factors accounting for the heightened physiological and subjective distress shown by these people.

Two recent studies by May (1977, in press) are relevant here. He found that snake-phobic subjects become physiologically and subjectively aroused just by thinking about the phobic object, as might be expected. Of particular interest, however, is the fact that the subjects seemed sensitized to their own thoughts, in that it became increasingly difficult for them to turn the snake imagery off. This suggests that the usual blunting strategies that nonphobic individuals employ to "tune out" (such as distraction) are unavailable to snake-phobic individuals. This helps to explain how a phobic can both recognize that the fear is irrational and yet still be afraid. As long as the individual lacks the skills to remove him or herself psychologically from the danger signal, he or she will suffer the emotional consequences, *even though the person may recognize that the danger signal is physically (objectively) absent.*

The preceding argument would be particularly applicable to people suffering from the subset of somatic syndromes that is psychogenic, such as hypertensives, ulcer-prone, and asthma-prone individuals. Consider the case of an asthma-prone anxiety neurotic. She (or he) has to go out on an important date and there are no danger cues for asthma around. However, she starts to think to herself, "What if I *do* have an attack?" That is, she starts brooding or ruminating about her breathing. Being in the psychological presence of the danger signal (cell C of Table 8.1) makes her anxious and so her breathing becomes labored. She is now in the presence of real danger cues, from which she is unable to distract herself. This leads to a full-fledged asthma attack.

With regard to the treatment of asthma neurotics, Yorkston, McHugh, Brady, Serber, and Sergeant (1974) have recently employed a variant of systematic desensitization that focuses on the anxiety-engendering thoughts and images of the client. Therapy involves the construction of a graded hierarchy of such images, beginning with the thoughts that typically initiate an asthma attack (e.g., "I feel tight across my chest."), and progressing on to the thoughts that further maintain and exacerbate the attack (e.g., "Am I going to die?"). Clients who have been desensitized in this fashion show treatment gains up to 2 years later, and such gains included reduced usage of all asthma-controlling drugs.

In the same way, then, that behavior therapists have developed replicable techniques for assertive training, relaxation training, and social skills training, it would seem important to develop techniques for training in distraction as well as other blunting strategies to reduce anxiety syndromes. Meichenbaum (1977) has recently reported on a package of "cognitive-behavior modification" techniques, aimed at modifying what clients say to themselves. The core theme of these techniques, which have been successfully applied to the treatment of phobias and related anxiety disorders, involves changing the client's self-statements by building up a set of coping skills such as the ones we have outlined.

Let us illustrate this approach with respect to the "cognitive desensitization" of test-anxious college students. As in the standard desensitization procedures, subjects are taught to relax and are presented with a graded set of fear-evoking imagery. In addition, however, while visualizing the fearful stimuli, subjects are instructed to imagine themselves coping with any anxiety they may feel, by means of relaxation and appropriate self-statements (e.g., "See yourself coping with this anxiety by use of the breathing procedures that we have practiced."). In this way, the subject learns to relabel his or her experience of anxiety as a positive factor, as a "cue to cope," rather than as a debilitating factor. Within our framework, there are essentially two crucial aspects to this therapy. The first aspect consists of training the client to attend to safety signals (cell D of Table 8.1), thereby forestalling the emergence of physical danger signals, such as rapid breathing and increased heart rate. However, should the client fall into cell C and the psychological presence of danger signals ("I may not be able to finish this exam."), thereby generating real danger signals in the form of heightened anxiety (cell A), the person is then taught to view this anxiety as a discriminative stimulus for placing him or herself in the psychological presence of safety signals (cell B). This, in turn, should serve to lower the level of anxiety, and thus the client should gradually be able to work back to cell D and safety. An expanded version of this approach, called "stress inoculation" training, involves building up a general set of such coping skills, which the client can then apply across diverse stress situations. Similarly, Goldfried, Decenteceo, and Weinberg (1974) train anxious clients to use a variety of blunting strategies, such as reinterpretation of the anxiety-inducing situation, as a means of accomplishing psychological withdrawal from danger signals.

In conclusion, we have proposed a hypothesis that integrates the literature on the human stress response to predictable versus unpredictable aversive events. The hypothesis states, and the evidence bears out, that humans generally prefer predictable to unpredictable aversive events, because predictable aversive events provide more safety signals. However, the hypothesis also states, and the evidence bears out, that there is one salient class of exceptions: When individuals are allowed to distract themselves, they prefer unpredictable aversive events, because distraction and other blunting techniques provide the most effective means of reducing stress. In addition, the hypothesis states, and the evidence bears out, that anticipatory arousal should be greater with predictable than with unpredictable aversive events and that impact may not differ. Finally, we have speculated that anxiety neurotics may be deficient in the cognitive strategies that would remove them psychologically from the presence of danger signals, and that training these skills may be an important part of therapy.

ACKNOWLEDGMENTS

We thank E. Freed, H. Lief, W. Miller, J. Nelson, M. Seligman, and S. Silverstein for their comments and ideas.

REFERENCES

Averill, J. R. Personal control over aversive stimuli and its relationship to stress. *Psychological Bulletin*, 1973, *80*, 286–303.

Averill, J. R., & Rosenn, M. Vigilant and nonvigilant coping strategies and psychophysiological stress reactions during the anticipation of an electric shock. *Journal of Personality and Social Psychology*, 1972, *23*, 128–141.

Badia, P., McBane, B., Suter, S., & Lewis, P. Preference behavior in an immediate versus variably delayed shock situation with and without a warning signal. *Journal of Experimental Psychology*, 1966, *72*, 847–852.

Badia, P., Suter, S., & Lewis, P. Preference for warned shock: Information and/or preparation. *Psychological Reports*, 1967, *20*, 271–274.

Barber, T. X., & Cooper, B. J. Effects of pain on experimentally induced and spontaneous distraction. *Psychological Reports*, 1972, *31*, 647–651.

Beck, A. T. *Cognitive therapy and the emotional disorders*. New York: International Universities Press, 1976.

Berlyne, D. E. *Conflict, arousal and curiosity*. New York: McGraw-Hill, 1960.

Bloom, L. J., Houston, B. K., Holmes, D. S., & Burish, T. G. The effectiveness of attentional diversion and situation redefinition for reducing stress due to a nonambiguous threat. *Journal of Research in Personality*, 1977, *11*, 83–94.

Bowers, K. S. The effects of UCS temporal uncertainty on heart rate and pain. *Psychophysiology*, 1971, *8*, 382–389. (a)

Bowers, K. S. Heart rate and GSR concomitants of vigilance and arousal. *Canadian Journal of Psychology*, 1971, *25*, 175–184. (b)

Chaves, J. F., & Barber, T. X. Cognitive strategies, experimenter modeling, and expectation in the attenuation of pain. *Journal of Abnormal Psychology*, 1974, *83*, 356–363.

Coles, M. G. H., Herzberger, S. D., Sperber, B. M., & Goetz, T. E. Physiological and behavioral concomitants of mild stress: The effects of accuracy of temporal information. *Journal of Research in Personality*, 1975, *9*, 168–176.

Cook, J. O., & Barnes, L. W., Jr. Choice of delay of inevitable shock. *Journal of Abnormal and Social Psychology*, 1964, *68*, 669–672.

D'Amato, M. R., & Gumenik, W. E. Some effects of immediate versus randomly delayed shock on an instrumental response and cognitive processes. *Journal of Abnormal and Social Psychology*, 1960, *60*, 64–67.

Elliott, R. Tonic heart rate: Experiments of the effects of collative variables lead to a hypothesis about its motivational significance. *Journal of Personality and Social Psychology*, 1969, *12*, 211–228.

Epstein, S. The nature of anxiety, with emphasis upon its relationship with expectancy. In S. D. Spielberger (Ed.), *Anxiety: Current trends in theory and research* (Vol. 2). New York: Academic Press, 1972. Pp. 291–337.

Epstein, S. Expectancy and magnitude of reaction of a noxious UCS. *Psychophysiology*, 1973, *10*, 100–107.

Folkins, C. H. Temporal factors and the cognitive mediators of stress reaction. *Journal of Personality and Social Psychology*, 1970, *14*, 173–184.

Furedy, J. J. Test of the preparatory adaptive response interpretation of aversive classical autonomic conditioning. *Journal of Experimental Psychology*, 1970, *84*, 301–307.

Furedy, J. J. Auditory and autonomic tests of the preparatory-adaptive-response interpretation of classical aversive conditioning. *Journal of Experimental Psychology*, 1973, *99*, 280–283.

Furedy, J. J., & Chan, R. M. Failures of information to reduce rated aversiveness of unmodifiable shock. *Australian Journal of Psychology*, 1971, *23*, 85–94.

Furedy, J. J., & Doob, A. N. Autonomic responses and verbal reports in further tests of the preparatory-adaptive-response interpretation of reinforcement. *Journal of Experimental Psychology*, 1971, *89*, 258–264. (a)

Furedy, J. J., & Doob, A. N. Classical aversive conditioning of human digital volume–pulse change and tests of the preparatory-adaptive-response interpretation of reinforcement. *Journal of Experimental Psychology*, 1971, *89*, 403–407. (b)

Furedy, J. J., & Doob, A. N. Signalling unmodifiable shocks: Limits on human informational cognitive control. *Journal of Personality and Social Psychology*, 1972, *21*, 111–115.

Furedy, J. J., Fainstat, D., Kulin, P., Lasko, L., & Nichols, S. Preparatory-response versus information-seeking interpretations of preference for signalled loud noise: Further limits on human informational cognitive control. *Psychonomic Science*, 1972, *27*, 108–110.

Furedy, J. J., & Ginsberg, S. Effects of varying signalling and intensity of shock on an unconfounded and novel electrodermal autonomic index in a variable and long-interval classical trace conditioning paradigm. *Psychophysiology*, 1973, *10*, 328–334.

Furedy, J. J., & Klajner, F. Unconfounded autonomic indexes of the aversiveness of signalled and unsignalled shock. *Journal of Experimental Psychology*, 1972, *92*, 313–318. (a)

Furedy, J. J., & Klajner, F. *Preference, verbal ratings and autonomic data on the preparatory-response theory: Subjects believe in it, but it is false.* Paper presented at the 7th Annual Conference of the Australian Psychological Society, Canberra, 1972. (b)

Gaebelein, J., Taylor, S. P., & Borden, R. Effects of an external cue on psychophysiological reactions to an external event. *Psychophysiology*, 1974, *11*, 315–320.

Geer, J. H., & Maisel, E. Evaluating the effects of the prediction-control confound. *Journal of Personality and Social Psychology*, 1972, *23*, 314–319.

Glass, D. C., Singer, J. E., & Friedman, L. N. Psychic cost of adaptation to an environmental stressor. *Journal of Personality and Social Psychology*, 1969, *12*, 200–210.

Goldfried, M., Decenteceo, E., & Weinberg, L. Systematic rational restructuring as a self-control technique. *Behavior Therapy*, 1974, *5*, 247–254.

Grings, W. W. Cognitive factors in electrodermal conditioning. *Psychological Bulletin*, 1973, *79*, 200–210.

Jones, A., Bentler, P. M., & Petry, G. The reduction of uncertainty concerning future pain. *Journal of Abnormal Psychology*, 1966, *71*, 87–94.

Kanfer, F. H., & Goldfoot, D. A. Self-control and tolerance of noxious stimulation. *Psychological Reports*, 1966, *18*, 79–85.

Kanfer, F. H., & Seidner, M. L. Self-control: Factors enhancing tolerance of noxious stimulation. *Journal of Personality and Social Psychology*, 1973, *25*, 381–389.

Kilpatrick, D. G. Differential responsiveness of two electrodermal indices to psychological stress and performance of a complex cognitive task. *Psychophysiology*, 1972, *9*, 218–226.

Klemp, G. O., & Rodin, J. Effects of uncertainty, delay, and focus of attention on reactions to an aversive situation. *Journal of Experimental Social Psychology*, 1976, *12*, 416–421.

Lacey, J. L. Somatic response patterning and stress: Some revisions of activation theory. In M. H. Appley & R. Trumbell (Eds.), *Psychological stress: Issues in research*. New York: Appleton-Century-Crofts, 1967. Pp. 14–37.

Lovibond, S. H. The aversiveness of uncertainty: An analysis in terms of activation and information theory. *Australian Journal of Psychology*, 1968, *20*, 85–91.

Maltzman, I., & Wolff, C. Preference for immediate versus delayed noxious stimulation and the concomitant G.S.R. *Journal of Experimental Psychology, 1970, 83,* 76–79.

Mansueto, C. S., & Desiderato, O. External versus self-produced determinants of fear reaction after shock threat. *Journal of Experimental Research in Personality, 1971, 5,* 30–36.

May, J. R. Psychophysiology of self regulated phobic thoughts. *Behavior Therapy, 8,* 1977, 150–159.

May, J. R. A psychophysiological study of self and externally regulated phobic thoughts. *Behavior Therapy,* in press.

Meichenbaum, D. *Cognitive-behavior modification. An integrative approach.* New York: Plenum Press, 1977.

Miller, S. M. Controllability and human stress: Method, theory, and evidence. *Behavior Research and Therapy,* in press. (a)

Miller, S. M. Why having control reduces stress: If I can stop the roller coaster, I don't want to get off. In M. E. P. Seligman & J. Garber (Eds.), *Human helplessness: Theory and application.* New York: Academic Press, in press. (b)

Miller, S. M. *Coping with impending stress: Psychophysiological and cognitive correlates of choice.* Psychophysiology, in press. (c)

Miller, S. M. *Monitors versus blunters: A laboratory validation of two cognitive styles for information-seeking under stress.* Unpublished manuscript, University of Pennsylvania, 1979.

Miller, S. M., & Grant, R. P. *Predictability and human stress: Evidence, theory, and conceptual clarification.* Unpublished manuscript, 1978.

Miller, S., Mangan, C. E., Freed, E., & Burtnett, M. *Which patients benefit from information before a gynecological procedure?: When the doctor should tell all.* Unpublished manuscript, University of Pennsylvania, 1979.

Monat, A. Temporal uncertainty, anticipation time, and cognitive coping under threat. *Journal of Human Stress, 1976, 1,* 32–43.

Monat, A., Averill, J. R., & Lazarus, R. S. Anticipatory stress and coping reactions under various conditions of uncertainty. *Journal of Personality and Social Psychology, 1972, 24,* 237–253.

Peeke, S. C., & Grings, W. W. Magnitude of UCR as a function of variability in the CS–UCS relationship. *Journal of Experimental Psychology, 1968, 77,* 64–69.

Perkins, C. C., Jr. The stimulus conditions which follow learned responses. *Psychological Review,* 1955, 62, 341–348.

Perkins, C. C., Jr. An analysis of the concept of reinforcement. *Psychological Review,* 1968, 75, 155–172.

Price, K. P., & Geer, J. H. Predictable and unpredictable aversive events: Evidence for the safety-signal hypothesis. *Psychonomic Science, 1972, 26,* 215–216.

Rescorla, R. A. Pavlovian conditioning and its proper control procedures. *Psychological Review,* 1967, 74, 71–79.

Rothbart, M., & Mellinger, M. Attention and responsivity to remote dangers: A laboratory simulation for assessing reactions to threatening events. *Journal of Personality and Social Psychology, 1972, 24,* 132–142.

Seligman, M. E. P. Chronic fear produced by unpredictable shock. *Journal of Comparative and Physiological Psychology, 1968, 66,* 402–416.

Seligman, M. E. P. *Helplessness. On depression, development, and death.* San Francisco: Freeman & Co., 1975.

Seligman, M. E. P., Maier, S. F., & Solomon, R. L. Unpredictable and uncontrollable aversive events. In F. R. Brush (Ed.), *Aversive conditioning and learning.* New York: Academic Press, 1971. Pp. 347–400.

Sokolov, Ye. N. *Perception and the conditioned reflex.* New York: MacMillan, 1963.

Yorkston, N. J., McHugh, R. B., Brady, R., Serber, M., & Sergeant, H. G. S. Verbal desensitization in bronchial asthma. *Journal of Psychosomatic Research, 1974, 18,* 371–376.

9

Central Stimulant Drugs and the Nature of Reinforcement[1]

MELVIN LYON

In the practice of behavior therapy, the fundamental importance of the concept of reinforcement is commonly acknowledged. However, in recent years, classical interpretations of reinforcement have become more and more strained in attempts to cover phenomena such as shock-maintained fixed-interval responding (Kelleher & Morse, 1968b; Stretch, 1972), apparently paradoxical effects of punishment upon behavior (Fowler, 1971), and "auto shaping" (Williams & Williams, 1969). In addition to these experimental demonstrations, which have a direct relevance for behavior therapy, there are specific problems of interpretation with respect to the origin of neuroses. One example is the so-called "Napalkov phenomenon" referred to by Eysenck (1968, 1976) in relation to the gradual increase (incubation) of anxiety occurring long after a single traumatic event (see also Koranda & Freedman, 1976; Morley, 1977). A closer inspection of the events described in all of these cases indicates that the classical conceptions of reinforcement may have some difficulty in explaining the effects observed.

[1]This chapter is based on empirical work with central stimulant drugs, which was supported by the Danish Medical Research Council (Grants no. 512-2542 and 512-3507) and by the Danish Hospital Foundation for Medical Research: Region of Copenhagen, the Faroe Islands, and Greenland (Grant no. 73/74, 47).

TRENDS IN BEHAVIOR THERAPY

Copyright © 1979 by Academic Press, Inc.
All rights of reproduction in any form reserved.
ISBN 0-12-647450-8

The nature of reinforcement has been of great interest to me in connection with central stimulant drug effects. During the last several years, I have been engaged with Trevor Robbins in working out a general theory of central stimulant drug effects (Lyon & Robbins, 1975, in press). In the course of this work we have been struck by the difficulty of explaining certain central stimulant drug effects, in particular effects following amphetamine treatment, by means of the usual reinforcement concept. Recently it has occurred to us that the reason for this difficulty may be that our description of the reinforcement process itself is not yet complete and may be misleading. It appears that the behavioral process of reinforcement under drug action can be used to describe the reinforcement effect in a new way, which makes it easier to understand the problems mentioned here. If this new means of description, as derived from our theory, is correct, it would have wide implications for behavior therapy, the understanding of drug addiction, and psychology in general. However, the present exposition is still at the speculative stage and the following discussion indicates a new way of thinking about the reinforcement process rather than a finished theoretical product.

WHAT DO DRUGS HAVE TO DO
WITH REINFORCEMENT?

One of the interesting facts about many central stimulant drugs is that they seem to be addictive even though, in many cases, the strong physiological addiction produced by morphine and other drugs is lacking. This is true, for example, for the amphetamines, which seem to act, in a general way at least, as positively reinforcing agents. If taking a pill or performing an injection is followed by a strong amphetamine effect, the frequency of pill taking or injecting tends to increase. This is one of the operations normally used for the definition of positive reinforcement. However, the drugs themselves are not positively reinforcing under all conditions, since injections can also be used to establish taste aversions (Cappell & LeBlanc, 1973; Carey, 1973; Martin & Ellinwood, 1974), indicating that amphetamines can act as aversive stimuli under certain conditions. Furthermore, the effects produced by amphetamine in human addicts (Rylander, cited in Schiørring, 1977), and in laboratory studies (see Lyon & Robbins, 1975) seem to indicate a strong component of forced repetitive behavior, described by humans as not necessarily pleasurable. In spite of this, the immediate behavioral result often reported is an increase in positive reinforcing action (Hill, 1967, 1970, 1972; Stein, 1964), with the implication that stimulant drugs have some direct effect upon the reinforcing value of stimuli. A relationship between central stimulant reinforcement effects and the release of the transmitter substances nor-adrenaline and dopamine has been suggested (Kety, 1970; Stein & Wise, 1973). Many investigators have adduced clear evidence that nor-adrenaline may be less important in this connection than dopamine (Baxter, Gluckman, & Scerni, 1976; Yokel & Wise, 1976). However, dopamine precursors such as L-Dopa do not seem to act as positive reinforcing agents. Here, there is an intriguing closeness between the behavioral changes produced by drugs and their biochemical action, yet the exact nature of the relationship to positive reinforcement remains elusive.

Another important point concerning the behavioral effect of central stimulant drugs is that repeated administrations to a subject, whether human or rodent, tend to induce stereotyped behavior, the form of which is often specific to the individual. This is not simply a mechanical stimulation of whatever the organism happens to be doing at the moment the drug takes effect. The effect may be limited to certain types of behavior, but a specific individual pattern is developed, which is associated with the drug state and which is gradually strengthened with repeated treatments (see Lyon & Robbins, 1975). Also, since the drug state itself is highly discriminable, whatever happens to the behavior during this state becomes in some way associated with the state (Rosecrans, Chance, & Schechter, 1976; Silverman & Ho, 1976; Stretch & Gerber, 1973).

All of the preceding points seem to implicate central stimulant drugs directly in some sort of reinforcement process. However, there is as yet no clear explanation of how this happens. Even self-administration studies show that ineffective or dangerously persistent behavior can be induced by repeated self-injections of central stimulant drugs (Ellinwood & Kilbey, 1975; Johanson, Balster, & Bonese, 1976). Thus, the question arises: How do these drugs produce effects that so closely resemble those produced by reinforcement processes, at the same time containing elements of a stereotyped or forced nature, which distinguish this state from normal reinforcement? Since Goldberg (1973) could maintain equal operant responding with *post-session* cocaine, d-amphetamine, or food, a simple drug–response interaction alone is unlikely. If drugs, unlike food, can reinforce when given before *or* after responding, then a new reinforcement model is needed.

CLASSICAL DEFINITIONS OF REINFORCEMENT AND THEIR SHORTCOMINGS

In order to discuss the basic issues of a definition of reinforcement, it is necessary to return to some of the classical models used to describe the reinforcement process. Figure 9.1 briefly sketches two of these models. The upper arrow in Figure 9.1 shows the strengthening of the associative bond between the stimulus (S) and the response (R), which was originally proposed by Thorndike and later developed in detail by Hull (1943). It is

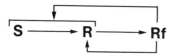

FIGURE 9.1. *Diagram of stimulus (S), response (R), and reinforcement (Rf) relationships according to Thorndike and Hull (upper arrow to the left) and Skinner (lower arrow to the left).*

important to note that a motivational state is implied as a necessary condition for the appearance of the strengthened bond. Also, repeated R-reinforcement (Rf) presentations ensure an increasing strength of the S–R bond by regular increments.

Models such as this, requiring a motivational state for the strengthening of the associative bond and for the performance of the R have been increasingly difficult to defend. Early arguments against such theories were derived from situations in which latent learning seemed to occur, despite the lack of a close connection between S and R in the presence of the appropriate motivational state. Although variations on the basic S–R model have proved capable of dealing with the early criticisms (e.g., Spence, 1956), more serious problems have been raised recently by studies of shock-maintained behavior (Kelleher & Morse, 1968b; Stretch, 1972). These studies have shown that monkeys can be conditioned to maintain performance on a fixed-interval schedule in which the only response-contingent event is that they obtain a strong electric shock with the last R in the interval. Their behavior may be maintained for months under these conditions, despite the implication from motivational models that the production of a punishing state should lead to a loss of performance. Furthermore, there are many paradoxical effects of punishment (Fowler, 1971), indicating that under a wide variety of conditions, an aversive S can be used to strengthen behavior that increases the frequency of the aversive event, and possibly even its intensity.

Fowler's (1971) review shows the generality of these findings and indicates that the apparent "paradoxical" effects of punishment must somehow be related to the extremely clear stimulus properties of the aversive S in these situations. To any researcher working with aversive events, in particular in situations where the shock itself may be the only distinct S, it is apparent that animals do not behave so as to minimize the production of the noxious event, even when they have the opportunity to eliminate it completely (e.g., Lyon & Randrup, 1972). Badia and his colleagues (Badia & Culbertson, 1972; Badia, Culbertson, & Harsh, 1973) have documented the positive nature of these signaling properties even when the choice of a schedule containing a signal event results in a greater frequency or intensity of punishment. Of course, it may be argued that uncertain (i.e., nonsignaled) events produce an internal state that is highly aversive (Seligman, 1968). Furthermore, the lack of typical autonomic responses to aversive events associated with a positive consequence was already documented by Pavlov's coworkers (Pavlov, 1960) and has since been confirmed many times.

There is a further problem with models implying a motivational state related to the original reinforcing event: Avoidance behavior may occur with increasing strength after some time has elapsed since the occurrence of a highly traumatic event. Eysenck (1968, 1976) cites the early work of Napalkov with animals and suggests a close correspondence with the delayed increase (incubation) of anxiety in human neurotics. Motivational explanations face some difficulty here, since it might be expected that the motivation originally engendered by the traumatic event would decrease with time. In any case, one would not expect this motivation to be strong enough, at a much later date, to support an increasing strength of an avoidance response related to the initial aversive event. Eysenck has proposed that this effect may be the result of classical conditioning of autonomic responses to stimuli (CS), immediately preceding or present during the initial aversive state (unconditioned stimulus, UCS). This original conditioning forms the basis for later conditioning of an operant nature, which is said to acquire its strength from the termination of anxiety associated with avoidance of stimuli present in the original situation. In this example, as in the others noted earlier, the theoretical notions arising from classical descriptions of reinforcement effects are strained to their limits and require postulation of complicated secondary (drive) reactions in order to avoid being refuted.

The lower arrow in Figure 9.1, connecting the Rf event with the preceding R, is meant to illustrate the operant model of reinforcement (Skinner, 1969), where reinforcement is defined as an effect related to any event that increases the future frequency of a preceding R. This is an ex post facto definition, since events are considered to have reinforcing properties only after they have been demonstrated to affect response frequency. This is a powerful descriptive model and it ensures that reinforcing properties are not erroneously assigned to events before such properties have been demonstrated. However, in therapeutic settings it is frequently difficult or even impossible to test possible reinforcing events if the *consequences* of these events, including the probability of harmful or negative outcomes, cannot be predicted with certainty. It is a weakness of this model that in therapeutic practice, where predictability is especially important, the descriptive model demands the production of the event before its effect can be tested. Premack (1965), in an attempt to revise this model, has suggested that the reinforcing properties of behavioral activities are related to their relative position in a hierarchy of behavioral probabilities at any given point in time. According to Premack, events having a high probability of occurrence will act as reinforcing events for activities having a lower probability of occurrence. However, this model requires some prior knowledge of: (*a*) response probability under specific deprivation conditions; (*b*) the relationship between response frequency and the future probability of the response; or (*c*) the relative strength of two different responses widely separated on a continuum, without regard to the possible changes in stimulus properties related to these events because of their wide separation. The Premack principle (Premack, 1965) operates well within the framework of general classes of activities that have similar stimulus properties. However, it is unlikely to be very accurate in therapeutic situations where experience with response probability is limited and where testing of these probabilities under specific deprivation conditions may be difficult to achieve.

In both of the general types of models described in Figure 9.1, the reinforcing effect is often closely related to an object (food pellet, token, etc.) or to a specific response (lever press, licking, etc.). The reinforcement process is rarely discussed in relation to a change in the state of the organism. Despite warnings that the reinforcing effect is not to be found directly in the reinforcing object, it is characteristic of these models to avoid a discussion of what determines the general pattern of behavior. The result is often that great emphasis is placed upon the specific objects and the individual responses related to reinforcement rather than on how the relationship between them may be altered. In contrast to this, in the following discussion, the term *reinforcing (Rf) effect* will be used, which will be shown to be related to changes in the general behavioral pattern of the organism, rather than to any specific object or response event.

A CONTIGUITY MODEL

A focus on the change in the state of the organism produced in association with the Rf effect, suggests a conception very similar to that originally proposed by Guthrie (1952, 1959). This model has some properties that I consider important for the final development of the present theoretical position. In Figure 9.2, an attempt has been made to diagram the Guthrie model. Here, a chain of responses is designated as R1–R4, and the final response of the sequence (R4) is followed by an abrupt change in the state of affairs, which is indicated to be an Rf condition. As proposed by Guth-

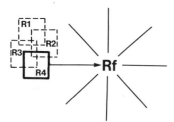

FIGURE 9.2. *Diagram of response (R1–R4) to reinforcement (Rf) relationships according to Guthrie.*

rie, the important feature of this conception is not the quality of the Rf event or the responses producing it. Rather, the focus is on the fact that the occurrence of the Rf event takes the organism out of the response sequence that it was performing. The Rf event induces a powerful stimulus change that "breaks off" the ongoing behavior and thus protects the final response in the sequence from being "unlearned." Guthrie's model is based on a change of state that will be referred to as a *stimulus change*. Thus, this conception does not depend upon identifying positive or negative motivational properties surrounding the Rf event. This is an essential feature of the present formulation also. The relative change in the stimulus state of the organism is presumed to be important rather than the positive or negative sign associated with this change. Furthermore, as is implied by this formulation, the earlier response elements in the chain leading to the response that is followed by the Rf event are more easily subject to interference by competition from other responses than the response that abruptly terminates upon production of the Rf event. The protective action of the Rf event in relation to the final response in the chain is also an important element in the present theoretical conception.

NEWER MODELS—THE FLIGHT FROM CONTIGUITY

The close similarity of Guthrie's principle of contiguity and the Skinnerian definition of a reinforcing event in terms of its immediate relationship to the preceding response, has long been recognized (Skinner, 1953, 1969). In recent years, a number of alternative conceptions have been proposed. Most of these have arisen from attempts to explain an increase in response frequency associated with events that have had only a remote connection in time with the subsequent so-called reinforcing event. An example of this type of model is Baum's (1973) "correlation-based law of effect," which is structured around the time allocation of responses occurring in, for example, two general categories such as the two ends of a shuttle box. Figure 9.3 illustrates this type of analysis, with the larger square on the right-hand side indicating the larger number of different response types generally correlated with the reinforcement obtainable at one end of the box. The fewer responses in the box at the left indicate the correlation with the reinforcement available at the other end of the box. In

FIGURE 9.3. *Diagram of Baum's "correlation-based law of effect" model. The two squares represent ends of a shuttle box with reinforcement correlated (r) .80 with the right end and .20 with the left end. Letters represent individual responses.*

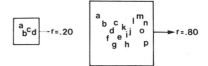

such a model, it is assumed that the form and timing of individual responses are not particularly important elements in the reinforcement relationship. Indeed, emphasis is placed upon the general categorizing of responses, either in geographical location or in time in relation to the events most often producing a reinforcing event. It is important to consider such models here, since it has already been indicated that contiguity will be considered an important element in the present model, whereas the contiguity of individual responses is not considered to be a prime factor in Baum's (1973) model.

The same reticence to accept a contiguity model is found in the theory of Staddon (1972), who has proposed a "relative proximity principle," according to which response events in relative proximity (although not in precise contiguity) to reinforcing events will increase in strength, and in Killeen's (1975) model in which the essential events controlling the behavioral change are the different temporal orders induced by the rate of responding itself. These points of view share an antithesis to a closer analysis of specific responses. In general, they all make or imply the criticism that the definition of responses is always arbitrary and may even be virtually impossible. However, this criticism is not acceptable, since the arbitrary nature of response definition is an ever-present condition in behavioral analysis. Even for the Staddon and Killeen models, arbitrary response definitions have been made in advance, and the substance of their arguments rests more upon the relationship between the grouping of these responses in time and the reinforcing events than upon the problem of arbitrary response defintion. Since the definition of a response is necessarily arbitrary, it must be equally clear that rejection of the contiguity principle must be based upon an analysis of the subsequent changes of individual response strength and not upon the experimenter's arbitrary redefinition of the response category.

Recent studies on "collateral" or "adjunctive" behavior (Henton & Iversen, 1978; Iversen, 1976; Staddon, 1977) indicate the inadequacy of defining responses solely as lever pressing, tube licking, etc. The point here is to indicate the prematurity of the theoretical leap from problems of response definition to suggestions that general correlations of events or relative proximity in time are the most appropriate defining parameters for reinforcing events. In fact, the substance of the present model and its supporting data suggest that giving up the contiguity principle, or assigning it a minor role, may be a serious mistake. As is true for the tendency to define reinforcing events in terms of concrete reinforcing objects (see the preceding discussion), the tendency to revert to less powerful models of description than those related to specific response events, may depend on the difficulties common to operant behaviorists of disengaging their thinking from the specific apparatus used. A complete detailing of these arguments and relevant counterarguments is beyond the scope of the present chapter. However, the theoretical view presented in the following section may indicate a fresh approach built upon the stronger elements of the classical descriptions of the conditioning process together with the salient points that research with central stimulant drugs appears to confirm.

DEVELOPMENT OF THE PRESENT THEORY

In order to illustrate the development of the present theory, its three main features will be presented briefly. The three main elements are stimulus change, repetition, and acceleration/deceleration. This is followed by a discussion of each element separately.

Stimulus Change

Stimulus change is the Guthrian element referring to the change in the state of affairs for the organism that follows closely after "the-response-to-be-reinforced." In Guthrie's (1959) interpretation, this change did not have the status of a reinforcing effect element, but only of a sharp change in the stimulus condition. Its function was to remove the final response of the chain preceding the stimulus change from any further association with responses of the kind given earlier in the situation. This is a basic element of the present model, and, because of its nature, it is presumed to work best when the stimulus change occurs immediately following the response that is to be reinforced or changed. In general, the further in time a response is removed from the stimulus change condition, the less will be the influence of the stimulus change. The stimulus change is conceived as an indicator of a change in the internal state of the organism, which can be measured indirectly by behavioral methods and which may be directly influenced, for example, by a central stimulant drug.

Repetition

Repetition is a common feature of reinforcing situations and conditioning procedures in general, and its importance has been recognized from the first formulations of associationistic psychology. It was given the status of a "law of frequency" by Thorndike, but as both Skinner (1953, 1969) and Guthrie (1952, 1959) have pointed out, under clear stimulus conditions, responding may achieve almost full strength in one trial. As long as the analysis of behavior is relegated to the examination of external muscular behavioral events, it appears that repetition is made superfluous by these demonstrations of one-trial learning. The point of view taken here is that, *even in these cases*, there is an important repetitive element in the nervous activity following the one-trial event, which, in fact, continues the repetition internally. The effect of such internal changes can easily and rather accurately be measured indirectly by behavioral methods. This is illustrated in the extensive literature on short-term memory during verbal learning and retention in humans (Dixon & Horton, 1968) and by techniques for measuring so-called "memory consolidation" following one-trial learning in animals as it is affected by electroconvulsive shock or posttrial injections of central stimulant drugs (McGaugh & Herz, 1972).

It is important to note that in the description of behavioral effects, the meaning of the term "repetition" may be difficult to distinguish from "perseveration." In the present context, *repetition* is taken to refer to the repeated initiation of a short behavioral chain. The reason for this emphasis is that the shorter the chain, the closer all of its elements are likely to be associated with the reinforcing event and the less interference is to be expected from other behaviors. *Perseveration* refers to the length of time during which the organism engages in a certain behavior. It is thus partially independent of a very rapid repetition rate within limited bursts of a given behavior occurring as separate elements in a larger pattern containing other behaviors. In this case, the perseverative effect is relatively weak even though, for some single chains, the repetition rate may be high. The strength of a given perseverative tendency can be tested by making reinforcement contingent upon a reduction in the perseverative response. Examples of how this might be done are found in the "stochastic reinforcement of waiting" (SRW) schedule of Weiss and Laties (1964, 1967) and in the combined differential reinforcement of low and high rates (DRL versus DRH) in the same session (Stitzer & McKearney, 1977). Furthermore, it is necessary to emphasize the analysis of the local interresponse time (IRT) *sequences,* as well as their average distribution, if the contribution of repetition and perseveration to a given behavioral pattern is to be properly assessed.

Increased repetition and perseveration are of special interest here since they are not only properties of normal responding, but are also characteristic of the effects of those central stimulant drugs that are often claimed to have a direct Rf effect (Lyon & Robbins, 1975, in press). It is therefore suggested that repetition be raised to the status of a major element, not only in the presence of, but also in the production of reinforcing effects. Consequently, agents that induce repetitive behavior, whether behavioral conditions or drugs, will also influence the frequency and thus the final strength of reinforcing effects.

Acceleration/Deceleration

Changes in response rate are also characteristic of learning situations and have been suggested to constitute a major basis for reinforcing effects (Killeen, 1975; Morse & Kelleher, 1970). In the present formulation, rate changes during their dynamic phase are considered to be important elements and are assigned the status of direct involvement in the reinforcing effect. The term "acceleration/deceleration" is used descriptively to indicate that it is the change itself, and not the final rate difference, that is assumed to be most important for the Rf effect.

The features described in the preceding sections—stimulus change, repetition, and acceleration/deceleration—have all been considered previously by various researchers, but mainly in the context of qualities produced *by* Rf, whereas here they *are* the Rf effect. It is proposed that these factors interact to yield the Rf effect. *Essentially, the behavior itself is said to be the reinforcing effect.* This may be regarded as an extension of the suggestion by Morse and Kelleher (1970) that schedules of reinforcement produce behavior that may be self-propagating. The present model goes further in that it involves elements of stimulus change and repetition, whereas the Morse and Kelleher conception is based mainly on rate changes induced by schedules. Likewise, the present model has certain similarities to suggestions by Glickman and Schiff (1967). It differs, however, from their theory in that it does not specifically suggest any natural units of behavior (in an ethological or evolutionary sense) as necessary basic elements in learning processes. The latter point will be further developed in a coming publication (Lyon & Robbins, in press), but the other main features of the present theory will be presented in more detail in the three sections that follow.

THE STIMULUS CHANGE ELEMENT OF THE Rf EFFECT

As was noted previously, the notion of stimulus change has been used in other models, but the specific use in the present formulation requires a clarification of some points. Figure 9.4 illustrates the basic nature of the stimulus change effect. In this figure, an arbitrarily chosen series of re-

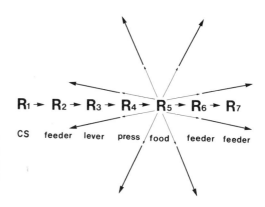

FIGURE 9.4. *Diagram of selected response sequence (R1–R7) to certain stimulus elements (below each R). CS = conditioning stimulus. Short and long arrows represent weak and strong Rf effects, respectively.*

$R_1 \rightarrow R_2 \rightarrow R_3 \rightarrow R_4 \rightarrow R_5 \rightarrow R_6 \rightarrow R_7$

CS   feeder   lever   press / food   feeder   feeder

sponses (R1–R7) is used to illustrate the stimulus change effect upon a behavioral sequence. The spreading arrows around the Rf effect region indicate that the Rf effect influences other regions of the behavioral complex, presumed to be occurring in parallel to the sequence arbitrarily chosen for description. Thus, the Rf effect as related to stimulus change will spread to nearby response chains (which are not diagramed) and will affect them in their order of proximity to the chosen chain. The responses of the chain in Figure 9.4 are associated with stimulus elements, shown underneath the various responses. For instance, R1 refers to the conditioning stimulus and the response to that stimulus; R2 refers to a response to the feeder apparatus; R3 is the response to the lever, but one by which the lever is not depressed; R4 has a special importance in that it involves depression of the lever, and it is the response leading to the strongest stimulus change, since R5 is a response to food, produced by the lever press. Thus, R5 abruptly changes the sequence of stimulus events in that a very strong stimulus change, the presence of food, accompanies this consummatory response.

In Figure 9.4, two types of arrows have been drawn radiating from R5. The small, thin arrows indicate a weak stimulus change, and the presumed Rf effect is restricted to the responses localized in proximity of the R5 event. Thus, the major influence of a weak reinforcer will be upon the response yielding depression of the lever *or upon the response to the feeder*, since this follows immediately. It should be noted that there is a forward-directed Rf effect influencing the strength of responses that follow immediately after the presentation of food. This feature is consistent with the nondirectional implications of a stimulus change model, and it is based on the supposition that each response elicits some sort of neural "trace" that will be available for association with subsequent events. Thus, this model will predict both an increase in lever pressing, which is followed by the presentation of food, and an equal or even larger increase of the response to the feeder, which follows closely after the stimulus change.

The large, bold arrows drawn radiating from R5 in Figure 9.4 represent the effect of a strongly reinforcing event. In this case, the effect spreads in the same manner as for a weak reinforcer. In addition, it causes an increase of responses performed in the vicinity of the lever, but which did not yield depression (R3). Also, responses to the conditioning stimulus (R1) are possibly increased. In the forward direction, subsequent responses to the feeder (R7) are also affected. The strong Rf effect also spreads to a larger "lateral" area (not shown), which includes possible associations with a great number of response chains, related topographically to the one arbitrarily chosen for the Rf event. Most of the changes diagramed are commonly referred to as occurring by "induction" in standard reinforcement models. An important point of the present exposition is that the neural "traces" from events occurring *before* the Rf change are assumed to be present and to be affected simultaneously with the immediate changes produced by responses occurring immediately *after* the Rf event.

It should be noticed that the wording *Rf event* refers to the exact moment of the initiation of the *Rf effect*, which spreads over a considerable period of time. Under all conditions, however, the response of lever pressing (R4) and the response to the feeder (R6) will have the greatest chances of survival in subsequent training. The R4 response will be especially strengthened because of the contiguity effect, which will protect it from being interfered with to the same extent as earlier elements in the response chain. The R6 response to the feeder is strengthened by a somewhat different mechanism: Like R4, it occurs in close association with the strong stimulus change produced by the food, but since it is not necessarily followed by yet another stimulus change (not even another food pellet will have the initial effect), subsequent responses will interfere with R6 more than with R4. In standard reinforcement analyses, it is striking how often repeated responses to the food tray or to the water tube have been ignored. Such responses show an increasing conditioned strength derived from the stimulus change that took place immediately *before* they occurred. The latter feature, referring to the local strengthening effect of response repetition during the Rf effect, leads to another important feature of the present model.

There are at least two ways in which the Rf effect can be weak. It may occur, as noted earlier, because the stimulus change is weak in itself, but it can also occur if the next stimulus change is initiated before the full effect of the previous one can be realized. This can happen because the full Rf effect, in comparison with a stimulus event or single response may require a longer duration for its full effect. Thus, this assumption allows the possibility that too rapidly occurring Rf effects may have a particular interference effect of their own. If these events occur rapidly enough, they may lead to an extreme localization of the Rf effect within the response area related directly to the initiating Rf event. This is an important consideration for models that purport to explain central stimulant drug effects, in that the neural changes associated with increasingly rapid repetition of responses under the drug may be associated with an increasing frequency of Rf events and with an increasing localization of these effects. If the model is correct, this would be true especially for high doses of central stimulant drugs, that is, if the localized stereotyped repetitive responding engendered by the drug can be "blended" with the conditioned response requirements.

On the other hand, considering the strong Rf effect indicated by the large arrows of Figure 9.4, there are also at least two ways in which this effect can be produced. The first is when the stimulus effect itself is strong. The second is produced by making the system more sensitive to stimulus changes of certain types, either by deprivation or by the use of drugs or other means of directly affecting the central nervous system. Central stimulant drugs are particularly effective in this respect (Key & Bradley, 1960), but only in low dose ranges or in drug-tolerant animals. At high dose levels, the extreme stimulation produced by all stimuli, including the conditioning stimuli, may prevent these drugs from having independent stimulus change value, as required by the present model.

Figure 9.4 thus summarizes stimulus change effects, which derive their main strength primarily from contiguity, especially to the immediately preceding response. However, they also have consequences extending beyond the immediate Rf event itself. In a sense, the model suggests that "backward conditioning" is a standard feature of all conditioning situations. This phenomenon has often been ignored because it does not strengthen responses appropriate to the conditions immediately preceding the Rf event. The latter point deserves a fuller exposition than can be given here, but it is an important part of the forward-acting Rf effect in the present model. Another important point is that deprivation conditions and other changes frequently described as motivational are seen as methods of increasing the stimulus change level produced by a given Rf event, rather than having any immediate positive or negative reinforcement implication. This is consistent with the fact that theories attempting to encompass central stimulant drug effects upon behavior have great difficulties in using motivational explanations for behavioral changes (Kelleher & Morse, 1968a).

THE REPETITION ELEMENT OF THE Rf EFFECT

As already noted, a very rapid repetition of the Rf effect will reduce the possibility of interference by response elements not in close proximity to the Rf event. It was noted that behavioral repetition is a cardinal feature of central stimulant drug action. Repetition, and in particular perseverative bursts of repetitive behavior, can limit behavioral possibilities so that certain responses become highly favored in the conditioning process. How this occurs is described in more detail by Lyon and Robbins (1975). We diagramed some of the changes induced by increasing doses of d-amphetamine, as reproduced in Figure 9.5. Here, the abscissa represents increasing doses of d-amphetamine from 0 to 10 mg/kg. The latter dose reliably produces a completely stereotyped behavioral pattern in rats. On the ordinate of Figure 9.5, an illustration is provided of rat behavior under normal conditions. Normal behavior is characterized by a division into many categories, such as feeding, grooming, locomotion, and social and investigatory responses.

The time sample chosen here serves to indicate an average distribution of behavior patterns over an extended period of time, since daily rhythms

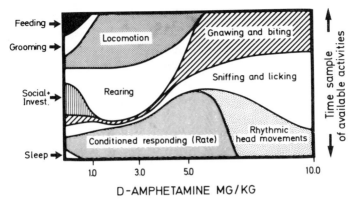

FIGURE 9.5. *The relative distribution and availability of various rat behavior patterns within a given time sample as related to the dose of d-amphetamine. (From Lyon & Robbins, 1975. Copyright 1975 by Spectrum Publications, Inc. Reprinted by permission.)*

would, at any given point in time, lead to certain of these factors having a greater weight than others. However, a customary finding is that these several types of behavior patterns are exhibited in repeated samples of rat behavior. It should be noted that a certain amount of time is devoted to "conditioned responding," which, in this case, may be a task occurring within the animal's living environment. While this diagram has some obvious inaccuracies, which experienced observers of rat behavior may notice, the essential features concerning the changes produced by spaced single injections of increasing drug doses are correct (see Norton, 1969, 1973; Schiørring, 1971). For the present purposes, the major points are (*a*) an increase of the amphetamine dose from 1 to 3 mg/kg yields a substantial increase of the amount of locomotion and rearing, and (*b*) at the same time, feeding, grooming, social and investigatory behaviors, and sleep disappear completely.

Thus, certain response categories appear in great quantities and begin to crowd out other responses in the animal's response "economy." How this occurs is the major concern of the Lyon and Robbins' (1975) theory, which allows for substantial increases in conditioned responding under the condition that this responding is characterized by a short behavioral chain, not requiring very much time before the next initiation (e.g., lever pressing or licking). Another important effect shown in Figure 9.5 is the change induced between 5 and 10 mg/kg, where the behavior becomes excessively stereotyped in rats. Figure 9.5 shows that only responses that occur extremely rapidly and that are capable of almost immediate and constant repetition remain in the behavioral repertoire. This is a change consistently produced by the continuing and increasing hyperstimulation of the rate with which behaviors are generated during the drug effect. The result is that conditioned responding may also disappear, unless it can be "mixed" favorably with an extremely short behavioral chain such as licking a drinking tube (Teitelbaum & Derks, 1958). The main purpose of Figure 9.5 is to illustrate that increasingly limited response categories become available to the organism due to the persistent repetition at very high rates within a few specific response categories.

The manner in which the central stimulant drug may produce this response change is indicated more specifically in Figure 9.6, also taken from Lyon and Robbins (1975). Figure 9.6 illustrates changes in normal responding caused by the increasing stimulation effect. Lines A–G denote increasing dose effects of the drug and the related changes of a response sequence. Line A illustrates normal responses separated by an interresponse time (IRT), which, in Line B is decreased without much change of response time. In Lines C and D, the IRT decreases further or disappears entirely and the behavior occurs so rapidly that its normal form is changed. In Line E, there are no IRTs during response periods, although pauses in responding may occur. The behavior is now quite abnormal in the sense that responses occur so rapidly that they may be incomplete and may not be capable of producing significant changes in the animal's environment. When responses no longer produce Rf events outside the organism, they can only have an effect upon the behavior itself, as is suggested by the present model.

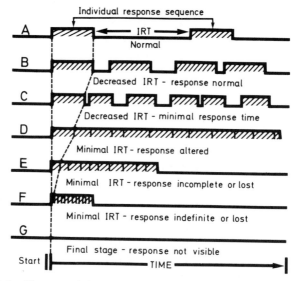

FIGURE 9.6.   *The proposed theoretical effect on single response components produced by a continuously increasing psychomotor stimulation caused by increasing doses (A–G) of d-amphetamine. Time is on the abscissa. (From Lyon & Robbins, 1975. Copyright 1975 by Spectrum Publications, Inc. Reprinted by permission.)*

In interpreting Figure 9.6, it is suggested that the increasing speed of responding may, at first, lead to an increase of Rf events, and that the effect of these Rf events will become more and more localized due to their rapidity of occurrence. Gradually, the relative value of an Rf effect produced by a given stimulus change will be reduced if no intervening pauses occur, preventing comparison of the stimulus change with the preceding "baseline" condition. However, the stimulus change potential of the Rf event may be increased by low doses of central stimulant drugs, so that this feature of the Rf effect initially may benefit from the drug action. This benefit will not be long lasting, since an increase in the drug effect will make pauses too brief and the repetition rate too rapid for the stimulus change event to exercise any significant effect, even upon the localized responses. For these reasons it is postulated that response repetition is a significant feature of the Rf effect. Thus, externally caused stimulus change events are not the only ones acting to modify the Rf effect, and response repetition *itself* is suggested to be an important aspect of central stimulant drug action upon the Rf effect.

The repetition element is probably not as strong as the stimulus change element described earlier, since considerable evidence shows that mere repetition of stimulus events in close conjunction with each other is not a sufficient condition for strong increases in conditioning effects (Ray & Sidman, 1970). However, although constant pairing of stimuli, irrespective of the animal's behavioral necessities, does not automatically lead to a strengthening of the conditioned association between paired stimulus elements, there is a special feature of central stimulant drug action in that the entire economy of the animal's behavior becomes limited to very few response categories. This increases both the repetition possibilities and the perseveration of repetitive chains of behavior far above the typical conditioning situation. With central stimulant drugs, there is also a strong element of drug-induced behavior that is "naturally" blended with the animal's ongoing response patterns. Thus, this situation cannot be directly compared with the rather artificial presentation of two stimuli arbitrarily chosen and presented at arbitrary times to the organism. Rather, there is *a connection between responses generated by the organism itself* under the coexisting conditions of central stimulant drug action and the conditioning contingencies to which it is exposed.

Figure 9.7 illustrates this point in more detail. The figure is idealized but is based on actual data from experiments by Robbins (1976b). He studied rats using a fixed ratio of 10 responses (FR 10) for water reinforcement in a Skinner box equipped with separate lever (L) and liquid feeder (F) mechanisms positioned at the right- and left-hand sides of the front panel. In the no-drug condition, a fixed ratio, represented in Figure 9.7 as a 5-response requirement, leads to a regular rapid performance of 5 re-

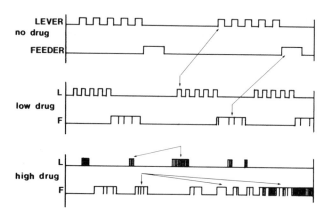

FIGURE 9.7. *Diagram showing lever- and liquid feeder-oriented behavior of a rat on a fixed ratio 5 schedule with liquid reinforcement. Responses to the lever or liquid feeder and their duration are indicated by upward deflections. The upper pair of lines represents a no drug control condition, the middle and lower pairs show behavior after low and high doses of the central stimulant drug methylphenidate. The upper two arrows indicate reductions in response duration and interresponse times for lever and feeder, respectively. The middle two arrows indicate too few (< FR5) versus too many lever responses. The bottom arrows indicate perseverative feeder responses in the absence of water reinforcement.*

sponses, followed by a drinking period, during which the animal presses open a plastic panel, allowing access to the liquid feeder. A low dose of the central stimulant drug methylphenidate produced more rapid responding to the lever and an increased number of approaches to the feeder. It should be noticed that the animal goes briefly away from the feeder and comes back again in the manner proposed in Figure 9.4. However, other changes also occur. The duration of the individual responses is probably decreased, and although the animal spends more time at the feeder, responding is broken up into several short periods, closely concentrated in time. The lower two lines of Figure 9.7 illustrate the effects of a high dose of the drug. Although responses to the lever are performed very rapidly with almost no measurable IRT, they are often either fewer than 5 (and thus do not give food reinforcement), or they are repeated well beyond this number. The same phenomenon occurs at the feeder, where discrete periods of nosing become briefer and briefer and frequently occur at inappropriate times. Toward the end of the lower line, the animal responds continuously to the feeder, which may last for periods up to 1 hour. It is as if responding to the feeder has become self-perpetuating without regard to the production of the originally reinforcing water (see also Robbins, 1976a).

In further experiments Robbins (1976b) has observed, although less often, that some animals respond continuously to the lever, ignoring the possibility of obtaining reinforcements at the feeder. There is considerable evidence that the discriminative abilities of animals are not severely disturbed by central stimulant drugs (Laties & Weiss, 1966; McMillan & Morse, 1967). It thus appears that the drugs induce repetitive behavior that seems to be self-perpetuating in many respects. It is suggested that part of the basis for the constant repetition is that it operates directly as a feature of the reinforcing effect itself. This is important since it will then affect subsequent behavior, but perhaps *only while under the drug*. A point that has clouded this issue in previous accounts is that central stimulant drugs produce a clearly discriminable "state," such that animals discriminate the drug state from the no-drug state (Stretch & Gerber, 1973). This leads to a sharp separation of effects between the two states and, normally, special training is required to obtain generalization between the two states. However, this also increases the possibility that whatever Rf effect may be produced by the excessive repetition will be evident mainly while the animal is on the drug. This sharp unconditioned stimulus control due to the "state" effect may have prevented investigators from associating the strong increases in particular forms of stereotyped behavior in animals under the drug as being partly due to reinforcing effects, since they are not seen in the no-drug state. It is therefore precisely this association to which we wish to draw attention here. The possible relevance of such repetitive changes for the understanding of similar phenomena during central stimulant drug states in humans, as well as for stereotyped behavior produced in psychotic states, is intriguing but remains to be explored.

THE ACCELERATION/DECELERATION ELEMENT
OF THE Rf EFFECT

It should be apparent from the preceding discussion that central stimulant drug treatment causes increases of repetitive behavior in a manner leading to excessive acceleration. This acceleration may cause local rates of responding that exceed those obtained with schedules normally inducing maximum response rates (Gage, 1970; Knowler & Ukena, 1973; Wuttke, 1970). The possible importance and stability of schedule-induced accelerations and decelerations of behavior has been pointed out by Morse and Kelleher (1970). They have emphasized that learned accelerations of rate, produced by a multiple schedule, may become fixed elements in the animal's pattern of responding. This may, in a sense, act to maintain behavior when the initial shaping events are removed. Likewise, Killeen (1975) has suggested that the temporal order of responses is of prime importance and that rate changes are the major discriminative component acting to maintain the animal's behavior. It is proposed here that both of these conceptions (Killeen, 1975; Morse & Kelleher, 1970) are relevant and that they represent an important third element of the Rf effect. A more detailed discussion of rate changes and their relationship to the well-known "rate dependency" hypothesis of amphetamine effects (Dews & Wenger, 1977) is found in Lyon and Robbins (1975, in press).

Figure 9.8 is designed to show how behavioral acceleration, however produced, relates to behavioral chains in a spatially defined situation (upper part of Figure 9.8) and in a temporal sequence (lower part of Figure 9.8). In the spatially defined setting, a response sequence (R1–R6) places the animal in a certain geographic position such that returning to a previous activity is to some extent limited by the spatial localization of the Rf event. Since the Rf event occurs while the animal is on the lever, and is followed by an approach to the feeder, the R6 response to the feeder is the part of the chain that requires the least time for immediate repetition. Following this, the spatially second closest element is R4, which is an approach to the feeder occurring before the lever press. The third closest element is the response to the lever (R5). Figure 9.8 is, of course, a theoretical diagram, but it illustrates an appropriate condition for the production of the behavioral changes under the high drug dose shown in the lower part of Figure 9.7. Here, the animal's most frequent response was to the feeder (R6), the second-most frequent response was a short detour from the feeder, followed by a return (R4), and the third-most frequent a return to the lever. Of course, we have omitted consideration of the "pauses" between responses at the feeder or the lever, which contain other behavior directed somewhere between these two parts of the apparatus. No analysis would be complete without a consideration of these elements (Henton & Iversen, 1978). However, since the animal's behavior after the high drug dose is, in the end, completely dominated either by the lever or by the feeder, these two elements seem to be the most important in the present analysis.

In the lower part of Figure 9.8, the temporal analysis of behavior suggests some further implications. If we arrange responses purely in terms of temporal sequence and if, in addition, the responses are increasingly removed in time from the Rf effect, which is maximal at R6, then it may be possible to predict the effect of rate increases upon the order of

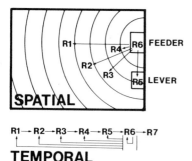

FIGURE 9.8.   *Diagram of spatial and temporal relationships within a series of responses (R1–R6). The spatial portion represents an experimental box with physical location of responses. The temporal part shows the temporal sequence of responses and the response-limiting effect of increasingly briefer time for repetition of the sequence (see arrows). When time is very short, stereotypy occurs (see R6).*

responses. An acceleration of rate would effectively prevent the animal's return to earlier elements of the chain, temporally distant from the R6 event, thus localizing the behavior more and more in the vicinity of the feeder. The final result may be that the R6 event alone completely monopolizes behavior, since the animal does not have sufficient time to return to other elements in the chain. Furthermore, even if it manages to reach some earlier point, the intermediate members of the sequence might be missing in a rapid attempt to continue responding. In both models diagramed in Figure 9.8, temporal and spatial contiguity is important, especially when acceleration of activity occurs. Acceleration is a very common property of response repetition and hence of learning situations in general. The contiguity factor is made less obvious in the Skinner box as indicated in the spatial part of Figure 9.8, since the box is designed to limit behavior to only a few categories. This increases the chance that the "correct" response appears among those produced.

It should be observed that the temporal pattern of Figure 9.8 provides the most convenient model for detecting accelerative effects. If the animal has very little time to respond, it will be more and more likely to respond locally, and finally, it will respond with R6 alone. *This is exactly what we would call stereotypy*, which is a major characteristic of central stimulant drug effects (Randrup & Munkvad, 1967) and of the amphetamine psychoses that so closely resemble paranoid schizophrenia (Kalant, 1966; Snyder & Banerjee, 1973).

It is even possible that an extremely rapid acceleration of behavior may not leave the animal enough time to repeat fully the response R6 itself. In that case, it might simply go on to other behavior, R7 and R8, which may contain partial elements of normal responding and which are never repeated. This would resemble the loss of control exhibited by hebephrenic schizophrenics, another major category of patients. However, this point remains speculative as it still lacks the necessary empirical support to make it a major element of the present model.

In any case, the accelerative factor, together with repetition, may contribute to the self-propagating character of the behavior. If the acceleration is rapid enough, it effectively prevents other responses and, almost by default, strengthens the remaining stereotyped responses. This may be the way in which stereotyped responses are learned in the characteristic individual pattern exhibited, within limits, by each animal.

IMPLICATIONS OF THE PRESENT MODEL FOR DRUG ADDICTION AND BEHAVIOR THERAPY

The present model postulates that there are three main interdependent elements in the Rf effect. There are several features of these elements that are directly related to behavior itself more than to specific objects or events that are produced by given responses. The three theoretical features are stimulus change, repetition, and acceleration/deceleration.

Most behavior therapists act according to the first of these principles, that of stimulus change contiguous to individual responses. This is an essential feature of both the development of behavioral disorders and their treatment. It should be remembered, however, that according to the present model, the stimulus change element cannot be considered independently of the repetition or the acceleration features. Thus, producing a stimulus change contiguous to an individual response may fail to increase its frequency if repetition and acceleration factors work against this particular change. This is a problem particularly with drug addicts, who frequently operate under a sharply discriminable drug state that contains strong elements of repetition and acceleration, which are not entirely under the person's control. The implications are that treatment in the no-drug condition may not be expected to generalize easily to the drug condition, and treatment in the drug condition may be made difficult by the forced repetition and acceleration effects produced by the drug.

The repetition element seems to be the least recognized feature of behavioral processes. If the model is correct, excessively repetitive responding and training, or therapy based on such responding, must be viewed with some caution until the general relationship to the Rf effect is understood. It has been suggested in this chapter that some behaviors, if extremely frequent and repeated at very high rates with accelerating effects, may become self-propagating in the sense that they are maintained after the initial shaping consequences are withdrawn. This has implications for the use of behavior therapy techniques such as negative practice, flooding, and some avoidance procedures. While these techniques may yield temporary benefit, and even very sharp stimulus control due to the nature of the highly repetitive behavior, according to the present theory, they increase the risk of strengthening the behaviors treated. The increased strength of these behaviors may not be evident as long as the person is not exposed to the schedule conditions that were originally present. However, a renewed presentation would be expected to produce the behavior at greater strength than before treatment. This could mean that if these techniques fail, relapses may be difficult to treat by alternative measures, especially if the person treated is unable to avoid the schedule conditions producing the original problem. While I consider these warnings relatively serious because of our present lack of knowledge about the features involved, it is important to note that the relationship between behaviors affected by central stimulant drugs and normal behavior is not yet firmly established. However, the potential implications are serious enough to suggest that investigations of this relationship should be given first priority rather than a further development of the previously noted therapy procedures.

With respect to such relatively intractable behavioral disturbances as those found in childhood autism and schizophrenia, it may be noted that a cardinal symptom is stereotyped, repetitive responding (Bleuler, 1950). In line with the present model, in these cases, treatment should aim at preventing the repetitive behaviors *at once*, a conclusion also reached by Lovaas and Newsom (1976), on the basis of other evidence. Also, an early appearance of this kind of symptom should be given much weight in diagnostic procedures. To judge from animal experiments with central stimulant drugs, it would seem possible to devise tests that are sensitive to this type of behavioral change at stages where the deviant behavior is not outwardly visible and has had no severe social consequences. In any case, the change of emphasis in diagnosis and treatment would be essential, since standard Rf techniques based on strong stimulus change (and, for that matter, electroshock as well) can briefly interrupt, but may have difficulty counteracting, these self-maintaining behaviors once strong stereotypy has developed. Furthermore, in concordance with a conception prevalent among behavior therapists about cases where strongly repetitive behavior is present, no time should be wasted in waiting for the symptoms to abate. Also, even if drug treatment is necessary following an acute breakdown and admission to a hospital, it should be centered on medications that would lessen the possibility of self-maintaining elements of the Rf effect, and of "supersensitivity" to these actions when the drug is withdrawn. While it is impossible to go into detail here, it may be noted that contemporary selections of antipsychotic drugs are not necessarily based on such criteria. In some cases, drugs are included that, in the long run and after drug withdrawal, are ineffective or even exacerbating with respect to these behavioral signs.

In general, with drug addiction, psychotic states, and normal behavior, it is suggested that the greatest changes of the strength of a given behavior will occur if all three of the critical features of the Rf effect are present. Furthermore, it is suggested that it may be possible to make up for a lack of one of the three elements by emphasizing one of the others. Despite the emphasis on the negative side of the self-maintaining aspect of repetitive behavior here, it should be remembered that the same element can be used to build desirable, socially adaptive behavior with a long-lasting importance for the person in treatment. If the present formulation is correct, research on the central stimulant drugs has forced us to a new interpretation of reinforcing effects with important implications far beyond the narrow limits of drug addiction and disturbed behavioral patterns.

REFERENCES

Badia, P., & Culbertson, S. The relative aversiveness of signaled vs. unsignaled escapable and inescapable shock. *Journal of the Experimental Analysis of Behavior*, 1972, *17*, 463–471.
Badia, P., Culbertson, S., & Harsh, J. Choice of longer or stronger signalled shock over

shorter or weaker unsignalled shock. *Journal of the Experimental Analysis of Behavior*, 1973, *19*, 25–32.

Baum, W. M. The correlation-based law of effect. *Journal of the Experimental Analysis of Behavior*, 1973, *20*, 137–153.

Baxter, B. L., Gluckman, M. I., & Scerni, R. A. Apomorphine self-injection is not affected by alphamethylparatyrosine treatment: Support for dopaminergic reward. *Pharmacology, Biochemistry, and Behavior*, 1976, *4*, 611–612.

Bleuler, E. *Dementia praecox*. New York: International Universities Press, 1950.

Cappell, H., & LeBlanc, A. E. Punishment of saccharin drinking by amphetamine in rats and its reversal by chlordiazepoxide. *Journal of Comparative and Physiological Psychology*, 1973, *85*, 97–104.

Carey, R. J. Long-term aversion to a saccharin solution induced by repeated amphetamine injections. *Pharmacology, Biochemistry, and Behavior*, 1973, *1*, 265–270.

Dews, P. B., & Wenger, G. R. Rate-dependency of the behavioral effects of amphetamine. In T. Thompson & P. B. Dews (Eds.), *Advances in behavioral pharmacology* (Vol. 1). New York: Academic Press, 1977. Pp. 167–227.

Dixon, T. R., & Horton, D. L. (Eds.). *Verbal behavior and general behavior theory*. Englewood Cliffs, N.J.: Prentice-Hall, 1968.

Ellinwood, E. H., & Kilbey, M. M. Species difference in response to amphetamine. In B. F. Eleftheriou (Ed.), *Psychopharmacogenetics*. New York: Plenum Press, 1975. Pp. 323–375.

Eysenck, H. J. A theory of the incubation of anxiety/fear responses. *Behaviour Research and Therapy*, 1968, *6*, 319–331.

Eysenck, H. J. The learning theory model of neurosis—a new approach. *Behaviour Research and Therapy*, 1976, *14*, 251–267.

Fowler, H. Suppression and facilitation by response contingent shock. In F. R. Brush (Ed.), *Aversive conditioning and learning*. New York: Academic Press, 1971. Pp. 537–604.

Gage, M. I. *Amphetamine and pentobarbital effects on interresponse time distributions of monkeys reinforced for low sequential variability of interresponse times*. Unpublished doctoral dissertation, University of Rochester, 1970.

Glickman, S. E., & Schiff, B. B. A biological theory of reinforcement. *Psychological Review*, 1967, *74*, 81–109.

Goldberg, S. R. Comparable behavior maintained under fixed-ratio and second-order schedules of food presentation, cocaine injection or *d*-amphetamine injection in the squirrel monkey. *Journal of Pharmacology and Experimental Therapeutics*, 1973, *186*, 18–30.

Guthrie, E. R. *The psychology of learning* (Rev. ed.). New York: Harper, 1952.

Guthrie, E. R. Association by contiguity. In S. Koch (Ed.), *Psychology: A study of a science* (Vol. 2). New York: McGraw-Hill, 1959. Pp. 158–195.

Henton, W. W., & Iversen, I. H. *Classical conditioning and operant conditioning: A response pattern analysis*. Berlin: Springer, 1978.

Hill, R. T. *A behavioral analysis of the psychomotor effect of a drug: The interaction of pipradrol with conditioned reinforcers*. Unpublished doctoral dissertation, Columbia University, 1967.

Hill, R. T. Facilitation of conditioned reinforcement as a mechanism of psychomotor stimulation. In E. Costa & S. Garattini (Eds.), *Amphetamines and related compounds*. New York: Raven Press, 1970. Pp. 781–795.

Hill, R. T. *Animal models of the euphorigenic action of amphetamine-like psychomotor stimulant drugs*. Invited address at the meeting of the American Psychological Association (Div. 28), Honolulu, 1972.

Hull, C. L. *Principles of behavior*. New York: Appleton-Century-Crofts, 1943.

Iversen, I. H. Interactions between reinforced responses and collateral responses. *The Psychological Record*, 1976, *26*, 399–413.

Johanson, C. E., Balster, R. L., & Bonese, K. Self-administration of psychomotor stimulant drugs: The effects of unlimited access. *Pharmacology, Biochemistry, and Behavior*, 1976, *4*, 45–51.

Kalant, O. J. *The amphetamines: Toxicity and addiction.* Toronto: University of Toronto Press, 1966.

Kelleher, R. T., & Morse, W. H. Determinants of the specificity of behavioral effects of drugs. In *Reviews of physiology, biochemistry, and experimental pharmacology* (Vol. 60). Berlin: Springer, 1968. Pp. 1–56. (a)

Kelleher, R. T., & Morse, W. H. Schedules using noxious stimuli. III. Responding maintained with response-produced electric shocks. *Journal of the Experimental Analysis of Behavior,* 1968, *11,* 819–838. (b)

Kety, S. S. The possible role of the adrenergic systems of the cortex in learning. *Research Publications of the Association for Nervous and Mental Disease,* 1970, *50,* 376–389.

Key, B. J., & Bradley, P. B. The effects of drugs on conditioning and habituation to arousal stimuli in animals. *Psychopharmacologia,* 1960, *1,* 450–462.

Killeen, P. On the temporal control of behavior. *Psychological Review,* 1975, *82,* 89–115.

Knowler, W. C., & Ukena, T. E. The effects of chlorpromazine, pentobarbital, chlordiazepoxide and d-amphetamine on rates of licking in the rat. *Journal of Pharmacology and Experimental Therapeutics,* 1973, *184,* 385–397.

Koranda, L. G., & Freedman, P. E. Effects of generalization of fear on incubation in a response suppression paradigm. *Bulletin of the Psychonomic Society,* 1976, *8,* 97–100.

Laties, V. G., & Weiss, B. Influence of drugs on behavior controlled by internal and external stimuli. *Journal of Pharmacology and Experimental Therapeutics,* 1966, *152,* 388–396.

Lovaas, O. I., & Newsom, C. D. Behavior modification with psychotic children. In H. Leitenberg (Ed.), *Handbook of behavior modification and behavior therapy.* Englewood Cliffs, N.J.: Prentice-Hall, 1976. Pp. 303–360.

Lyon, M., & Randrup, A. The dose-response effect of amphetamine upon avoidance behaviour in the rat seen as a function of increasing stereotypy. *Psychopharmacologia,* 1972, *23,* 334–347.

Lyon, M., & Robbins, T. The action of central nervous system stimulant drugs: A general theory concerning amphetamine effects. In W. Essman & L. Valzelli (Eds.), *Current developments in psychopharmacology* (Vol. 2). New York: Spectrum Publications, 1975. Pp. 80–163.

Lyon, M., & Robbins, T. *A behavioral theory of central stimulant drug action.* New York: Spectrum Publications, in press.

Martin, J. C., & Ellinwood, E. K., Jr. Conditioned aversion in spatial paradigms following metamphetamine injection. *Psychopharmacologia,* 1974, *36,* 323–335.

McGaugh, J. L., & Herz, M. J. *Memory consolidation.* San Francisco: Albion, 1972.

McMillan, D. E., & Morse, W. H. Schedules using noxious stimuli. II: Low intensity electric shock as a discriminative stimulus. *Journal of the Experimental Analysis of Behavior,* 1967, *10,* 109–118.

Morley, S. The incubation of avoidance behaviour: Strain differences in susceptibility. *Behaviour Research and Therapy,* 1977, *15,* 363–367.

Morse, W. H., & Kelleher, R. T. Schedules as fundamental determinants of behavior. In W. N. Schoenfeld (Ed.), *The theory of reinforcement schedules.* New York: Appleton-Century-Crofts, 1970. Pp. 139–185.

Norton, S. The effects of psychoactive drugs on cat behavior. *Annals of the New York Academy of Sciences,* 1969, *159,* 915–927.

Norton, S. Amphetamine as a model for hyperactivity in the rat. *Physiology and Behavior,* 1973, *11,* 181–186.

Pavlov, I. P. *Conditioned reflexes.* New York: Dover, 1960.

Premack, D. Reinforcement theory. In D. Levine (Ed.), *Nebraska Symposium on Motivation* (Vol. 13). Lincoln: University of Nebraska Press, 1965. Pp. 123–180.

Randrup, A., & Munkvad, I. Stereotyped activities produced by amphetamine in several animal species and man. *Psychopharmacologia,* 1967, *11,* 300–310.

Ray, B. A., & Sidman, M. Reinforcement schedules and stimulus control. In W. N. Schoenfeld (Ed.), *The theory of reinforcement schedules.* New York: Appleton-Century-Crofts, 1970. Pp. 187–214.

Robbins, T. Relationship between reward-enhancing and stereotypical effects of psychomotor stimulant drugs. *Nature (London),* 1976, *264,* 57–59. (a)

Robbins, T. Personal communication, 1976. (b)

Rosecrans, J. A., Chance, W. T., & Schechter, M. D. The discriminative stimulus properties of nicotine, d-amphetamine and morphine in dopamine depleted rats. *Psychopharmacology Communications,* 1976, *2,* 349–356.

Schiørring, E. Amphetamine induced selective stimulation of certain behaviour items with concurrent inhibition of others in an open-field test with rats. *Behaviour,* 1971, *39,* 1–17.

Schiørring, E. Changes in individual and social behavior induced by amphetamine and related compounds in monkeys and man. In E. H. Ellinwood & M. M. Kilbey (Eds.), *Cocaine and other stimulants.* New York: Plenum Press, 1977. Pp. 481–522.

Seligman, M. E. P. Chronic fear produced by unpredictable electric shock. *Journal of Comparative and Physiological Psychology,* 1968, *66,* 402–411.

Silverman, P. B., & Ho, B. T. Discriminative response control by psychomotor stimulants. *Psychopharmacology Communications,* 1976, *2,* 331–337.

Skinner, B. F. *Science and human behavior.* New York: The Free Press, 1953.

Skinner, B. F. *Contingencies of reinforcement: A theoretical analysis.* New York: Appleton-Century-Crofts, 1969.

Snyder, S. H., & Banerjee, S. P. Amines in schizophrenia. In E. Usdin & S. H. Snyder (Eds.), *Frontiers in catecholamine research.* New York: Pergamon, 1973. Pp. 1133–1138.

Spence, K. W. *Behavior theory and conditioning.* New Haven: Yale University Press, 1956.

Staddon, J. E. R. Temporal control and the theory of reinforcement schedules. In R. M. Gilbert & J. R. Millenson (Eds.), *Reinforcement: Behavioral analyses.* New York: Academic Press, 1972. Pp. 212–257.

Staddon, J. E. R. Schedule-induced behavior. In W. K. Honig & J. E. R. Staddon (Eds.), *Handbook of operant behavior.* Englewood Cliffs, N. J.: Prentice-Hall, 1977. Pp. 125–152.

Stein, L. Amphetamine and neural reward mechanisms. In H. Steinberg (Ed.), *Animal behavior and drug action.* Boston: Little, Brown, 1964. Pp. 91–113.

Stein, L., & Wise, C. D. Amphetamine and noradrenergic reward pathways. In E. Usdin & S. H. Snyder (Eds.), *Frontiers in catecholamine research.* New York: Plenum Press, 1973. Pp. 963–968.

Stitzer, M., & McKearney, J. W. Drug effects on fixed-interval responding with pause requirements for food presentation. *Journal of the Experimental Analysis of Behavior,* 1977, *25,* 51–59.

Stretch, R. Development and maintenance of responding under schedules of electric-shock presentation. In R. M. Gilbert & J. R. Millenson (Eds.), *Reinforcement: Behavioral analyses.* New York: Academic Press, 1972. Pp. 67–95.

Stretch, R., & Gerber, G. J. Drug-induced reinstatement of amphetamine self-administration in monkeys. *Canadian Journal of Psychology,* 1973, *27,* 168–177.

Teitelbaum, P., & Derks, P. The effect of amphetamine on forced drinking in the rat. *Journal of Comparative and Physiological Psychology,* 1958, *51,* 801–810.

Weiss, B., & Laties, V. G. Drug effect on the temporal patterning of behavior. *Federation Proceedings,* 1964, *23,* 801–807.

Weiss, B., & Laties, V. G. Comparative pharmacology of drugs affecting behavior. *Federation Proceedings,* 1967, *26,* 1146–1156.

Williams, D. R., & Williams, H. Auto-maintenance in the pigeon: Sustained pecking despite contingent non-reinforcement. *Journal of the Experimental Analysis of Behavior,* 1969, *12,* 511–520.

Wuttke, W. The effects of d-amphetamine on schedule-controlled water licking in the squirrel monkey. *Psychopharmacologia,* 1970, *17,* 70–82.

Yokel, R. A., & Wise, R. A. Attenuation of intravenous amphetamine reinforcement by central dopamine blockade in rats. *Psychopharmacology,* 1976, *48,* 311–318.

III

APPLICATIONS: SELECTED PROBLEM AREAS

___ 10 _____

Behavioral Analysis of Alcohol Abuse[1]

STEN RÖNNBERG

There are now more than 500 scientific publications dealing with behavior therapy for alcohol abuse. Some recent reviews have covered most
of these publications (Briddell & Nathan, 1976; Hamburg, 1975; Miller &
Barlow, 1973; Nathan, 1976; Nathan & Briddell, 1977). Also, behavioral
analysis and treatment of alcoholism has recently been comprehensively
presented in a book by Miller (1976). Since this field has been competently
reviewed by several authors, I intend this chapter to serve a somewhat
different purpose. By examining the ways in which behavioral analysis can
be applied to alcohol abuse, I hope to provide directions for research and
suggest practical implications.

MODELS OF CLINICAL BEHAVIOR THERAPY

All behavior therapy can be said to depend on some model of application. Unfortunately, the models are seldom made explicit in the writings of
behavior therapists. When there are presentations of the structural models
from which clinical treatments have been derived, these are generally re-

[1]The research for this chapter was supported in part by Grant B79-25X-05458-01 from the
Swedish Medical Research Council.

TRENDS IN BEHAVIOR THERAPY
Copyright © 1979 by Academic Press, Inc.
All rights of reproduction in any form reserved.
ISBN 0-12-647450-8

stricted to an outline of the most important technical points or to treatment aspects. It is very rare to find a detailed description of the theoretical background and guiding principles of the whole course of a behavior therapy. Descriptions of the models used for the initial behavioral analysis and assessment are notable by their absence in behavior therapy studies. Often, there is merely a description of the problem, some background information is given, and the functional contingencies of the problem are detailed. This is usually followed by a description of the intervention and the empirical evaluation of the treatment procedures. Usually, there is no explanation of the important steps taken before the therapists arrive at a point of agreement with their clients about treatment objectives.

At least six main models for clinical behavioral analysis and assessment are widely recognized and currently used by behavior therapists: (a) the operant model (e.g., Stuart, 1970); (b) Kanfer and Saslow's (1969) model; (c) Wolpe's (1973) model; (d) the multimodal model (Lazarus, 1976); (e) Goldfried and colleagues' model (e.g., Goldfried & Davison, 1976); and (f) the procedure for the assessment and modification of behavior in open settings (PAMBOS) (see Carter, 1973; Gambrill, 1977). There are quite a few additional publications presenting variations of these clinical models of behavior analysis and assessment. (Most of these have been reviewed by Rönnberg, 1978.)

The models of behavioral analysis can be seen as bridges between, on the one hand, basic theoretical work in behavior therapy (reviewed by Bandura, 1977; Honig & Staddon, 1977; Maser & Seligman, 1977; Yates, 1970) and, on the other hand, practical behavior therapy work. I believe that these connecting points, or juxtapositions, need to be explained in detail in most behavior therapy studies (see Feldman & Broadhurst, 1976). Several authors have recently voiced similar opinions concerning the need for more comprehensive and detailed behavioral analyses and assessments (e.g., Cautela, 1977; Ciminero, Calhoun, & Adams, 1977; Cone & Hawkins, 1977; Hersen & Bellack, 1976; Mash & Terdal, 1976).

MAIN IDEAS IN CLINICAL BEHAVIOR ANALYSIS

Most authors who deal with clinical behavioral analysis would seem to agree with the following statements concerning this subject:

1. Current psychiatric diagnoses have little value in behavior therapy.
2. Assessment should include both responses and their most important controlling factors.
3. Individualized treatment programs have to be prepared for each client, since topographically "identical" problems may have different causes in different individuals.

4. Establishing problem priorities is a complex process influenced by the therapist's skills, research about the problems, the client's resources, ethical considerations, and the client's preferences.
5. The behavioral alternatives that are available and the resources that can be mobilized by the client should be assessed and utilized in the treatment program.
6. Measurement and evaluation are essential to all behavior therapy.
7. Decisions made during the behavioral analysis process may heavily influence the outcome of therapy.

It is my impression that few of the conclusions drawn in the literature on clinical behavior analysis and assessment have been respected in most behavior therapy research on alcoholism.

A MODEL FOR BEHAVIORAL ANALYSIS OF ALCOHOL ABUSE

Rönnberg (1978) has presented an outline of a comprehensive model of clinical behavior analysis and assessment. The model consists of nine detailed steps for behavioral therapeutic work: (1) assessment of major complaints; (2) contingency analysis of major complaints; (3) assessment of alternatives; (4) contingency analysis of alternatives; (5) historical analysis; (6) analysis of change; (7) treatment plan and contract; (8) intervention; and (9) followup. The remainder of this chapter will be devoted to a discussion of alcohol abuse, using these nine steps as a guide. The purpose of this discussion is to point out some of the issues that are of particular concern in clinical practice and research on alcohol abuse. Step by step, the discussion presents a way of viewing the problems of analysis and treatment of alcohol abuse.

Assessment of Major Complaints

The first stage of the behavior therapy process includes listing the problems as experienced by the client, and as seen by the therapist, as well as a summary of the general impression the therapist has of the priorities of the problems, more precise problem descriptions, and baseline measurement.

The client's listing of the problems is often influenced by prevalent conceptions of what constitutes an alcoholic. Many of these conceptions are based on folklore and are manifested in statements such as: "Once an alcoholic, always an alcoholic"; "Take one drink, and you are on a drinking bout"; "An alcoholic has a strongly felt craving for alcohol"; "A typical alcoholic is a male who has lost his job and family and is living poorly on skid row"; and "Alcoholism is like an allergy." It is quite probable that the client will use such terms in describing the problems. Even if such labeling is not wholly satisfactory, thorough problem descriptions as recounted by the client are indispensable to establish and enhance the intimate, emotional contact that is necessary in most behavior therapy (compare Redl, 1959). This first stage can be regarded as mainly nondirective.

The therapist's own values are more noticeable in the second stage when problems are described as the therapist sees them. The therapist looks for behavior problems in motor, physiological, and cognitive dimensions, trying to complete the picture presented by the client. The descriptions given by the client are often clarified and reformulated by the therapist.

The third stage involves coming to an agreement about what the behavior problems are and how they can be described in general terms, for example, in traditional psychiatric nomenclature. At this stage, the problems of an alcohol abuser may be described for example, as muscle tension, lack of social skills, anxiety attacks, depression, and insomnia, in addition to drinking problems.

Establishing priorities is seldom discussed in the literature on behavior therapy. Rönnberg (1978) suggests the following procedures: The client makes a list of priorities; the therapist makes a list of priorities according to research results and his or her own knowledge about the problems; the therapist and the client make priorities according to the resources available for therapy; and, finally, the therapist and the client coordinate their priorities. This should result in decisions about a starting point that fully involve both client and therapist in the decision-making process. This mutual involvement is very important, especially when alcohol abuse is one of the problems. The client has to be responsible and feel involved in therapy to be able to carry out a treatment program, which, to a large extent, is conducted without the therapist over a long period of time.

The final stages of the first step of the therapeutic process are well known in behavior therapy praxis: making precise descriptions and measuring the baseline (e.g., Hersen & Barlow, 1976).

MAIN COMPLAINTS AND THE DRINKING RESPONSE

The main complaint is seldom excessive drinking alone. An assessment confined merely to the drinking response is therefore rarely sufficient. The main complaints examined by the client and the therapist jointly during the first step of the treatment program usually number four, five, or more behavior problems—in addition to the obvious, excessive drinking and its many variations. The drinking response is, however, a central one, and the one we shall deal with in this chapter. Let us therefore look at some facts about this particular problem before proceeding to the next step of the behavior therapy process.

There exists a wide cultural variation in drinking patterns. Figure 10.1 illustrates these differences in alcohol consumption for 36 different countries. Not only do the total amounts consumed vary widely between countries, but so do the kinds of beverages. In most industrial countries of the world, the percentage of adult teetotalers is very small (in Sweden, for instance, about 10% of the males and 25% of the females). A majority of the people who drink alcoholic beverages (in Sweden, approximately 80% of the adult male population) drink in a controlled, socially and medically acceptable manner. The rest, a small but significant portion of the adult population, are problem drinkers. (In Sweden, they constitute approximately 10% of the adult male population.) Most of these problem drinkers (60–80%) are usually not openly recognized as such; they carry on with

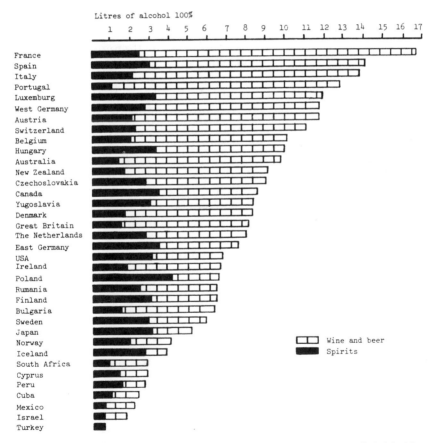

FIGURE 10.1. *Alcohol consumption per resident, per year in litres of pure alcohol for 36 countries. (Adapted from* Rapport 76. Alkohol och narkotika—fakta och debatt. Centralförbundet för alkohol och narkotikaupplysning. Stockholm: CAN, 1976.)

their work and may have more or less satisfactory social relations for many years. They are the hidden alcoholics (Rubington, 1972).

The consumption of alcohol in most industrial countries increased after World War II, especially among women and teenagers. In Sweden, for instance, the total consumption has doubled since the 1950s. The increase is especially noticeable among young women. Approximately 90% of both males and females in Sweden now consume alcohol at the age of 16. There exists a relationship between the total amount of alcohol consumed in a country and the proportion of the population who could be classified as problem drinkers: The larger the amount of alcohol consumed, the more problem drinkers there are. This relationship shows trends of positive acceleration. In Sweden, for instance, contemporary estimates indicate that about 40% of the male alcohol consumption and 47% of the female alcohol consumption can be counted among the 10% of the population who have the largest consumption (Socialstyrelsen, 1978). When consumption increases further, it can be expected that more than half of the total amount of alcohol will be consumed by about 10% of the drinking population.

Medically, an individual can be considered to risk developing into a problem drinker when he or she consumes more than .7 grams of alcohol per kilogram of body weight per week for about 10 years. This corresponds to approximately 15 centiliters of distilled spirits, 25 centiliters of fortified wine, 70 centiliters of table wine, about 5 bottles of strong beer, or about 8 bottles of light beer per week (Rydberg & Skerfving, 1974). The risks of liver cirrhosis, damage to the central nervous system, cancer, accidents, heart disease, and probably pneumonia and stomach ulcers as well, increase when such doses (or higher) are consumed for many years (Lindgren, 1977).

Whether or not someone is labeled a problem drinker, however, depends on social factors. In the Scandinavian countries, for instance, it seems to be acceptable to get heavily drunk now and then, but it is not acceptable to drink a little alcohol every day. In France, the situation is almost the opposite: A moderate daily consumption is socially accepted by most people, whereas occasional heavy drinking is not. Thus, a drinker is labeled "a problem" according to the rules of conduct customary in his or her society. A beginning drinker may have a number of years before drinking produces physical damage, but the chances are great that social sanctions will be felt much earlier.

There exists a great deal of evidence now that most problem drinkers can control their drinking in certain situations (Lloyd & Salzberg, 1975; Pattison, 1976). Sobell and Sobell (1978) list 80 studies that have demonstrated that controlled drinking is a worthwhile goal for some alcoholics. (Miller and Muñoz [1976] have published a book for self-help to achieve such controlled drinking.) It has been shown that even skid-row alcoholics can control their drinking occasionally (Vogler, Weissbach, & Compton, 1977). Thus, a simple, straightforward interpretation of Jellinek's (1960) "loss of control" hypothesis can no longer be defended. However, there is evidence that in some settings, especially in the natural environment, self-control is more difficult to apply. Also, it seems that the more advanced alcoholics find it harder to abide by pre-set rules, although controlled drinking may never be totally impossible, even for this group.

The hypothesis that intake of even minute amounts of alcohol by abstinent alcohol abusers inevitably leads to a craving for alcohol arises from a conceptualization of alcoholism as biologically determined. This idea has been repeatedly challenged in recent years. Not only has it been possible to modify drinking habits by the use of psychological methods (e.g., Emrick, 1974), but it has also been shown that predictions from a model viewing alcoholism as a disease have not been verified. Bromet and Moos (1977) estimate that endogenous factors account for no more than 10–20% of the variance in treatment outcome. The "disease" model (Begelman, 1976) of alcoholism seems to be applicable only to a minority of problem drinkers, especially heavy drinkers, and those who have organic injuries following long-term abuse of alcohol.

It should be pointed out, however, that controversies about controlled drinking, craving for alcohol, biological causes, etc., to a large extent consist of obscure and irrelevant questions. These are poorly defined concepts, which are of little value in research and therapeutic practice (Maisto & Schefft, 1977). Of more importance from a therapeutic point of view are behavior analytic questions such as: What are the specific responses that are considered problematic by an alcoholic and those in the immediate environment? What are the controlling variables of alcohol consumption? How should this information be used in a treatment program?

Contingency Analysis of Current Behavior Problems

The behavioral analytic model used here is based on the contingency model. An outline of a model for contingency analysis is presented in Figure 10.2. Let us briefly discuss each one of the variables mentioned in this model.

THE ANTECEDENTS OF THE DRINKING RESPONSE

There are numerous factors that may facilitate the abuse of alcohol. Some of them are ever present in our environment, some are temporary but exert their effects through a history of reinforcement, and some consist of prompts and probes from people around the drinker. Little research has been done in a behavioral analytic context to determine the exact nature of the factors that seem to facilitate the abuse of alcohol. There is a great deal of variation both within and between individuals. Strict experimentation is

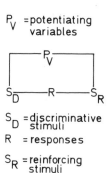

P_V = potentiating
      variables

S_D = discriminative
       stimuli
R = responses

S_R = reinforcing
       stimuli

FIGURE 10.2.   *A general model for clinical contingency analysis.*

necessary to determine the stimuli that act on each individual in specific situations. What follows, therefore, is a list of general areas that should be covered in future experimental work.

Alcoholism is related to many factors in the environment that may act as more or less constant stimuli, for example, marital status, conditions at work, group membership, socioeconomic status, and health. These are areas that should be assessed and examined in any behavior therapy program. Deficits in these areas undoubtedly stimulate the abuse of alcohol.

Most abusers do not seem to be particularly influenced by the sight and smell of alcohol (Miller, 1976). Drinking sprees are not often touched off by the mere sight and smell of alcohol. Neither is a craving for alcohol elicited solely by a simple display of alcohol, whether real, advertised, or imaginary. Nor does a strongly felt need or craving for alcohol seem to precede alcohol consumption (MacDonough, 1976).

Much effort has been exerted to alter the stimulus value of alcohol by aversive methods (Davidson, 1974). Used alone in the treatment of alcoholism, this method has generally not been very successful, but as a stimulus control technique it may be of use in a more comprehensive treatment plan (Nathan & Briddell, 1977). According to leading researchers in the field (Nathan, 1976), the best aversive method for most cases is chemical aversion, rather than electrical aversion or covert sensitization.

Modeling stimuli are probably a very potent source of influences facilitating alcohol abuse. It is likely that heavy drinking is started by such influences (Caudill & Marlatt, 1975). Smoking (Craig & van Natta, 1977) and hunger (Mello, 1972) may also act as triggers for alcohol consumption. Many alcoholics may have had their start in a gang of drinking, smoking, and hungry adolescents.

There is still much research to be done before we know which stimuli should be assessed and focused on in behavior therapy programs for alcoholism. More information about the antecedents of alcohol abuse will hopefully be available within the next few years.

THE REINFORCEMENT OF ALCOHOL ABUSE

An important reinforcing effect of alcohol is that it acts as a sedative, especially for the moderate consumer. For the heavy consumer, however, moderate amounts of alcohol may even increase anxiety and depression. Another reinforcing effect of alcohol, mainly negatively reinforcing, is that it gives the drinker a means of avoiding stress situations (Sobell & Sobell, 1973). Alcohol can also be used as an excuse to discard one's inhibitions, as evidenced by the fact that most alcohol consumers believe that they are less responsible for their actions when they are drunk (Lang, Goeckner, Adesso, & Marlatt, 1975). The negative reinforcement interpretation of excessive drinking should, however, be used with caution (Cappell, 1975). For most heavy drinkers, anxiety and discomfort are unlikely to be significantly reduced by drinking. There is even some data indicating that anxiety and depression may increase in heavy consumers as a result of drinking (Nathan, 1976).

Positive social reinforcement is more likely to contribute to the maintenance of alcohol abuse. Foy, Miller, Eisler, and Hemphill O'Toole (1976) have estimated that social pressure was the cause of approximately 50% of relapses into alcoholism. Peer problem drinkers often provide the only social reinforcement available, and often, this is forthcoming only after a period of drinking. It is not only the skid-row alcoholic groups that provide such social reinforcement; drinking is a notable means of enhancing social acceptance and attention at parties, business meetings, and other social events in a variety of groups.

Loss of status, job, or money may be consequences that can often keep problem drinkers from drinking. Hunt and Azrin (1973) tested this time-out from reinforcement interpretation and found that alcoholics were in fact heavily influenced by withdrawal and threats of withdrawal of positive reinforcers, such as jobs, family, and social relations.

VARIABLES POTENTIATING ALCOHOL ABUSE

The most important potentiating variables for alcohol consumption seem to be the social skills of the consumer, marital support available, reinforcing work opportunities, and the level of experienced stress. Distinctions between constant stimuli and potentiating variables are often arbitrary in natural settings.

Pre-alcoholic male teenagers seem to possess significantly fewer social skills than nondrinking peers (O'Leary, O'Leary, & Donovan, 1976). Furthermore, the nonsocially skilled ways alcoholic-prone individuals solve problems result in loss of opportunities to train adequate responses. Thus, they lag farther and farther behind their peers.

Many studies support the theory that a satisfactory marital life helps to keep people from heavy drinking. However, it is interesting to note that some wives of alcoholics in fact reinforce their husbands' drinking by paying extra attention to alcoholic themes in family interactions (Hersen, Miller, & Eisler, 1973). Bromet and Moos (1977) produced some data to support the hypothesis that a large part of environmental influences on the abuse of alcohol can be explained by marital and work relations.

As to stress and alcohol, there is a widespread belief that stress increases the consumption of alcohol. However, very little conclusive research data is available to support this belief. Most studies have been confined to animals in restricted environments.

ADDITIONAL CONTINGENCIES OF
CURRENT BEHAVIOR PROBLEMS

This description of a general contingency analysis of alcohol problems is a very rough approximation of what a contingency analysis would be like if we knew more about its different components in the analysis and treatment of alcoholism. We have yet to pinpoint the real-life factors that correspond to discriminative stimuli, potentiating variables, responses, and reinforcers. We cannot even guess how other contingencies influence alcoholism, such as schedules of reinforcement, chaining, and, to some extent, punishment. We have obtained some evidence about a few other contingencies, such as avoidance, response cost, prompts, and probes. But in fact, we are just beginning to uncover the basic structure of a contingency analysis of alcohol problems.

We have not yet fully explored the possibilities of contingency analyses of all kinds of responses. We have confined ourselves primarily to motor responses but have left out the cognitive and physiological responses that are of equal importance. In the future, behavioral analyses of alcohol abuse should include extrinsic, cognitive, and physiological control within an operant framework (Biglan & Kass, 1977). At present, our knowledge is insufficient for such a comprehensive behavioral analysis.

The relationships that exist between different problem behaviors (and their contingencies) are, to a large extent, unexplored. Alcohol abuse is often related to physical health problems, to interpersonal relations, to problems at work, and to various subjectively experienced problems such as anxiety, depression, and aggression. How these relationships should be dealt with and how priorities should be determined is seldom discussed in literature on behavior therapy.

The Alternatives to Alcohol Abuse

Problem behaviors are often seen as something that should be eliminated. A person with such behaviors should be helped, cured, freed, etc. But this focus upon problem behaviors is not necessarily the most efficient one. Goldiamond (1974) supports what he calls "a constructional approach to human problems" where the focus in treatment is upon the positive alternatives the client would need. This educational approach has made some impact on behavioral analyses as well as on treatment.

Miller and Mastria (1977), for instance, have outlined a treatment strategy for alcoholics that includes relaxation and assertion training, social and marital skills training, sex counseling, self-control training, and training of occupational skills. The treatment is based on the idea that if the alcoholic is trained in these skills, he or she will have less need for alcohol. If the client has all the skills necessary for a socially reinforcing life, he or she will not need to drink. This is a plausible hypothesis that I believe should be considered in most behavior therapy programs.

Alternatives to each individual's problem behaviors must be assessed and contingency analyses made with the same thoroughness as in the assessment and analyses of the main complaints and problem behaviors. A similar procedure can be followed in assessing and analyzing alternatives, as was outlined previously for the assessment and analysis of problem behaviors.

Background Information

Behavior therapy focuses on the here and now. It is believed that what is learned earlier in life will manifest itself in some way in the current functioning of the organism. Therefore, the history of a patient's problem as taken in behavior therapy generally extends over a shorter period of time than in psychiatric practice in general. However, historical information about a problem should never be totally left out. The "original learning," if such can be traced, the development of the problem, the contingencies that have been functionally related to it, and the alternatives that have been available, all give important information needed for setting up a program for change, assessing what would be suitable for each particular individual in terms of treatment, and setting goals for the maintenance of a better way of living.

To obtain the problem history of the alcoholic client it is necessary to keep in mind a few points about research findings on the etiology of alcoholism. It has been found that children in families where one or both parents are heavy drinkers and children in families where neither of the parents drink are much more likely to become alcoholics than are children of parents who are "normal" drinkers. The obvious interpretation of this observation is that only children whose parents drink "normally" have effective social models of controlled drinking (Miller, 1976).

A career of drinking usually begins during adolescence. Learning to drink during that period may lead to alcoholism later on (Vogler, Weissbach, Compton, & Martin, 1977). Drinking alcohol may appear to the adolescent to be a way of growing up and becoming a member of the drinking adult society (Jessor & Jessor, 1975). It is important that interventions be made before physical deterioration and detrimental social effects become pronounced (Sclare, 1977). Taking this into consideration, it is surprising to find so few studies that focus on adolescent drinking and its treatment (Teicher, Sinay, & Stumphauzer, 1976).

The abuse of alcohol is related to various kinds of deviant behaviors (Moos, Moos, & Kulik, 1976). For example, it has been estimated that about 50% of the increase in violent crimes during the 1960s in Sweden can be explained by the increase in alcohol consumption (Rexed, 1977). The causal relationship between deviant behaviors and the abuse of alcohol is, however, in no way established. We do not know if deviant behaviors cause alcoholism, or if alcoholism often leads to various transgressions and aggressions, or if both alcoholism and deviant behaviors are primarily caused by particular personality disorders, the environment, or other contingencies. Perhaps there is a multifactorial determination that varies in configuration over time and situations.

Analysis of Change

The sixth step in the model presented in this chapter is an analysis of change. It includes discussions about the most ideal development in the problem areas, alternatives to problem behaviors, and the effects of the planned development on friends, relatives, and other persons related to the client. Different treatment alternatives are discussed with the client, who is encouraged to choose an alternative that he or she feels can be believed in and accepted. This entails the therapist making a prognosis for the various treatments proposed. As to alcoholism, the therapist should know that some studies point to certain patient characteristics as positively related to recovery: stability of social relaionships, a high level of education, motivation for treatment, late onset of drinking, and early hospitalization (Baekeland, Lundwall, & Kissin, 1975). At the same time, this knowledge should be used with caution in the individual case, because, strictly speaking, results from group studies are not fully generalizable to individual cases (e.g., Nordlund & Rönnberg, 1976). In general, however, this step implies discussions about the treatment goals and final results that are of a client-centered nature.

Treatment Plan and Contract

In initial behavior analyses, final decisions about the treatment methods are not made until step seven. Here, treatment targets are determined, and decisions are made about techniques of intervention, the tasks of the client and therapist, contingencies for the therapist's and the client's work, methods for measuring progress, and contract details. However, most of the work is a review and classification of what has already been discussed at the earlier stages. It is mostly intended for structuring the situation and for motivating the client.

Intervention

Intervention and techniques of intervention have received the most extensive coverage of all aspects of the behavior therapy process in literature on behavior therapy. Technical books such as those by Kanfer and Goldstein (1975), Krumboltz and Thoresen (1976), Lazarus (1971), and Rimm and Masters (1974), present numerous behavioral techniques that can be used for intervention. The proper use of techniques in the treatment of alcoholism has been the focus of many publications (for references, see Miller, 1976; Nathan, 1976; Sobell & Sobell, 1978). The main point to be made here is that the techniques chosen should be based on the initial behavioral analyses and thus adapted to the unique problem constellation of each client.

Followup

In behavior therapy, there has been a long-standing interest in methods of changing behavior in natural settings. It is only recently, however, that maintenance problems have become a central concern. At the same time, there is a growing awareness among behavior therapists of the complexities of the problems of maintenance and followup (Mash & Terdal, 1977). It is not only a question of whether or not the client has stopped drinking for some time after the termination of the treatment, but it is also a question of how the individual feels about his or her new life style and how he or she is getting along in other areas of life. Followup assessment should cover as many areas as were covered by measurement during treatment. As with treatment, followup checks must also be individually planned for each client, and his or her particular problems and contingencies must be taken into consideration. Maintenance can be seen as a problem of generalizing the results of treatment in time and over situations and responses (Lovaas, Koegel, Simmons, & Long, 1973; Mash & Terdal, 1977; Tennow & Jacobson, 1977). Generalization can be increased by broad-spectrum treatment programs, full involvement of the client in the treatment, successive fading of the treatment, and successive training in normal life. There is no standard way of doing this, however. Followup, like treatment, must be individualized and based on an initial and ongoing behavioral analysis of each client's problems and their maintaining contingencies.

CONCLUSIONS

An outline of a clinical behavioral analytic framework that should be employed in most practical applications of behavior therapy, including work on alcoholism, was presented in this chapter. The review of some of the results of work on alcoholism has made it clear that treatment must be based upon thorough behavior analyses and assessment, and that an adequate treatment program will have to include a number of behavioral techniques depending on the different characteristics of each individual. Treatment programs will thus differ in each individual case.

The approach presented in the present chapter is, broadly speaking, in agreement with the main ideas recently formulated by several other independent authors, namely Azrin (1976); Lovibond (1977); Miller (1976); Miller and Eisler (1976); Pattison, Sobell, and Sobell (1977); and Sobell and Sobell (1978). All have strongly emphasized treatment designs adapted to each particular individual and following rules obtained from comprehensive models of clinical behavior analysis and assessment.

An obvious conclusion is that there is no simple treatment for alcoholism. Alcoholism is not considered a disease as long as physical ill-health does not dominate the clinical picture. Alcoholism is neither a simple behavioral problem nor merely the result of unsolved emotional conflicts. What we have to deal with is a set of undesirable responses controlled by factors which, although they may not be manifest in many cases, nevertheless must always be checked in each individual case. Behavior therapy is a set of principles that could be used for the analysis and modification of many of the responses and many of the controlling factors of alcoholism.

REFERENCES

Azrin, N. H. Improvements in the community-reinforcement approach to alcoholism. *Behaviour Research and Therapy*, 1976, *14*, 339–348.

Baekeland, F., Lundwall, L., & Kissin, B. Methods for treatment of chronic alcoholism: A critical appraisal. In R. J. Gibbins, Y. Israel, H. Kalant, R. E. Popham, W. Schmidt, & R. G. Smart (Eds.), *Research advances in alcohol and drug problems* (Vol. 2). New York: Wiley, 1975. Pp. 277–327.

Bandura, A. *Social learning theory.* Englewood Cliffs, N.J.: Prentice-Hall, 1977.

Begelman, D. A. Behavioral classification. In M. Hersen & A. S. Bellack (Eds.), *Behavioral assessment: A practical handbook.* New York: Pergamon, 1976. Pp. 23–48.

Biglan, A., & Kass, D. J. The empirical nature of behavior therapies. *Behaviorism*, 1977, *5*, 1–15.

Briddell, D. W., & Nathan, P. E. Behavioral assessment and modification with alcoholics: Current status and future trends. In M. Hersen, R. M. Eisler, & P. M. Miller (Eds.), *Progress in behavior modification* (Vol. 2). New York: Academic Press, 1976. Pp. 1–51.

Bromet, E., & Moos, R. H. Environmental resources and the posttreatment functioning of alcoholic patients. *Journal of Health and Social Behavior*, 1977, *18*, 326–338.

Cappell, H. An evaluation of tension models of alcohol consumption. In R. J. Gibbins, Y.

Israel, H. Kalant, R. E. Popham, W. Schmidt, & R. G. Smart (Eds.), *Research advances in alcohol and drug problems* (Vol. 2). New York: Wiley, 1975. Pp. 177–209.

Carter, R. D. *Outline for procedural guide to behavioral case management.* Unpublished manuscript. Ann Arbor: School of Social Work, University of Michigan, 1973.

Caudill, B. D., & Marlatt, G. A. Modeling influences in social drinking: An experimental analogue. *Journal of Consulting and Clinical Psychology,* 1975, *43,* 405–415.

Cautela, J. R. *Behavior analysis forms for clinical intervention.* Champaign, Ill.: Research Press, 1977.

Centralförbundet för alkohol och narkotikaupplysning. *Rapport 76. Alkohol och narkotika—fakta och debatt.* Stockholm: CAN, 1976.

Ciminero, A. R., Calhoun, K. S., & Adams, H. E. (Eds.), *Handbook of behavioral assessment.* New York: Wiley, 1977.

Cone, J. D., & Hawkins, R. P. (Eds.). *Behavioral assessment: New directions in clinical psychology.* New York: Brunner/Mazel, 1977.

Craig, T. J., & van Natta, P. A. The association of smoking and drinking habits in a community sample. *Journal of Studies on Alcohol,* 1977, *38,* 1434–1439.

Davidson, II, W. S. Studies of aversive conditioning for alcoholics: A critical review of theory and research methodology. *Psychological Bulletin,* 1974, *31,* 571–581.

Emrick, C. D. A review of psychologically oriented treatment of alcoholism. I. The use and interrelationships of outcome criteria and drinking behavior following treatment. *Quarterly Journal of Studies on Alcohol,* 1974, *35,* 523–549.

Feldman, M. P., & Broadhurst, A. (Eds.). *Theoretical and experimental bases of the behaviour therapies.* London: Wiley, 1976.

Foy, D. W., Miller, P. M., Eisler, R. M., & Hemphill O'Toole, D. Social-skills training to teach alcoholics to refuse drinks effectively. *Journal of Studies on Alcohol,* 1976, *37,* 1340–1345.

Gambrill, E. D. *Behavior modification. Handbook of assessment, intervention, and evaluation.* San Francisco: Jossey-Bass, 1977.

Goldfried, M. R., & Davison, G. C. *Clinical behavior therapy.* New York: Holt, Rinehart, & Winston, 1976.

Goldiamond, I. Toward a constructional approach to social problems. Ethical and constructional issues raised by applied behavior analysis. *Behaviorism,* 1974, *2,* 1–84.

Hamburg, S. Behavior therapy in alcoholism. A critical review of broad-spectrum approaches. *Journal of Studies on Alcohol,* 1975, *36,* 69–87.

Hersen, M., & Barlow, D. H. *Single-case experimental designs: Strategies for studying behavior change.* New York: Pergamon, 1976.

Hersen, M., & Bellack, A. S. (Eds.). *Behavioral assessment. A practical handbook.* New York: Pergamon, 1976.

Hersen, M., Miller, P. M., & Eisler, R. M. Interactions between alcoholics and their wives: A descriptive analysis of verbal and nonverbal behavior. *Quarterly Journal of Studies on Alcohol,* 1973, *34,* 516–520.

Honig, W. K., & Staddon, J. E. R. (Eds.). *Handbook of operant behavior.* Englewood Cliffs, N.J.: Prentice-Hall, 1977.

Hunt, G. M., & Azrin, N. H. A community-reinforcement approach to alcoholism. *Behaviour Research and Therapy,* 1973, *11,* 91–104.

Jellinek, E. M. *The disease concept of alcoholism.* Highland Park, N.J.: Hillhouse Press, 1960.

Jessor, R., & Jessor, S. L. Adolescent development and the onset of drinking. *Journal of Studies on Alcohol,* 1975, *36,* 27–51.

Kanfer, F. H., & Goldstein, A. P. (Eds.). *Helping people change: A textbook of methods.* New York: Pergamon, 1975.

Kanfer, F. H., & Saslow, G. Behavioral diagnosis. In C. M. Franks (Ed.), *Behavior therapy: Appraisal and status.* New York: McGraw-Hill, 1969. Pp. 417–444.

Krumboltz, J. D., & Thoresen, C. E. (Eds). *Counseling methods.* New York: Holt, Rinehart, & Winston, 1976.

Lang, A. R., Goeckner, D. J., Adesso, V. J., & Marlatt, G. A. Effects of alcohol on aggression in male social drinkers. *Journal of Abnormal Psychology*, 1975, *84*, 508–518.

Lazarus, A. A. *Behavior therapy and beyond*. New York: McGraw-Hill, 1971.

Lazarus, A. A. (Ed.). *Multi-modal behavior therapy*. New York: Springer, 1976.

Lindgren, Å. *WHO-rapport om alkoholpolitik. Rapport från TSAs litteraturgrupp. Nr. 1*. Stockholm: TSA & CAN, 1977.

Lloyd, R. W., Jr., & Salzberg, H. C. Controlled social drinking: An alternative to abstinence as a treatment goal for some alcohol abusers. *Psychological Bulletin*, 1975, *82*, 815–842.

Lovaas, O. I., Koegel, R., Simmons, J. Q., & Long, J. S. Some generalization and follow-up measures on autistic children in behavior therapy. *Journal of Applied Behavior Analysis*, 1973, *6*, 131–165.

Lovibond, S. H. Behavioral control of excessive drinking. In M. Hersen, R. M. Eisler, & P. M. Miller (Eds.), *Progress in behavior modification* (Vol. 5). New York: Academic Press, 1977. Pp. 63–109.

MacDonough, T. S. The validity of self-recording reports made by drug and alcohol abusers in a residential setting. *International Journal of the Addictions*, 1976, *11*, 447–466.

Maisto, S. A., & Schefft, B. K. The constructs of craving for alcohol and loss of control drinking: Help or hindrance to research. *Addictive Behaviors*, 1977, *2*, 207–217.

Maser, J. D., & Seligman, M. E. P. (Eds.). *Psychopathology: Experimental models*. San Francisco: Freeman, 1977.

Mash, E. J., & Terdal, L. G. (Eds.). *Behavior therapy assessment. Diagnosis, design, and evaluation*. New York: Springer, 1976.

Mash, E. J., & Terdal, L. G. After the dance is over: Some issues and suggestions for follow-up assessment in behavior therapy. *Psychological Reports*, 1977, *41*, 1287–1308.

Mello, N. K. Behavioral studies of alcoholism. In B. Kissin & H. Begleiter (Eds.), *The biology of alcoholism. Physiology and behavior* (Vol. 2). New York: Plenum, 1972. Pp. 219–291.

Miller, P. M. *Behavioral treatment of alcoholism*. New York: Pergamon, 1976.

Miller, P. M., & Barlow, D. H. Behavioral approaches to the treatment of alcoholism. *Journal of Nervous and Mental Disease*, 1973, *157*, 10–20.

Miller, P. M., & Eisler, R. M. Alcohol and drug abuse. In W. E. Craighead, A. E. Kazdin, & M. J. Mahoney (Eds.), *Behavior modification. Principles, issues, and applications*. Boston: Houghton Mifflin, 1976. Pp. 376–393.

Miller, P. M., & Mastria, M. A. *Alternatives to alcohol abuse. A social learning model*. Champaign, Ill.: Research Press, 1977.

Miller, W. R., & Muñoz, R. F. *How to control your drinking*. Englewood Cliffs, N. J.: Prentice-Hall, 1976.

Moos, R. H., Moos, B. S., & Kulik, J. A. College-student abstainers, moderate drinkers, and heavy drinkers: A comparative analysis. *Journal of Youth and Adolescence*, 1976, *5*, 349–360.

Nathan, P. E. Alcoholism. In H. Leitenberg (Ed.), *Handbook of behavior modification and behavior therapy*. Englewood Cliffs, N.J.: Prentice-Hall, 1976. Pp. 3–44.

Nathan, P. E., & Briddell, D. W. Behavioral assessment and treatment of alcoholism. In B. Kissin & H. Begleiter (Eds.), *The biology of alcoholism. Treatment and rehabilitation of the chronic alcoholic* (Vol. 5). New York: Plenum, 1977. Pp. 301–349.

Nordlund, O., & Rönnberg, S. Reasons for $N = 1$ designs in educational research. *Scandinavian Journal of Educational Research*, 1976, *20*, 73–83.

O'Leary, D. E., O'Leary, M. R., & Donovan, D. M. Social skill acquisition and psychosocial development of alcoholics. A review. *Addictive Behaviors*, 1976, *1*, 111–120.

Pattison, E. M. Nonabstinent drinking goals in the treatment of alcoholism. *Archives of General Psychiatry*, 1976, *33*, 923–930.

Pattison, E. M., Sobell, M. B., & Sobell, L. C. *Emerging concepts of alcohol dependence*. New York: Springer, 1977.

Redl, F. The life space interview. *American Journal of Ortopsychiatry*, 1959, *29*, 1–18.

Rexed, B. Alkohol och välfärd. In D. H. Ingvar (Ed.), *Att dricka. Fakta och diskussioner om alkoholens inverkan på kropp och själ.* Stockholm: Bonniers, 1977. Pp. 78–103.

Rimm, D. C., & Masters, J. C. *Behavior therapy. Techniques and empirical findings.* New York: Academic Press, 1974.

Rönnberg, S. *Beteendeanalys: Riktlinjer för analys, datainsamling och utvärdering i beteendeterapi.* Stockholm: CBM/Rönnberg, 1978.

Rubington, E. The hidden alcoholic. *Quarterly Journal of Studies on Alcohol,* 1972, *33,* 667–683.

Rydberg, U., & Skerfving, S. Alkoholens giftighet. Ett försök till riskvärdering. *Läkartidningen,* 1974, *71,* 2275–2277.

Sclare, S. B. Treatment of alcoholism in Scotland. *International Journal of Offender Therapy and Comparative Criminology,* 1977, *21,* 153–165.

Sobell, M. B., & Sobell, L. C. Individualized behavior therapy for alcoholics. *Behavior Therapy,* 1973, *4,* 49–72.

Sobell, M. B., & Sobell, L. C. *Behavioral treatment of alcohol problems. Individualized therapy and controlled drinking.* New York: Plenum, 1978.

Socialstyrelsen. *Vården av alkoholmissbrukare.* Stockholm: Socialstyrelsen, 1978.

Stuart, R. B. *Trick or treatment. How and when psychotherapy fails.* Champaign, Ill.: Research Press, 1970.

Teicher, J. D., Sinay, R. D., & Stumphauzer, J. S. Training community-based paraprofessionals as behavior therapists with families of alcohol-abusing adolescents. *American Journal of Psychiatry,* 1976, *133,* 847–850.

Tennow, D., & Jacobson, J. W. Maintenance and generalization through unpredictable reward in applied settings. *European Journal of Behavioral Analysis and Modification,* 1977, *1,* 276–284.

Vogler, R. E., Weissbach, T. A., & Compton, J. V. Learning techniques for alcohol abuse. *Behaviour Research and Therapy,* 1977, *15,* 31–38.

Vogler, R. E., Weissbach, T. A., Compton, J. V., & Martin, G. T. Integrated behavior change technique for problem drinkers in the community. *Journal of Consulting and Clinical Psychology,* 1977, *45,* 267–279.

Wolpe, J. *The practice of behavior therapy* (2nd ed.). New York: Pergamon, 1973.

Yates, A. J. *Behavior therapy.* New York: Wiley, 1970.

_11_

Behavioral Treatment of Obesity:
Maintenance Strategies and
Long-Term Efficacy

G. TERENCE WILSON

In the years that have followed Stuart's (1967) landmark paper, we have seen a dramatic increase in research on the behavioral treatment of obesity (Bellack, 1977; Franks & Wilson, 1975, 1976; Jeffery, Wing, & Stunkard, 1978; Stunkard & Mahoney, 1976). Some consistent conclusions can be drawn from the numerous and often diverse studies produced in this upsurge of research on the treatment of obesity. First, most of the research is limited by several methodological shortcomings (Wilson, 1978). Second, despite these methodological inadequacies, behavioral treatments appear to be significantly more effective than alternative methods in the short term. Third, the outcome of behavioral treatment of obesity has been marked by substantial intersubject variability. Fourth, attempts to identify accurate predictor variables of treatment outcome have been notably unsuccessful. Fifth, the magnitude of weight loss in most studies has fallen short of clinical significance. Finally, long-term evaluations of treatment outcome have been conspicuously lacking. The latter problem—the paucity of long-term outcome studies—is the subject of this chapter. More specifically, the available evidence on the long-term efficacy of behavioral treatment of obesity is critically reviewed, the reasons behind the lack of studies explored, the conceptual considerations governing outcome evaluation analyzed, and explicit strategies for facilitating maintenance of treatment-produced weight loss discussed.

TRENDS IN BEHAVIOR THERAPY

Copyright © 1979 by Academic Press, Inc.
All rights of reproduction in any form reserved.
ISBN 0-12-647450-8

EVIDENCE OF LONG-TERM EFFICACY

The relative lack of long-term followup studies is a problem that transcends the literature on the behavioral treatment of obesity. It constitutes one of the major shortcomings in the behavior therapy—indeed, in all psychotherapy—literature as a whole. Consider, for example, the results of two recent analyses of the contents of leading behavior therapy journals. In their appraisal of four behavioral journals[1] for the year 1973, Cochrane and Sobol (1976) found that only 35% of studies where followup was appropriate actually included followups. Less than one-third of these followup evaluations (a mere 10 out of 113 studies reviewed) took place more than 6 months after the end of therapy. In a similar analysis of three behavioral journals[2] for the years 1972–1973, Keeley, Shemberg, and Carbonell (1976) estimated that only about 12% of studies reported followup data of more than 6 months in duration. There is little reason to suspect that matters have changed appreciably over the past 4 or 5 years (Franks & Wilson, 1973, 1975, 1976, 1977; Kazdin & Wilson, 1977; Leitenberg, 1976).

The data on the treatment of obesity paint a similarly poor picture. In a review of the research literature in 1974, Hall and Hall reported that only 2 of 19 controlled studies included followups of more than 6 months in duration. In one of these studies (Harris & Bruner, 1971), significant weight reduction over a 3-month treatment period was not maintained at a 7-month followup. In the other, Foreyt and Kennedy (1971) found that behavioral treatment was significantly superior to a no-treatment control condition 9 months after therapy. Interpretation of this finding, however, is complicated by experimental confounding: Subjects in the treatment group were younger than those in the control group. A 1-year followup of the Penick, Filion, Fox, and Stunkard (1971) study that compared a group behavioral program with traditional group therapy showed that both treatments produced continued weight loss at 6- and 12-month followup evaluations (Stunkard, 1972). While the behavioral treatment appeared more effective, statistical analyses of the followup findings were not described, making it impossible to draw any firm conclusion about long-term efficacy.

Hall, Hall, Hanson, and Borden (1974) found that a multifaceted and a more circumscribed, "simple" behavioral self-management treatment produced significantly greater weight loss than an attention-placebo treatment at posttreatment and at a 3-month followup. At a 6-month followup, however, these differences were no longer significant and both behavioral groups had regained significant amounts of weight. Hanson, Borden, Hall,

[1] *Journal of Applied Behavior Analysis, Journal of Behavior Therapy and Experimental Psychiatry, Behavior Therapy,* and *Behaviour Research and Therapy.*
[2] *Journal of Applied Behavior Analysis, Behavior Therapy,* and *Behaviour Research and Therapy.*

and Hall (1976) compared a therapist-administered behavioral self-control treatment method with two programmed text conditions differing only in degree of therapist contact, an attention-placebo, and a no-treatment control group. The three behavioral treatment groups were collectively superior to the two control groups at posttreatment and at a 10-week followup. A 1-year followup showed that this difference had disappeared. As in the Hall *et al.* (1974) study, there was a marked subject attrition rate during treatment (21.8%), and an additional 11% of subjects dropped out during followup. Since program drop-outs are usually failures (Franks & Wilson, 1975), these results have particularly negative implications for long-term efficacy of the treatment procedures.

More encouraging data were reported by Mahoney (1974). A self-reinforcement treatment aimed at modifying inappropriate eating patterns resulted in significantly greater weight loss at posttreatment than either self-monitoring alone or self-reinforcement contingent upon weight loss. A 1-year followup indicated "marked superiority" in maintenance of weight loss in the self-reinforcement of habit change group. However, no statistical analyses of the data were presented. Mahoney and Mahoney (1976b) reported the results of the behavioral treatment of 13 obese subjects. Their improvement at posttreatment was even more pronounced at a 6-month followup, after which weight loss was shown to have stabilized at 1- and 2-year followups. Aside from the absence of any controls, the fact that only 7 and 5 subjects respectively—of the initial 13—were contacted at the two followups vitiates the significance of the findings. Furthermore, it should be noted that Hanson *et al.* (1976) conducted their followup over the telephone and Mahoney and Mahoney (1976b) obtained some of their data by mail. The validity of self-report of weight maintenance has not been established. Öst and Götestam (1976) conducted a 1-year followup of a comparative outcome study of a behavioral treatment versus a pharmacological (fenfluramine) treatment. Consistent with previous research, the behavioral treatment was significantly superior at posttreatment but not at the long-term followup. The 1-year results indicated that the majority of subjects in both treatment groups had regained substantial amounts of weight, although the mean weight of the behavioral group was still significantly lower than the pretreatment level.

Perhaps the most impressive findings of long-term efficacy of behavioral treatment have been those of Levitz and Stunkard (1974) and McReynolds and Paulsen (1976). The former study demonstrated that behavioral treatment produced significantly lower client attrition rates and greater weight reduction than either nutrition education or self-help (TOPS—Take Off Pounds Sensibly) control groups at posttreatment and at a 9-month followup. The latter study compared a comprehensive behavioral self-control treatment to one emphasizing stimulus control procedures. There was no difference at posttreatment, but the stimulus control program was significantly superior at 3-, and 6-month followups, but not at 9-, 12-, and 18-month followups. Although groups tended to regain weight increasingly after the 3-month followup, reasonably impressive rates of maintenance of treatment-produced weight loss of approximately 75% and 80%, respectively, were obtained at the 1-year followup. The superiority of a component part of the usual behavioral self-control treatment package over the complete program raises important theoretical and practical issues concerning the effective components of what have become standardized treatment regimens.

REASONS FOR THE RELATIVE LACK OF LONG-TERM FOLLOWUPS

Like other addictive behaviors (e.g., Hunt, Barnett, & Branch, 1971), obesity is characterized by a high relapse rate following treatment. Clients who lose weight during treatment usually regain it (Stunkard, 1958; Stunkard & Mahoney, 1976). In view of this problem the relative lack of long-term followup studies constitutes a major shortcoming. The reasons behind this state of affairs bear investigation (Wilson, 1978).

Of particular significance in this respect are the influences that govern the research behavior of investigators concerned with the evaluation of treatment outcome. Long-term followups require the investment of considerable time, effort, and often expense. Whether or not they are completed successfully is frequently uncertain and unpredictable. These characteristics of long-term followup are less than optimal if not anathema for the graduate students and faculty in primarily academic settings who conduct most of the research on obesity. Consider doctoral dissertation research, at least in the United States. Graduate students do not have the time to conduct long-term followups themselves. Rather, the exigencies of the situation reward more manageable, more predictable, time-limited studies. As a result of these practical constraints and, in some instances, conceptual biases about pure versus applied research, the importance of treatment outcome evaluation (especially long-term followup) is relegated to a secondary status (Azrin, 1977). The contingencies affecting the research behavior of young faculty members seeking promotion and tenure in the increasingly competitive job market situation may exercise a similar effect. Outcome research emphasizing long-term followup is a risky business. Relatively quick, laboratory-based studies are clearly better suited to boosting publication frequencies and enhancing curricula vitae.

In sum, remedying the current lopsided emphasis on short-term treatment studies seems to require that specific steps be taken to encourage long-term followups of treatment evaluation in both university and applied settings. For example, a student's participation in one facet (e.g., the followup) of a broader research program might be viewed as a legitimate dissertation topic. This can and must occur without relaxing rigorous standards of scholarship and methodological sophistication. Faculty should be encouraged to engage in treatment evaluation that requires lengthy followups. Specifically, research grants might be awarded for this very purpose and for the duration that such time-consuming studies necessarily require.

THE SOCIAL LEARNING MODEL OF OUTCOME EVALUATION OF PSYCHOLOGICAL TREATMENT

Another factor that has contributed to the paucity of research on maintenance strategies and long-term followup of treatment effects has been the traditional approach to outcome evaluation. In this quasi-disease model, abnormal behavior is a function of some intrapsychic personality conflict that remains relatively unaffected by environmental events. To the degree that the underlying conflict is resolved, abnormal behavior is supposedly altered independent of specific environmental changes. There is no emphasis on explicit strategies to maintain treatment-produced improvement. In terms of the social learning framework, psychological functioning involves a reciprocal interaction between an individual's behavior and the environment; the client is both the agent and the object of environmental influence. Outcome evaluation must distinguish among the initial induction of therapeutic change, its transfer to the natural environment, and its maintenance over time (Bandura, 1969; Kazdin & Wilson, 1977). These different phases of the overall treatment strategy may be governed by different processes, and maintenance can be ensured only to the extent that procedures designed to accomplish this goal are included in the treatment program.

The behavioral treatment of obesity is geared to teaching clients self-regulatory functions that enable them to control their eating patterns. However, continued self-regulatory behavior requires reinforcement; as with other behavior it will extinguish in the absence of appropriate reinforcement. Newly acquired self-control, such as eating less, is particularly vulnerable to competing response tendencies. In contrast to the instant gratification afforded by consuming food, self-regulation over eating has few sources of immediate reinforcement. It cannot be assumed that the relatively minimal weight losses achieved at the end of typical behavioral treatment programs are sufficient to reinforce persistent self-regulatory efforts. Additional maintenance strategies are needed.

In terms of this social learning analysis, Yates' (1975) verdict that the treatment of obesity is an example of "where behavior therapy fails" is premature. Behavioral treatment is clearly effective in producing initial weight reduction, even though maintenance of improvement has yet to be shown convincingly. The effect of maintenance strategies—and thus behavioral treatment accurately conceived of—has yet to be properly evaluated.

STRATEGIES FOR MAINTAINING
TREATMENT-PRODUCED WEIGHT LOSS

It is instructive to compare Stuart's (1967) series of multiple systematic case studies with subsequent controlled outcome studies. The failure to replicate Stuart's (1967) results could be due to a variety of factors, including subject and therapist variables. However, Stuart's (1967) procedure differed from subsequent studies in at least two other important respects. First, each client was treated on an individual basis. Second, following 16–17 weeks of therapy, booster sessions were scheduled "as needed" for the remainder of the 12 months of followup. Accordingly, O'Leary and Wilson (1975) advocated the use of the following three maintenance strategies in the treatment of obesity: (a) treatment that is individually tailored to each client's particular weight problem instead of the group application of standardized techniques that has been typical of behavioral outcome studies; (b) the use of explicit booster sessions to provide feedback and reinforcement for continuing self-regulatory behaviors and newly acquired eating habits; and (c) the inclusion of family members in the treatment process so as to ensure reinforcement of appropriate behavior in the natural environment. The following describes the program[3] of research undertaken by the author and his colleagues aimed at evaluating the contribution of these three maintenance strategies to the long-term efficacy of behavior therapy for obesity.

Individualized Treatment and Booster Sessions

Both theoretical considerations (e.g., Mischel, 1968) and clinical lore (e.g., Lazarus, 1971) suggest that individualized treatment should improve the durability of behavior change. Emphasizing the importance of such a strategy in their treatment of over 200 obese clients, Stuart and Davis (1972) concluded that "it was found expedient to individualize specific procedures within the rubric of a general approach to situational management [p. 95]." Wilson (1976) similarly pointed out the necessity of individualized

[3]Several of the studies reported here were part of a research program directed by the author and supported by a grant from the Busch Foundation Endowment Fund, Rutgers University.

treatment of obesity in clinical practice. Booster sessions have long been proposed as a means of enhancing the persistence of behavior change (Bandura, 1969; Eysenck & Rachman, 1965). Uncontrolled findings from the treatment of alcoholics (Voegtlin, Lemere, Broz, & O'Hallaren, 1942) and enuretic children (Lovibond, 1964) have indicated the potential value of booster sessions. Accordingly, in the first of the series of studies, Kingsley and Wilson (1977) evaluated the effects of individualized therapy and post-treatment booster sessions on long-term outcome.

STUDY I

Subjects were assigned randomly on the basis of within-sample matching from stratified blocks of percentage overweight to one of three treatment groups (described below) with an N of 26 in each group.

Group behavioral treatment. Treatment consisted of the sequential presentation of the various techniques commonly included in behavioral self-control programs modeled after Stuart and Davis (1972). These methods include self-monitoring, self-reinforcement, stimulus control, relaxation training, imagery techniques, and behavior management procedures such as disrupting the usual eating pattern and substituting incompatible behaviors for eating. Food-related problems were analyzed in the group on the basis of information derived from subjects' self-monitoring records. Group members were encouraged to suggest solutions to particular problems and were praised by the therapist for suggesting and implementing appropriate self-control methods. The attempt was made to provide as personalized a program as possible within the constraints of the group setting by discussing techniques in connection with the specific circumstances of individual group members.

Individual behavioral treatment. Therapists conducted behavioral assessments of each subject in individual sessions. The treatment techniques included those used in the group condition. However, they were not limited to those of the group behavioral program. Therapists were instructed to go beyond the standardized group program by using any social learning procedure that appeared necessary for comprehensive therapy.

Social pressure treatment. This procedure was modeled after Wollersheim's (1970) social pressure treatment. Similar to the TOPS method and emphasizing that the critical factor in weight reduction is high motivation, this procedure was designed to constitute a stringent control condition for nonspecific treatment influences. Posttreatment ratings indicated that this was a credible treatment that was successful in creating expectancies of favorable treatment outcome.

The therapists were three male graduate students in clinical psychology with a minimum of 2 years' experience in conducting therapy. All three therapists conducted each of the two group treatments. Each subject in the individual behavior treatment condition was seen by the same therapist throughout.

Treatment consisted of eight weekly sessions. At the end of this period, half the subjects in each treatment condition were assigned to a booster condition and half were assigned to a no-booster condition. Those in the booster condition participated in four additional treatment sessions during the 14 weeks following the end of therapy. Subjects in the no-booster condition attended only the followup weigh-ins at 3, 6, 9, and 12 months after treatment. The attrition rate was only 7.7% during treatment and 10% during the 1-year followup.

The results show that both behavioral treatments were significantly superior to the social-pressure treatment at posttreatment, but this greater efficacy was not maintained over followup. Although slightly superior, the group behavioral treatment was never significantly different from the social pressure treatment across followups; moreover, both group treatments showed significantly greater maintenance of treatment-produced weight reduction than the individual behavioral treatment at the 9- and 12-month followups.

The booster sessions resulted in continued weight loss while they were in effect. Independent of the specific treatment, booster sessions significantly facilitated maintenance of weight loss at the 3-, 6-, and 9-month followups.

Contrary to the prediction that individualizing behavioral treatment for obese clients would facilitate maintenance of improvement, individual behavior therapy resulted in significant relapse. At posttreatment, subjects in the individual behavioral treatment had lost the most weight. During the next 3 months, subjects in the individual behavioral group who received booster sessions continued to lose weight, whereas the individual behavioral subjects not receiving booster sessions showed a weight gain over the same period. Following completion of booster sessions, subjects in the individual behavioral booster group, like their no-booster counterparts, began to regain lost weight.

Kingsley and Wilson (1977) interpreted the greater long-term efficacy of group as opposed to individual treatment as evidence of the fact that successful maintenance of treatment-produced weight loss is due to subjects' *motivation*. Behavioral self-control methods equip subjects with the necessary skills to regulate their eating behavior, hence their superiority over the less structured, less didactic social pressure condition at posttreatment. Maintenance, however, is a function of whether these self-regulatory skills are applied. If this function is dependent on motivation, as Kingsley and Wilson (1977) suggest, the comparable success of the two group treatments is not surprising. Group cohesiveness and pressure to implement self-control may make group treatment more powerful than individual therapy in terms of sustaining commitment and motivation.

Group behavior therapy might be the optimal treatment modality for obesity, with the adjunctive use of associated individual sessions to address idiosyncratic problems revealed by a thorough behavioral assessment. It must be emphasized, however, that Kingsley and Wilson's (1977) failure to assess subjects' actual adherence to the behavioral programs renders this interpretation tentative at best.

Given these promising results on booster sessions as an effective maintenance strategy, a second study was conducted in which the nature and the frequency of booster sessions were evaluated over a 1-year followup (Ashby & Wilson, 1977). It was predicted that if successful maintenance depends upon subjects' motivation to implement self-regulatory behaviors, booster sessions that are nonspecific and merely expose subjects to group support and encouragement might be as effective as formally structured rehearsals of specific behavior change methods. Whether different frequencies of booster sessions exercised an effect was also investigated.

STUDY II

Seventy-five obese women who had participated in an 8-week group behavioral treatment program similar to that used by Kingsley and Wilson (1977) were assigned to one of five different maintenance conditions from stratified blocks based on pretreatment percentage overweight and percentage overweight lost during therapy.

1. *Behavioral/two-week condition.* Subjects met every 2 weeks in what was an extension of the original 8-week treatment program. The focus was on the acquisition and implementation of behavioral skills as long-term adaptive habits.

2. *Behavioral/four-week condition.* This was identical to the behavioral/ 2-week condition except that the maintenance groups met every 4 weeks.

3. *Nonspecific/two-week condition.* Fortnightly meetings were held in which the original external structure provided by the therapist was discontinued. The therapist acted as a relatively passive facilitator rather than as an active behavioral instructor. Discussion was kept as general and nonspecific as possible, with groups arranged so as to foster a sense of mutual concern and with group subjects offering each other encouragement and reinforcement. Subjects were informed that they should continue applying what they had learned during treatment but that in the maintenance phase it was important that they manage their own weight loss independent of the therapist.

4. *Nonspecific/four-week condition.* This was the same as the nonspecific/2-week condition except that the group met every 4 weeks.

5. *Control condition.* Following treatment, subjects had no contact with the therapist except for weigh-ins at the 3-, 6-, 9-, and 12-month fol-

lowups. Subjects were told that it was important that they learn to apply on their own the techniques learned during treatment.

The 2-week conditions met every fortnight during the first 4 months and the 4-week conditions met every month during the first 4 months of the followup period. During the second 4 months of followup the frequency of maintenance sessions was gradually decreased. The 2-week conditions met in 3 weeks, then 4, then 5, and so on. There were no maintenance sessions during the final 4 months of followup. The study was completed in two replications.

The results indicated that neither booster session frequency nor nature had a significant effect on maintenance of weight loss. All five groups continued to lose weight during the first 3 months of followup. Thereafter subjects in the first replication showed a significant increase in weight over the next 9 months, whereas subjects in the second replication maintained the weight they had lost in treatment. The attrition rates were 7.4 and 5.3% during treatment and the 1-year followup, respectively.

The lack of a significant difference between the booster and control conditions is inconsistent with the Kingsley and Wilson (1977) findings. In the latter study, however, although a significant overall effect of booster versus no-booster sessions was obtained, the individual comparison between the group behavioral treatment condition with and without booster sessions fell short of statistical significance. Moreover, Hall, Hall, Borden, and Hanson (1975) reported that booster sessions failed to facilitate maintenance of weight loss over control conditions in a 3-month followup of a behavioral treatment program. Clearly, booster sessions have yet to be demonstrated to be reliably effective strategies for the maintenance of weight loss. The discrepancy between the two replications of the Ashby and Wilson (1977) study is not readily explained. It is typical, however, of the variability in outcome that has characterized the obesity treatment literature.

Incorporating Family Members in the Treatment Process

The role of spouse or family support in the treatment of obesity has been surprisingly neglected, although scattered observations have indicated its potential importance. On the basis of recorded mealtime interactions between overweight women and their husbands, Stuart and Davis (1972) concluded that some husbands ''. . . are not only contributors to their wives' efforts to lose weight, but may actually exert a negative influence [pp. 19–20].'' Specifically, husbands were more likely than their overweight wives to initiate conversation on food-related topics and were more likely to criticize their wives' eating behavior than they were to praise moderation. Mahoney and Mahoney (1976b) reported an apparent relationship between treatment outcome and estimated family support of subjects. These authors computed a family support index based upon family attendance at therapy sessions and subjects' reports of encouragement that they received. A positive correlation between weight loss and family support was statistically significant at the end of the 10-week treatment program but not at the 6-month followup. Similarly, Jeffery *et al.* (1978) reported a significant positive correlation between weight loss and social support in their uncontrolled clinical treatment series.

An initial controlled investigation of the influence of family involvement in the treatment process was conducted by Wilson and Brownell (1978) using a 2 × 2 factorial design. Obese women, similar in age and percentage overweight to the population treated by Kingsley and Wilson (1977) and Ashby and Wilson (1977), were assigned to a family member present or family member absent condition. Subjects in the family present group were required to attend all treatment sessions with a member of their family. The purpose of having family members present was to: (*a*) acquaint them with the principles of behavior change and the philosophy underlying behavioral weight reduction treatments; (*b*) instruct them to cease criticizing their partners' weight and/or eating behavior; (*c*) teach them to provide positive reinforcement for improved eating habits; and (*d*) provide assistance in their partners' attempts to monitor eating activities and restructure some of the conditions and consequences of eating. In all but three cases, husbands were the family members in treatment. All subjects received the 8-week group behavioral treatment program described by Kingsley and Wilson (1977).

Following treatment, subjects within each of the family member present and absent conditions were randomly assigned to either a booster session or a no-booster session group. The booster session groups met at monthly intervals over the 6-month followup period. These sessions were essentially an extension of the 8-week treatment sessions. Subjects in the no-booster groups attended followup weigh-ins at 3 and 6 months after treatment. The results failed to show a significant effect for either the family member present or the booster session condition. The latter finding conflicts with the Kingsley and Wilson (1977) data but is consonant with Ashby and Wilson's (1977) and Hall *et al.*'s (1975) results.

Interpretation of these results is complicated by a 20% attrition rate over followup and the fact that Wilson and Brownell (1978) failed to determine whether subjects adhered to treatment instructions. No independent evaluation of the behavior of the family members was undertaken. Furthermore, it is possible that a more extensive family intervention program than the limited procedure employed in the Wilson and Brownell (1978) study might be more effective in facilitating maintenance of weight loss. Accordingly, Brownell (1977) conducted a better controlled investigation to explore further the role of family support.

Ten men and 19 women who were an average of 55.7% overweight and whose mean age was 45.3 years were assigned to one of three treatment conditions:

1. *Cooperative spouse-couples training.* Subjects attended all treatment sessions with their spouses. Spouses were trained to model appropriate eating habits, to reinforce such behavior in subjects, and to engage subjects in activities incompatible with eating at times when subjects were especially vulnerable to food. The importance of stimulus control was emphasized and spouses were asked to refrain from eating in subjects' presence at other than mealtimes. Spouses self-monitored their own behavior toward subjects as well as subjects' compliance with treatment instructions.

2. *Cooperative spouse-subject only.* Although spouses in this condition had agreed to participate in the full treatment program, subjects were asked to attend sessions alone.

3. *Noncooperative spouse-subject only.* Spouses of subjects in this condition had refused to participate in the treatment program even though they had been informed at the outset that treatment was contingent on their participation. Subjects were subsequently told that a special group had been formed to provide treatment even without spouse participation. Treatment consisted of 10 weekly group sessions. Thereafter monthly sessions were conducted over a 6-month maintenance phase.

The results show that all three groups achieved significant weight losses at posttreatment with no differences among groups. However, the cooperative spouse-couples training treatment produced significantly greater weight loss and reduction in percentage overweight at the 3- and 6-month followups. Particularly impressive is the magnitude of weight loss in the couples training conditions. At the final followup, 66.7% had lost more than 20 pounds, 44.4% had lost more than 30 pounds, and 22.2% had lost more than 40 pounds. As Brownell (1977) suggests, these are the most favorable results yet obtained in any controlled outcome study. In contrast to most treatment studies, the attrition rate was zero, and the method was clearly cost effective. The total cost for the 8½-month program was $130 per subject.

These findings constitute the strongest evidence yet that the active involvement of family members in the treatment process might significantly improve the treatment of obesity. However, some cautions should be borne in mind in evaluating the data. First, all three treatment groups continued to lose substantial amounts of weight over the followup period, especially the first 3 months. Although couples training resulted in optimal improvement, even subjects with uncooperative partners continued to lose weight. This atypically favorable outcome may be attributable to the monthly sessions, which in effect acted as booster treatments. Second, while the couples training group was significantly superior in terms of absolute weight loss and percentage overweight lost, there were no statistically significant intergroup differences at any point if outcome is measured in terms of the weight reduction quotient. This is an unusual finding, since previous studies have indicated a high correlation between the weight reduction quotient and other indices of weight loss (Wilson, in press). Third, the final followup was only 6 months in duration. The results of a longer followup can only be guessed at, although it appears as though the couples training condition had "bottomed out" at 6 months and no further weight loss was to be expected.

RESEARCH ON THE TREATMENT OF OBESITY: WHERE NEXT?

There are few controlled studies on the long-term efficacy of behavioral treatment of obesity and the data that do exist raise more questions than they provide answers. Clearly the long-term efficacy of behavioral treatment has *not* been convincingly demonstrated. Yet some promising strategies for producing long-term maintenance have begun to be explored and it is premature, to say the least, to conclude that behavioral treatment has been shown to be ineffective. The relevant evidence is nonexistent rather than nonsupportive. What is apparent is that the onus is on behavioral investigators to conduct the necessary studies to evaluate treatment procedures that are derived rationally from the social learning model of behavior change and that incorporate necessary maintenance strategies.

Wanted: Long-Term Followup Studies

Long-term followups of treatment studies must become a research priority. Commitment to this objective will have to take into account the considerations discussed earlier concerning the practical problems and personal payoff for behavioral researchers. Conceptually, the design and evaluation of treatment studies must distinguish between initial weight loss and its maintenance over time (Kingsley & Wilson, 1977). Jeffery *et al.* (1978), for example, found that weight loss at posttreatment was poorly correlated with weight loss at a 1-year followup.

Attenuating Attrition

Attrition rates that are frequently high during treatment itself are likely to be even higher over the course of long-term followup (e.g., Mahoney &

Mahoney, 1976b; Wilson & Brownell, 1978). Explicit steps need to be taken to reduce the number of drop-outs. The following are some procedures that seem to be useful in this respect:

1. Maintenance procedures and long-term followup should be an integral part of the design of a treatment outcome study and should be presented to subjects as such. In commiting themselves to the treatment program, subjects also explicitly commit themselves to the followup. It is *not* something to be tacked on following treatment almost as an afterthought.

2. Frequent personal contact between the investigators and subjects might minimize attrition (Sobell & Sobell, 1976). Regular telephone calls or contact via the mail are cost-efficient means of accomplishing this goal. This continuing contact might well be reactive and function as a form of maintenance strategy in its own right.

3. Contingency contracting—a refundable deposit that subjects lose if they miss followup evaluations—reduces drop-outs (e.g., Hagen, Foreyt, & Dunham, 1976).

The relatively low attrition rates reported by Kingsley and Wilson (1977), and Brownell's (1977) success in following 100% of his subjects attests to the feasibility of reducing drop-outs using the procedures mentioned in the preceding list.

Adherence to Maintenance Strategies

Behavioral treatment attempts to equip clients with self-regulatory skills that they can implement in order to alter eating habits. Clients might acquire these functions but not adhere to the therapist's instructions to implement them in the natural environment. Instigating or motivating clients to adhere to treatment prescriptions might be the key to superior maintenance of treatment-produced weight loss. As is typical of the literature in general, one of the weaknesses of the Kingsley and Wilson (1977) and Ashby and Wilson (1977) studies was their failure to conduct independent evaluations of subjects' compliance with the treatment regimen. Other findings suggest that adherence might be unsatisfactory (e.g., Brownell, 1977; Green, 1976). Some of the variables influencing adherence to behavioral prescriptions are discussed more fully by Bellack (1975), Blackwell (1976), and Wilson and Evans (1976).

Time-Limited versus Target-Oriented Treatment

Controlled outcome studies, as in the research discussed in this chapter, have typically evaluated standardized treatment programs that range from 4 weeks to 3 months in duration. Since behavioral treatment is designed to promote slow but gradual weight loss (ideally about 1–2 pounds per week) this means that the magnitude of weight loss in most studies is about 10–12 pounds (see Jeffery *et al.*, 1978). The logic of the treatment is that clients will continue to apply the self-control methods they have learned and continue to lose additional weight. Unfortunately, it seems that clients do not always continue to implement self-control methods (adherence); and continued weight loss is the exception rather than the rule.

It seems inescapable that the sort of weight loss that is typically produced in treatment outcome studies is not sufficiently reinforcing in itself to ensure continued weight-reducing efforts. But what if treatment were continued until sizeable amounts of weight loss were produced? More particularly, what if treatment were continued until the subject's individual target weight is reached, however long that treatment takes? It might be that at this level subjects will be more motivated to adhere to weight control methods. Since so many overweight clients are seriously overweight, renewed attention might be given to rapid methods of facilitating substantial weight loss, such as drugs or special diets. These methods, which perhaps have been too readily dismissed by behavior therapists, might be useful *adjuncts* as part of the initial treatment program. They could then be faded out as progress toward the ultimate goal of *behavioral self-control* over eating habits and exercise patterns is gradually established.

New Concepts and Treatment Innovations

Behavioral treatment of obesity has been formalized prematurely in terms of a relatively restricted operant conditioning approach. As a result, not only flexibility, but also greater emphasis on cognitive mediating influences have been ignored and even discouraged (Mahoney, 1975; Wilson, 1976). This tendency should change, and the use of a broader social learning model should be encouraged. The role of cognitive factors, such as expectancies on the maintenance of treatment-produced improvement in addictive behaviors, has been emphasized by Mahoney and Mahoney (1976a) and Wilson (in press).

Consider, for example, Bandura's (1977) theory of self-efficacy (Wilson, in press). Specifically, he has argued that changes in an individual's expectations of personal efficacy determine whether or not self-regulatory behavior will be initiated, how much effort will be expended, and how long the person will persist in these behaviors in the face of adverse experiences. Bandura (1977) summarizes evidence showing that self-efficacy expectations can be significantly better predictors of subsequent generalized behavior change than past behavioral performance. In the case of obesity, the treatment target would be more than the modification of overt eating habits; perhaps more importantly it would involve the development of strong, reality-based efficacy expectations about the maintenance of self-control. For example, two clients might show the same degree of behavior change following treatment but differ in terms of their efficacy expectations that might determine the generalization and maintenance of that initial behavior change. Some recent data are consistent with this view. Although strictly correlational in nature, Green (1976) found a significant positive correlation between weight loss and perceived control. In a related fashion, Stuart (1977) reported that one of the most powerful correlates of successful weight reduction is perceived control in coping with food-related situations.

Another question that should be researched is Lazarus' (1976) claim that durable therapeutic change will be effected only to the extent that multimodal therapy that addresses itself to the "basic id" is administered. Lazarus (1976) would insist that present behavioral treatment programs are too narrow in scope to produce lasting change. Certainly the current emphasis on multifaceted behavioral treatment programs is in line with this reasoning. On the other hand, Bellack (1975) has criticized what he calls the "smorgasbord" approach to the treatment of obesity, and there are data that are inconsistent with predictions from multimodal therapy (e.g., McReynolds & Paulsen, 1976).

REFERENCES

Ashby, W. A., & Wilson, G. T. Behavior therapy for obesity: Booster sessions and long-term maintenance of weight loss. *Behaviour Research and Therapy*, 1977, *15*, 451–463.

Azrin, N. H. A strategy for applied research: Learning based but outcome oriented. *American Psychologist*, 1977, *32*, 140–149.

Bandura, A. *Principles of behavior modification*. New York: Holt, Rinehart, & Winston, 1969.

Bandura, A. Self-efficacy: Toward a unifying theory of behavioral change. *Psychological Review*, 1977, *84*, 191–215.

Bellack, A. S. Behavior therapy for weight reduction. *Addictive Behaviors*, 1975, *1*, 73–82.

Bellack, A. S. Behavioral treatment for obesity: Appraisal and recommendations. In M. Hersen, R. M. Eisler, & P. M. Miller (Eds.), *Progress in behavior modification* (Vol. 4). New York: Academic Press, 1977. Pp. 1–38.

Blackwell, B. Treatment adherence. *British Journal of Psychiatry*, 1976, *129*, 513–531.

Brownell, K. D. *The effect of spouse training and partner cooperativeness in the behavioral treatment of obesity*. Unpublished doctoral dissertation, Rutgers University, 1977.

Cochrane, R., & Sobol, M. P. Myth and methodology in behaviour therapy research. In M. P. Feldman & A. Broadhurst (Eds.), *Theoretical and experimental bases of the behaviour therapies*. New York: Wiley, 1976. Pp. 365–404.

Eysenck, H. J., & Rachman, S. *The causes and cures of neurosis*. London: Routledge & Kegan Paul, 1965.

Foreyt, J., & Kennedy, W. Treatment of overweight by aversion therapy. *Behaviour Research and Therapy*, 1971, *9*, 29–34.

Franks, C. M., & Wilson, G. T. *Annual review of behavior therapy: Theory and practice* (Vol. 1). New York: Brunner/Mazel, 1973.

Franks, C. M., & Wilson, G. T. *Annual review of behavior therapy: Theory and practice* (Vol. 3). New York: Brunner/Mazel, 1975.

Franks, C. M., & Wilson, G. T. *Annual review of behavior therapy: Theory and practice* (Vol. 4). New York: Brunner/Mazel, 1976.

Franks, C. M., & Wilson, G. T. *Annual review of behavior therapy: Theory and practice* (Vol. 5). New York: Brunner/Mazel, 1977.

Green, L. *The temporal and stimulus dimensions of self-monitoring in the behavioral treatment of obesity.* Unpublished doctoral dissertation, Rutgers University, 1976.

Hagen, R. L., Foreyt, J. P., & Dunham, T. W. The dropout problem: Reducing attrition in obesity research. *Behavior Therapy*, 1976, 7, 463–471.

Hall, S. M., & Hall, R. G. Outcome and methodological considerations in behavioral treatment of obesity. *Behavior Therapy*, 1974, 5, 352–364.

Hall, S. M., Hall, R. G., Borden, B. L., & Hanson, R. W. Follow-up strategies in the behavioral treatment of overweight. *Behaviour Research and Therapy*, 1975, 13, 167–172.

Hall, S. M., Hall, R. G., Hanson, R. W., & Borden, B. L. Permanence of two self-managed treatments of overweight. *Journal of Consulting and Clinical Psychology*, 1974, 42, 781–786.

Hanson, R. W., Borden, B. L., Hall, S. M., & Hall, R. G. Use of programmed instruction in teaching self-management skills to overweight adults. *Behavior Therapy*, 1976, 7, 366–373.

Harris, M. B., & Bruner, C. G. A comparison of self-control and contract procedures for weight control. *Behaviour Research and Therapy*, 1971, 9, 347–354.

Hunt, W. A., Barnett, L. W., & Branch, L. G. Relapse rates in addiction programs. *Journal of Clinical Psychology*, 1971, 27, 455–456.

Jeffery, R. W., Wing, R. R., & Stunkard, A. J. Behavioral treatment of obesity: The state of the art, 1976. *Behavior Therapy*, 1978, 9, 189–199.

Kazdin, A. E., & Wilson, G. T. *Evaluation of behavior therapy: Issues, evidence and research strategies.* Cambridge, Mass.: Ballinger, 1977.

Keeley, S. M., Shemberg, K. M., & Carbonell, J. Operant clinical intervention: Behavior management or beyond? Where are the data? *Behavior Therapy*, 1976, 7, 292–305.

Kingsley, R. G., & Wilson, G. T. Behavior therapy for obesity: A comparative investigation of long-term efficacy. *Journal of Consulting and Clinical Psychology*, 1977, 45, 288–298.

Lazarus, A. A. *Behavior therapy and beyond.* New York: McGraw-Hill, 1971.

Lazarus, A. A. *Multimodal behavior therapy.* New York: Springer, 1976.

Leitenberg, H. *Handbook of behavior modification and behavior therapy.* Englewood Cliffs, N.J.: Prentice-Hall, 1976.

Levitz, L. S., & Stunkard, A. J. A therapeutic coalition for obesity: Behavior modification and patient self-help. *American Journal of Psychiatry*, 1974, 131, 423–427.

Lovibond, S. *Conditioning and enuresis.* Oxford: Pergamon Press, 1964.

Mahoney, M. J. Self-reward and self-monitoring techniques for weight control. *Behavior Therapy*, 1974, 5, 48–57.

Mahoney, M. J. Fat fiction. *Behavior Therapy*, 1975, 6, 416–418.

Mahoney, K., & Mahoney, M. J. Cognitive factors in weight reduction. In J. D. Krumboltz & C. E. Thoresen (Eds.), *Counseling methods.* New York: Holt, Rinehart, & Winston, 1976. Pp. 99–105. (a)

Mahoney, M. J., & Mahoney, K. Treatment of obesity: A clinical exploration. In G. J. Williams, S. Martin, & J. Foreyt (Eds.), *Obesity: Behavioral approaches to dietary management.* New York: Brunner/Mazel, 1976. Pp. 30–39. (b)

McReynolds, W. T., & Paulsen, B. K. Stimulus control as the behavioral basis of weight loss procedures. In G. J. Williams, S. Martin, & J. Foreyt (Eds.), *Obesity: Behavioral approaches to dietary management.* New York: Brunner/Mazel, 1976. Pp. 43–64.

Mischel, W. *Personality and assessment.* New York: Wiley, 1968.

O'Leary, K. D., & Wilson, G. T. *Behavior therapy: Application and outcome.* Englewood Cliffs, N.J.: Prentice-Hall, 1975.

Öst, L., & Götestam, K. Behavioral and pharmacological treatments for obesity: An experimental comparison. *Addictive Behaviors*, 1976, *1*, 331–338.

Penick, S. B., Filion, R., Fox, S., & Stunkard, A. J. Behavior modification in the treatment of obesity. *Psychosomatic Medicine*, 1971, *33*, 49–55.

Sobell, M. B., & Sobell, L. C. Second year treatment outcome of alcoholics treated by individualized behavior therapy: results. *Behaviour Research and Therapy*, 1976, *14*, 195–216.

Stuart, R. B. Behavioral control of overeating. *Behaviour Research and Therapy*, 1967, *5*, 357–365.

Stuart, R. B. Comments during symposium on obesity, International Congress of Behavior Therapy, Uppsala, Sweden, August 1977.

Stuart, R. B., & Davis, B. *Slim chance in a fat world.* Champaign, Ill.: Research Press, 1972.

Stunkard, A. J. The management of obesity. *New York Journal of Medicine*, 1958, *58*, 79–87.

Stunkard, A. J. New therapies for the eating disorders. *Archives of General Psychiatry*, 1972, *26*, 391–398.

Stunkard, A. J., & Mahoney, M. J. Behavioral treatment of the eating disorders. In H. Leitenberg (Ed.), *Handbook of behavior modification and behavior therapy.* Englewood Cliffs, N.J.: Prentice-Hall, 1976. Pp. 45–73.

Voegtlin, W. L., Lemere, F., Broz, W. R., & O'Hallaren, P. Conditioned reflex therapy of chronic alcoholism. *Quarterly Journal of Studies on Alcohol*, 1942, *2*, 505–511.

Wilson, G. T. Obesity, binge eating, and behavior therapy: Some clinical observations. *Behavior Therapy*, 1976, *7*, 700–702.

Wilson, G. T. Methodological considerations in treatment outcome research in obesity. *Journal of Consulting and Clinical Psychology*, 1978, *46*, 687–702.

Wilson, G. T. Booze, beliefs, and behavior: Cognitive factors in alcohol use and abuse. In P. E. Nathan & G. A. Marlatt (Eds.), *Experimental and behavioral approaches to alcoholism.* New York: Plenum Press, in press.

Wilson, G. T., & Brownell, K. D. Behavior therapy for obesity: Including family members in the treatment process. *Behavior Therapy*, 1978, *9*, 943–945.

Wilson, G. T., & Evans, I. M. Adult behavior therapy and the therapist–client relationship. In C. M. Franks & G. T. Wilson (Eds.), *Annual review of behavior therapy: Theory and Practice* (Vol. 4). New York: Brunner/Mazel, 1976. Pp. 771–792.

Wollersheim, J. P. Effectiveness of group therapy based upon learning principles in the treatment of overweight women. *Journal of Abnormal Psychology*, 1970, *76*, 462–474.

Yates, A. *Theory and practice in behavior therapy.* New York: Wiley, 1975.

12

Bereavement: A Behavioral Treatment of Pathological Grief[1]

R. W. RAMSAY

INTRODUCTION[2]

In this chapter I shall be dealing with the behavioral treatment of pathological grief. The first part will be mainly theoretical, dealing with the characteristics of grief. Then I shall go on to a description of the structure of grief, what it consists of. From there we can branch off into some behavioral theorizing on depression and on grief in particular. From a comparison of phobic behavior and the behavior of pathological grievers, a possible therapeutic approach is proposed, based on flooding and pro-

[1]The Dutch version of this chapter can be found in J. W. G. Orlemans (Ed.), *Handboek voor Gedragstherapie*. Deventer: Van Loghum Slaterus, 1979. The English version appears by permission.

[2]From the psychoanalytic literature we have descriptions of grief processes and the emotions involved, so that the therapist knows in advance what to expect in the way of the nature and content of the emotional responses. Most people are emotionally inhibited, they have learned to suppress feelings; part of the therapist's task is to help the client give structure to the process of feeling and expression, to relearn how to feel, to code it correctly, and to express it in an appropriate way. From the Rogerian school we have learned a lot about how to listen to the client, to know "where the client is" (Gendlin, 1974), and then to help him further in his emotional work. From the psychoanalysts we have learned about the structure of bereavement processes. From the Gestalt therapists we have learned much, but the present treatment basically remains a behavior therapy approach of flooding, repeated confrontation, with prolonged exposure and response prevention where the client tries to escape or avoid.

TRENDS IN BEHAVIOR THERAPY   ISBN 0-12-647450-8

longed exposure. The major part of the chapter will be devoted to a detailed look at the therapy, with the emphasis on how the clinician can actually go about the treatment. We shall deal with topics like indications and contraindications for therapy, preparation for treatment, how to begin, a typical session, when to end, and some of the difficulties and pitfalls that may be encountered. I have tried throughout to illustrate what I have to say by citing actual case material.

Some people may want to skip the theory, with the idea, "Don't bore me with the background, just tell me what to do." I would suggest that you not skip too lightly over the background structure of a bereavement process. The therapy is not easy, and the background knowledge is the best guide for how to do a good job. The knowledge of the structure is a sort of road map to help in planning the therapy and to give you leads when you get lost and bogged down in dead ends.

BACKGROUND

In clinical practice we sometimes see clients presenting us with a reactive depression caused by a significant loss, where the link between the present problems and the precipitating event is beyond doubt. More often, we see clients with a mixture of symptoms—depression, psychosomatic ailments, phobias, relationship problems, etc.—where it is difficult (or impossible) to make out the causes. In some of these cases, we can form a hypothesis, a clinical hunch, that the problems are the result of an unresolved bereavement process. As an example: In one study of 135 severe agoraphobics, Roth (1959) found that bereavement played a major role in the onset of problems:

> The association (of the first breakdown) with calamitous circumstances was striking. The illness had frequently followed closely on a bereavement or a suddenly developing illness in a close relative or friend (37%), illness in, or an acute danger to the patient himself (31%), and frequently severance of family ties or acute domestic stress, which often constituted threat to marriage (15%) [p. 16].

Thus in more than half the cases, a bereavement process or a threat thereof was the precipitating factor for the phobia.

If the stress of bereavement plays such an important part in many clinical problems, it is useful to look into it in detail, to understand what this process is, and to be able to help people through when they get "hung up." In this chapter we shall be looking closely at what bereavement is and how we can deal with it when it goes wrong.

The loss of a significant object, a close relative, a marriage relationship, a valued possession, wealth, or position, the loss of a part of one's body due to illness or accident, are extremely stressful experiences that will occur in each individual's lifetime, and possibly on a number of occasions. Changes in life, leaving school, changing jobs, or moving to another neighborhood, may entail some bereavement concerning what is left behind, but these changes usually produce little stress, since they are planned in advance, time is available to prepare for the losses, and the experience of change may be positive. However, the loss of one's parents, a husband or wife, a child, or the refugee's loss of his homeland is usually the loss of a valued relationship that the individual cannot be prepared for ahead of time and where what is lost can never be completely replaced. The stress in these cases can be severe. In this chapter, for convenience, we shall mainly deal with bereavement due to the loss of a partner, and, for further convenience, we shall usually refer to the grieving widow. What we have to say on the bereavement process though, can be translated to other forms of loss.

MOURNING AND GRIEF

Averill (1968) used the term bereavement behavior to denote the total response pattern, psychological and physiological, displayed by a person following the loss of a significant object. This response pattern has two aspects, mourning and grief. Mourning refers to the conventional behavior as determined by the mores and customs of the society; grief is the stereotyped set of psychological and physiological reactions of biological origin.

Mourning as a ritual may contain little or no affect, and grief may occur outside the mourning procedure—the two patterns may occur independently of each other, but they are generally closely related and implement each other. The grief reactions, however, are the therapist's only concern. Averill (1968) summarized the major features of grief as follows:

1. Grief is a complex but stereotyped response pattern that includes such psychological and physiological symptoms as withdrawal, fatigue, sleep disturbances, and loss of appetite.
2. It is elicited by a rather well-defined stimulus situation, namely, the real or imagined loss of a significant object (or role), and it is resolved when new object relations are established.
3. It is a ubiquitous phenomenon among human beings and appears in other social species as well, especially in higher primates.
4. It is an extremely stressful emotion, both psychologically and physiologically, and yet behavior during grief is often antithetical to the establishment of new relations, and hence the alleviation of the stress.

PHASES OR COMPONENTS?

Some people talk about *phases*, while others use the term *components*. Bugen (1977) criticizes the phases (stages) concept on a number of grounds:

> The "stage" concepts of grieving contain a number of theoretical weaknesses and inconsistencies. First, the stages are not separate entities, but subsume one another or blend dynamically. Second, the stages are not successive; any individual may experience anger, for instance, prior to denial, or perhaps disorganization before shock. Third, it is not necessary to experience every stage. Depression, or for that matter any volatile emotion, may never be a recognizable response to loss. Fourth, the intensity and duration of any stage may vary idiosyncratically among those who grieve. For one mourner, sadness may be a short-lived experience, while anger is a more protracted stage; the duration of these two emotional stages might be reversed for someone else. Finally, little empirical evidence is offered by proponents to substantiate the theory of stages [pp. 196–197].

In spite of Bugen's criticisms of the stages model, we feel that in planning and carrying out therapy, it is useful to have a general idea of what a grief process consists of, even though individual differences are great. For example, there is almost invariably a stage of desolation, with uncontrollable crying outbursts. If this has not occurred, we can be fairly sure that the whole process has been delayed or distorted. If there has been no experience of protest and aggression, that lends weight to our hypothesis of pathology. Add to all this continuing searching behavior long after the death of the loved one, and we can safely say that the process has not yet been worked through. We do not find it sufficient just to say, as Bugen (1977) does, "that the existence of *a variety of emotional states* is the essential point, and *not* the need to order them [p. 197]." We agree, however, that the muddle of stages and components has caused theoretical and practical difficulties. Emotions of yearning and pining, motor behavior of searching, illusory perception of seeing and hearing the deceased; the condition of shock; the cognition of denial; these are dissimilar articulations of the grief process. To try to get some order into the confusion, we would like to propose a scheme (see Figure 12.1), knowing that it is not the last word, and hoping that others will revise it. We do not know whether one will have to experience *all* phases and components. Probably not, as individual differences are so great, but it is important that the therapist knows which phases and components *can* exist so that explorations can be made to check if one component is causing problems.

Shock

Shock can be only momentary or it can be prolonged even for weeks. The subjective experience is one of numbness, an inability to let the fact of

Shock
Disorganization
Denial
```
                    ┌ Searching behavior
                    │ Emotional components
                    │   Desolate pining
                    │   Despair
                    │   Guilt
                    │   Anxiety
                    │   Jealousy
                    │   Shame
                    └ Protest, aggression
```
Resolution and acceptance
Reintegration

FIGURE 12.1. *Phases of grieving.*

the death come through, often coupled with feelings of depersonalization and derealization. It seems likely that the duration and intensity of this phase corresponds with the amount of difficulty with which the rest of the bereavement process will be worked through.

Disorganization

The disorganization phase varies enormously from one person to another, with some people being completely paralyzed and incapable of doing anything, ranging to the exact opposite, where the griever efficiently and seemingly without difficulty organizes everything from the funeral to the pension legalities to the disposing of the deceased's clothes. In these two phases of shock and (dis)organization, the social network plays the major supportive role, with possibly some medical assistance from the family doctor, or some religious help, and some professional legal advice. A therapist would seldom be involved at this stage, although Raphael (1975) advocates some, limited, psychiatric intervention for high-risk persons.

Searching Behavior

Searching behavior can range from mild restlessness without knowing the cause, through catching oneself waiting for the deceased to come home at the usual hour, or listening for his footsteps, to an active searching in various places where earlier he could have been found. This heightened alertness for the lost person often results in the griever "seeing" him on the street, hearing his voice, or at least feeling his presence. These illusions can be very real and very frightening. The searching and the illusions usually drop away gradually, or extinguish, as the behavior is never followed by the reinforcement of finding the lost person. When the grief is pathological and needs professional intervention, response prevention may be necessary, if the searching is still in evidence.

Emotional Components

Emotional reactions occur concomitantly with the searching, but usually last longer. These we prefer to call *components*, since they can appear in any order, with varying intensity and importance for different persons. These emotions are not constant and always present; they ebb and flow, coming in waves, one giving way to another in quick succession. They have in common, though, that they are all extremely painful. This is the important part for any therapy, and therefore we explore the origins of these components.

What we call *desolate pining* has often been called depression. This latter word we prefer not to use; it is too broad and all-encompassing, bringing with it connotations of psychiatric symptomatology that are inappropriate (e.g., the overwhelming feelings of worthlessness seen in psychotic depressions are seldom encountered in grief). What we want to describe may be called grief, but with an aspect of yearning. This is the deep, empty feeling, interspersed with waves of intense psychic pain, with frequent outbursts of crying, often uncontrollable. There is a sense of yearning and longing that cannot be fulfilled. There are often physical symptoms accompanying these feelings: restlessness, nausea, vomiting, loss of appetite, poor sleep, choking sensations, and various hyperventilation phenomena. The uncontrollable aspect of the crying usually soon disappears; the griever learns to "save" the anguish, not be overwhelmed by it, but to give in to it at times when it will not be disruptive (e.g., when alone at home). If this component is not in evidence by the time of the funeral, it is a sign of a poor prognosis, yet mourners are often praised by the social network for being brave and not breaking down. (The stiff upper lip, the "Jackie Kennedy Syndrome," is not universal. In certain societies, paid mourners, brought in to cry and howl, will continue wailing the deceased's name until the griever joins in.)

Despair is the term we can use for the feelings of helplessness and hopelessness. The pining is an active feeling, going along with the searching, whereas the despair is the dark bleakness of realizing the full impact of the impotence to change things.

Guilt can arise from many sources, and it is not of much value to try to distinguish "real" from "imagined." A thought of "Drop dead" in a quarrel before a fatality can be just as troublesome as causing a traffic accident in which a loved one is killed. Where the relationship was an ambivalent one, this component is particularly complex. There is often the feeling of release from a difficult partnership, with the accompanying guilt for not feeling sad. There is the guilt arising from aggressive feelings and thoughts toward the dead; guilt from omissions or commissions of deeds prior to the death; guilt for being selfishly busy with yourself and not being able to give enough attention to others, usually the children. This aggression against oneself can be severe enough to lead to suicide.

Anxiety comes from many sources, with questions such as "What is going to happen to me? How am I going to cope? What changes will have to be made? Can we manage financially?" There is also anxiety from what at the moment is happening to the griever: the loss of control over the emotions, the feeling of going mad, the fear of aggressive acts and thoughts, the inability to cope with even the smallest task.

Jealousy as a component, we thought for some time, was only associated with grief reactions arising from separation and divorce—the person imagining the ex-partner with another. However, jealousy also seems to be common after a death. The widow envies other women who still have husbands; parents who have lost a child will envy and hate other parents with children. As these feelings are often intense while at the same time regarded as unnatural and unacceptable, guilt is an added burden.

Shame as an emotional component can take the form of the griever being ashamed to allow others to see her feelings, and in trying to suppress them, the process is made more difficult and prolonged. Many people, because of the shame they feel, isolate themselves from family and friends and then resent the fact that they have little contact with others. The griever can also be ashamed of the position in which he or she has been placed. Widows often report that they are ashamed of their status as widows and break off contact with former friends who are married couples.

Aggression is the most difficult of the emotional components to accept and to work through, probably because of the social taboos on aggressive thoughts and deeds, especially toward the dead. There is an irritability directed against family and friends, often regarded as unjustified and therefore adding to the guilt, and aggression against those surrounding the death, doctors and nurses, who did not prevent it from occurring. There is often diffuse protest against God or fate—anguished cries of "Why did you do this to me? Why me?" The most difficult part, though, is the primitive anger against the person who died, leaving the griever in the lurch and in so much pain and misery. The aggression is usually expressed in far subtler ways than the other emotions. Where the grief is usually expressed in obvious outbursts of crying, the anger often is not obvious and may easily be missed if the therapist is not alert for it. Nor is it necessary for the anger to be expressed in an outburst for it to be dealt with adequately; an imagined conversation with the deceased containing veiled aggression may be all that is needed.

Denial

In Figure 12.1, denial has been placed outside the phases and components, as it plays a part throughout the process. The searching and the
illusions are a manner of denial; with the emotional components, the denial ebbs and returns, breaks down and then comes back again in full force.
It can be interpreted as a defense mechanism, and it is a protection from
too much pain all at once, yet it prolongs the process and thus lengthens
the duration of that pain. There is not only denial that the loss has occurred, but also denial of the emotions connected with the loss. Many
people suppress their feelings, do not or cannot feel the guilt, anger, or
grief. For these people, emotional training with modeling and prompting
will be needed to stimulate the client to experience feelings again.

Resolution and Acceptance

Resolution and acceptance can take place suddenly or gradually over
time. As the searching diminishes, as the emotional components gradually
extinguish so that the waves of feelings become less intense, of shorter
duration, and with longer periods between them, as the denial breaks
down more and more and becomes unnecessary, there is a resolution of
the process and an acceptance that the calamity has occurred; it is a taking
leave of the dead and an acceptance that life must go on, in a changed form
where the departed has no central place.

Reintegration

We see reintegration as the long, difficult process of putting the resolution and acceptance into practice in everyday life—carrying out the consequences of the psychic changes. This is not a smooth process but suffers
many interruptions and setbacks, especially at anniversaries and festive
occasions. Reintegration can take a long time and can be painful at times.
There are many habits that are only meaningful within a relationship;
when the partner dies these habits will tend to persist, and only slowly will
the remaining partner realize that the carrying out of these is no longer
adequate. There are so many of these habits, in so many different areas,
that it will take years to change. Examples would be: deciding in a super-
market to buy a certain food—why, because he liked it; putting on the blue
dress—why, because he always admired it; asking, should we go to Spain
this year for our holiday—why, because he always enjoyed the Cuba Libre;
let's watch that program on TV—he always found it amusing. These habits
die hard, and it is only in the continuing to live on that one catches oneself
in this way of thinking. There is a moment of pain and a realization that
things are different now. And different means difficult.

PATHOLOGICAL GRIEF REACTIONS

The grief responses to a significant loss are not always present—the "normal" reactions of shock, despair, and recovery are often distorted, exaggerated, prolonged, inhibited, or delayed. These terms are, of course, for easy reference, and no hard dividing line can be drawn between normal and pathological. However, there is reasonable agreement in the literature that grief *has* to be worked through; if it is not, the person will continue to have troubles of some sort. Lindemann (1944) states with regard to the grief work that "one of the big obstacles to this work seems to be the fact that many patients try to avoid the intense distress connected with the grief experience and to avoid the expression of emotion necessary for it [p. 143]." Hodge (1972) puts it more strongly:

> The problems must be brought into the open and confronted, no matter how unpleasant it may be for the patient. *The grief work must be done.* There is no healthy escape from this. We might even add that the grief work *will* be done. Sooner or later, correctly or incorrectly, completely or incompletely, in a clear or a distorted manner, *it will be done.* People have a natural protective tendency to avoid the unpleasantness of the grief work, but it is necessary and the more actively it is done the shorter will be the period of grief. If the grief work is not actively pursued, the process may be fixated or aborted or delayed, with the patient feeling that he may have escaped it. However, almost certainly a distorted form of the grief work will appear at some time in the future [pp. 230–231].

DIFFICULT PROCESSES

Some bereavement processes may be more difficult to work through than others. Parkes (1975) states: "It has often been asserted that sudden unexpected bereavements are a likely cause of pathological grief [p. 119]." In a study conducted in Boston, Parkes found that "many of the members of the Short Preparation Group are still, two to four years after bereavement unable to throw off their ties to their dead spouse. . . . So strong are the memories of the world now passed that the present world seems unreal by comparison [pp. 133–134]." It thus appears that anticipatory grief plays an important part in the successful working through of this process. Where no time for preparation has been given, the chance of chronicity increases.

Bereavement after a suicide is another important complicating factor. Shneidman (1973) states that in the case of suicide, the largest public health problem is neither the prevention of suicide nor the management of suicide attempts, but the alleviation of the effects of stress in the survivor-victims of the suicidal deaths, whose lives are forever changed and who, over a period of years, number in the millions. Guilt and aggression in these cases can be so strong and painful that the victim is unable to work them through. We have only limited clinical experience with survivor-victims of murders, and, as was expected, aggression was the most important and difficult of emotional components.

Another factor making for difficulties is the death of a child. Many authors report that people can accept the death of an adult far more easily than that of a child. We have no evidence on this, but clinical experience inclines us to believe it to be true. Length of relationship does not seem to be an important factor influencing outcome, but the type of relationship does. A good relationship with the partner before death is a favorable prognostic sign; a love/hate or a passive clinging relationship will make a bereavement process more complex and intense.

No work on personality factors has yet, to our knowledge, been done, but we would predict that emotionally labile people, those high on Eysenck's personality factor of neuroticism, would fare less well than stable people; the labile person will experience more intense subjective pain.

PHOBIAS

Eysenck (1967) has proposed a theoretical course of development of phobic behavior. In the first place, there is a single traumatic event, or else a series of subtraumatic events producing unconditioned but strong emotional reactions. At the second stage, conditioning takes place, in the sense that previously neutral stimuli become connected with the unconditioned stimulus or stimuli. From now on, the conditioned (CSs) as well as the unconditioned stimuli (UCSs) produce strong emotional behavior. Stimulus and response generalization take place, and the complex of maladaptive reactions becomes persistent. In order to account for lack of extinction in certain cases, the third stage is as follows: Approaching the CS gives rise to conditioned fear and anxiety reactions; withdrawing from the CS would reduce the emotional response, thus being reinforcing; hence the subject would become conditioned to avoid the CS, making extinction unlikely. It is not always possible to avoid all the CSs completely, so an additional factor is postulated to account for the lack of extinction in these cases. This is incubation, or the "Napalkov phenomenon" (Eysenck, 1967). Under certain conditions, not yet clearly understood, it has been found that the response strength increases over time with or without further presentation of unreinforced CSs. Thus, an originally fairly weak unconditioned stimulus–unconditioned response bond can result in time in a conditioned response (CR) that is of such strength as to seem out of proportion to the situation. In clinical practice, when using systematic desensitization and flooding, it has been observed that when strong CRs are aroused for short periods of time, they tend to increase in strength instead of extinguish.

PHOBIAS AND GRIEF

Here we would like to propose a link between grief and phobias. Phobic reactions are characterized by anxiety in, and avoidance of, an objectively harmless situation (Barendregt, 1973; Marks, 1969). A person whose prepotent response pattern is to avoid confrontations and escape from difficult situations is a potential phobic. The loss of a significant object entails the consequence that numerous stimuli and situations will evoke the pain and anguish that the loss causes. A person whose prepotent response pattern is to avoid confrontations and to escape from difficult situations will not tackle the "grief work" and will tend to get "stuck" in the grief reactions. If these two suppositions are correct, then we should expect to find a number of reactive depressives with phobic patterns of life and a number of phobics suffering pathological grief. In clinical practice it is not rare to hear statements such as: "The problems started just after the death of my mother" or "After we moved from X to Y, I started having trouble going out and meeting people." The main point to be made here is that there are some superficial similarities between phobias and pathological grief reactions, and if we take it further and look at the behavior of people suffering from unresolved grief, we see avoidance behavior similar to that of phobics. Many of the former will not enter situations that will evoke the sense of loss: Certain streets are avoided, personal belongings are not touched, "linking objects" (Volkan, Cilluffo, & Sarvay, 1976) are locked away, certain tunes are never played. The stimuli and situations that could get the grief work going, that could elicit the undesired responses so that extinction could take place, are avoided. From Eysenck's theoretical explanation of how phobic reactions develop and are maintained, we would expect some grieving people to get "hung up" or even to become more depressed and miserable over time as they avoid and escape.

This explanation can, of course, be supplemented by the social reinforcement theory (Seitz, 1971) that depression is a function of inadequate or insufficient reinforcers. A widow whose reinforcers consisted of doing everything with and for her husband suddenly finds herself left with no positive reinforcers when he dies. Everything is now meaningless to her. A further supplement to the theorizing about depressions is Seligman's (1975) concept of "learned helplessness" (see Abramson, Seligman & Teasdaler, Chapter 6 of this volume). We are powerless in the face of death or an important loss, all action is futile, and so the person stops responding in ways that would eventually alleviate the stress. No "working through" of the bereavement takes place.

To summarize so far, a person suffering from pathological grief has lost a major portion of the positive reinforcers in life, has learned that nothing helps to relieve the stress, and so either does nothing in the way of confronting herself with the situations that could lead to an extinction of the negative conditioned emotional responses, or, like the phobic, actively avoids those situations.

Treatment of phobics by means of flooding and prolonged exposure to the CSs that arouse the conditioned emotional responses has been shown to be highly effective (Marks, 1972). In a limited number of single case studies carried out by myself and colleagues, flooding and prolonged exposure has been found to be highly effective in the treatment of pathological grief reactions. This is not to say that the technique is simple. Systematic desensitization has been shown to be effective with phobics, but for grief we have found no gentle equivalent; the therapist can grade the confrontation in a roughly hierarchical fashion, but the emotional reactions, when they occur, are usually intense. In the selection of stimuli that elicit phobic reactions, the procedure is usually fairly straightforward: Most phobics can produce lists of situations that frighten them and that are regularly avoided. With grief, it takes much searching to find the stimuli that will elicit the conditioned emotional responses.

TREATMENT

Most people get over their grief reactions in their own way and at their own rate, albeit with difficulty, and, therefore, never need treatment. Some never even start on their grief work; for example, if after 50 years of married life the husband suddenly dies, the wife will often go on setting a place for him at the table, talking to the empty chair, and talking to others about what they are doing together. In such cases, no one would try to break down the denial. In some cases, though, the person gets hung up on one or more of the components and will need to be helped through. This proposed treatment is not intended to take away grief, but to normalize it in some cases where it goes wrong.

Indications for Bereavement Therapy

CLEAR-CUT CASES

As we said in the introduction, some people come for help with a clear-cut case of unresolved grief. If the loss has been within the previous year, this is a normal reaction and it would probably be better if the professional encouraged the griever to try and work it through on her own, with help from others in the social network. Where there is no adequate social network, a supportive, empathic treatment of a nondirective nature, as suggested by Raphael (1975) may be indicated, but certainly not the type of treatment to be described here. Only in exceptional circumstances would we advocate a flooding approach within the first year of loss. One such exception was a 34-year-old woman, who, 6 months after her husband's death, threatened to kill herself and her 6-month-old daughter. The choices were, homicide and suicide, an intensive flooding treatment, or a long period of hospitalization where it was estimated that it would take her years to work it through, with the consequent deleterious effects on her and her daughter. (This case is described in Ramsay, 1976.)

For those still grieving more than a year after the loss, one would have to assess the client's ability to withstand the stress of the treatment, the efficacy of the social network to support the client during the treatment, and the possibilities open to the client for making a new life. A person with a long history of psychiatric problems prior to the loss would probably not be able to withstand the stress of the therapy; a widow with three young children and no close family to fall back on would not be a candidate unless someone could be found to temporarily take over the responsibilities of looking after the children; a widow of 65 could profit more from a supportive contact than a flooding approach. As in all therapies, the fewer the complications, the safer the therapist can feel in offering this treatment. Measuring against young, attractive, verbal, intelligent, social (YAVIS) persons in a supportive social network (they would not need treatment), the therapist has to use his clinical judgment as to where he draws the line and chooses a less drastic but possibly less effective approach. An example of a good candidate has been a 48-year-old woman, married to a doctor, with two daughters, who lost her 18-year-old son in an unsuccessful heart operation; after 3 years she was still severely depressed. Another example of a good candidate was a Jewish woman, 54 years old, intelligent, introspective, married, with three children, whose parents were liquidated in Nazi concentration camps during the war; after more than 30 years she asked for help to finally bury her parents.

Where there is a danger of suicide, the therapy would need to be carried out in a hospital with appropriate facilities. As with most other forms of psychotherapy, psychosis is a contraindication for treatment, although there have been cases successfully treated where the MMPI psychotic scales showed frighteningly high scores. These scores returned to normal after treatment, indicating that it was the pathological grief itself that was inflating them, not that the client had a psychotic personality structure.

EMBEDDED GRIEF REACTIONS

More often than the clear-cut cases, one sees various neurotic problems where, on careful examination, a hypothesis can be formed that an unresolved bereavement plays an important or vital part in the problems. An example would be a 26-year-old woman with typical agoraphobic complaints that had started after her divorce. She was afraid of meeting her ex-husband on the street and had a diffuse aggression against men in general. Where the grief reaction is embedded, treating this alone *can* result in dramatic changes, the phobia evaporating rapidly. More often there is still a need for some conventional therapy, although the obstinacy of the neurosis will have been substantially weakened.

Preparations for Treatment

Let us assume that the therapist is faced with a clear-cut bereavement problem and has decided that a behavior therapy is indicated and possible. I find it important that the client be told in advance what this form of treatment entails, the harshness of it, and what alternatives are available. Some clients decide on the basis of this information on a less implosive but more protracted alternative; two clients so far have, out of fear of the therapy, gone to work on themselves and pulled themselves through without the need of professional help. The client must know that it will be difficult and painful and that things will get worse before they get better.

RULES

I lay down certain ground rules that the client must agree to abide by:

1. You may not break off the treatment halfway. There will be a tendency at the low points to want to stop, but that is exactly when you have to go on. I then set a time limit of X weeks or months, X being a rough estimate of how long the therapy will take, multiplied by two. If we are not finished within that time, we can renegotiate.
2. You may not commit suicide during the treatment; afterward you may do what you like, but no suicide during therapy. Most clients laugh at this, but it has helped on a number of occasions that the client is bound by a promise for a limited time.
3. If there is a real danger of suicide and/or breaking off the treatment, you must be prepared for a short period of hospitalization.
4. You may become angry with me during the therapy, but you may not hit me or break up the furniture.
5. Finally, you and I will be working together as a team on a problem—your grief. If I go too fast or push too hard, say so and we can come to a compromise; if my probing becomes too painful, tell me to ease up. You have as much say in the matter as I have.

MEDICATION

If the client is on tranquilizers or antidepressants, this is fully discussed with the client and the prescribing physician. I have the impression, shared by many colleagues, that medication inhibits or at least slows down the working through of grief. If the client and the physician can agree, antidepressant medication is stopped, tranquilizers and sleeping pills are limited to an absolute minimum, with no tranquilizers on the day of a session, before we go to work. It is difficult enough for the therapist to break through the inhibitions to get at the client's emotions; with an added barrier of tranquilizers this is often impossible.

IMPORTANT OTHERS

After describing the treatment and outlining the rules, and in most cases giving the client a pamphlet on bereavement to take home and read, the client is asked to take time to think it over and discuss it with others before making a decision. If, at the next contact, the client agrees to this form of therapy, another appointment is made with the client and a significant other in the client's life—usually the partner. If there is a partner, I regard this contact as vital; if the support is from various family members or friends, a contact with them may not be necessary. The therapist can usually get some impression of the patterns of interaction within the relationship, which may play a part in the therapy; for example, having met the partner may make the therapist decide to advise the client that between sessions it would be better not to discuss certain topics with the partner. On the other hand, the partner may be a valuable co-therapist.

I usually outline once again the goals of therapy and what we expect to take place. If the partner knows what is going on, where and with whom, he/she is much more likely to be able to do the right thing. I repeat the rules, so that the partner knows of the promise of no suicide. I also give my telephone number, business and private, to both the client and the partner, with the invitation that they can always phone if in difficulty. This has so far not been abused. The partner is also asked to go easy on the client during the period of the therapy, sometimes taking over the care of the children, doing the household chores, or not planning a busy social program. The partner is also warned that there will be changes in the relationship after the therapy, especially where the client's depression has been of long standing. I cannot predict what changes will take place, but where one partner has been low and depressed for years and then, usually in the space of a few weeks, alters drastically, adjustments that have been made to incorporate the depression will need to be reversed. Where both partners have suffered the loss, I invite both to take part in the therapy, but until now this has been consistently declined. In some therapies that I have supervised but have not carried out myself, it has been possible to involve the whole family and have them grieve together.

The partner has the opportunity to ask questions that may have been bothering him, to get to know the therapist, and to assure himself that the therapist is a person competent to deal with the problems. (Most partners express pleasure at having been able to meet and talk to the therapist and to know that they can make further contact if necessary.) The most frequent question asked is: "If she is acting strange, must I encourage her to talk about it, or ignore her?" The only answer I know to this question is to ask the partner to be prepared to listen empathically if the client wants to talk, but not to force it if the client wants privacy.

THE PHYSICAL SETTING

A setting can facilitate or inhibit the therapy. It is easier to cry in dim light than in bright, and the client is going to have to cry. A box of tissues discreetly placed within view and reach not only gives implicit permission but is an invitation to cry. The client is going to be making some noise, anything from low sobbing to piercing shrieks. If the client can only deal with anguish by screaming, the therapist will need some sound-proofed room (a video studio is ideal, and you might even get permission to turn on the cameras as well). One telephone interruption can ruin a whole session, so install a switch to be able to turn it off. Comfortable chairs make the long sessions more bearable.

PLANNING THE SESSIONS

I used to think that daily sessions were best to get the client through the depths of despair and pain as quickly as possible. Experience has shown that for most people, daily sessions do not allow enough time between sessions to deal emotionally with what has happened within a session. Three per week is probably best, but difficult for most therapists to arrange. Further, clients differ in their need for time between sessions— one client needed about 3 weeks to work through and digest the experience of each session. The ideal is to work out a way to get through the client's deep, dark despair as quickly as possible, without exhausting the client to the point that no work can be done. If the client starts complaining in terms like, "I almost phoned you today to cancel the appointment"; "I don't feel up to doing any work today, please can't we take a break," then you are probably going too fast and too hard. What happens between sessions is just as vital as what is going on within a session.

I find the traditional 50-minute hour too short for this type of therapy; to be on the safe side I find I need 2 hours before the next appointment. One and one-half hour is planned for the actual therapy, and a margin of one-half hour is allowed for two possibilities:

1. A reaction may get out of hand and may not be worked through in the allotted time. This occasionally happens and it is unpleasant to ask a client to leave in the middle of an emotional outburst, or else the next appointment has to be delayed.
2. The therapist often needs time after a session to get back to a frame of mind where other tasks can be tackled. More on this later.

Some therapists make the sessions last up to 6 hours. This I would consider too tiring for the client, and I personally would not be able to last. If possible, the next appointment after a session should be for some type of work totally different from bereavement. It would be inadvisable to plan the start of a bereavement therapy when a vacation will be a disruption in the middle of the process. A behavior therapy for phobic complaints can usually withstand an interruption due to the absence of the therapist or client. This is not the case with bereavement, since the client gets worse before getting better, and it is unfair to the client if the therapist goes on a holiday while the client is in the depths of a depression.

Starting Therapy

After the initial diagnostic interviews, an appointment is made to begin the actual therapy. The client is usually terrified of what is going to happen, so that it is best to start as quickly as possible. Discussing the anxiety is only prolonging the agony and is an escape behavior on the part of both therapist and client. The therapist can briefly review what he will be trying to do and then should launch in. The question is, where to begin?

In many cultures, part of the rituals surrounding death entails that the family and friends call round and ask to be told the whole story of how it happened, so that the mourner is forced to review, over and over again, the situation as it was, before, during, and after the death. There is a lot of wisdom in some of these customs, and it seems to be a good way for the therapist to start. Humans have the ability to re-create events from the past, and the mourner during that period was more than likely in a state of shock, not capable of feeling in an appropriate way. Also, not having had time enough to feel, as everything went too fast, re-creation of the sequence of events will give the opportunity and time to bring the feelings into tune with what happened.

A possible start may be as follows: Therapist: "Good morning Mrs. X, we'll be getting to know each other quite well, so let's drop the formalities right away. My name is Ron, yours is...? Anne? Okay, Anne, you remember that last time I said that the purpose of the therapy is to get at your feelings; if you want to cry, do it! If you feel like getting angry, do it! Now, I guess you're scared of what is going to happen, so let's get into it. Could you tell me once again how he died, how you first knew about it, what happened afterward? Take your time and tell me in as much detail as you can remember." Most people will start crying at some time during the relating of this and will then try to stifle their sobs, apologizing for breaking down and not being able to continue with the story. The therapist can then encourage the client to continue with the crying by saying: "Please don't say I'm sorry, and please let go and have a good cry. You couldn't cry properly then, take the time now to do it. That's what we're here for."

In listening to the story, the therapist can be forming hypotheses as to which parts may be potential trouble spots: guilt or aggression, despair, protest, etc. For example, a 48-year-old woman whose 18-year-old son died after an unsuccessful heart operation, related: "We went to visit him on the Saturday evening, and after visiting hours ended at 9 o'clock, my husband and I went back to the hotel for a bite to eat. At about 11 o'clock we got a message to come back to the hospital where we were told that he had died." *Hypothesis:* She feels guilty that she left him at such a crucial time—she abandoned him when he most needed her, and she went off with her husband. She went on to relate that as they were in a foreign country, they thought that their duty was to get back to their two daughters as quickly as possible, so they went home on the Monday, leaving friends to see to the cremation and the scattering of the ashes. *Hypothesis:* She deserted him again. In her story she went on to say that she had wanted to have the body flown home, but her husband and one of the doctors had dissuaded her from doing this. *Hypothesis:* Anger against the husband and the doctor for making her desert her son, anger against herself for allowing herself to be dissuaded.

After the story is finished, the therapist can discuss points of possible importance, or omissions, ask for further clarification, or request that the client repeat a particular part: "When you were telling me about standing in that room being told by the doctor that your son was dead, you were crying just now. That is a difficult scene for you—can you tell me again how it went." Or, the therapist could say: "I could imagine that you feel that you deserted him on that Saturday evening. You didn't know it then that he was dying, but you know it now. Could you tell me again how you left the hospital after visiting hours." In this way the client is forced to confront the situation, to stay with that confrontation in a prolonged exposure, and to allow the emotions that are coupled with the stimulus situation to be evoked and to extinguish.

After a number of emotional outbursts, I usually end the first session within about an hour, so as not to be too hard on the client too soon. The amount of emotionality should be regulated to what the client can take, without destroying her motivation to continue therapy. One way of ending a session is to review with the client what has taken place during the session: "Okay, Anne, I think you've done enough work for one day. You told me about what happened, and there were a few scenes that were very difficult for you. You did very well. What happened is something to cry about, and you need space and time to cry. That's what we're here for. You'll probably feel tired for the rest of the day, but you probably won't be able to switch off in your mind what we did this morning. If you have the opportunity, go over it again at home, and if you have to cry again, do it. Now, I suggest a visit to the washroom to freshen up, and then a walk around the block before driving home."

If relating the story does not evoke any emotional response, the therapist will need to find situations where he thinks a particular feeling would be appropriate and probable and discuss this with the client, keeping distance for the time being: "The nurse only allowed you one minute to be with his body after he died, before bustling you out of the room. Now, if you heard that that had happened to someone else, would it surprise you if that person became angry with the nurse? No, it wouldn't surprise you. You can accept on an intellectual level that the anger in that situation is a possibility? But you neither feel nor felt anger? Okay, let's go back to the situation and re-create it not as it went but as you would have liked it to go. The nurse tells you to leave, but you now refuse. Say to her, 'Nurse, that was my son, he's dead now and will soon be buried; I surely deserve a little time with him; I've got so little left, please don't send me away so soon.' But she did send you away. You had only one minute with him and now he's gone forever. That nurse took him away from you before you had time to say goodbye. If you could see that nurse again, what would you like to say to her?" In this way the therapist first gets agreement on the reasonableness of an emotion and then sets the stage for a possible reaction of anger or grief. If necessary, the therapist goes further with modeling and prompting: "Imagine that she is sitting here now, sitting in that chair. Tell her how you feel, tell her, 'You gave me so little time, I wanted to be with him, but you wouldn't let me.'"

Progression

A new session begins with inquiries about things that have happened since the previous visit. How did the client feel after the last session, did she do any "homework," are there any leads that suggest how we are to progress? If no leads are given, I usually repeat that we are working as a team, therefore she has as much say as I have in the therapy, and then ask her if she has any suggestions as to where we can begin.

This initial exploration at the beginning of a session should be kept brief and to the point. Because working on the problem is difficult and painful, for both client and therapist, there is a natural tendency for both to enter into a collusion to work on a substitute problem. The client may relate that she feels guilty toward the children because she is spending so much time thinking about herself and not giving enough time and attention to the children; that's a real problem at the moment, and maybe it would be worthwhile to deal with. However, in the bereavement therapy, this is a sidetrack that is enticing but should be avoided with a remark like: "Let's rather work on the main problem, then you'll have more time for your children and your guilt will disappear by itself."

The question to the client, "Where shall we begin today?" is invariably answered with the reply, "I don't know." Sometimes with "I don't know, and even if I did I would not tell you." However, the client is given the feeling that she has a say in the way the therapy is conducted, even if she does not make use of it.

The therapist must be prepared to present stimulus situations that he thinks will be fruitful: "Yesterday you found it difficult to talk about the way some family members behaved at the funeral. Can we go over that again? Start where the car came round to pick you up." There are invariably a number of false starts. The negative emotions associated with an episode may have extinguished, in which case the therapist will be able to see this in the way the client handles the situation with ease. It is also possible that the client is not ready yet to allow the full impact of a situation to come through; in this case the client feels nothing, can't concentrate, blocks, sidetracks, and nothing therapeutic happens. As Reeves (1974) points out, we grieve at various levels, and at times the client is ready to tackle an aspect and work it through, at other times no amount of prompting will elicit anything.

> Intellectual acceptance of loss is one thing: acceptance of loss at the gut level is another. Reason may be reconciled: but then memories start coming back, slumbering emotions begin to stir again, and the pain may be so acute as to force again the cry, "No—it isn't so!" Or anger because "It isn't fair," or guilt because "It is my fault." And this can happen many times, as strata after strata of memories and feelings are uncovered [pp. 282–283].

If there is too much sidetracking and blocking, the therapist must be prepared to try another scene and/or another emotion, presenting stimuli, modeling, cueing, prompting, until one "hits home."

How to Probe, or Selecting Stimuli

Denial can take the form of not believing that the loss has occurred: "I can't believe it, I won't believe it, it isn't true!" Denial can also take the form of not feeling. The therapist constantly has to form hypotheses about what emotions would be appropriate to a certain situation and then to check whether these emotions have in fact occurred in this situation. Further, it is a question not only as to whether these responses have occurred or not, but also as to whether they have been sufficient for extinction to have taken place. Let me give an example where only partial extinction had taken place, and where there was denial of an emotion. A 22-year-old woman, divorced, two children, had the idea that with two children she had little chance of remarrying. There had been fantasies of getting rid of the youngest son. One evening the youngest son became ill, she knew that he was desperately ill and would possibly die, but she did not call a doctor until the following morning. By noon the child was dead, a case of meningitis. The staff in the hospital assured her that even had she summoned the doctors earlier, the child would still have died. This assurance, however, did not help, and in the following 2 years there were waves of overwhelming guilt during which she took overdoses of pills and slashed her wrists, resulting in several hospitalizations. In one of the institutions she was told by a staff member that it was stupid to feel guilty and that she was disturbing the other patients with her suicidal behavior. Her reply to this was, "Okay, then I'll stop feeling guilty" which she somehow managed to do, but she remained severely depressed. In the behavior therapy 2 years after the son had died, it was hypothesized that guilt was still playing a vital role in the depression, but was in some way being inhibited. The client was asked to go back in her imagination to the scene of the conversation with the staff member in the mental hospital, when she had stopped feeling guilty, to get angry with him, become emotionally aroused, and then the therapist gave the cues of: "He says that it wasn't your fault, but it was, you didn't call the doctor, it was your fault that your son died, you knew that he was sick and you did nothing about it." The result was a massive emotional upheaval in which the suicidal feelings returned, but with response prevention for carrying out the act and a prolonged flooding with stimuli to maintain the guilt reaction. Extinction did finally take place, to the point where she could calmly say: "I don't know if it was my fault or not, but at that time I could do nothing else." I have this complete therapy, 10 sessions, on videotape, with the client's permission to use it for teaching purposes (in Dutch).

Misfires

Where the whole session threatens to be a fiasco, it is best to end early, before both the client and therapist become too discouraged. When this happens the therapist can explain to the client that it sometimes occurs that the client is too emotionally exhausted to work and that it would be better to let things rest for a day or so. If this happens often, the therapist is probably setting too fast a pace for the client to catch up emotionally between sessions. It is also a signal that the therapist may be on the wrong track and has missed something important. Discussing the case with colleagues in the form of intervision (supervision with colleagues of equal level) usually produces valuable leads to which the therapist has until now been blind. Where the opportunities for intervision are limited, I often make use of my supervision groups with students to present my therapy just as they have to tell what they are doing with their clients. My experience is that not only do the students appreciate hearing about my problems, doubts, toils, and troubles, but often they give sound advice or ask searching questions that lead to new insights and altered strategies.

When a stimulus "hits home" and an emotional response ensues, it is a matter of individual choice as to whether the therapist continues talking, or remains silent while the client continues in her own way until the outburst subsides. Some clients require continual prompting to stay with a stimulus situation, others find it disturbing to have the therapist continually at them, at times doing things not exactly as the client herself would do them, hindering rather than helping the process. With any given stimulus, the client may vacillate swiftly between two violent emotions, say anger and despair, and the therapist may impede this if he is prompting her in only one direction. I personally prefer to give the client a clue and then let her carry on from there, but the client's needs prevail over my preferences. One advantage, though, of being able to be silent during outbursts is that the therapist has a chance to plan new strategies; another advantage is that there is less chance of the client involving the therapist in the emotions. If the client is angry and the therapist is constantly a part of the stimulus situation, there is a fair chance that the anger will be directed against the therapist. This is an undesirable state of affairs. The main point I want to make here is that the therapist may at times be silent for long periods of time without getting the feeling that he is not working. As long as the client is working, the therapy is progressing. Periods of up to 20 minutes can ensue in a therapy where there is not a word said, and where I as therapist hardly dare to move for fear of disturbing the process, but where I know that important events are taking place. Many clients have said afterward that they appreciated the uninterrupted time and space to work things out; others have said that without my constant guidance and presence they would not have been able to get anywhere. The same client will at times need constant prompting and at other times will need silence to explore. The therapist will need to get to know his client well and be able to follow whatever needs are prevalent at a particular time. Flexibility and sensitivity are an integral part of this type of therapy, as with every other.

Humans not only have the ability to re-create scenes from the past, but also to create ones that did not happen. This ability can be useful in finishing unfinished business. The mother who left her son to be cremated in a foreign country while she went home to the rest of the family could create in her fantasy what happened at the cremation, but with herself present at the last rites. Another example: A widow who was being eaten up with anger toward the dead husband could re-create fights that had taken place before his death, but then change the outcome so that now she beat him up instead of vice versa. In this latter case, she needed the help of the therapist in her fantasy to fight against her husband, and in the first battle the scene ended for her with the therapist being beaten up; only with repeating the scene again and again did the fantasy go according to plan (Ramsay, 1976).

In some cases, the denial that the loss has occurred is so strong that the client feels the presence of the deceased and may even hallucinate it. This denial can at times be useful to the therapist as an aid in the creation of scenes to evoke various emotions. For example, if guilt plays an important part, the client could be asked to close her eyes and then the therapist can instruct her to: "Imagine that John is present, tell him that you did things wrong, tell him what you did, ask him if he can ever forgive you." When the guilt has finally extinguished, the client will be able to report that he has forgiven her, meaning of course that she has forgiven herself.

With clients who have difficulty using fantasy and who find the third chair artificial, photos can be a powerful substitute. In most cases, the first time that the client looks at the photos in the therapy, there is an outburst of crying. At home there may be photos displayed, but avoidance reactions are always possible so that little of the pain of grief need be experienced. In the therapy situation the possibility of avoidance is decreased, and the emotions can be more easily elicited. When the first reactions begin to die down, to extinguish, the client can be asked to carry out various conversations with the photos, the type of conversation depending on which emotion the therapist thinks is important at that moment. A possible conversation for pining may be, therapist: "Tell him how much you miss him, tell him how often in the mornings breakfast isn't the same any more; toward six o'clock you feel the pain of knowing he won't be walking through the front door. Tell him that dinners are quiet and empty and the food doesn't taste good any more. The evenings are so long, but you don't want to go up to the cold, empty bed. Tell him how long and bleak the weekends are, that you've tried to keep his garden going but that it's now in ruins . . ." All this is addressed to the photo as prompting to elicit various emotions associated with different situations.

Linking Objects

During the therapy the client is asked to be on the look-out for the presence of linking objects. According to Volkan *et al.* (1976)

> these objects are typically treasured by people unable to resolve their grief— something that magically provides the illusion of communication with the dead. The pathological mourner can control this illusionary communication, turning it on by musing over the object and turning it off by putting the object out of sight in an inaccessible place [pp. 179–180].

Often the linking object is never touched—just the knowledge that it is there, locked away, is sufficient. The Jewish woman whose parents had been liquidated during the war had a pendant containing a photo of her mother kept in a drawer for more than 30 years—untouched. When I explained to her what a linking object was, she immediately understood and promised to bring the pendant next time. It cost her many hours of pain to handle it and to open the pendant, but at the next session her face was radiant as she showed me the photo inside. Another client had 45 hours of film of his wife and daughter, which had been locked away in a cupboard when the wife divorced him. The film had not been touched for 10 years.

A linking object might be some trivial article, a piece of music, an article of clothing, a letter, a piece of jewelry, or a photograph of the loved one. I do not attribute magical powers to these objects, as clients do, but see them rather as stimuli that can elicit strong emotional reactions, most times negative, but that can, under special conditions or ways of thinking, produce positive affect during denial fantasies. Strangely enough, the pleasant emotions that can be elicited by the linking object do not extinguish. The explanation for this is complex, but it is likely that the negative and positive emotions associated with the object both extinguish, and then, as the object was so important, it still has the ability to bring back happy memories, which, by a selective process, tend over time to be mainly positive in nature.

Following the Client

In working through the various emotions, the therapist will need to be alert and to listen carefully to where the client is at a particular moment, which emotion is the dominant, and to prompt in that direction. It is no use probing for anger if the client is on the verge of tears, no use looking for pining while the client is in the throes of powerless desolation. The therapist must follow the client and also be prepared to switch quickly from one feeling to another at a moment's notice. This switching is not an escape reaction, as any one stimulus situation will be associated with a number of mixed emotions. As Izard (1972) points out, emotions are rarely pure, and as long as the client stays in the situation, the mixture will gradually extinguish.

Expression of Emotions

Many psychotherapists believe that for anything psychotherapeutic to occur, the client must express the feelings; some even go so far as to insist that the feelings must be expressed in words. I do not agree with this. Few people are so verbally gifted that under severe strain, they can report to another person what is happening to them. With most people, words fail them. I maintain that the important thing is to be able to evoke the various emotions, by means of appropriate stimuli, and then to allow time for these feelings to extinguish. The way to express these feelings is left to the client (with some restrictions, like not breaking up the furniture or attacking the therapist). The client does not have to put it into words during an emotional outburst. It is useful to the therapist if the client can say afterward what has happened, but this is not necessary during the process itself. It is often frustrating to have to sit and see that something is going on, without knowing what it is; however, interruptions to satisfy the curiosity of the therapist are undesirable. Colleagues have often asked me why I do not use some form of scream therapy. Clients sometimes do scream as a form of expression, but the choice of how emotions are to be expressed is left to the client. Some curl up like wounded animals, some rock back and forth in the chair, some pace around the room, some wring their hands or bite their fingers, others scream at the top of their voices. The form of expression is up to the client, the main thing is to be able to elicit the feelings and to hold them as long as is necessary to get extinction.

Some clients prefer to work with their eyes closed, as in systematic desensitization, whereas others find this unnatural. With closed eyes, extraneous stimuli can be excluded and the client can usually concentrate more easily on the stimulus and work on the feelings. This is not necessary, however, as a client hard at work will be oblivious to the surroundings, including the therapist.

Nearing Completion

Both therapist and client will be able to see progression in the therapy in that various scenes and situations, which previously caused trouble, can now be viewed and talked about with ease. The therapist will need to review, from his knowledge of the structure of the bereavement process, whether he has probed all the emotional components that may be important. Usually, the last to appear is the aggression against the dead person: He died and is at rest; the mourner is left in pain and strife. I do not know if this is a necessary component to be found in all cases of bereavement; my doubts are especially strong where the deceased was a child, but it *is* necessary to look for this. If this aggression is present and is not dealt with, the last step cannot be taken. A possible way for the therapist to probe might be: "Look at that photo again, tell him how much pain and misery his death has caused you, tell him that he left you in the lurch, tell him how difficult it has been for you because of his death, he deserted you . . ." This aggression may be combined with the last step, which is letting go of the deceased. The mourner has to relinquish the lost person, object, or role before new ways of life can be found in which the lost object does not play a major part. The young widow has to say farewell to her dead husband before she can think of remarrying. The mother of a dead child has to let the child go before she will be ready for another child for its own sake and not as a substitute for the loss. The man fired from his job must settle all emotional accounts if he is to function adequately in a new role or position. The divorcee must totally relinquish the ex-partner before a new relationship is possible. The blind man must die as a sighted person in order to be reborn as a blind one.

This letting go of the lost object is extremely difficult, both emotionally and in finding ways to do it. Most people are terrified of doing this, "because then I will have nothing left." In a sense, this is true—they will have nothing left of that past life in which the lost object plays a major role. Clients protest that if they let go they will be losing an integral part of themselves; this is also true—but if a client is in therapy, the therapist has to assure himself that there will be enough of the person left over to be able to build up a new way of life. If the integral part that must be relinquished is so great that there is not enough left over to make life worthwhile and possible, the client should not be in this type of therapy. Clients also have the idea that if they let him go, there will be nothing left in the way of images or memories—they will never be able to think of him again or ever recall what he looked like or what they did together. These fears need to be discussed with the client, and although the client cannot imagine how she could ever think of him again if she said farewell forever, I ask her to take on faith my assurance that she will get him back again, in another form, in another way of feeling about him, in memories without pain.

Most people find letting go too passive a process and do not know how to do it. Sending the dead person away is more active and combines letting go with an aggressive deed. Any aggressive feeling toward the deceased is evoked and given expression in deeds, the violence of the act being proportional to the amount of the anger felt. In another case, a medical colleague who had been forced out of a job imagined using scalpels to cut up her former boss in order to get rid of him. The 34-year-old woman who threatened to kill herself and her 6-month-old daughter after the husband had died, spent many stormy sessions trying to get rid of him. At first he would not leave, and she had to have imaginary physical fights with him; then he stood at the door and taunted her but would not leave. Next he went to stay with a girlfriend, which he had done in real life after some bitter quarrels; finally, after he had returned, she killed him and placed his body in the coffin. As can be imagined, this last case is a severely disturbed woman who needed much more than a short behavior therapy for her problems. (In her case, she went back to her original therapist after the behavior therapy, spent 3½ years in an analytic therapy, which was broken off by the analyst when the transference got out of hand, then came back to me for a further bereavement treatment for the broken relationship with her ex-therapist.)

The letting go must be absolute if the process is to be resolved so that the client can move into the reintegration phase. There needs to be an acceptance that this catastrophe has occurred, there can be no denial any more, and the farewell must be final. One client, when asked to take leave of her mother, spent a restful 5 minutes with her eyes closed, then reported that she had done it. When asked to give details of how she had done it, her choice of words implied a leave-taking in the form of "Bye for now, see you again." When this was pointed out to her, she could immediately see that this was *auf Wiedersehen* and not goodbye. The real thing then caused a long and painful upheaval.

How do you know if the "real thing" has taken place or not? In the first place, this is probably *the* most difficult thing to do in the whole process, so that if there is no obvious emotionality, the client has not done it. After such a step, the client is completely spent, exhausted, and empty. If this is not the case, do it again. If the client becomes angry with the therapist, this is a positive sign: Many clients feel that the therapist has taken their loved one away from them. The therapist need not "deal" with this anger except by allowing time for it to extinguish—it is best to stop the session here, since the client will not be able to do any more work, nor is there much more to do.

Finishing

How do you know when the client is finished, is through the main bereavement process and into the reintegration phase? This is usually obvious for both client and therapist, yet it is difficult to put into words what the changes are. The client looks different, is brighter, more alert, more spontaneous. Subjective reports are in the form of, "I feel different; it's as if a weight has been lifted off me; I can breathe again; the world is once more in color; I can look around me again and see things." One client reported that the deceased was no longer directly in front of her, blocking every thought and movement, but had moved to the side so that she was now free to move forward. The change is usually dramatic and obvious, but the therapist should still check to make sure that there are no further major obstacles. A number of stimuli can be presented which, in the past, had caused trouble: looking at photos, listening to a piece of music, handling a linking object. If the responses are not negative, then you may be reasonably sure that the client is "through." If she is not altogether through, this is not a catastrophe, since the client will come back with further depressive thoughts and actions, indicating that some extra work needs to be done.

The Reintegration

As was said earlier, the reintegration phase is a long process with many pinpricks of pain, as old memories surge back or as old habits have to be changed. The client may need occasional support from the therapist during this period, but most can do it on their own. It is a good idea for the therapist to arrange to phone or write after a month, and certainly on the anniversary of the death to offer his condolences; the clients have expressed appreciation of this thoughtfulness, and if a client needs further help in clearing up the remainders of the process, contact is made much easier.

SOME COMPLICATIONS

If a person has been depressed for years and the partner has adjusted to this state of affairs, a sudden lifting of the depression will cause large changes in the balance between the partners. This can cause problems in the relationship that may need professional help. If the two people came together while the one was still grieving, this is bound to cause upheaval. The 22-year-old woman who lost her young son because of meningitis, had just got to know her future second husband when the tragedy hit. He was a psychologist, and apparently he had few difficulties with the fact that his future wife was depressed. They married soon after the therapy. At the 6-month followup they asked for marriage guidance, but in spite of this, 2 years after the therapy, they were separated.

Another complication is that a therapy like this often triggers off other unresolved conflicts from the past, either during the course of treatment or a short time later. During the treatment, the therapist has to decide for himself whether to temporarily stop work on the main problem and clear up the earlier ones before proceeding, or to wait until the end and then to mop up the remnants. It is not usually possible to switch back and forth from one problem to another. If, while working on one problem, the client reaches a difficult period and then changes to another problem, the result is usually chaos and a worsening of the depression. This switching would be the equivalent of an agoraphobic reaching a high level of anxiety for shops, then switching to trains, then to crowded streets, and so on, changing whenever the anxiety reaches a peak. When this happens, extinction will not occur. Where multiple unresolved grief processes are present, it is best to settle one problem, then tackle the next.

In other cases, the other unresolved processes become apparent only later. One client came back to me for divorce problems after having previously been in therapy with me for two other bereavement problems: his parents and a man whom he had had to kill during the war. One may argue here that I should have explored further during the first therapy and then should have done all the necessary work at the same time. Against this, it may be argued that the client was not motivated to work on the divorce at that time, was not ready for it, and did not see it as a problem. When it became a problem for him, which he could not solve on his own, he came back into therapy. Two clients have returned after a time with other, previously unresolved bereavement problems. Two others have returned with new problems, one who had lost her analytic therapist and one with the impending loss of his mother who had multiple sclerosis, which was causing him so much trouble that he could not cope alone. In the latter case, two sessions were enough to bring the anticipatory grief reaction to within normal limits.

SOME RESULTS TO DATE

I shall report only on those clients who have been in treatment with me, not those where others have done the work under my supervision. These results are not to be taken as hard facts, but are given only as an indication. Of 23 cases so far, 16 were clear-cut, and 7 embedded in other problems. No one has broken off the treatment before finishing, and no one has become worse. In one case, I feel that the therapy did not help, although the client says that it did. The average number of sessions per client is 9, the range is 1 to 60, and the median is 5. The one case of 60 sessions is an exception. The average time between the loss and the time of coming into therapy is 11 years, the median being 2½ years. The range is 0 (anticipatory) to over 30 years (among those over 30 years there is a cluster of 5 clients, showing that it is still possible to deal with some problems of very long standing). My subjective ratings of improvement, for what they are worth, are 9 highly improved, 9 moderately improved, 4 slightly improved, 1 unchanged, and none worse. The clients' ratings are higher than mine. These ratings are only to be taken as indicators of a trend. All I want to say here is that selected clients can be helped considerably in a short period of time, even when the problems are of long standing.

THE EFFECT ON THE THERAPIST

If this treatment is hard on the client, it is also hard on the therapist. Many people shy away from dealing with death, but the therapist has to be able to handle the subject without fear and without the meaningless clichés that most laymen use. In hearing the moving stories of clients, the therapist has to strike a balance between empathic feeling with the client and taking distance so as to stay in control. A sobbing therapist is not going to be of much help to a client, nor is a cool, detached therapist—there has to be a balance, which is emotionally demanding of the therapist. Letting the client see that you are emotionally involved can sometimes help, sometimes hinder, the client. A client in telling the story of his daughter drowning, said that seeing tears in my eyes gave him implicit permission to cry, which he had not been able to do until then. Another client seeing the same thing burst out with, "What is wrong with you? It's not your problem."

What I want to say here is that all therapy is hard work, and this type is especially demanding of the therapist. Hence the extra half hour tacked on to the therapy time for each session: It is often necessary for the therapist. Further, I find that I can do other types of therapy at the same time as tackling a bereavement problem, but not two bereavements at the

246 R. W. RAMSAY

same time—that is too much. It is neither easy nor pleasant to "hit home" with a stimulus and then sit back, powerless to ease the suffering and pain that you have elicited, even if you have not caused it.

THE CLIENT–THERAPIST RELATIONSHIP

As with all therapies, the client–therapist relationship is vital, but it is not used in the same way as in therapies along analytic lines. Here, there is a working relationship, a teamwork on a problem, where the relationship is only discussed when it tends to interfere with this work. The therapist can build up the working alliance during the preparation for the treatment and use it to get the client to take difficult steps during the treatment, alternating between being a hard taskmaster and then repairing any damage by being an empathic, understanding person. At the end of a therapy the client is glad that it is over and the parting is usually not difficult. There is a mutual respect, a bond such as soldiers build up who have fought side by side during a short battle, but this bond is not what analysts would call transference. It does not have to be worked through. There is usually a feeling at ending of "We've gotten to know each other in our work, it would be pleasant to get to know each other in other ways as well, but you have your life and I have mine. We may bump into each other occasionally. Till then." The client knows that it is always possible to come back, which makes the parting easier; further, I shall be contacting the client for followups. It is clear to the client, though, that any further contact will be on a working and not on a social basis.

WARNINGS

I would like here to give some warnings. In presenting the results earlier I used the words "selected clients." This type of therapy is not suitable for everyone with bereavement problems. Once again, grief is a *normal* reaction to loss, and it is only if it goes wrong in some way that we may consider whether an intervention is possible or desirable. This is a difficult and harsh treatment; flooding always is, and not all people in trouble can or want to go through it. The chances of suicide are high, and great care has to be taken in the way we use our techniques.

That was about the clients, now for the therapists. This is not a therapy for beginners. Flooding with phobics is difficult, demanding a good basic knowledge of background theory, plus the experience to know when to push and when to ease up. In bereavement this is even more difficult, and the problems are compounded by having to search constantly for stimuli to get and keep the process going. The therapist has to switch back and forth from the hard taskmaster to the empathic, warm supporter, while staying in control of violent outbursts of emotions, keeping them going as long as possible, but not allowing them to get out of hand. The therapist has to continually make decisions as to whether the material that the client brings into the therapy is relevant to the problem, or whether it is a sidetrack. The therapist has to continually make decisions as to whether to intervene or to allow the client to continue undisturbed. The client has to be helped to experience various emotions by means of rational emotive training, cognitive restructuring, modeling, prompting, and assertive training, with successive approximations and shaping to deal with difficult parts. Almost the whole arsenal of the behavior therapist is brought into play in each and every session. I would suggest that only if a therapist has some considerable experience in more conventional forms of therapy should he launch into this type of work.

REFERENCES

Averill, J. R. Grief: Its nature and significance. *Psychological Bulletin*, 1968, *70*, 721–748.

Barendregt, J. T. Onderzoek van fobieën. In A. P. Cassee, P. E. Boeke, & J. T. Barendregt (Eds.), *Klinische Psychologie in Nederland*. Deventer: Van Loghum Slaterus, 1973. Pp. 102–116.

Bugen, L. A. Human grief: A model for prediction and intervention. *American Journal of Orthopsychiatry*, 1977, *47*, 196–206.

Eysenck, H. J. Single-trial conditioning, neurosis and the Napalkov phenomenon. *Behaviour Research and Therapy*, 1967, *5*, 63–65.

Gendlin, E. T. Client-centered and experiential psychotherapy. In D. A. Wexler & L. N. Rice (Eds.), *Innovations in client-centered therapy*. New York: Wiley, 1974. Pp. 211–246.

Hodge, J. R. They that mourn. *Journal of Religion and Health*, 1972, *11*, 229–240.

Izard, C. E. Anxiety: A variable combination of interacting fundamental emotions. In C. D. Spielberger (Ed.), *Anxiety: Current trends in theory and research* (Vol. 1). New York: Academic Press, 1972. Pp. 50–106.

Lindemann, E. Symptomatology and management of acute grief. *American Journal of Psychiatry*, 1944, *101*, 141–148.

Marks, I. M. *Fears and phobias*. New York: Academic Press, 1969.

Marks, I. M. Perspective on flooding. *Seminars in Psychiatry*, 1972, *4*, 129–138.

Parkes, C. M. Unexpected and untimely bereavement: A statistical study of young Boston widows and widowers. In B. Schoenberg, I. Gerber, A. Wiener, A. H. Kutscher, D. Peretz, & A. C. Carr (Eds.), *Bereavement: Its psychosocial aspects*. New York: Columbia University Press, 1975. Pp. 119–138.

Ramsay, R. W. A case study in bereavement therapy. In H. J. Eysenck (Ed.), *Case studies in behaviour therapy*. London: Routledge & Kegan Paul, 1976. Pp. 227–235.

Raphael, B. The management of pathological grief. *Australian and New Zealand Journal of Psychiatry*, 1975, *9*, 173–180.

Reeves, R. B. Reflections on two false expectations. In B. Schoenberg, A. C. Carr, A. H. Kutscher, D. Peretz, & I. K. Goldberg (Eds.), *Anticipatory grief*. New York: Columbia University Press, 1974. Pp. 281–284.

Roth, M. The phobic anxiety-depersonalization syndrome. *Proceedings of the Royal Society of Medicine*, 1959, *52*, 587–595.

Seitz, F. C. Behavior modification techniques for treating depression. *Psychotherapy: Theory, Research, and Practice*, 1971, *8*, 181–184.

Seligman, M. E. P. *Helplessness. On depression, development, and death*. San Francisco: Freeman, 1975.

Shneidman, E. S. *Deaths of man*. New York: Quadrangle/New York Times Book Co., 1973.

Volkan, V. D., Cilluffo, A. F., & Sarvay, T. L. Re-grief therapy and the function of the linking object as a key to stimulate emotionality. In P. Olsen (Ed.), *Emotional flooding*. New York: Human Sciences Press, 1976. Pp. 179–224.

13

Behavioral Group Therapy[1]

ROBERT PAUL LIBERMAN AND JAMES TEIGEN

The work of behaviorally oriented clinicians with groups is distinguishable from other approaches by the emphasis on: (*a*) specifying problems and goals in concrete, behavioral terms; (*b*) measuring change in behavior from the problematic to the desirable; and (*c*) using principles of learning to facilitate behavioral change. Specification of the problem leads naturally to an elaboration of *therapeutic goals* for the individuals and the group as a whole. Goal planning should be a mutual, collaborative effort between the therapist and the patients. The development of a simple but reliable recording or measurement system for monitoring the targeted behavior provides an opportunity to evaluate *therapeutic progress* that the therapist and clients should frequently review for decisions about changing goals and interventions. Principles of learning, such as positive and negative reinforcement, modeling, shaping, extinction, punishment, satiation, time-out from reinforcement, prompting, stimulus control, fading, and counterconditioning, form the basis for formulating *treatment tactics and strategies*.

[1]The opinions stated in this article are those of the authors and should not be construed as official policy of the California Department of Health or the Regents of the University of California. The writing of this chapter was supported in part by NIMH Grants 09-000005-02-0 (Hospital Improvement Project) and MH 19880 (Behavioral Analysis and Modification in a Community Mental Health Center).

Copyright © 1979 by Academic Press, Inc.
All rights of reproduction in any form reserved.
ISBN 0-12-647450-8

A thorough understanding of behavioral principles permits the therapist to formulate working clinical hypotheses, or experimental analyses in the case of research, about the environmental influences that maintain problem behaviors and make it difficult for the patients to function more adaptively. The single most important feature of behavior therapy, however, is its inextricable bond with empirical values. As in other sciences, the science of human behavior relies completely on measurement. The implication for clinicians is that they should not use techniques for their own sake, but only for their effective impact on behavior. The clinical application of behavioral and learning principles with therapy groups was stimulated by experiments with contrived laboratory groups in which contingencies of reinforcement were shown to powerfully influence the sequencing of conversations, the contributions of group members, and the distribution of status and leadership among the group members.

Conducting therapy in groups makes eminently good sense from the perspective of behavioral or learning principles. If we assume that psychotherapy is a learning process, then group therapy affords some natural advantages over individual therapy for learning new behaviors and attitudes. In a group there are multiple opportunities for suggestions and prompts from peers as well as from the therapist. These suggestions can serve as effective antecedents of new behavior and actions by receptive group members. Much of our learning goes on through the process of imitation, also called modeling, or identification. In the group situation, each individual has a variety of social and role models to imitate and hence the potentially assimilable repertoire is much greater than in individual therapy. It is also known that imitation occurs more rapidly and thoroughly when the models have features in common with the imitator; thus, having peers present as well as a therapist facilitates observational learning.

Adaptive behavior is strengthened as it is reinforced by the social environment. There are many sources of reinforcement in the group—co-members and therapist—and some may be more effective than others. The stimulus situation in group therapy is closer to naturally occurring social situations than that in individual treatment. Thus, the interpersonal skills learned in group therapy should generalize more readily to real-life situations. There is the opportunity to structure the group therapy situation so that it closely simulates the problematic situations of a patient, using various members of the group in role-playing or behavioral rehearsal scenes. The accepting, cohesive climate in therapy groups also promotes symptomatic improvement and an atmosphere conducive to taking risks in trying out new problem-solving strategies.

There are two general categories of behavioral approaches to group therapy. The earliest efforts were made by those clinicians who infused behavioral specification, recording, and technology into conventional or nondirective group formats. Behavioral techniques are superimposed upon the ongoing group dynamics that unfold without prestructuring by the leader. Many of these clinicians were themselves trained in the analytic, nondirective modes of doing therapy and developed expertise in behavioral principles at a later stage in their careers. The second type of approach, which is gaining in popularity, involves the structuring of the group format in ways that maximize the directed input of behavioral techniques, with less encouragement of spontaneous group process. The approaches differ in the degree to which the leader is directive in structuring and prompting what happens in the group.

BEHAVIORAL METHODS IN UNSTRUCTURED GROUP THERAPY

A variety of behavioral methods have been used in conventional group therapy settings in which there is little or no interference by the leader in the spontaneous group interaction. Verbal prompting and reinforcement have been used to increase "personal" and "group-centered" references made by group therapy patients. Whenever the desired responses were expressed by patients, the therapist "rewarded" them by giving verbal approval. Silences were effectively eliminated in a therapy group of chronic psychotics by surreptitiously introducing a noxious noise whenever the group fell silent for more than 10 seconds. The noise was turned off as soon as a group member broke the silence; thus the group avoided the aversive stimulus by increasing their talk (Heckel, Wiggins, & Salzberg, 1962). Shapiro and Birk (1967) showed how systematic, preplanned use of approval and attention from the therapist can serve effectively as a therapeutic tactic in dealing with patients' problems, such as hogging the group's attention, distancing maneuvers, and lack of assertiveness. Birk (1974) has extended this approach to an intensive, five sessions per week model of group therapy in which each patient's targeted problem behaviors and their adaptive alternatives are given negative and positive feedback, respectively, by the leader and by other members of the group as they emerge in the natural social interaction. Anecdotal reports indicated that this format was helpful for patients who suffered from severe depressions, social isolation, drug abuse, suicidal behavior, and depersonalization and who had not responded to other forms of psychotherapy.

In a controlled study of two matched therapy groups of nonpsychotic out-patients, Liberman (1970, 1971) found that an experimental group led by a therapist who systematically reinforced intermember expressions of cohesiveness and solidarity experienced faster symptomatic improvement than a comparison group led by a therapist who used a more intuitive, psychodynamic approach. The patients in the experimental group also showed significantly greater cohesiveness, measured sociometrically, and changes on personality tests that assessed dimensions of interpersonal competence and comfort. In both groups, whether or not the therapist was aware of the contingencies of reinforcement, a lawful positive relationship was evident between the group members' expression of *cohesiveness* and the therapist's activity in prompting and acknowledging this dimension of group dynamics.

Reinforcement methods have been applied to children's play therapy groups (Clement, Fazzone, & Goldstein, 1970). Second- and third-grade boys who were referred to the clinic by their teachers because of shy, withdrawn behavior were randomly placed in groups of four that met once a week for 20 consecutive sessions. In the behavior modification group, the boys received tokens for social approach behavior directed at each other during spontaneous play. The giving of the tokens was paired with praise by the therapist and the tokens were exchanged for small toys and candy after the session. A comparison group of boys was given verbal praise for socializing and playing together, but did not receive tokens. The boys in the token group improved more than the comparison group and no-treatment control groups, and they continued to be better adjusted at a 1-year, posttherapy followup. Token reinforcement has also been shown to be effective in significantly increasing the verbal interactions of a group of hospitalized "silent" adolescents who were considered poor candidates for psychotherapy (Hauserman, Zweback, & Plotkin, 1972). After verbalizations increased, group peer pressure, exerted via social reinforcement and prompts, reduced silly, off-topic comments and increased appropriate and relevant contributions to the group process.

Modeling or learning through imitation has also been effectively used to increase the social skills of withdrawn children. Withdrawn and socially isolated nursery school children who viewed a narrated film showing sociable peer models increased their level of social interaction in the school playroom as compared to nonisolate, normal children (O'Connor, 1969). Grade school children from poverty backgrounds were exposed to group-wide or individual reinforcement contingencies during arithmetic tasks. It was found that giving reinforcement on the basis of the total group's performance increased cooperative behavior among the students significantly more than individually based contingencies (Wodarski, Hamblin, Buckholdt, & Ferritor, 1973).

Token reinforcement was used in a clinical investigation by Liberman (1972b) in an attempt to increase social interaction among four chronic schizophrenic women, each of whom had been hospitalized for over 15 years. Reliable, quantitative records were made of their social conversation during 50-minute meetings. During the baseline period, conversational interchanges occurred at an average rate of one per minute. Contingent reinforcement for conversation among themselves was introduced using tokens that could be exchanged for candy, cake, cigarettes, and jewelry. The tokens were distributed at the end of each session. A noncontingent reinforcement phase was next introduced with the patients receiving their tokens before the session. This was done to assess the causal influence of the contingent use of tokens. A final phase returned the patients to reinforcement contingent upon their social conversation. Using the same design, another series of sessions was run using a table game that the patients played, which evoked conversation. Contingent token reinforcement increased participation in an open-ended conversation 10 times over the baseline and noncontingent reinforcement phases. Although the game situation alone produced a high baseline rate of conversation, introduction of contingent reinforcement doubled the rate of the baseline. Also, with chronically hospitalized psychotic patients, the amount of verbal participation in a ward-wide "community" meeting has been shown to be a direct function of the amount of prompting and acknowledging by staff members (Licker, Perel, Wallace, & Davis, 1976).

TOKENS AND TASKS IN GROUP THERAPY WITH DELUSIONAL SCHIZOPHRENICS

A clinical research approach to the use of behavioral interventions with a group of paranoid schizophrenics is presented here in some detail to illustrate the effects of reinforcement and task structure on the amount of rational speech. Delusional speech and social withdrawal are two major contributors to the labeling of individuals as mentally ill and to their confinement in mental institutions. Epidemiological studies indicate that the most frequent type of abnormal behavior leading to readmission of previously hospitalized patients is verbalization of delusional and bizarre ideas (Wing, Monck, Brown, & Carstairs, 1964). One of the most disastrous effects of long-term institutionalization of mental patients is the constriction of interpersonal responses and withdrawal from social interaction, an outcome termed the "social breakdown syndrome" (Zusman, 1967). In custodial settings, patients are not encouraged or reinforced for interacting with each other or with staff. When attention is given by staff, it is often contingent upon the patients' acting in a disturbing way or expressing delusional and bizarre talk. The study reported here aimed to enhance social conversation and rational speech concomitantly in a group therapy situation. The interventions that were assessed include instructions and prompts from the therapist, acknowledgments and social approval from the therapist, token reinforcements exchangeable for a variety of tangible rewards, and a structured task situation in which the patients played a game. The overriding purpose of this clinical research endeavor was to develop and test simple and practical procedures that could be applied to similar patients in a variety of therapeutic settings.

Methods

SUBJECTS

Four patients (described below) from Camarillo State Hospital with 12 to 25 years of hospitalization took part in the study. They had been diagnosed by different clinicians many times as paranoid schizophrenic and were chosen because they had high rates of verbally expressing persecutory and grandiose delusions.

Herman D.: A 38-year-old, single veteran with 4 years of college education whose delusions included a belief that he was a "five, golden-cluster major general" sent by the president to investigate sex racketeers in California. He was well groomed, intelligent, sociable and well mannered.

Jane V.: A 47-year-old widow on welfare assistance with a musical and acting background whose delusions focused on her alleged wealth. She accused staff and other patients of wearing her clothes and claimed that she had been injected with "monkey's blood." She was shrewdly manipulative and alternated between maudlin sweetness and hostile abusiveness.

Jack E.: A 63-year-old divorced college graduate with a prefrontal lobotomy. His delusions included concerns that his extensive financial holdings were taken by "plastic look-alikes" of his family and that rays from space were destroying him. He was polite, friendly, and a conscientious gardener on the hospital grounds.

Mary N.: A 62-year-old single woman who voiced delusions regarding her age (claiming she was 17), name, and family background. She was fastidious and worked regularly and competently in a hospital storeroom.

SETTING

During the 6-month course of the study, the patients were living at Camarillo State Hospital's Clinical Research Unit, a 12-bed coeducational ward employing a token economy. While the group study was ongoing, contingencies placed on the subjects' behavior in any individual program were not applicable during the group meeting. Three times weekly, the patients were brought to a "social-interaction room," which was comfortably furnished and which contained an observation room behind a one-way mirror. The facility was equipped with an intercom and a remote control electronic prompting device (Farrall Model B102 Bug-in-the-ear). The apparatus was shown to the patients and it was explained that observers would be present during the meetings.

RESPONSE MEASURE

The subjects met for 30 minutes during each session, seated in a semicircle in view of the one-way mirror. At every session a psychiatric social worker sat in the group as therapist and gave instructions at the start of the session. During the previous 2 months, a content analysis was performed on the conversational speech of the patients. An exhaustive search of records and interviews with relatives revealed what topics of speech were delusional. A glossary of delusional topics was compiled and used by the raters in this study.

Interval recordings were made by raters seated behind the one-way mirror. Consecutive 1-minute time segments were rated for the presence or absence of delusional speech or for silence for each patient. Any delusional statement made during the interval produced a delusional rating for that patient for that interval. The individual's data were summarized for each 30-minute session by calculating the percentage of rational time segments (time segments totally rational/time segments totally rational + time segments delusional) without including the silent segments. The group data represent "pooled individual measures," or the sums of individual data for all intervals as differentiated from data summed for all patients across each interval.

Interrater agreement ranged from 75 to 95.5% with a mean of 87.5% for five meetings in which two observers independently rated the speech content. This compares well with the interrater reliability of the measurement of the onset of delusional speech in staff–patient conversations reported elsewhere (Liberman, Teigen, Patterson, & Baker, 1973).

EXPERIMENTAL DESIGN

Phase 1: Baseline. Baseline conditions were in effect during the first four meetings. The therapist was present with the four subjects and verbally acknowledged their discussion on a time-contingent basis. Approximately every 30 seconds the therapist would face whomever was talking and attend to that person, regardless of content. Phrases were used such as: "Oh?" "Tell me more," "That's interesting," "Uh-huh," and "Do you have anything else to say about that?" The therapist attempted to promote conversational flow rather than to affect verbal content.

When no one spoke, the therapist would prompt with such phrases as: "What have you to say about that?" "I'd like to hear what you have to say," or "I'm interested in listening to you, too." These were directed toward a subject who had been remaining silent. Two tokens per meeting were given to each subject contingent upon attendance rather than participation. This contingency to facilitate voluntary attendance was maintained throughout all but the token reinforcement phases of the experiment. The tokens could be exchanged three times each day for coffee, candy, cigarettes, grounds privileges, and private room time.

Phase 2: Social reinforcement. Social reinforcement consisted of placing delusional talk on "extinction" while socially "reinforcing" rational talk. The therapist showed interest in and attended to any subject speaking rationally. Acknowledgements were given continuously and immediately for any rational speech. Whenever two subjects spoke at the same time, both were acknowledged. Any topic was considered appropriate as long as it did not include delusional material. Effort was made to foster communication between subjects rather than between the therapist and a subject by prompts to address the group or by prompting silent group members to respond. Two tokens were again given each subject contingent upon attendance. This phase covered eight consecutive meetings.

Phase 3: Social reinforcement plus structured conversation. This intervention included the same methodology as Phase 2, but the therapist added a structured topic for discussion. A topic for conversation was introduced by the therapist and comments were invited. Topics were: "The token economy," "Unit business," "Industrial therapy jobs" and "Vocations." Acknowledgments by the therapist were still given to any subject speaking rationally, regardless of topic. However, the therapist used his judgment to redirect the conversation to preselected topics whenever there were pauses of 30 seconds or more. This phase consisted of four sessions.

Phase 4: Game. The third intervention involved further structuring of interaction through introduction of a task. A table game ("Group Therapy") was played that consisted of questions read from cards specially prepared for use with a group of institutionalized patients. A roll of dice established whether the player landed on a "question space" or won a sum of play money (which had no exchange value). Sample questions were

> "Tell the group about something that makes you angry and ask them to do the same."
> "Find out from the group what would be some of the first things that they would do if they were discharged from the hospital."
> "Ask people in the group what they would most like to do in their lives. Get reasons why."
> "Get the two people sitting next to you to tell each other how they like each other."
> "Which activity do you like the most on the unit?"

The subjects were instructed to read the questions aloud and then to answer them as best they could. The therapist participated in the game but drew from a different stack of cards that had questions worded slightly differently than the subjects' cards. Lengthy discussion could ensue from the questions and answers, but the rules were to adhere to the game format. The game was played for five meetings.

Phase 5: Baseline. Baseline conditions were reinstituted for two meetings identical to the four original baseline sessions.

Phase 6: Token reinforcement. The next intervention involved token rein-forcement of rational talk. Tokens, exchangeable for coffee, candy, off-unit time, movies, and other "goodies," were given contingent upon avoidance of delusional conversation. The ratio used to determine the amount of reinforcement was one token per every six intervals with no delusional talk. Thus, 1–6 rational intervals were rewarded with one token and 7–12 rational intervals earned two tokens. Every subject earned at least one token and could earn a maximum of five, regardless of the performance of others. The tokens were given to the subjects at the end of the session. Rational speech was also socially "reinforced" as before by the therapist who led the group discussion. Additional cues and reinforcers were given to the subjects during the course of the meeting. The therapist placed a special chip in a cup labeled for each subject at the end of each 1-minute time segment that was not rated delusional by the observers. This was to serve as feedback on progress and as immediate reinforcement for refrain-ing from delusional speech. The chips were then counted at the end of the meeting and were exchanged for real tokens at the rate of 6:1. This im-mediate feedback was discontinued after four meetings, although delayed token reinforcement continued for two additional sessions.

Phase 7: Token reinforcement plus game. A structured task was combined with token reinforcement for five sessions. A card game (blackjack) was played with toy money for two sessions, and the question-and-answer table game for the final three sessions. However, data were lost for one of these meetings due to an error in which the rater mistakenly labeled silent segments as rational. The data from this one session is thus omitted from the results and the graphs. The latter structured activity again focused on subjects that typically evoked delusional comments from all of the subjects.

Token reinforcement was given using the same contingencies as in Phase 6. Verbal acknowledgment and prompts for rational speech were again provided by the therapist.

Phase 8: Baseline. Contingencies were removed and baseline conditions resumed for an additional five meetings.

Phase 9: Token reinforcement with group contingency. Tokens were paid on a group-contingent basis for the final six nonstructured meetings. The content of the discussion was rated as before, but individual earnings were affected by the participation of each other subject. Delusional talk on the part of any one subject reduced the average amount of rational speech upon which token reinforcement for each group member was computed. The number of time segments during which rational talk *only* was heard was divided by the total of all time segments in which speech occurred. One token was given to each subject for every 3 intervals with only rational talk over 15 such intervals. Thus each subject received three tokens if rational talk for the group as a whole ranged between 22 and 24 intervals, four tokens if between 25 and 27 intervals. As in the token reinforcement

Phases 6 and 7 using individual contingencies, the maximum number of tokens that a subject could earn was five.

Results and Comments

The data for the group as a whole are pictured in Figure 13.1. During baseline conditions, the discussion tended to be more delusional than rational. For the group as a whole, rational speech ranged from 32 to 60% of total time segments in which talking occurred, with a mean of 44%.

The first two interventions, social "reinforcement" with and without structured conversation, yielded no different responses from the group's baseline performance. With a mean of 39%, these two conditions can be considered as extensions of the baseline period and are so designated in Figure 13.2.

A more highly structured format, the game, resulted in a range of response from 52 to 94%, with a mean of 68%. Individual differences in

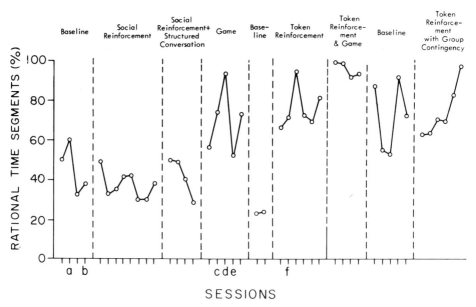

FIGURE 13.1. *Percentage of 1-minute time segments based on sums of pooled individual scores that contained rational speech in 30 minutes of group therapy with four chronic, paranoid schizophrenic patients. Approximately three group sessions were held each week. Sessions are noted with letters a–f due to absence from the session by Herman, Jane, or Mary. (a) Herman out for the last 29 minutes; (b) Jane out for the last 14 minutes; (c) Jane out in the middle for 10 minutes and Mary for 6 minutes at the beginning; (d) Jane out the entire time; (e) Herman out the entire time; (f) Herman out the last 16 minutes.*

attendance explains the increased variability in this phase. Herman and Jane were far less rational than either of the other two group members. During this phase, Jane was absent for 40 minutes of two sessions and Herman for one entire session. Thus, the group data for this phase show a peak of rational speech during the session that Jane missed completely. The stated reason for refusal to join the group or to remain with the group was anger directed at another group member.

Baseline contingencies were reinstituted with a dramatic reduction in rational talk. The group data show the lowest percentage of rational talk throughout the experiment during this phase.

Token reinforcement was about as effective in increasing rational talk as was the game; however, there was less variation in attendance, and the data are more stable, with a mean of 76%. The two most effective contingencies, a structured task and token reinforcement, were then combined. The results reflect the additive effects of these interventions. The mean was 96% of intervals rated rational with a range of 92 to 99%. The blackjack card game appeared to prompt a slightly higher level of rational speech than the question-and-answer game.

Baseline conditions were reinstituted and a decrement in rational speech was noted. The group data range from 53 to 92%, with a mean of 72%. Individual data shown in Figure 13.2 indicate that neither Jane nor Herman became as delusional as under previous baseline conditions.

The final phase in which a group contingency was used to dispense tokens produced an increasing percentage of rational talk, with a range from 63 to 97%. Most of the session-to-session variation is due to Jane's variability of from 0 to 92% rational talk.

It is clear from Figure 13.2 that individuals responded quite differently to the various conditions used. Herman responded best to the structure that the game provided, remaining practically delusion-free during Phases 4 and 7. Mary consistently maintained almost delusion-free speech throughout all phases, even during the baseline conditions. This was similar to her general pattern of conversation on the unit where she avoided "sensitive" topics that might evoke delusional talk. Of all the subjects, Mary was most discreet and controlled in verbalizing delusional content. Interestingly, the variability in Mary's speech narrowed as the experiment proceeded.

Jack responded well to both the game and token reinforcement interventions. His lowest levels of rational speech occurred during the three baseline conditions. While the third baseline condition produced only a moderate decrease in his rational speech, it produced a large increase in the session-to-session variability.

Jane showed the least response to the therapeutic interventions. She showed no improvement during the game condition (Phase 4) in which she refused to participate. While the others played the game, Jane sat to one

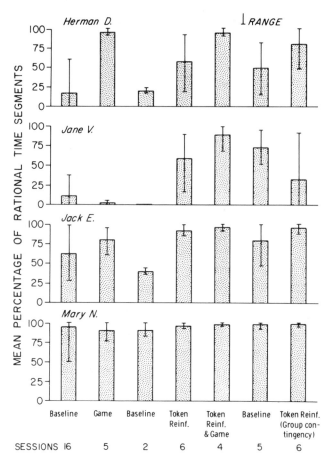

FIGURE 13.2. *The mean percentage of 1-minute time segments that contained rational speech in each experimental condition for each of the four chronic, paranoid schizophrenic patients in a group therapy situation. The number of group sessions held during each condition is noted at the bottom of the figure. The first three conditions in Figure 13.1 are grouped as "Baseline" in Figure 13.2. The bar graphs also show the range for individual sessions under each condition.*

side of the table, talking delusionally virtually the entire time. She also missed one session and part of another one during Phase 4.

Jack and Herman showed the clearest discrimination in their responses to the token contingencies and the games. The sharp reduction in rational speech during the second baseline condition for the group data is an effect contributed primarily by Jack and Herman's decrease in rational talk.

This study represents a small step toward the application of basic principles of learning to complex social behavior—delusional speech in chronic, paranoid schizophrenic patients. The relative merits of task structure and token reinforcement for enhancing rational conversation were demonstrated to be nearly equal. A combination of task structure and tokens proved to be the most powerful intervention, doubling the amount of rational talk from the baseline period. On the other hand, verbal prompting and feedback from the therapist were ineffective in improving the content of speech of these chronic patients. Group-contingent token reinforcement appeared to be no more effective than individualized token reinforcement. Because the amount of rational talk was increasing during the group contingency condition, this phase should have been continued for a few more sessions to determine its steady-state level. However, clinical considerations prevailed when it became possible to concentrate on discharge planning.

A question that remains is the failure of rational speech to dramatically regress to lower levels when the contingencies were removed for the second time during the baseline conditions in Phase 8. The lack of deterioration in verbal content may have been the result of natural contingencies of social reinforcement coming to control the conversation. Group interaction may have become more socially reinforcing to the patients because of the 10 consecutive sessions with predominantly rational conversation during Phases 6 and 7. An alternative explanation for the lack of a clear-cut "reversal" is that the value of each token as a reinforcer may have been reduced during Phase 8 by virtue of greater token earnings by the patients in ward routines outside of the group sessions.

Of clinical import is the demonstrated effect of task structure, through game playing, on the flow of rational speech in the group sessions. Simple games such as the ones used in this experiment can be employed easily in most treatment settings. The games seemed to provide a series of prompts for rational speech that the social environment naturally reinforced in the form of sequential questions and answers (Marlatt, 1972). At least for paranoid schizophrenics, the structure of a task needs to be well defined, as in a game, since conversational topics suggested by the therapist proved ineffective. It is of interest that token reinforcement and game playing also have been demonstrated to increase the amount of social interaction among a group of four withdrawn, chronic psychotics (Liberman, 1972b).

A pathological modeling effect seemed to occur in the group that multiplied the impact of any delusional material that was presented. This "ripple" effect does not appear to occur when paranoid patients are placed in heterogeneous groups, suggesting that groups of paranoids alone should be avoided. The existence of marked individual differences in responses to the various interventions must also be noted. While Jack and Herman showed expected changes in rational speech according to the imposition of games and token reinforcement, Mary showed almost no variation in speech, with an average of 90% or more rational talk throughout each of the conditions. Jane's responses were almost totally unpredictable and not clearly under the influence of the experimental variables. With the exception of Mary, the patients also exhibited marked session-to-session variability within each of the experimental conditions.

A change in medication for Jane confounds the results of her response to the various interventions and may help to explain her variability. Because Jane had been suspected of "cheeking" and spitting out her tablets, her phenothiazine medication was changed to liquid form just prior to the first token reinforcement phase. Although the amount of medication—800 mg of Chlorpromazine daily—remained constant, her in-therapy verbal behavior may have been affected by differential absorption of the phenothiazines as well as by the environmental conditions. Jane's daily dosage of Chlorpromazine remained at 800 mg until two sessions into Phase 8, the final baseline period, when it was reduced to 400 mg/day. Two sessions later it was reduced to 200 mg/day and was then discontinued after two more sessions.

It is of interest that while Jane received no medication at all during the final five sessions of the experiment, at the same time her rational speech climbed steadily from 0 to 91.7% of the segments. Other studies indicate that phenothiazines have greater effects on social withdrawal than on the content of psychotic speech (Liberman, Davis, Moore, & Moon, 1973). It is important that all published accounts of behavioral interventions include descriptions of the type and dose of medication given during the study (Spohn, 1973), since drugs have such a powerful effect on behavior. In the current study, Herman's medication (400 mg/day of Chlorpromazine) remained constant throughout the entire experiment and Mary and Jack had no medication whatsoever.

Thirty months after the last session and 28 months after the four Ss were discharged, Jack and Mary continued to live in a small residential care facility in the community. They both frequently visit a nearby shopping center, and Jack pursues his gardening and photography hobbies. Jane has been rehospitalized twice since her discharge but has remained out of the hospital longer than in the past. Herman was rehospitalized at a Veteran's Administration hospital briefly but is presently living in a residential care home in Los Angeles. He occasionally phones and visits the clinical research unit to report that he is "doing fine." Thus, as a group, these subjects have been markedly successful in maintaining themselves in the community since their course of behavior therapy.

The group experience was, of course, only part of a more comprehensive behavior therapy program aimed at reducing delusional speech and improving socialization. Changing long-standing and highly ingrained behavior patterns, such as delusional speech, requires a controlled milieu and staff therapists who can provide consistent contingencies of social attention over very long periods of time. Nursing staff require enthusiastic support from their professional consultants and supervisors in ignoring "crazy talk" and warmly attending to realistic talk among delusional patients. These contingencies need to be applied consistently 24 hours a day for many months. Even with optimal treatment conditions, generalization of improved conversational content into new settings and the future must be specifically and energetically programmed, rather than expected to occur spontaneously.

In summary, controlled experiments using within-subject or group designs with a variety of patient populations have clearly demonstrated the effectiveness of systematic and contingent reinforcers (social and tangible) in improving the amount and content of social conversation in relatively unstructured therapy groups. A further extension of these findings has been speculatively applied to the behavior of individuals in sensitivity and encounter groups (Houts & Serber, 1972). The creative and stimulating techniques used by group leaders in the "humanistic" or human growth movement can be made more effective in generating long-term and generalizable changes in members' behavior by an infusion of social learning principles without sacrificing the immediacy of their impact on feelings.

BEHAVIORAL METHODS IN STRUCTURED GROUP THERAPY

In this section, we will describe group therapy formats that have been structured by the leader with objectives for behavioral change planned prior to the session. Spontaneous and free-flowing group process and interaction is limited and focused and may be discouraged by the leader if it interferes with achieving the predetermined objectives. The therapist takes a task-oriented, educational role by prompting in-group interaction and by giving and reinforcing "homework" assignments. However, as in any work group, group dynamics such as cohesiveness do inevitably develop and enhance the learning that goes on at a more explicit level.

Systematic Desensitization

Systematic desensitization, one of the first of the behavioral therapies, is used for patients with avoidance problems based upon fear or anxiety, such as phobias. Desensitization has been applied in group settings for patients with various anxiety reactions. A group of individuals with a similar problem are taken through the steps of the desensitization program simultaneously. Patients with fears of traveling (Lazarus, 1961), public speaking (Paul, 1969), examinations (Ihli & Garlington, 1969), and socializing (Paul & Shannon, 1966), have been successfully treated in group settings with a substantial saving of therapists' time. The use of desensitization in groups appears to be as effective as individual desensitization, and in several controlled studies, it proved to be more effective than conventional psychotherapy. The group situation can be engineered so that patients with different avoidance problems can be treated at the same time. This is done by providing each person with an index card or note paper on which his or her individualized hierarchy is written. After the group has been taught to master deep muscle relaxation together, the therapist cues their moving through their own particular hierarchy by saying, "Now, picture the next scene on your list as vividly as you can while remaining deeply relaxed." Each person moves at his or her own pace, so that some individuals will complete their desensitization before others. The exposure or desensitization *in vivo* method of anxiety management, demonstrably more efficient than desensitization with imagery, has also been conducted in groups of phobics with results more favorable than obtained through individual therapy.

Social Skills Training

Social skills training is a generic term that includes any structured group situation that facilitates the acquisition of emotionally expressive behaviors and interpersonal goals. Behavioral goals can include learning how to "stand up for yourself," saying "no" to people who are exploiting you, obtaining instrumental role needs in everyday life, expressing affection, anger, tenderness, or sadness. Other terms in use to describe this type of group are personal effectiveness training, assertion training, and structured learning therapy. The behaviorist position assumes that once the appropriate overt expressions of emotions are learned, practiced, and reinforced, the correlated inward or subjective feelings will be experienced.

The process of social skills training involves a series of steps:

1. Identify the problems in expressing feelings and specify the "where, when, how, what, and with whom" of the problem.

2. Target the goals of training, which usually consist of new behaviors to rectify deficits in performance or modulation of excessive or overly intense emotional expressiveness.

3. Simulate the problem situation using the group members to role play or rehearse the relevant scenes. These are usually scenes that have occurred in the recent past or those that are likely to occur in the near future.

4. Use modeling and shaping (reinforcing successive approximations) to gradually modify the client's expressive behaviors. Elements of the total behavioral gestalt are added one by one, such as facial expression, vocal tone and loudness, posture, accessory body movements, eye contact (nonverbals), and speech content.

5. Have the group give feedback to the individual on his or her improving performance—positive feedback for improvements rather than confrontation for failure is emphasized.

6. Give the individual assignments to practice the behaviors learned in the group setting in real-life situations and then use group approval to reinforce successes.

While social skills training methods are used in individual and family psychotherapy, their most efficient application lies in therapy groups. The ingredients of assertion training—problem specification, goal setting, behavioral rehearsal, modeling, prompting, and feedback—can be effectively used with homogeneously or heterogeneously composed groups. Currently under clinical development and research evaluation are structured learning groups for hospitalized chronic psychotics, divorced and separated individuals, alcoholics, drug addicts, depressed out-patients, mothers learning more effective child management skills, and women in the female consciousness-raising movement. A large amount of evidence has been collected to demonstrate the effectiveness of structured learning in groups for poor and underprivileged patients, for training paraprofessionals in therapy skills, and for supervisors and managers in business enterprises (Goldstein, 1974).

Social skills or personal effectiveness training in groups has been introduced as a fundamental component of the clinical services offered by a comprehensive community mental health center (Liberman, 1972a; Liberman, King, DeRisi, & McCann, 1975). Patients with a variety of problems are taught to improve their interpersonal communication in six-session, crisis intervention groups. Groups of adolescents practice problem solving with peers and adults, and children undergo social skills training with the aid of videotape feedback and token reinforcement. Anxious and depressed out-patients participate in a combined format utilizing both a variant of desensitization (anxiety management training) and personal effectiveness training. Married couples in distress receive group training in communication skills, such as giving empathy, initiating requests, giving positive feedback, and expressing negative feelings directly. The married couples also learn to recognize and reinforce pleasing behaviors in the spouse and to negotiate and agree on a contingency contract.

Personal effectiveness training, a more generic form of assertion training, is the keystone of treatment for a mixed group of psychotic and marginally functioning patients at the day treatment program of the community mental health center. Patients referred to the day treatment program as an alternative to hospitalization have major deficits in their repertoires of emotional expressiveness and family and work roles. Many of them are passive and withdrawn and reluctant to stand up for their rights. They fail to generate reinforcers from their families and work settings, but instead allow the world to ignore or exploit them. Some patients are deficient in expressing affection, anger, or sadness. Expressing these emotions, with convincing nonverbal correlates, is the goal of personal effectiveness training.

The training is carried out in small groups of 6 to 15 patients with two staff members as leaders. The patients participate in four group sessions per week for 1 to 3 months, since the community mental health center emphasizes short-term treatment. Each patient is given a "report card" that lists the targeted goals for their "homework" between training sessions. The start of each session is set aside for setting goals and getting feedback from the patients on their progress. When a goal has been achieved in the community (i.e., when the training has been generalized), a new goal is selected. Examples of specific goals that are set include: (a) expressing enthusiasm and desire for help to a vocational rehabilitation counselor; (b) expressing affection to husband; (c) persisting with one's rights at the welfare office; (d) asking a girl out for a date; (e) keeping on a single subject in a conversation; (f) requesting that husband allow wife to drive the car; (g) initiating a conversation with a stranger; (h) telling roommate to bathe more often; (i) confronting a subordinate at work with his poor performance; (j) "selling" oneself at a job interview; and (k) inviting a neighbor over for coffee.

An evaluation of personal effectiveness training showed that 78% of 50 unselected, consecutive interpersonal scenes or situations that were rehearsed in the day treatment program were reported by the patients as having been performed successfully outside the group in their natural milieus. In a second phase of the evaluation, 50 additional scenes were rehearsed in the group. Direct observation in the community by research assistants indicated that 80% of these practiced scenes were actually performed by the patients. This evaluation demonstrated that structured group therapy is effective with a broad range of psychiatric patients, enabling them to transfer the behaviors learned in the mental health center to everyday problem situations (King, Liberman, Roberts, & Bryan, 1977). More controlled, experimental data from several research centers indicate that the assertion training "package" of methods is causally related to improvements in behavior (Hersen & Bellack, 1976).

Social skills training is a general label that currently includes many different approaches, having in common only their dependence upon behavioral and learning principles. These approaches will be more specifically formulated and evaluated during the next 5 to 10 years, but they already promise to be a major movement for generating change through groups.

CONCLUSIONS

The behavioral approach to group therapy, with its more systematic and specific guidelines, makes it less likely that a therapist will adventitiously reinforce or model contradictory behavior patterns. The behavioral approach, consistently applied, is a fast and effective means of modifying maladaptive behavior in groups. While the technology of the behavioral clinician, based on empirical laws of learning, is important in treatment, the relationship with the group members also contributes to the outcome. A therapist who does not have a positive alliance with the group does not possess reinforcing or modeling properties. As an educator and lever for initiating changes in the group reinforcement contingencies, the therapist depends in part on a capacity to show empathy, warmth, and concern for those he or she is working with.

Further clinical and research progress made by behavior therapists will challenge all group therapists, regardless of their theoretical leanings, to specify more clearly their interventions, their goals, and their empirical results. Only when this happens can we develop a compendium of techniques with known and predictable effects on a wide variety of clinical problems.

ACKNOWLEDGMENTS

The authors acknowledge the therapeutic skill and commitment of the nurses and technicians of the Clinical Research Unit whose consistency and competence made this work possible. The authors appreciate the support and encouragement of Robert Coombs, Chief of Research, Clinton Rust, Executive Director of Camarillo State Hospital, and Louis Jolyon West, Medical Director of the Neuropsychiatric Institute.

REFERENCES

Birk, L. Intensive group therapy: An effective behavioral-psychoanalytic method. *American Journal of Psychiatry*, 1974, *131*, 11–16.

Clement, P. W., Fazzone, R. A., & Goldstein, B. Tangible reinforcers and child group therapy. *Journal of the American Academy of Child Psychiatry*, 1970, *9*, 409–427.

Goldstein, A. P. *Structured learning therapy: Toward a psychotherapy for the poor.* New York: Pergamon, 1974.

Hauserman, N., Zweback, S., & Plotkin, A. Use of concrete reinforcement to facilitate verbal initiations in adolescent group therapy. *Journal of Consulting and Clinical Psychology*, 1972, *38*, 90–96.

Heckel, R. W., Wiggins, S. L., & Salzberg, H. D. Conditioning against silences in group therapy. *Journal of Clinical Psychology*, 1962, *18*, 216–217.

Hersen, M., & Bellack, A. S. Social skills training for chronic psychiatric patients. *Comprehensive Psychiatry*, 1976, *17*, 559–580.

Houts, P. S., & Serber, M. (Eds.). *After the turn-on, what? Learning perspectives on humanistic groups.* Champaign, Ill.: Research Press, 1972.

Ihli, K. L., & Garlington, W. K. A comparison of groups vs. individual desensitization of test anxiety. *Behaviour Research and Therapy*, 1969, *7*, 207–209.

King, L. W., Liberman, R. P., Roberts, J., & Bryan, E. Personal effectiveness: A structured therapy for improving social and emotional skills. *Behaviour Analysis and Modification*, 1977, *2*, 82–91.

Lazarus, A. A. Group therapy of phobic disorders by systematic desensitization. *Journal of Abnormal and Social Psychology*, 1961, *63*, 504–510.

Liberman, R. P. A behavioral approach to group dynamics. *Behavior Therapy,* 1970, *1,* 140–175.

Liberman, R. P. Reinforcement of cohesiveness in group therapy: Behavioral and personality changes. *Archives of General Psychiatry,* 1971, *25,* 168–177.

Liberman, R. P. Behavioral methods in group and family therapy. *Seminars in Psychiatry,* 1972, *4,* 145–156. (a)

Liberman, R. P. Reinforcement of social interaction in a group of chronic mental patients. In R. Rubin, H. Fensterheim, J. D. Henderson, & L. Ullmann (Eds.), *Advances in behavior therapy* (Vol. 3). New York: Academic Press, 1972. Pp. 151–160. (b)

Liberman, R. P., Davis, J., Moore, J., & Moon, W. Research design for analyzing drug-behavior-environment interactions. *Journal of Nervous and Mental Disease,* 1973, *156,* 432–439.

Liberman, R. P., King, L. W., DeRisi, W. J., & McCann, M. *Personal effectiveness training: A manual for teaching social and emotional skills.* Champaign, Ill.: Research Press, 1975.

Liberman, R. P., Teigen, J., Patterson, R., & Baker, V. Reducing delusional speech in chronic paranoid schizophrenics. *Journal of Applied Behavior Analysis,* 1973, *6,* 57–64.

Licker, L., Perel, I., Wallace, C. J., & Davis, J. It's the staff that keeps the patients talking. *Journal of Psychiatric Nursing and Mental Health,* 1976, *14,* 11–14.

Marlatt, G. A. Task structure and the experimental modification of verbal behavior. *Psychological Bulletin,* 1972, *78,* 335–350.

O'Connor, R. D. Modification of social withdrawal through symbolic modeling. *Journal of Applied Behavior Analysis,* 1969, *2,* 15–22.

Paul, G. L. Outcome of systematic desensitization. In C. M. Franks (Ed.), *Behavior therapy: Appraisal and status.* New York: McGraw-Hill, 1969. Pp. 63–159.

Paul, G. L., & Shannon, D. T. Treatment of anxiety through systematic desensitization in therapy groups. *Journal of Abnormal Psychology,* 1966, *71,* 124–134.

Shapiro, D., & Birk, L. Group therapy in experimental perspective. *International Journal of Group Psychotherapy,* 1967, *17,* 211–224.

Spohn, H. E. The case for reporting the drug status of patient subjects in experimental studies of schizophrenic pathology. *Journal of Abnormal Psychology,* 1973, *82,* 102–106.

Wing, J. K., Monck, E., Brown, G. W., & Carstairs, G. M. Morbidity in the community of schizophrenic patients discharged from London mental hospitals in 1959. *British Journal of Psychiatry,* 1964, *110,* 10–21.

Wodarski, J. S., Hamblin, R. L., Buckholdt, D. R., & Ferritor, D. E. The effects of different reinforcement contingencies on cooperative behaviors exhibited by fifth graders. In R. Rubin, J. P. Brady, & J. D. Henderson (Eds.), *Advances in behavior therapy* (Vol. 4). New York: Academic Press, 1973. Pp. 255–262.

Zusman, J. Some explanations of the changing appearance of psychotic patients: Antecedents of the Social Breakdown Syndrome Concept. *International Journal of Psychiatry,* 1967, *3,* 216–237.

_14_

Behavioral Group Therapy for Obsessions and Compulsions: First Results of a Pilot Study

IVER HAND AND MARLEN TICHATZKY

INTRODUCTION

To our knowledge, no systematic group treatment for obsessions and compulsions has been published in the behavior therapy literature. In-patient group treatment has been attempted by Meyer and his colleagues, but it proved to be difficult (Chesser, 1976). Early in 1976 we started an out-patient group project for severely handicapped obsessive–compulsive patients with multiple problems. This group of patients seems unlikely to benefit sufficiently from behavioral treatment techniques directed merely at their obsessions and compulsions. Successful "symptom"[1] treatment with these patients probably includes considerable skillful intervention in other problem areas. Unfortunately, behavior therapy publications in the past have often tended to overemphasize symptom-directed specific treatment techniques, whereas so-called unspecific interventions in other problem areas are hardly mentioned. We intended to develop a treatment package that would deal systematically with all those problem areas that frequently plague obsessive–compulsive patients. In the context of our

[1]The term _symptom,_ as we use it here, does not have the same meaning as it does in psychoanalytic usage. Rather, the term merely covers the problem area that the patient initially presents for treatment, as distinguished from other problem areas.

TRENDS IN BEHAVIOR THERAPY

Copyright © 1979 by Academic Press, Inc.
All rights of reproduction in any form reserved.
ISBN 0-12-647450-8

community-oriented work, emphasizing training in the natural environment, we aimed for an out-patient program involving the social micro-unit most relevant for the patient in her[2] daily life. So far, most behavior therapy studies with individual obsessive–compulsive patients have included an in-patient period of a minimum of 6 weeks. However, there is evidence that obsessive–compulsives can be helped equally effectively on an out-patient basis (Boersma, DenHengst, Dekker, & Emmelkamp, 1976; Meyer, Robertson, & Tatlow, 1975).

Before describing the details of our study, we will briefly review the reasons for the use of this treatment in a group setting.

Use of Group Dynamics in Problem-Homogeneous Groups

Systematic use of group dynamic processes is still a neglected field in behavior therapy. An extensive review of the English and American behavior therapy literature (Hand, 1975) shows that, until recently, the small number of "group" treatments has largely been limited to the application of individual treatment techniques to several patients simultaneously. Except for Liberman's studies (1970, 1971a, 1971b; see also Liberman & Teigen, Chapter 13 of this volume), few systematic applications or even observations of interactional phenomena in behavior therapy groups were published until 1974. An integration of experimental findings on small-group dynamics (Hare, 1976; Shaw, 1976), with data on objectifiable group processes described in the rather heterogeneous "group therapy" literature, into a behavioral group therapy model appears to be possible and useful (Hand, 1975). Since the mid-1970s, we have witnessed increasing efforts in this direction (Goldstein, 1973; Grawe, 1977; Lazarus, 1974; Liberman, King, DeRisi, & McCann, 1975).

Liberman (1970, 1971a, 1971b) was the first to show that the enhancement of group "cohesion" (as defined by Shaw in 1976) by systematic reinforcement increases the beneficial effect of group treatment for patients with a variety of problems (problem-heterogeneous groups). Hand, Lamontagne, and Marks (1974) investigated whether high group cohesion can be an additional therapeutic agent in symptom-directed treatment of a problem-homogeneous group. Their study of group therapy for agoraphobics compared groups with high and low cohesion. There was some evidence that the highly cohesive condition produced better followup results than the low-cohesion condition; the former type of group was also easier for the therapist to conduct. A replication by Teasdale, Walsh, Lancashire, and Mathews (1977) did not confirm this particular effect during followup. Further work on the long term effects of highly cohe-

---

[2]Since the majority of our obsessive–compulsive patients are female, we have consistently referred to patients as females in this chapter.

sive groups for agoraphobics is currently under way in our behavior therapy outpatient unit at the Department of Psychiatry, Hamburg University.

The group dynamics that are systematically reinforced are restricted to items usually subsumed under the term "cohesion," that is, mutual understanding and mutual help during treatment exercises, including reduction of self-centeredness by increased concern for others; decrease of dependence on the therapist; provision of a chance to meet people with whom a trusting and helpful relationship can be established beyond therapy; and mutual reduction of anxiety regarding discussion of problem areas other than the symptom. These items seem to be essential in defining a collection of patients as a treatment group and in calling the procedure a group treatment.

"Group exposure" in which cohesion and helpful interaction is furthered by the therapist (Krumboltz & Potter, 1973) is now used for agoraphobics in several clinics in England (Hafner & Marks, 1976; Hand et al., 1974; Teasdale et al., 1977), Norway (Holm, 1973), and Germany (Hand & Wedel, 1978). It is applied to symptom-homogeneous groups with the clear goal of symptom reduction by graded exposure *in vivo*. (For a definition and review of laboratory and clinical studies of this method, see Marks, 1975). Group exposure for agoraphobics is only directed at the phobias. Other problem areas are merely identified in group discussions and attempts are made to motivate the patients for changes in these areas, if necessary in therapy at a later date.

Our current project for severely disturbed obsessive–compulsives goes beyond this aim toward simultaneous improvement of other important problem areas and of problem-solving skills in general. Group-specific processes are used in a much broader way, particularly to change interpersonal behavior in close dyadic, as well as in general social interactions.

Motivation and Goal Setting

The trend in behavioral group procedures noted in the preceding section parallels a recent development in individual behavior therapy: the concept of therapy as an ongoing behavioral and motivational analysis, particularly for those patients who enter therapy either unable to face their "real" problem or suffering without being able to specify their problems (Gottman & Leiblum, 1974; Kanfer, 1977; Kanfer & Saslow, 1969). This approach implies a continuous motivational procedure to help patients face problems that give rise to high anxiety and a chronic feeling of helplessness. When treating such patients in a group setting, it is important to provide a similar opportunity for a continuous behavioral and motivational analysis and to allow for successive problem solving until major problem areas can be tackled. Such a treatment program may well start with the symptom that brought the patient into treatment.

A note of caution may be necessary: Since two decades of behavior therapy practice has shown that numerous patients do benefit from a straight, short, and standardized single-problem-directed treatment. It is also well known that the more treatment that is offered, the more a patient may "need." Thus, using a short and standardized technique with a certain patient may indicate high therapeutic skill, or it may reflect poor technological thinking. Unfortunately, we often lack prognostic criteria to safely predict the most appropriate intervention.

Our program is meant for patients who are unlikely to benefit from the single-problem-directed approach. So far, the criteria for selecting patients for this study have been derived only from "clinical experience." We have now started a second step of research to look into the time factor as well as the necessary level of complexity of the treatment package for this kind of patient.

TREATMENT

Treatment Model

RESEARCH STRATEGY

We decided to design a package approach to fit the everyday practices of an out-patient psychotherapy unit in an average-sized city. In such a setting, the therapist usually gets few obsessive–compulsive patients at a time, and the group model requires five to seven patients appearing together on the waiting list. Matching of groups for sex, age, specific sub-symptoms, and background problems receives much less emphasis in this approach than in the usual kind of controlled study. Otherwise, the problem of group composition may increase the waiting time so much that this negative effect outweighs the advantages of the group approach. A treatment package for such groups also has to be organized so that the whole course of treatment is clearly structured, with successive stages of different content, and yet open enough to permit individual variation as group composition dictates. Only after experience with several randomly composed groups can conclusions be reached about the specific group constellations that naturally appear and how their varying needs can best be met.

TREATMENT PACKAGE

We wanted to investigate an out-patient treatment model that utilized *in vivo* training as much as possible, while employing a group setting in which cohesion was systematically reinforced. Some of the factors that increase cohesion, like common complaints and goals and high external pressure on the group, are easy to achieve in the agoraphobia groups during their emotion-arousing *in vivo* exposure outside the hospital (Hand *et al.*, 1974). Obviously, it is more difficult to create situations in which a group of obsessive–compulsive patients can share similar *in vivo* exercises. One solution to this problem will be described in a later section of this chapter.

Whenever possible, we arranged for systematic spouse and family involvement. A study by the Oxford group (Mathews, Teasdale, Johnston, Munby, & Shaw, 1977) has shown that this may lead to continued improvement during followup, at least with agoraphobics. Marks (1975) found spouse groups very helpful as an adjunct to individual treatment of obsessive–compulsive patients. There is at present a general trend in behavior therapy to involve spouses and families in a variety of treatments. Haley (1976) has recently formulated a "problem-solving therapy" model that combines treatment techniques from behavior therapy with interventions on the spouse and family levels, mainly derived from communication theory. This conceptualization has influenced our interventions.

Our package had to include systematic group training for transfer into a goal-oriented self-help group, not only for mutual help in symptom reduction, but also for the development of new, alternative behavior. The assumption was that a self-help group would be particularly useful for patients with long-lasting complaints and repeated treatments, since going to the therapist may have become a habit for some patients over the years. On the other hand, self-help groups can produce undesirable effects by actually reinforcing illness behavior rather than reducing it (Hand, 1975). An important task for the therapist is therefore to guide the patients to establish therapeutic group norms. The feasibility and efficacy of transfer to a posttreatment self-help group need further experimental investigation (Hand, 1975; Mathews *et al.*, 1977). The present study is intended as a contribution in that direction.

Finally, we did not want to exceed the average time of patient–therapist contact used in the standard individual treatment of obsessive–compulsive patients.

A BEHAVIORAL OUT-PATIENT GROUP THERAPY MODEL

The content and setting of each phase of the Behavioral Out-Patient Group Therapy Model (BOGTMO) are outlined in Chart 14.1. The treatment program is divided into three phases. Before the first group session, patients and, whenever possible, their spouses have had two to three individual interviews for a first behavioral analysis and goal setting.

Phase I. Phase I consists of 12 weeks of intensive patient–therapist contact. The treatment starts with group sessions in the hospital twice weekly, initially lasting 3 hours, then gradually reduced to 2 hours. In a second step, the frequency is reduced to once a week, with sessions again lasting 3 hours, later reduced to 2 hours. In addition, the patients receive

CHART 14.1

A Behavioral Out-Patient Group Therapy Model (BOGTMO)

Phase	Weeks	Content	Setting
IA	2	*Patients:* Mutual information about "symptom," other problem areas and life style *Spouses:* Similar to patients *Therapist:* Reinforcing group interaction; avoiding expert role; trusting relationship to patient and spouse *Together:* Goal setting Main emphasis: Cohesion	PATIENTS THERAPIST SPOUSES THERAPIST PATIENTS SPOUSES THERAPIST
IB	6	*Therapist:* Takes expert role in "symptom" area and group management; models helping skills *Patients:* Learn coping techniques for "symptom"; receive training as co-therapist and group leader Main emphasis: "Symptom" behavior	PATIENTS HOME VISITS (*in vivo* training) 1 PATIENT THERAPIST 1 PEER SPOUSE FAMILY THERAPIST
IC	4	After first "symptom" reduction, reevaluation of treatment goals; extension of treatment to other problem areas; establishment of alternative behavior Main emphasis: Other problem areas Conjoint reevaluation of treatment goals	Video playback of home visits PATIENTS SPOUSES THERAPIST
II	6	Fading out of therapist Main emphasis: Alternative behavior	PATIENTS (therapist)
III	12	Beginning of self-help group Spouses as potential reinforcing agents for ongoing self-help group	PATIENTS (therapist) PATIENTS (+ SPOUSES) (OPEN ENDED)

five home visits or *in vivo* training sessions, with members of the family, one peer patient, and the therapist present.

During the first 2 to 3 weeks of Phase I (IA), the therapist's main goals are to create a trusting relationship not only with the patients, but also with the spouses in order to gain their cooperation from the start and to reduce their anxiety regarding a possible patient–therapist coalition against them.

The therapist must also establish cohesion among the patients and the patients' spouses. In this context it is critical to diminish the role differentiation that usually occurs when the therapist treats one person in the dyad as "patient" and the other as "normal" (Haley, 1976). To achieve these goals, the therapist must use expert knowledge of group dynamics before accepting the expert role for symptom treatment. He or she reinforces and encourages mutual information about the symptom, other problem areas, and general life style. For many patients, this is their first chance to talk openly about problem areas other than the obsessions and compulsions, and it allows them to extend their treatment goals.

After a few sessions with the patients, the therapist meets the spouses as a group. This session is conducted under the assumption that "being close to people who have problems means having problems oneself." Therefore, the therapist emphasizes open discussion about the spouses' life situation, their problems, and their feelings before a discussion of the patients' problems is started. This *spouse-group session* early in treatment serves to increase spouses' motivation for active participation. It also gives the spouses a defined role for the *conjoint patient–spouse–therapist session*. Without this group session for themselves, spouses may feel insecure in the conjoint session with their partners, in which only the symptoms of the patients would be discussed. Before the start of the symptom-treatment period, final goal setting occurs in the conjoint session. Ideally, on this occasion treatment goals should already have evolved in other problem areas in addition to the obsessions and compulsions. The therapist must ensure that the goals are defined in behavioral terms. At this early stage, patients typically want: better communication with others; less distrust in others; less dependency upon others; higher self-esteem; and ability to develop and fight for one's own standards in the area of socially acceptable anancastic (see Beech, 1974) behavior, as well as in other areas.

After this session, the intensive symptom treatment begins (Phase 1B). Initially, the therapist accepts the expert role and gives explanations of and treatment advice for obsessive–compulsive symptomatology, particularly regarding the methods of *in vivo* exposure, response prevention, and modeling (hereafter referred to as exposure exercises). Therapist skills concerning the proper application of these techniques are also modeled. For most patients, it is possible to find at least one situation in the hospital that is difficult to tolerate. The therapist then demonstrates, in front of the group, how treatment is properly conducted with at least one exposure exercise for a difficult situation for each patient. This gives the members of the group an opportunity to learn about each other and to observe possible treatment effects. After a few demonstrations, the patients are gently but firmly pushed into a cotherapist role, so that eventually the group members work out specific treatment steps for each other.

Soon after the start of these symptom exercises in the hospital, the *in vivo* training begins, usually as home visits for 3 hours. Unfortunately, obsessive–compulsive patients whose most severe symptomatology occurs in the home setting, generally refuse to have the whole group present during the first few home visits. In fact, at the start it is even difficult for them to accept the therapist and one group member in their home. The first session is therefore videotaped and shown in parts at the subsequent group session, which is conducted by the peer who had been present during the home visit. This ensures maximum possible information as well as an opportunity for mutual advice and help for the group. This, to some extent, compensates for the lack of group participation in the home visit. With respect to emotional arousal and rapid behavior change, these home visits resemble the *in vivo* exposures in agoraphobia groups much more than the exposure exercises in the group setting in the hospital.

The first home visit includes another behavioral analysis, followed by the exposure exercises. A behavioral contract is also established between patient and family on how to cope with obsessions and compulsions. In subsequent home sessions, occurring approximately once a week, marital counseling may become the main focus of treatment after patient and spouse have grasped the principles of the exposure technique. The therapist guards against marital counseling being used to avoid work on obsessions and compulsions. Presence of a peer is required not only to further group cohesion, but also because patients need to know each others' real-life problem areas well in Phase III of treatment if they are to function as a self-help group for mutual support. The home visits also have an important diagnostic function. Often, the most problematic obsessive–compulsive behavior and family interactions can only be observed in the home setting.

At the end of Phase IB, which consists of home visits and a number of homework assignments for the days in between group meetings, the first major reduction of obsessions and compulsions can be expected. Group members now ought to be "experts" regarding the application of the exposure techniques. In the next step they learn to become group leaders. They are trained to take responsibility for the timing and task achievement of the group session, to encourage peers to report progress and failures in homework, and to interrupt peers who make conversation to avoid goal-oriented work. In this stage the patient also learns to accept the high subjective risk of making mistakes, hurting peers, or being attacked. For obsessive–compulsive patients this is a particularly difficult step, which must be mastered before the group can progress to goal-oriented self-help in Phases II and III. At the end of Phase I (IC), patients should have learned how to cope with obsessions and compulsions and how to progress further, individually or with help. The therapist now consistently redirects questions regarding obsessive–compulsive behavior to the group. The establishment of alternative behavior and necessary tasks in other problem areas, which were identified during the continuous behavioral analysis, are also emphasized. Phase I ends with *a second conjoint patient–spouse–therapist meeting*. The spouses are now ideally fully involved in treatment, having participated in the spouse group, the first conjoint group, and in home exercises. The second conjoint meeting is devoted to an evaluation of the positive and negative treatment effects, as well as to a reevaluation of general treatment goals. At this stage of the program, decisions may be made to start marital therapy, join an assertiveness training group, or implement major changes in daily life, such as taking up a job or regular free-time activities.

Phase II. Phase II consists of six weekly meetings in which patients gain more experience in taking over responsibility for treatment and in conducting the group sessions. The time spent on exposure exercises is reduced in favor of work on other problem areas and the establishment of alternative behavior. Every second group session in Phase II is conducted by a patient, without the therapist being present. These sessions are taperecorded to provide information for the therapist.

Phase III. Phase III lasts for another 12 weeks, with meetings once a week to establish self-help skills. The therapist participates sporadically to enhance the group members' self-help skills. Phase III may be regarded as a structured followup. The study by Hand *et al.* (1974), suggested that high group cohesion may lead to better followup results, possibly by creating higher patient motivation to continue exercises in the followup period (Gelder, 1977). When designing the present program, we thought that integration of regular group meetings without a therapist into the treatment program might increase the likelihood of successful self-help activities and further reduce obsessions and compulsions, as well as increase mutual assistance in other problem areas and development of alternative behavior. In the last area, the group setting might be particularly helpful for socially isolated patients.

Application of the Treatment Model

PATIENTS

So far, we have treated 17 patients in three successive groups. The first author treated Groups 1 and 2, with the second author acting as cotherapist. The second author treated Group 3, along with a new cotherapist. Group 1 was an "experimental" group in which we deliberately allowed the patients to influence the content of every session, since we wanted to discover whether the patients behaved differently in a group setting as compared with individual treatment. Groups 2 and 3 were treated in a much tighter structure as a result of our experience with Group 1. The 17 patients treated in the present study represent one-third of the 53 obsessive–compulsive patients whom we saw in our behavior therapy out-patient unit over a period of 18 months. When this report was written, 17 of the remaining patients were still on the waiting list. The others received individual or couple treatment. Only 5 of them were admitted into the hospital, for reasons related to the traveling time from home to hospital, rather than to the severity of obsessions and compulsions.

The upper section (Patients) of Chart 14.2 shows the patient characteristics for each group. The by-chance composition from the waiting list produced three rather different groups with respect to important variables such as age, sex, marital status, work adjustment, duration of obsessions and compulsions, and duration of previous treatments. Regarding the type of obsessions and compulsions, the groups appeared to be rather homogeneous. Only a few patients suffered from ruminations; several had had periods of ruminating during the earlier course of their illness. Those patients who held jobs had serious difficulties at work because of their illness. With a few exceptions, the patients, as well as the doctors who referred them for treatment, had expected in-patient therapy because of the severity of the problems. Duration of obsessive–compulsive symptoms, as well as duration of previous treatments, varied in all groups from a few years to approximately 20 years. Reliable assessment of problem and treatment duration was difficult, however. Group 2 may seem to be more disturbed, showing the longest average duration of previous treatment and having three of the four patients in the whole study who received a pension because of their illness. However, this impression is not confirmed in the ratings of the current severity of their illness (discussed later). All four married patients in Group 2 reported long-lasting and severe marital discord. Some authors (e.g., Beech, 1974) claim that, on the average, no more than half of obsessive–compulsives are married. However, two-thirds of the total sample of our patients were married. Unmarried obsessive–compulsive patients may tend to avoid treatment, whereas, at least in our sample, pressures from the spouse often seemed to contribute to the decision to seek treatment.

TIME STRUCTURE OF TREATMENT PHASES

The lower section (Treatments) of Chart 14.2 gives the actual time schedule for the three groups over the different treatment phases of the BOGTMO (see Chart 14.1). The treatment of Group 1 cannot be separated into phases because the therapists had a more passive, observational role than in the other two groups. Group 1 also had nearly twice as many treatment sessions in the hospital and far fewer home visits than the other groups. Groups 2 and 3 were treated with an identical systematic approach over three successive phases with minor differences in content, as seen in Chart 14.2. For reasons external to the research program, the Phase I interventions of Group 3 were more concentrated in time than those of Group 2. All home exercises were conducted during Phase I. The greater number

CHART 14.2
Patients and Treatment Time

Group

	Group 1				Group 2				Group 3			
Patients	N=6 (5F; 1M) Age: 33 (20–52) Married: 4 At work: 1 Years with "symptom": 7.5 (2–27) Years of treatment: 4.5 (2–10)				N=5 (5F) Age: 42 (36–50) Married: 4 At work: 1 Years with "symptom": 8.6 (5–20) Years of treatment: 8.0 (.5–20)				N=6 (3F; 3M) Age: 38 (26–62) Married: 4 At work: 2 Years with "symptom": 5.8 (2–17) Years of treatment: 3.3 (.5–10)			
Treatments	Phase	Group and Therapists	Home Visits	Group Alone	Phase	Group and Therapists	Home Visits	Group Alone	Phase	Group and Therapists	Home Visits	Group Alone
	No separate phases	117 hours	29 hours	20 hours	(I) 12 weeks	52 hours	45 hours	—	(I) 12 weeks	60 hours	72 hours	12 hours
					(II) 6 weeks	9 hours	10 hours	9 hours	(II) 6 weeks	9 hours	—	9 hours
					(III) 12 weeks	(6 hours)	—	(30 hours)	(III) 12 weeks	(6 hours)	—	(30 hours)
		117 hours	29 hours	20 hours	30 weeks	67 hours	55 hours	39 hours	30 weeks	75 hours	72 hours	51 hours
	Total therapist time: 146 hours Time/patient: 24.5 hours				Total therapist time: 122 hours Time/patient: 24.5 hours				Total therapist time: 147 hours Time/patient: 27.5 hours			

of treatment hours in Group 3 was mainly due to the additional patient. Group 3 also had a few more sessions with the therapist during Phase I and started with several "leaderless" sessions during this phase. Total therapist time was approximately equal in all groups when the smaller number of patients in Group 2 is taken into account. Of the total therapist time in Group 1, only 25% was spent on home visits or *in vivo* exercises, as compared with 45 and 50% for Groups 2 and 3, respectively.

Therapist time per patient was approximately 25 hours. However, this figure has to be qualified by a number of considerations. We arrive at this figure by dividing the group-with-therapist time in the hospital sessions plus the time spent on home visits by the number of patients in the group. For various reasons, all patients did not attend every group session and all did not receive the same number of home visits. Taking these factors into account, the actual number of therapist hours should be higher. One also has to add 3 to 5 hours of individual pretreatment interviews. The main problem in assessing the number of therapist hours actually required is owing to the fact that Groups 2 and 3 have not yet completed Phase III. Also, the followup phase remains to be performed.

During the usual individual 6 weeks' in-patient treatment, the time spent by a psychiatrist, a psychologist, and a qualified nurse behavior therapist easily amounts to 60 hours per patient. This is not intended as a measure of the level of effectiveness of the two treatment approaches. It just shows the range within which later comparisons will have to be made.

COURSE AND CONTENT OF TREATMENT PHASES

The treatment package was designed to bring about changes in several problem areas, such as obsessions and compulsions, decision making, risk taking and mood tolerance, general social interaction, and couple and family interaction. Most of the therapist-induced treatment steps were implemented in Phase I, whereas Phase II was used mainly to prepare the patients for the self-help activities of Phase III. In the following section, we will outline the procedures used to achieve improvement in the problem areas already mentioned.

Symptom behavior: Information and goal setting. The first part of Phase I (IA) was designed solely to create a group through the establishment of cohesion. The second step of Phase I (IB) started with information about obsessions and compulsions and the treatment method to be used, in a way similar to the approach of the Maudsley group (Röper, 1977). At the same time, we tried to lower the patients' expectancies by stressing the following: Treatment was not intended to free them entirely of their symptoms, nor will symptom reduction necessarily make their lives happier; due to a long learning history, they are prone to respond with obsessions and/or compulsions to any major stress situation that they feel unable to cope with. Therefore, training to cope with the obsessions and compulsions is combined with training to cope with and resolve complex problem situations. Treatment is designed only to initiate a process of change, and long-term results will depend largely on the patients' own efforts after the end of treatment.

At the start of Phase IB, each patient had to decide to what extent she wanted to reduce her problem behavior, particularly the compulsions. This process of norm finding was easier to deal with in a group setting than in individual treatment. In the latter context, inexperienced therapists easily get involved in fruitless struggles with the patient, particularly in the areas of exactness and cleanliness, where patients often regard their symptom as an exaggeration of frequency or duration but not as a problem of the topography of the behavior. We left it entirely to the patient groups to develop norms for each of the group members. Since patients did not have exactly the same compulsions, they usually made sensible proposals to each other. The individuals usually accepted the norms developed by group consensus, probably because group cohesion had been sufficiently established before this stage of treatment.

Exposure in-vivo. The symptom-directed exposure technique was applied in the manner described by Hodgson and Rachman (1976), Marks (1975), Marks, Hodgson, and Rachman (1975), Meyer and Levy (1973), Meyer, Levy, and Schnurer (1974), and Rachman (1976). Patients' cooperation for rapid confrontation with the trigger situations that provoke anxiety and compulsive rituals was firmly but gently enhanced (Röper, 1977). The patients were never pushed to do anything they did not feel ready for. We never employed "surprise" confrontation with situations that the patient tended to avoid. For ethical as well as for therapeutic reasons, we strongly disagree with therapists who expose patients to anxiety-arousing situations against their will, even if this is intended to be for their own benefit. Any patient who is motivated for change can be motivated to perform all necessary steps voluntarily. In fact, any time the patient hesitates is a good occasion to make motivation the object of treatment.

The patients were asked to use response prevention during exposure to discover their cognitive and emotional reactions. A common experience was that feelings of unreality, emptiness, unrest, aggression, or a dream-like state, rather than anxiety, occurred. At this point, "private events" could be analyzed and modified ("modification of expectancy," see Meyer, 1966), sometimes with application of parts of cognitive restructuring procedures (e.g., Mahoney, 1974). During the exposure-induced emotional arousal, patients may also "discover" the interpersonal function of a symptom. Resembling in its course Stampfl's (1967) pure "in-fantasy-exposure" (implosion), the *in vivo* exposure to a feared object in one patient induced spontaneous in-fantasy exposure to a close person toward whom there were strong but ambivalent feelings. In the subsequent session, the feared object was substituted by that particular person and the exposure *in vivo* to the "real" feared situation (i.e., the troublesome relationship), led to relationship counseling.

Decision making, risk taking, and mood tolerance. Obsessive–compulsive patients are generally reluctant to make a decision when there is a risk of making a mistake. This is seriously inhibiting in social interactions, and group sessions in the program dealt specifically with avoidance of decision making. This made the training of the group-leader role particularly difficult, since the patient/leader had to make risky decisions about interrupting a peer and judging without knowing the opinion of others. Even when asked to make personal comments about peer patients on a "secret" rating scale, several patients initially refused, thus offering another occasion to work on their anxiety about not being perfect, making a mistake, and afterward ruminating about the possible mistake.

Both the exposure exercises and the establishment of alternative behavior often resulted in hesitation to transform concepts into action, reflecting a phobia-like avoidance of risky unpredictability of future events. The emphasis of the treatment interventions on these occasions was on decision making, acting, and tolerance of insecurity. During treatment, patients frequently became aware of relations between the severity and frequency of obsessive–compulsive behavior and mood states like depression, guilty feelings, irritability, and aggression. They were then trained to identify such mood states at the beginning of compulsions or obsessions and to learn better ways of coping by dealing with the particular cognitive-emotional state rather than by concentrating on satisfactory performance of compulsive rituals.

Social interaction: General. During the 25 intensive group sessions there was extensive use of group dynamics. Already during the first few sessions, most patients began to talk about their low self-esteem and their distrust of others, at the same time indicating their desire for a close, safe, and predictable dyadic relationship. The latter was also an important aspect with regard to the relationship to the therapists. Lack of social skills and low self-esteem on the one hand (Belschner, Dross, Hoffman, & Schulze, 1974), and a strong desire for a close dyadic relationship on the other hand, may contribute to a typical communication pattern of obsessive–compulsives in close relationships, that is, a constant striving for dominance and testing of the partner's benevolence—possibly to avoid or to defeat criticism and to overcome insecurity regarding the partner's attitude toward oneself. This communication pattern may therefore be interpreted as a pseudoassertive, counterphobic behavior. In individual treatment this can lead to frustrating struggles during contracting, goal setting, and training. Therefore, treatment had to include training in social competence and interpersonal relations so that the patient ceased striving for dominance over others, possibly even using obsessions and compulsions for this purpose.

An example may illustrate the necessity of this training. One patient suggested to a female peer that she may have talked to her husband in a nonconstructive manner. This suggestion started lengthy explanations of how she was misunderstood and she could not admit making mistakes in relation to her husband. She tensed up, stared down at her feet, and talked faster and faster. Eventually, her peers were annoyed but did not dare to say anything, anticipating that this would make her feel even more hurt. After 20 minutes, the therapist intervened and described what had happened. Not looking at the others and not giving them a chance to respond had increased her anxiety of not being understood and had resulted in her talking even more. Through this vicious cycle of communication she disconnected herself completely from the group, and she made those who wanted to help her feel guilty. In the subsequent group discussion her problem was recognized as a common one. The situation was rehearsed and the patient was now asked to talk with constant eye contact and breaks every few minutes in order to get or ask for reactions. This role play resulted in most patients expressing great relief. In subsequent sessions the situation was rehearsed with other patients. The group was encouraged to interrupt anybody who made this mistake again. Additionally, adequate criticism of others and sensible coping with criticism was encouraged, that is, showing and accepting "bad" behavior without ruminating afterward. On a few occasions, we also tried to bring latent aggression into the open, with the assumption that verbally and emotionally congruent messages are a better basis for interpersonal problem solving than verbal denial of an obvious emotional conflict. Important as it may seem to use such interventions in a systematic way for this particular group of patients, so far we have only applied it intuitively.

The group setting was also used to induce "dereflection" (Frankl, 1975), which means withdrawing attention from oneself and one's problems toward something or somebody else. The patients' willingness to give mutual help was tested particularly in crisis situations between group sessions and in the group sessions without the therapists in Phases II and III. Our impression thus far is that mutual help is given quite frequently among obsessive–compulsive patients, who before treatment often seem very overconcerned with themselves.

Social interaction: Marital and family. Pretreatment contact with the patient and spouse separately gives the therapist a first impression of the state of their marriage and the function of the symptom. It also shows whether the patient herself wants to change through treatment, or whether she only complies with pressure from the family. To confirm such a first impression, observation of metaphoric communication and nonverbal messages in couples and families are necessary (Beier, 1966; Haley, 1976). Such information seems to be essential for the decision as to whether and in what way the spouse or other family members should be involved as cotherapists. If the relationship is characterized by marked role differentiation into "patient" and "normal," strenghthening of this differentiation by giving the "normal" the role of the co-therapist seems problematic if not countertherapeutic. In such cases, the therapist should try instead to include the spouse as a peer in conjoint therapy. Reluctant spouses can often be encouraged to accept an active involvement via the first spouse-group session. In Group 2, four couples reported that their marriages were very unsatisfactory, and three spouses initially refused to participate in treatment. Via spouse-group and conjoint patient–spouse–therapist meetings, they came to accept participation in home visits and eventually got so involved that in Phase III they appeared even more motivated for the self-help group than the patients themselves.

Considerable changes in spouse and family interactions could be achieved by a small number of home visits. In her first home exercise, one patient started excessive cleaning of the kitchen during which her husband happened to come home. Upon seeing her cleaning he got furious immediately and tried unsuccessfully to stop her ritual. We suggested that the husband's aggressive response was a result of helplessness and that it was similar to the wife's ritual. First, this appeared absurd to both of them. Eventually they accepted that the husband was unable to cope with his emotional reactions to that situation. Their vicious cycle of communication was replaced by a contract, based on the assumption that their behavior in the problem situation was an expression of joint helplessness. The husband agreed not to attempt to stop the wife's ritual and to leave the situation until she had overcome her problem by methods learned in treatment. The wife agreed to accept his leaving the scene as an expression of cooperation and not as owing to a lack of concern. After she had managed to stop the ritual by herself, they were to thank each other for having been understanding. Thus, in only one session a complete breakthrough was achieved in one of their most damaging interactions, which sometimes had disrupted communication for days.

Another example of what can be achieved in a few home sessions is an exposure exercise aimed at reduction of obsessive–compulsive behavior, ending with family counseling. A woman had restricted the living area for her husband and daughter to about 10% of the total space of their house. The daughter was allowed to use only one chair and the patient never touched it. Neither did she touch the telephone as her daughter kept using it. Before the home session, the patient had only mentioned problems with her husband, not with her daughter. During the first session we made the patient sit on her daughter's chair and touch the telephone for a prolonged period of time. After having talked for a while about the unpleasant feelings evoked by this, she started to report increasingly negative feelings about her daughter. Ongoing analysis of her feelings and cognitions made her report a traumatic experience of years ago, when she felt deeply betrayed by her husband and daughter. Finally the patient accepted *in vivo* confrontation with her daughter instead of exposure to chair and phone. In a subsequent session, she accused her daughter of a cold and unsympathetic response to her suffering. When the daughter later broke into tears, the patient abruptly turned away and started an irrelevant conversation. She was asked to look at her daughter and to describe how she felt seeing her suffering. She admitted that she had avoided seeing this in the past because of uncertainty about the outcome of an open discussion with her daughter. This session initiated helpful family counseling, and the chair and phone were no longer a problem.

The successful establishment of spouse and family involvement in Group 2 may have been aided by the fact that all group members' spouse relationships had been disrupted in similar ways over the years. In Group 3, we did not succeed in involving the spouses in a similar way.

The present treatment package does not include therapeutic work with sexual problems. With a few exceptions, sex was only rarely brought up in the groups. Groups 1 and 2 created a "group baby." When group members with a fear of getting pregnant from visiting public toilets were advised to go repeatedly to such places, the group offered to adopt any baby resulting from such visits. On these occasions, there was short, but evasive discussion about sexual behavior and problems.

Home visits, in vivo training. In general, *in vivo* training took place in the home setting, since, for the majority of patients, most severe problems occurred there. *In vivo* training in other situations was performed with a few patients who had problems such as compulsive litter picking in the streets. The home sessions are important for several reasons: (*a*) for assessment of patients' and spouses' problems; (*b*) for reduction of obsessions, and, particularly, compulsions; (*c*) for interventions in marital and family interaction; and (*d*) for fostering group cohesion.

With respect to assessment, home visits with family members present frequently showed important interpersonal functions of the obsessions and compulsions. In this respect, obsessions and compulsions do not seem to be different from other symptoms. In this context, it is also important to assess spouses' responses to the obsessions and compulsions: Spouses may obey and get completely involved in ritualistic behavior; they may fight against the rituals; or they may try a kind of time-out. We have seen these different types of spouse reactions, which appear to keep the symptom "going." As pointed out earlier, only on the basis of careful *in vivo* assessment can appropriate spouse involvement be designed.

In the obsessive–compulsive patient, a primarily anancastic life style may have been exaggerated by aversive social conditions. Thus, the obsessions and compulsions may not be a qualitatively new behavior but an exaggeration of a life style with which the patient was previously satisfied, and for which she may even have obtained considerable social reinforcement. In such cases, the social conditions producing this exaggeration (such as the family setting) should, whenever possible, become the major treatment concern.

Sometimes, home visits provide the only reliable assessment of the amount of symptomatology a patient exhibits. This may also apply to the spouses: Three of them had more severe obsessive–compulsive problems than the patients. These problems were not mentioned by the patient or the spouse in the pretreatment interviews. In three other patients this was true for close relatives living with the patient.

Home visits are a central part of the treatment package with regard to improvement of obsessions and compulsions. Group 1, with only a few home visits after Session 18, showed less "subjective improvement" (discussed later) during treatment than Groups 2 and 3. This is not surprising, since the group sessions in the hospital include a relatively small amount of symptom-directed exercises, except in Group 3. For most patients, the difficult situations created in the hospital setting apparently did not really resemble their real-life problem situations. This poses the question as to whether the number of home exercises should be increased. At the moment, five intensive home sessions seem sufficient to teach patients, spouses, and/or peers how to cope without the therapist. Furthermore, during this phase of treatment, home exercises and group sessions in the hospital are not parallel events but closely interconnected in their effects. The group meetings between and after the home sessions are to stabilize the reduction of obsessions and compulsions by increasing the likelihood of self-help activities and to help patients over periods of depression, irritation, or confusion after the first experience of symptom reduction induced by *in vivo* exposures and home visits. In Groups 2 and 3, we devoted an entire session toward the end of the series of home visits to the patients' discussion of depression, suicidal thoughts, and motivational problems. In these groups, there was an intense sharing of feelings and very helpful mutual support during this critical stage of treatment. Basic rules concerning peer help were agreed upon, as were criteria for contacting the therapist and for using the emergency services of the clinic. We feel that it was largely due to the self-help capacity of all groups that only one patient (in Group 1) has thus far been admitted to the hospital for a few days during treatment and followup.

We had difficulties in following the schedule of the home visits in Groups 1 and 3. In Group 1, only four out of six patients accepted home visits, with spouses willing to participate. In this group we did not emphasize home visits, since at that time we anticipated stronger effects from the exposure exercises in the group setting. In Groups 2 and 3, the home visit scheme was introduced as a condition of treatment that could not be waived. In general, patients accepted this in spite of high anticipatory anxiety before the first session. All patients in Group 2 had the five scheduled home visits with spouses present at least during the first visit. In several cases, spouses were also present on subsequent visits. We encountered problems regarding peer involvement. One patient was rejected by two of her peers because of her "unpleasant" compulsions, and they refused to visit her or let her into their homes. However, during the vast majority of Group 2 home visits, a peer patient was present, even in sessions in which we did marital counseling. This increased mutual understanding and readiness for mutual help. In Group 3, all patients agreed to five home visits, but in the end only three patients received all of them. Spouse involvement in Group 3 was minimal. On the other hand, Group 3 was the only one that started frequent meetings without the therapist in Phase I, in between the scheduled group sessions. These extra sessions were devoted to exposure *in vivo* exercises under mutual supervision.

Transfer to self-help groups. Phase II was difficult to carry out with all groups. When the therapist started to fade out from treatment sessions, there was heavy protest that the treatment was "much too short." In the end, however, most patients accepted the Phase II design. The optimum length or intensity of this kind of group treatment is difficult to determine. In Groups 2 and 3, which had only half as many hospital sessions as Group 1 but were much more work oriented, it may well have been useful to continue Phase I for a longer period of time—not necessarily with an increased number of home sessions.

Thus far, only Group 1 has completed Phase III, and our conclusion is that for that particular group, our plan failed. After a few sessions, the group members felt they were not able to proceed any further with symptom reduction or with the establishment of enjoyable alternative behavior without aid from the therapist. This may be due in part to their lack of systematic group training. Also, they did not develop any common goals beyond symptom reduction, in spite of their own emphasis on the establishment of alternative behavior early in treatment. Group 2 met a few times in the hospital and then decided to have the weekly meetings at a group member's home, with the intention of meeting in every member's home as soon as ongoing improvement would allow. Currently, this group is still meeting once a week. The amount of effective therapeutic work has declined in later meetings. The last few sessions with the therapist are designed to change this. Spouses participated during parts of most of these sessions without the therapist, although this was not required by the program. This group has also initiated joint alternative activities including the spouses.

Group 3 started leaderless meetings in Phase I and continued throughout Phases I and II. These meetings followed a structure similar to that of the sessions with the therapist. As Phase III approached, a spontaneous decision was made to hold some of the leaderless sessions outside the hospital for joint leisure activities.

MEASUREMENT AND INTERPRETATION OF TREATMENT PROCESS AND CHANGE

We have used rating scales in the areas of personality measurement, marital interaction, obsessive–compulsive symptomatology, and group cohesion. Most ratings were done by the patients, some also by spouses or family members. So far, only some of the data have been subjected to statistical analysis: (a) factor analyses of the cohesion ratings (see Table 14.1) and of the outcome variables (see Table 14.3); (b) multivariate analyses of variance (MANOVA) of the data in Tables 14.1 and 14.2 and in Figure 14.2 (discussed later). The following discussion includes only tentative conclusions concerning the treatment process and effects. The main aim of the present pilot study was to evaluate whether it is feasible and effective to work with obsessive–compulsive patients in the present manner and whether a long-range controlled study is worthwhile for further specification of the components of the group package, as well as for a comparison of group and individual treatments.

Group Cohesion

Cohesion among group members as well as patients' interaction with the therapists are treatment process variables of major importance in a treatment model meant to create cohesive self-help groups. Group cohesion was partly assessed in a manner employed with agoraphobic patients in previous studies (Hand et al., 1974; Teasdale et al., 1977). Patients rated items dealing with mutual sympathy and help, as well as subjective dependence on the therapists, on scales ranging from 0 to 8.

Table 14.1 shows the group means and standard deviations (SD) on the following cohesion variables: (a) liking of group (LOG); (b) liked by group (LBG); and (c) help from group (HFG). The data in Table 14.1 are from three different treatment stages: treatment sessions 1–9, 10–18, and for the last 9 treatment sessions. The relatively low ratings in the present study, particularly on HFG, may be partly due to the fact that the obsessive–compulsive patients had little opportunity for joint exposure *in vivo* training, especially as compared to the agoraphobics of previous studies (Hand et al., 1974; Teasdale et al., 1977). In these studies, group means over three treatment sessions ranged from 3.2 (noncohesive groups) to 5.9 (cohesive groups) for LFG; from 1.9 (noncohesive) to 3.4 (cohesive) for LBG; and from 4.0 (noncohesive) to 6.2 (cohesive) for HFG.

If our treatment program is successful, mutual help ratings should increase during Phase III. We have analyzed the three treatment stages separately, since we suspected that cohesion ratings might have decreased over treatment time. As the data show, there seems to be a slight decrease in all three variables for Group 1, and on variables LOG and HFG for

TABLE 14.1
Means and Standard Deviations (SD) of Cohesion Ratings for Each Group on Three Treatment Stages

Variable	Treatment stage[a]	Group 1 Mean	Group 1 SD	Group 2 Mean	Group 2 SD	Group 3 Mean	Group 3 SD
Liking of group	1	4.2	.7	4.5	.7	3.6	.8
(LOG)	2	3.4	1.6	4.2	.4	3.4	1.3
	3	3.5	.9	4.6	1.0	3.2	1.5
	Mean 1–3	3.7	1.1	4.4	3.4	3.4	1.2
Liked by group	1	2.7	1.0	3.4	.4	2.6	1.7
(LBG)	2	2.0	1.6	3.5	.5	2.6	1.3
	3	2.4	1.4	4.2	.7	2.8	1.8
	Mean 1–3	2.4	1.3	3.7	.6	2.7	1.5
Help from	1	2.2	1.8	3.1	.8	3.7	1.6
group (HFG)	2	1.6	1.8	2.9	1.1	2.5	1.3
	3	1.6	1.9	3.1	1.4	3.2	.9
	Mean 1–3	1.8	1.8	3.5	1.3	3.1	1.3

[a]Identification of treatment stages: (1) first 9 treatment sessions (1–9); (2) second 9 treatment sessions (10–18); (3) last 9 treatment sessions (19–27 in Groups 2 and 3; 39–47 in Group 1).

Group 3 (see Table 14.1). MANOVA of all groups combined over all three treatment stages revealed no significant changes and no interaction effects for LOG and LBG. For HFG there was a significant decrease over time ($p < .02$) but no significant difference between groups. This decrease in perceived help from the group may indicate that in Phases IC and II, we did not succeed in establishing independence and self-help skills with regard to obsessions, compulsions, and other problems. Patients may simply continue to follow the therapists' advice after the experience of extensive therapist involvement in Phase IB. This suggestion seems to be supported by patients' ratings of subjective dependence on the therapists (a negative cohesion rating) regarding goal-oriented treatment. Figure 14.1 shows that Group 2 rated very low dependence on the therapists during the systematic establishment of cohesion in Phase I, but when all patients had received their first home visit, the feelings of dependence increased and remained high until the end of Phase II (Session 27). In contrast, in Group 1, which had no systematic cohesion training at the start, the feeling of dependence was high initially and decreased considerably in the second half of their much longer treatment. In Group 3 (not shown), the feeling of dependence was at the same level as in Group 1, although the training of this group was meant to be identical to that of Group 2. In Group 2, the therapists could easily remain passive during the initial cohesion establishment process, which was greatly helped by high homogeneity of background problems in the form of marital discord in that group.

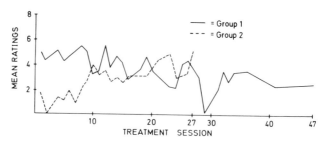

FIGURE 14.1. *Mean rated subjective dependence on therapists for Groups 1 and 2 for each treatment session.*

At this stage of the program, one cannot predict whether or not the differences in cohesion ratings in Table 14.1 and dependency ratings in Figure 14.1 will affect treatment outcome. Only Group 1 has finished Phase III. After initial attempts to achieve self-help skills had failed in this group, only a few loose contacts remained between individual patients. It is important to note that no systematic training for leaderless groups had been given to these patients. In spite of the low cohesion level in Group 1, most patients seemed to do surprisingly well during followup (discussed later).

Groups 2 and 3, who are now completing Phase III, both meet regularly about once a week. Just before this chapter was finished, Groups 2 and 3 had a joint meeting in the hospital at their own request. Only one patient from Group 1 attended, although this group had also been invited. Only the final followup analysis will reveal whether or not the nonattendance of Group 1 patients was a sign of improvement or of dissatisfaction with the treatment. For Groups 2 and 3, it remains to be seen whether their expanded group increases the opportunities for goal-oriented work by allowing better matching of patients for age, sex, marital status, general interests, and area of living.

Another cohesion measure, the number of patients preferring the group setting to individual treatment, may have some practical importance for the course of treatment. These ratings were performed at the end of each group session. Two patients in Group 1 and one patient in Group 2 who expressed no preference for group treatment during the second half of therapy showed no improvement during the followup period. Obsessive–compulsive patients may find it more difficult than others to leave a group, even if they feel they do not benefit from it. They may therefore be "hidden drop-outs." This raises the question whether such patients deteriorate in group treatment. With agoraphobics, Hafner (1976) found a drop-out rate of 25% from individual treatment as compared to 0% in a number of patients treated in a cohesive group condition. During followup, however, he found "fresh symptom emergence" in about 18% of the group patients, which led him to speculate that these might be potential drop-outs from individual treatment. Hafner's paper (1976) has provoked heavy criticism (Meyer & Reich, 1977; Stern, 1977). Nevertheless, the identification of patients who may deteriorate during group treatment remains an important task in order to reintegrate them into the group or to find better ways of helping them.

Change During and After Treatment

We have assessed change in three ways: (1) videotaped interviews ("clinical" assessment) with the patient and the spouse separately and, additionally, with both together in a group meeting, at the end of Phase I; (2) some of the recent Maudsley/Oxford rating scales for obsessive–compulsive patients; these are still in an experimental stage, and we made some modifications when translating them into German; and (3) a global scale on which the patient indicates how much improved she feels before every session as compared with her state before treatment. We will discuss these assessments of change separately.

1. In Group 1, two of the six patients felt they could cope without any further treatment at the end of Phase II, and even more so at 6 months' followup. One previously extremely disturbed young woman with a history of years of out- and in-patient treatments started a job early in the followup period and has kept it successfully for more than half a year with very little additional help. The fourth patient, with several hospitalizations in the 2 years prior to treatment, is still suffering from frequent mood changes but has managed to start a job three times and is holding her current job with very little extra support. The fifth patient is apparently doing well, but does not credit the treatment for this. Only one patient remained totally unchanged. Group 2 patients and spouses reported a symptom reduction of 50% in one patient, 60 to 80% in two patients, and 90% in the fourth patient, the fifth being unimproved and a drop-out. Similarly, in Group 3 two patients reported 50%, one patient 70%, and the fourth 90% symptom reduction, the fifth patient, having dropped out of treatment in the middle of Phase I, reported that she was doing well.

2. Table 14.2 shows the results on the Maudsley/Oxford scales. Variable 1 (range 0–117) consists of a listing of 39 everyday activities. For each activity, the patient indicates on a scale ranging from 0 to 3 how much, compared with "normals," her obsessions and compulsions extend the time necessary to perform these activities. Variable 2 (range 0–168) consists of a listing of 21 leisure activities. The patient indicates on 0–8 scales to what extent obsessions and compulsions prevent her from performance of these activities. Variable 3 (range 0–184) is the sum of the avoidance ratings on 0–8 scales for 23 phobic situations. Variable 4 (range 0–8) indicates the restrictions in daily life due to general anxiety. Variable 5 (range 0–72) is the

TABLE 14.2
Outcome Variables:[a] Means and Standard Deviations (SD) for Each Group over Treatment Time

Group	Testing[b]	Variable 1		Variable 2		Variable 3		Variable 4		Variable 5	
		Mean	SD	Mean	SD	Mean	SD	Mean	SD	Mean	SD
	Pre	20.7	10.3	69.3	25.3	57.7	26.6	6.2	3.1	37.7	13.7
1 (N = 6)	Middle	14.3	6.1	50.0	25.3	36.8	17.9	4.5	1.9	32.0	1.8
	Post	15.7	7.0	48.2	34.1	37.0	21.4	5.2	2.0	32.2	11.8
	Pre	28.0	24.6	46.0	25.6	47.3	44.5	7.0	1.2	38.5	9.9
2 (N = 4)	Middle	20.5	19.1	45.0	28.4	49.5	42.1	5.8	1.9	39.0	5.6
	Post	23.0	27.9	29.3	33.4	46.5	47.9	4.3	2.1	37.8	12.9
	Pre	32.8	7.2	55.4	32.3	57.4	11.1	7.0	.7	39.6	14.8
3 (N = 5)	Middle	27.0	6.1	58.2	34.2	51.0	21.7	5.8	.8	37.6	14.8
	Post	31.8	8.7	60.4	30.7	66.4	25.1	5.8	1.3	37.4	16.4

[a]Identification of outcome variables: (1) "symptom" behavior; (2) prevention of leisure activity by "symptom"; (3) phobia score; (4) general anxiety; (5) nonspecific "illness behavior."
[b]Pre = Pretreatment; Middle = end of Phase IA; Post = end of Phase II.

sum of 0–8 ratings for nine "nonspecific" complaints like restlessness. The ratings were made before treatment (Pre), at the end of Phase IA (Middle), and at the end of Phase II (Post). In Group 2, the one patient who dropped out of treatment at the end of Phase II was omitted from the analysis.

MANOVA for each variable (all groups combined over all rating occasions) revealed no significant changes or interactions in Variables 2, and 5. There is significant improvement on Variables 1 ($p < .04$) and 4 ($p < .01$) with no interaction effects (see Figure 14.2). On Variable 3, there is a trend toward improvement ($p < .12$), with an almost significant interaction effect ($p < .07$) (see Figure 14.2).

We have no explanation for the substantial improvement on the phobia scale (Variable 3) in Group 1, as opposed to the increase of phobic avoidance in Group 3 (see Figure 14.3). We did not directly tackle the phobias in any of the groups. The patients in Group 1 may have spontaneously applied the exposure technique to their phobias, but there is no ready explanation of why this did not happen in any of the other groups.

In general, the analysis of the outcome variables gives some tentative support for the much stronger clinical impression of improvement. If one considers that the most significant improvements occurred in Variables 1 and 4, it seems that our treatment package was mainly anxiety reducing, with some reduction of obsessive–compulsive symptomatology. It does not seem to have changed the restrictions of leisure activities or the nonspecific illness complaints. This poses the question as to whether Variable 5 is independent of obsessive–compulsive symptomatology. This could then imply that restrictions of leisure activities are not primarily due to obses-

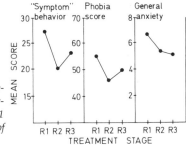

FIGURE 14.2. *Mean ratings of "symptom" be-havior, phobic behavior, and general anxiety (outcome Variables 1, 3, and 4 of Table 14.2) for all groups combined. R1 = pretreatment stage; R2 = middle of treatment (end of Phase IA); and R3 = end of Phase II.*

sions and compulsions but rather to factors important for nonspecific illness complaints (discussed later). This conclusion receives support from the results on our third change measure, the subjective improvement ratings.

3. The "subjective improvement" scale (range 0–8) was a very sensitive measure of changes over treatment in the Hand *et al.* (1974) study with agoraphobics. There, it correlated highly with the changes in the Marks/Gelder scales of phobic anxiety and avoidance: A reduction of phobias seemed to be combined with a general feeling of improvement for the agoraphobics (Hand *et al.*, 1974). In the present study, subjective improvement ratings remained low (around 3) as compared with ratings between 5 and 6 by the agoraphobics. For the obsessive–compulsive patients, subjective improvement ratings seem to be more in line with the low ratings on outcome Variables 2 and 5 (Table 14.2) than with the improvement ratings on obsessive–compulsive symptomatology and anxiety.

A factorial analysis was performed for each rating occasion, separately for the cohesion variables (Table 14.1) and together with the outcome variables (Table 14.2), with extraction of three factors. On all three rating occasions, outcome Variables 1 and 3 constituted one factor. Outcome Variable 2 appeared as a factor by itself on all rating occasions, with no loading on the previous factor. Outcome Variable 4 constituted a factor by

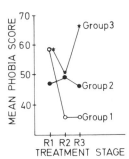

FIGURE 14.3. *Mean phobia score for all groups separately over three stages of treatment. R1 = pretreatment stage; R2 = middle of treatment (end of Phase IA); and R3 = end of Phase II.*

itself only on the first rating occasion. Variable 5 never constituted a factor by itself and had low loadings on all other factors. The extraction of three factors accounted for 92–96% of the variance on each occasion.

Interpretation of the MANOVA results on the basis of the factorial analysis allows further tentative conclusions. At this point, it seems evident that a lot of work has to be done before reliable assessment of complex problems in obsessive–compulsive patients is achieved. We have the impression that obsessive–compulsive patients are not only more difficult to treat than, for example, agoraphobics, but also that the use of rating scales with obsessive–compulsives presents particular problems. In these patients, the relations between their symptoms on the one hand and their general feelings of unhappiness and illness complaints on the other, seem to be different from the relations of the respective problem areas in agoraphobics. The present sample, at least, seems much less happy about any major symptom reduction than most agoraphobics. The self-ratings of change (especially improvement) may specifically interact with personality variables associated with the symptom picture.

SUMMARY

In behavior therapy two rather standardized group approaches for problem-homogeneous groups have been developed over the past few years: (a) for patients suffering from social anxiety (for a review see Heimberg, Montgomery, Madsen, & Heimberg, 1977; Ullrich & Ullrich, 1976); and (b) for agoraphobics (Hand et al., 1974). In the present study, we have attempted to develop a standardized out-patient group therapy model for the treatment of obsessive–compulsive patients. The model emphasizes dealing with the obsessive–compulsive problems per se, as well as with related problems of a social nature, for example, in marital and social interactions. There is an emphasis on training in the real-life problem situation involving each patient's most immediate social micro-unit, that is, family and spouses. For patients as well as spouses, treatment provided the opportunity for a continuous behavioral analysis intended as a motivational process and for continuous reformulation of treatment goals. Generalization of treatment effects to the followup period was trained for approximately one-third of treatment time. Patients were allowed to try out newly acquired self-help skills in group sessions without the therapists. For patients with long-lasting problems such as obsessions and compulsions it seems useful to try to help them cope with future relapses. This was partly done by establishment of group cohesion and by training the patients to seek help from one another before going to a therapist or to a clinic. Group cohesion, changes in unsatisfactory family interactions, and individual training in problem solving were expected to provide a sufficient basis for patients' coping attempts.

With regard to group cohesion, we apparently got better results in Phase III than the rather low cohesion ratings of Phases I and II indicated. This may be understandable in that the groups got their main chance for self-help and independent interaction in Phase III. Group 1, which did not receive training for leaderless groups, split up early in Phase III. Groups 2 and 3 kept meeting regularly and even initiated joint meetings on their own request. It needs to be seen during followup whether stable cohesion will preserve therapeutic group norms or whether cohesion will merely stabilize problem behaviors in a socially pleasant group of peers.

The clinical results from the first three groups treated for 3 months with intensive therapist involvement (two of them presently in the self-help phase), indicate considerable improvement in the majority of the patients. Within the 2 years prior to treatment, a number of these patients had been repeatedly hospitalized. During treatment, only one patient was hospitalized for a few days. In spite of their improvement, most patients still suffer from obsessive–compulsive symptoms, but either they feel able to cope sufficiently well or they are still working on their problems. Some have started treatment for other problems, such as marital discord.

Objective assessment of change appeared far more difficult with this group of patients than with agoraphobics, for example. We have the impression that in obsessive–compulsives, self-ratings of change (especially of improvement) do interact with personality variables associated with the symptom picture. Furthermore, in obsessive–compulsives the nonspecific illness complaints and feelings of unhappiness may be less closely connected with their symptoms than in agoraphobics. We are now working on the improvement of measures for treatment process and outcome. Improved measures should permit us to investigate the different package ingredients systematically and to perform controlled comparisons with individual treatment. Apart from the specific interventions for obsessions and compulsions, the Behavioral Out-Patient Group Therapy Model may also be useful for other severely disturbed patients with chronic courses of illness.

ACKNOWLEDGMENTS

We wish to thank Margaret Ackermann, Edda Stanik, and Helga Szelinski for their help in the design and performance of the treatment of Group 1, and Wolfgang Zaworka for his participation as cotherapist in Group 3. Many thanks are also due to Roland Müller and Wolfgang Zaworka for their help with the data analysis. Last, but not least, we gratefully acknowledge the laborious work the editors and some friends have performed on the first drafts of this chapter.

REFERENCES

Beech, H. R. (Ed.). *Obsessional states*. London: Methuen, 1974.

Beier, E. G. *The silent language of psychotherapy*. Chicago: Aldine, 1966.

Belschner, W., Dross, M., Hoffman, M., & Schulze, C. *Sozialangst und Normunsicherheit als Vorläufer von Zwangsverhalten*. Unpublished manuscript, Technische Hochschule Braunschweig, 1974.

Boersma, K., DenHengst, S., Dekker, J., & Emmelkamp, P. Exposure and response prevention in the natural environment: A comparison with obsessive–compulsive patients. *Behaviour Research and Therapy*, 1976, *14*, 19–24.

Chesser, E. S. Behaviour therapy: Recent trends and current practice. *British Journal of Psychiatry*, 1976, *129*, 289–307.

Frankl, V. E. Paradoxical intention and dereflection. In S. Arieti & G. Chrzanowski (Eds.), *New dimensions in psychiatry: A world view*. New York: Wiley, 1975. Pp. 305–326.

Gelder, M. Behavioural treatment of agoraphobia. In J. C. Boulougouris & A. D. Rabavilas (Eds.), *The treatment of phobic and obsessive–compulsive disorders*. Oxford: Pergamon, 1977. Pp. 7–12.

Goldstein, A. P. *Structured learning therapy. Toward a psychotherapy for the poor*. New York: Academic Press, 1973.

Gottman, J. M., & Leiblum, S. R. *How to do psychotherapy and how to evaluate it*. New York: Holt, Rinehart, & Winston, 1974.

Grawe, K. Verhaltensterapeutische Gruppentherapie. In L. Pongratz (Ed.), *Handbuch der Psychologie* (Band 8). Göttingen: Hogrefe, 1977. Pp. 20,696–20,724.

Hafner, R. J. Fresh symptom-emergence after intensive behaviour therapy. *British Journal of Psychiatry*, 1976, *129*, 378–383.

Hafner, R. J., & Marks, I. M. Exposure *in vivo* of agoraphobics: Contributions of diazepam, group exposure and anxiety evocation. *Psychological Medicine*, 1976, *6*, 71–88.

Haley, J. *Problem solving therapy*. San Francisco: Jossey-Bass, 1976.

Hand, I. Symptom-zentrierte Gruppentherapie bei Phobien—die Problemorientierte Arbeitsgruppe in der Psychotherapie. *Fortschritte der Neurologie und Psychiatrie*, 1975, *43*, 285–304.

Hand, I., Lamontagne, Y., & Marks, I. M. Group exposure (flooding) *in vivo* for agoraphobics. *British Journal of Psychiatry*, 1974, *124*, 588–602.

Hand, I., & Wedel, S. Verhaltenstherapeutische ambulanz an der psychiatrischen klinik der universität Hamburg. In *Deutsche Gesellschaft für Verhaltenstherapie: Verhaltenstherapie in der psychosozialen Versorgung*. Weinheim: Beltz, 1978. Pp. 59–71.

Hare, A. P. *Handbook of small group research* (2nd ed.). New York: The Free Press, 1976.

Heimberg, R. G., Montgomery, D., Madsen, C. H., & Heimberg, J. Assertion training: A review of the literature. *Behavior Therapy*, 1977, *8*, 953–971.

Hodgson, R., & Rachman, S. The modification of compulsive behaviour. In H. J. Eysenck (Ed.), *Case studies in behaviour therapy*. London: Routledge & Kegan Paul, 1976. Pp. 17–41.

Holm, H. Group exposure *in vivo* with agoraphobics in Modum Bads Nervesanatorium. Personal communication, Oslo, June 1974.

Kanfer, F. H. *Self-management therapy*. Workshop manuscript, University of Illinois, 1977.

Kanfer, F. H., & Saslow, G. Behavioral diagnosis. In C. M. Franks (Ed.), *Behavior therapy: Appraisal and status*. New York: McGraw-Hill, 1969. Pp. 417–444.

Krumboltz, J., & Potter, B. Behavioral techniques for developing trust, cohesiveness, and goal accomplishment. *Educational Technology*, 1973, *13*, 26–30.

Lazarus, A. A. Multimodal behavior therapy in groups. In G. M. Gazda (Ed.), *Basic approaches to group psychotherapy and group counseling* (2nd ed.). Springfield: Thomas, 1974. Pp. 150–174.

Liberman, R. P. A behavioral approach to group dynamics: Reinforcement and prompting of cohesiveness in group therapy. *Behavior Therapy*, 1970, *1*, 140–175.

Liberman, R. P. Behavioral group therapy. *British Journal of Psychiatry*, 1971, *119*, 535–544. (a)

Liberman, R. P. Reinforcement of cohesiveness in group therapy: Behavioral and personality changes. *Archives of General Psychiatry*, 1971, *25*, 168–177. (b)

Liberman, R. P., King, L., DeRisi, W., & McCann, M. *Personal effectiveness: Guiding people to assert themselves and improve their social skills*. Champaign, Ill.: Research Press, 1975.

Mahoney, M. J. *Cognition and behavior modification*. Cambridge, Mass.: Ballinger, 1974.

Marks, I. M. Behavioral treatments of phobic and obsessive–compulsive disorders: A critical appraisal. In M. Hersen, R. Eisler, & P. M. Miller (Eds.), *Progress in behavior modification* (Vol. 1). New York: Academic Press, 1975. Pp. 65–158.

Marks, I. M., Hodgson, R., & Rachman, S. Treatment of chronic obsessive–compulsive neurosis by *in vivo* exposure. *British Journal of Psychiatry*, 1975, *127*, 349–364.

Mathews, A. M., Teasdale, J. D., Johnston, D., Munby, M., & Shaw, P. A home-based treatment program for agoraphobia. *Behavior Therapy*, 1977, *8*, 915–924.

Meyer, V. Modification of expectancies in cases with obsessional rituals. *Behaviour Research and Therapy*, 1966, *4*, 273–280.

Meyer, V., & Levy, R. Modification of behavior in obsessive–compulsive disorders. In H. Adams & I. Unikel (Eds.), *Issues and trends in behavior therapy*. Springfield, Ill.: Thomas, 1973. Pp. 77–138.

Meyer, V., Levy, R., & Schnurer, A. The behavioral treatment of obsessive–compulsive disorders. In H. R. Beech (Ed.), *Obsessional states*. London: Methuen, 1974. Pp. 233–258.

Meyer, V., & Reich, B. Letter to the editors. *British Journal of Psychiatry*, 1977, *130*, 418–419.

Meyer, V., Robertson, J., & Tatlow, A. Home treatment of an obsessive–compulsive disorder by response prevention. *Journal of Behavior Therapy and Experimental Psychiatry*, 1975, *6*, 37–38.

Rachman, S. The modification of obsessions: A new formulation. *Behaviour Research and Therapy*, 1976, *14*, 437–443.

Röper, G. The role of the patient in modelling/flooding. In J. C. Boulougouris & A. D. Rabavilas (Eds.), *The treatment of phobic and obsessive compulsive disorders*. Oxford: Pergamon, 1977. Pp. 65–71.

Shaw, M. E. *Group dynamics: The psychology of small group behavior* (2nd ed.). New York: McGraw-Hill, 1976.

Stampfl, T. G. Implosive therapy: The theory, the subhuman analogue, the strategy and the technique: Part I, The theory. In S. G. Armitage (Ed.), *Behavior modification techniques in the treatment of emotional disorders*. Battle Creek, Mich.: V. A. Publications, 1967. Pp. 22–37.

Stern, R. Letter to the editors. *British Journal of Psychiatry*, 1977, *130*, 418.

Teasdale, J. D., Walsh, P. A., Lancashire, M., & Mathews, A. M. Group exposure for agoraphobics: A replication study. *British Journal of Psychiatry*, 1977, *130*, 186–193.

Ullrich, R., & Ullrich, R. *Das Assertiveness—Training Program ATP* (Parts I and II). München: Pfeiffer, 1976.

__ 15 _____

Marital Behavior Therapy:
A Research Reconnaissance

RICHARD B. STUART AND BRENDA L. ROPER

Operant technology grew from seeds planted in animal research laboratories, where every aspect of the experimental procedure was amenable to tight controls. When the technology moved into the community as the "social learning approach" (Bandura, 1977) in major efforts to improve the quality of human services in many settings, the potential for societal gain from the technology grew exponentially but so, too, did problems inherent in efforts to achieve rigorous experimental validation of the evolving programs.

Research in applied settings is difficult for many reasons. For example, service needs often compete with the demands of experimental designs, and intervention programs that are developed for testing are often warped by needs to respond to client distress that are unrelated to the experimental process. Also, various community groups with vested interests, not only in the experimental outcome, but in its process as well, often intervene in efforts to reshape experimental protocols; in addition, clients' lives are predictably affected by many situational factors and nonexperimentally controlled "therapeutic" experiences that often have a significant bearing upon intervention outcome. Superimposed upon these problems is the important and mandatory protection of subjects' human rights (Stuart, 1978), which often necessitates use of suboptimal experimental designs. Therefore, in contrast to the rigorous designs possible in laboratory re-

TRENDS IN BEHAVIOR THERAPY

Copyright © 1979 by Academic Press, Inc.
All rights of reproduction in any form reserved.
ISBN 0-12-647450-8

search, evaluations of community applications of social learning theory technologies commonly employ quasi-experimental designs, and hence, both their internal and external validity (Campbell & Stanley, 1963; Caporaso & Roos, 1973; Cook & Campbell, 1976) are subject to many threats.

The results of evaluations of these programs are impressive both with regard to the ingenuity with which the design issues have been handled and with regard to the results that have been achieved. Programs in schools (O'Leary & O'Leary, 1972; Stuart, 1974), for obesity (Stuart, in press) and developmental disabilities (Hamerlynck, in press), and in hospital settings (e.g., Agras, 1976; Stahl & Leitenberg, 1976) are but a few examples of applications in areas where great strides have been made. It is curious, however, that marital interaction has not received the same amount of research attention as have many other service areas. Elsewhere (Stuart, 1979) it has been suggested that marital interaction plays a pivotal role in the personal health and happiness of the spouses, in their professional productivity, and in their effectiveness as parents. Moreover, the rapid increase in the divorce rate, with all of the social dislocation and life stress that this entails, indicates that effective services are urgently needed for couples contemplating marriage, for those with preclinical marital adjustment problems when planning for parenthood or retirement, for those facing intense marital distress, and for those anticipating or adjusting to divorce. The marital treatment area is therefore a fertile arena for program development and evaluation.

This chapter will summarize the progress that has been made to date in this area. Laboratory-based analogue studies and clinical outcome studies are the two classes of research that have been reported. The former studies will be reviewed briefly, the latter in much greater detail. We shall show that the analogue studies have some heuristic value, although their contribution has been little realized to date; we shall also show that there has been startlingly little clinical research done in this area, and the work done has generally been of inferior quality, although some studies have reached highly suggestive conclusions. Throughout our discussion of the clinical research, we shall make our suggestions for ways in which such studies could be improved so as to increase their yields.

SELECTED ANALOGUE STUDIES

Virtually all of social psychology research on interpersonal interaction can be construed as analogue studies with potential application to the analysis of marital interaction. Therefore the selection of studies for review in this context is necessarily arbitrary. We shall limit our review to two of the lines of investigation that have been directly aimed at clinical marital therapy.

In general, analogue studies attempt to isolate the specific contribution of treatment components on a more circumscribed and, hence, supposedly better controlled basis than is possible in clinical outcome research. The precision that analogue studies achieve, however, is won at the expense of generalizability for three reasons. First, the subjects who participate in this research are often recruited from nonclinical populations and are therefore significantly different from clients. It has often been observed, for example, that social psychology generally tends to be the study of the college undergraduate. Second, the thoughts, affects, and actions studied in this research are often far removed from the same events in the natural environment. For example, Brehmer (1976) noted that conflicts induced in laboratory settings are less intense and expressed in very different ways than naturally occurring conflicts. Third, the manipulations used in analogue studies are often either inaccurate replications of the procedures used clinically (Bernstein & Paul, 1971), or they are used in isolation and out of the multimethod context that characterizes most clinical offerings. Therefore, writers such as Brehmer (1976) have raised serious questions about the relevance of analogue research for human service offerings. Clearly, the results of even the best of the analogue studies must be considered to be mainly heuristic until their recommendations have been tested in carefully controlled clinical trials. Only then can they be fed into active service programs.

With these caveats in mind, the first type of analogue research that we shall consider is the work of Eisler and his associates. In their first study (Eisler, Hersen, & Agras, 1973b), they attempted to establish the reliability and practical utility of videotape assessment of marital interaction. They concluded that observers' ratings of such nonverbal behaviors as eye contact and smiling were equally reliable when made from videotapes as when made from observation of live interaction. Moreover, they asserted their belief that videotapes may provide more effective observational data than live observations, because as permanent records they can later be coded from other perspectives. Tapes can, of course, also be used therapeutically as a source of feedback data (Bailey & Sowder, 1970; Danet, 1968), although the equivocal results of the client "self-confrontation studies" noted by Eisler, Hersen, and Agras (1973a, p. 420) would seem to support the need to add therapist-mediated feedback to the tapes. In addition, data summarized elsewhere (Stuart, 1979) point to the necessity of making this feedback positive rather than focusing on negative aspects of the interaction.

Eisler et al. (1973a) did, in fact, attempt to assess the specific contribution of videotape feedback as an intervention technique aimed at altering couples' nonverbal communication. While the couples were recruited from a clinical population (male psychiatric patients and their wives), they were not seekers of marital therapy. Twelve couples were sequentially assigned to one of four experimental conditions: (a) videotape feedback alone; (b) irrelevant television alone; (c) videotape feedback plus focused instruction; and (d) focused instruction alone. An ABAB reversal design was used with the three couples in each of the four conditions. The results are interesting but, at best, suggestive because of the small number of subjects and the lack of statistical evaluation of the outcome. Specifically, it was found that, as predicted, the placebo condition (irrelevant television) had no effect, whereas videotape feedback produced some increase in looking at each other, and focused instructions produced more dramatic changes in the target behaviors. Instructions alone had as much impact on the target behaviors as did instructions plus videotape feedback. These findings led the authors to question the usefulness of videotape feedback alone and to recommend that it be used solely in conjunction with focused instructions. Indeed, it is improbable that any clinician would rely on feedback without concomitant instruction.

Finally, Eisler, Miller, Hersen, and Alford (1974) reported three case studies in which spousal interactions were videotaped. Husbands were offered training in assertiveness in four 45-minute sessions in which training was or was not related to marital functioning. Interaction coding was used as a posttest. Data indicated that the couples' marital interaction improved most when training scenes simulated their interaction. Presumably, spouses offered such training can be expected to enjoy the greatest improvement in their marital interaction when the training is keyed to their specific concerns.

A second series of analogue studies was conducted at the University of Michigan. Couples were offered training in communication skills via an electronic feedback system similar to, although more sophisticated than, the system used by Stuart (1970) in attempts to modify interactions between parents and their delinquent adolescent children. Thomas, Carter, Gambrill, and Butterfield (1970) developed an electromechanical signal system that permitted multidirectional exchanges between spouses and an experimenter. In an application of the system, Carter and Thomas (1973a) found that collective feedback and instructions combined increased parity in interaction between spouses but that when they examined the relative impact of feedback and instructions on problem specificity, instructions alone increased problem specificity, with the electromagnetic feedback contributing little to this outcome. In a second report (Carter & Thomas, 1973b), data are reported on two couples, showing that corrective feedback instructions aimed at altering the rates of problematic verbal interactions produced a 44% increase in opinion-giving utterances by one husband, with no change in other targeted behaviors, and a 25% increase in content specificity in another couple. Stuart (1970) earlier pointed out that therapist interpretations of the evaluative quality of client behavior is a major source of therapeutic error, suggesting that the use of signal systems such as these (Stuart, 1970; Thomas et al., 1970) may function best when left in client hands, but "best" in this context is not particularly satisfying, given the present data.

The strongest statement that can be made about analogue studies such as those reviewed here is that they may prove to be a source of hypotheses about potentially effective therapeutic maneuvers but that, at present, their promise far surpasses their actual product.

STUDIES OF CLINICAL INTERVENTION

Evaluations of behavioral intervention programs aimed at relieving marital distress first appeared around 1969. As we shall demonstrate, the field still awaits its first definitive study of the effectiveness of the clinical applications of these methods.

The appendix presents a summary of the major characteristics and outcomes of the most representative studies produced since 1969. Studies included in this table: (a) are identified by their authors as evaluations of the behavioral management of marital distress; (b) are in print as opposed to being unpublished thesis research; and (c) report specific outcome data rather than merely offering anecdotal accounts. The third criterion led to the exclusion of nearly all case study reports that were offered mainly as illustrations of the applicability of general behavior therapy principles to marital intervention (e.g., Eisler & Hersen, 1973; Liberman, 1970). Studies were included in this table regardless of sample size and whether or not their results were statistically analyzed. When statistical tests were employed, only those results that proved to be significant are reported as positive outcomes.

As can be seen in the appendix, research in marital behavior therapy began with case studies involving one or more couples. While case studies, especially those of an anecdotal nature, are especially vulnerable with regard to internal validity, and therefore cannot provide conclusive support for causal hypotheses, they have been used within the behavioral framework with certain modifications. As used in the behavioral literature, case studies possess two virtues: First, they make use of intervention techniques that are more precisely defined than those of other approaches; and second, they do not rely upon simple pretest-to-posttest measures of change but instead offer frequent and repeated assessments of outcome. For example, Patterson and Hops (1972), Patterson, Hops, and Weiss (1975), Stern and Marks (1973), and Stuart (1969) all obtained baseline measures of specific target behaviors and then measured these behaviors repeatedly throughout treatment and into a followup period. While the results of these studies cannot be regarded as conclusive experimental proof, they resemble the results obtained thus far from analogue studies in this area in that they have important heuristic value and can lead to fully developed treatment packages (e.g., Azrin, Naster, & Jones, 1973; Patterson *et al.*, 1975; Stuart, 1975; Weiss, Hops, & Patterson, 1973). Because these studies are conducted with clinical populations in settings where treatment is normally offered, they overcome some of the limits to generalizability suffered by the analogue studies while at the same time preserving their seminal potential. These uncontrolled case studies have already begun to give way to studies that use small numbers of clients but build in single-subject design controls (e.g., Azrin *et al.*, 1973; Dixon & Sciara, 1977; Hickok & Komechak, 1974; Wieman, Shoulders, & Farr, 1974) and studies that use comparison or no-treatment control group designs (e.g., Harrell & Guerney, 1976; Jacobson, 1978; Liberman, Levine, Wheeler, Sanders, & Wallace, 1976), or both (e.g., Jacobson, 1977).

In the sections that follow, we shall first offer an overview of the studies presented in the appendix. This will be followed by a discussion of design issues, measurement concerns, and statistical considerations in this research. Finally, we shall offer our conclusions on the current "state of the art."

General Overview

The intervention studies listed in the appendix have attempted to produce maintainable changes in behaviors that the authors believe have an important bearing upon marital satisfaction and stability (Stuart, 1979). While the "product level" of case studies is believed not to be especially high (Paul, 1969, pp. 44–48), their results have tended to be positive. Indeed, there would be little justification for the publication of case studies having no noticeable effects. The case study by Stuart (1969) showed that intervention based on promoting the desired exchange of targeted behavior was associated with increases in conversation time, as well as with increases in the quality and frequency of sexual contact during treatment and through followup. In the same vein, Patterson and Hops (1972) noted improvements of problem-solving communication in the laboratory but not of negative communication patterns at home. (The low probability of such generalization was, in fact, observed many years ago by O'Rourke [1963].) Duration of interactions at home, however, did increase during treatment and was sustained afterward. Stern and Marks (1973) found decreases in negative behaviors as targeted positive behaviors increased in rate, a change that was maintained at followup. In addition, the Oregon group (Patterson *et al.*, 1975; Weiss *et al.*, 1973) found improvements in laboratory-based problem solving and in self-reports of pleasing and displeasing behaviors by spouses. After several months, followup data for half of the clients indicated improvement in marital satisfaction, whereas self-reported desire for changes in the spouses' behavior declined. Followup of all 10 couples at 1 to 2 years yielded equivocal results (see the appendix).

Finally, the case study (not listed in the appendix) with the largest number of subjects and the longest followup period has been briefly reported by Stuart (1976). He summarized preliminary descriptive data from a sample of 200 couples seen over a 10-year period, with followup intervals ranging from 1 to 5 years. Results indicated that all but 3 couples completed the Marital Precounseling Inventory (Stuart & Stuart, 1973), and all but 7 couples signed a contract committing themselves to intervention. In 87% of the couples, at least one spouse met the initial behavior change objectives. These objectives were met by both spouses in 81% of the couples. This was associated with an increased commitment to the marriage by one spouse in 84% of the remaining couples and by both spouses in 77% of the sample. At an average of 1 year after the end of treatment, 5 couples had divorced and 84% of those still married reported maintenance of their increased commitment to their marriages. After 5 years, 16 divorces were reported (still only 8% of the sample), while 89% of the couples reported maintenance of their commitment levels.

A quasi-control feature was introduced into the case study design used by Azrin et al. (1973) with 12 couples. They provided couples with 3 weeks of catharsis counseling in an attempt to control for attention-placebo effects and followed this with their brand of behavioral treatment, termed "reciprocity counseling." Results of this carefully described and innovative intervention indicate that the couples' ratings of their level of satisfaction in nine areas of functioning increased during the reciprocity counseling but not during catharsis counseling. Moreover, there is some support for the assumption that reciprocity counseling treatment effects generalized from the target behaviors to other, untreated behaviors.

The study by Azrin and his associates is impressive in the simplicity of its evaluation procedure and the precision with which the intervention method is described. However, the experimental design creates the illusion (but not the reality) of having achieved control of major threats to the validity of its conclusions. First, any conclusions about the effect of reciprocity counseling are, in fact, limited to reciprocity counseling preceded by catharsis counseling (Jacobson & Martin, 1976). Second, the positive results could also have been a reaction to the detrimental effects of the attention-placebo condition (Greer & D'Zurilla, 1975). Third, data collection methods calling for daily happiness ratings in areas in which clients knew that change was expected could have been highly reactive and susceptible to demand effects. Finally, it is, of course, possible that the catharsis procedure was not viewed as a credible therapeutic offering by clients, contributing an added potential weakness to the value of the comparative data in this study.

Hickok and Komechak (1974) employed a partial reversal (BAB) design with one couple in an attempt to demonstrate the controlling effect of a token economy approach. While the couple did increase their exchanges of positive target behaviors and maintained improvements at followup, the token economy procedure could not be credited with this result, because the data showed no reversal of therapeutic effect when the procedure was withdrawn during the A phase. The increase in target behaviors, then, could have been a function of some uncontrolled aspect of treatment, some extra-therapeutic factors, or may simply reflect the unwillingness of clients to give up intervention techniques or newly acquired skills that have proven helpful.

Wieman et al. (1974) used a multiple baseline design that is probably superior to reversal designs in this area of research. Working with a single couple, they were able to demonstrate successive increases in the rates of exchange of three sets of positive target behaviors as well as increases on two self-report satisfaction measures—changes that were maintained at followup. Therapist interventions were shown to be correlated with changes in two sets of the target behaviors, with the third set possibly showing the effects of generalization from attainment of the earlier therapeutic goals.

Dixon and Sciara (1977) also used a multiple baseline design as well as pre–post measures to assess their version of the reciprocity counseling procedures set forth by Azrin et al. (1973). Using a group treatment format with seven nonclinical couples (and thus exposing their work to some of the limitations of external validity that threatens the analogue studies), they found improvement in clients' self-reported levels of commitment to and optimism about their marriages. Using multiple baseline data (daily multi-area satisfaction inventory ratings) from three of the couples, they found treatment-correlated improvements in two of three target areas. As with the research of Wieman and his colleagues, it is possible that generalization may have helped to produce positive change in the untreated target area in this study.

Liberman et al. (1976) also used a group format in an attempt to assess the relative impact of behavioral and interactional treatment. The results of this painstakingly conducted research are unfortunately limited by several factors, including the facts that couples were assigned to treatment conditions consecutively rather than randomly and that the sample size was so small. In addition, considerable overlap clouds the meaningfulness of comparisons between the two approaches: For example, efforts to increase positive behaviors took place in both conditions. Moreover, the authors report that they attempted to do so much in their behavioral treatment program that their sessions were hurried and may have lacked the pacing that effective treatment demands. The same overburdening may also have complicated data collection insofar as the authors report that the clients complained about their boredom with and aversive reaction to long-term, intrusive data collection procedures. Given these limitations, it is not surprising that the evaluations along some 30 dimensions yield few significant differences. Moreover, some of the differences found between groups could have been due to chance and some appeared to be either relatively unimportant or perhaps only therapeutic artifacts. For example, the increased rate of client eye contact and smiles during sessions may have been a direct consequence of therapist prompting that was not used in the comparison group. Finally, those differences that were found during treatment and at termination were not reflected on followup measures. On the positive side, the couples in both groups appeared to value the treatment that they received as indicated by their positive testimonials. Also, they rated a lower perceived desire for change in their spouses and increased levels of marital satisfaction. This is a small return, however, from a study in which the effort was so great.

Harrell and Guerney (1976) also made use of a group format in comparing their behavioral group with a no-treatment control group. In behavior therapy they offered communication training and behavioral contracting. While they did randomly assign couples to conditions and employed a fairly large sample of 60 couples, they found statistically significant differences favoring the behavioral group on only 4 out of 13 dependent measures, with results on 1 measure appearing to favor the control group. Three of the 4 favorable outcome measures were independent assessments of communication in a laboratory exercise indicating some improvement in communication skills such as minimization of negative verbal behavior. In addition, the authors convincingly reinterpreted the apparently negative result, attributing their finding of decreased positive verbal behavior in the treatment group to an inadequacy in their coding system rather than viewing it as an adverse treatment effect. Unfortunately, no followup data are reported.

In addition, evaluation of the Harrell and Guerney (1976) study is hampered by inadequacy in the reporting of procedures and statistical methods. For example, it is not clear whether both pretests and posttests were administered or posttests only. In addition, the use of a number of univariate statistical tests naturally creates the possibility that some of the observed differences could have resulted from chance alone. Finally, as was the case with the study by Dixon and Sciara (1977) and, to some extent, with Azrin et al. (1973), couples in this study were drawn from a nonclinical population so that results may not be generalizable to distressed couples. For example, the fact that the participants may have been relatively well-functioning couples seeking marital enhancement may have rendered them less responsive to the treatment than treatment-seeking couples might have been. Indeed, many years of psychotherapy research support the notion that a high level of perceived stress at the start of treatment is a predictor of positive outcome (Hiller, 1959; Luborsky, 1962; Stone, Frank, Nash, & Imber, 1961; Strupp, Wallach, & Wogan, 1964).

The only study combining a group experimental design with single-subject controls is the work of Jacobson (1977). He randomly assigned 10 couples either to focal behavior therapy or to a minimum treatment, waiting-list control group. Using a covariance design to control for any pretreatment group differences, he found that treated couples outperformed the controls by emitting more positive and fewer negative responses in a laboratory problem-solving task as well as reporting greater marital satisfaction. While Jacobson (1977) states that the multiple baseline data support the specific efficacy of the treatment methods, data are reported only for husbands of 2 of the 4 couples for whom he said the method was relevant. Finally, while the author contends that the marital satisfaction pretest scores of his solicited couples do not differ significantly from the distressed clinical couples treated by Weiss *et al.* (1973), they were recruited through newspaper ads and may differ in significant respects from couples who made unprompted decisions to seek outside help in coping with marital distress.

In 1978 Jacobson attempted to both replicate and extend his prior study. Two of his conditions, the good faith and waiting-list groups, represent the attempt to replicate the earlier study. In addition, a quid pro quo contractive group was included to permit a comparison of two behavioral groups equivalent in all respects except for type of contracting procedure taught. The nonspecific group was included to control for all aspects of intervention except problem solving and communication skill training and contingency contracting skill training. Moreover, three therapists were employed so as to control for possible therapist or therapist X treatment interaction effects on outcome. Jacobson (1978) also attempted to check the adequacy of the independent variable manipulations by assessing possible differences in client ratings of therapists and treatment and in undergraduate students' credibility ratings of brief written descriptions of the three treatments.

Results were generally positive in that the behavioral groups performed better than the waiting-list group on the following four outcome measures, which included use of the Marital Interaction Coding System (MICS) (Weiss *et al.*, 1973) for coding negative and positive verbal problem-solving behavior; marital satisfaction ratings (Locke & Wallace, 1959); and marital happiness ratings in 12 areas (Stuart & Stuart, 1973). Only on the self-report measure of happiness in various areas did both behavioral groups fail to outperform the nonspecific group. The failure to find differences in outcome attributable to therapist or therapist X treatment interaction and the lack of differences in client and student credibility ratings of treatment and therapist are taken to suggest that the positive results of the behavioral groups may be attributed to the relevant treatment ingredients.

Jacobson (1978) is to be commended for the following features of his study: (a) the use of multivariate analysis of covariance, which minimizes capitalization on chance and statistically controls for any pretest differences; (b) treating couples', rather than individuals', scores as the unit of analysis; (c) the efforts that went into creating a credible, nonspecific control group as well as the rather thorough specification of its content; and (d) the attempts to assess the credibility and equivalence of the three therapists and the three treatments on all but the varied factors.

The main limitation of the study has to do with the small number of couples per cell, which makes lack of power a plausible explanation for some "no difference" findings, such as those findings taken to suggest that: (a) the two contracting procedures are interchangeable; (b) treatments and therapists were equally credible to clients; and (c) therapists were equally effective and did not interact with treatment conditions. Findings of no difference in conjunction with small sample size become especially problematic when the primary aim is to substantiate null hypotheses of "no differences." A minor problem is the ambiguity in the report of followup results. Jacobson (1978) reports that the followup data of any couples who returned the Marital Adjustment Scale (MAS) (Locke & Wallace, 1959) on at least two of the three occasions (1, 3, and 6 months) were averaged to get one followup score per couple. This, of course, means that followup may have been largely limited to 3 months for most couples. Finally, the fact that the "vast majority" of couples were recruited through advertisements (Jacobson, 1978, p. 443) and that therapists were relatively inexperienced (all, including Jacobson, were graduate students) suggests limitations to the generalizability of results.

In summary, the strongest conclusion that can be drawn about the outcomes in the studies reviewed here is that they offer some support for the potential usefulness of behavioral therapeutic methods for controlling marital distress. In no sense, however, can the results of this decade of research be interpreted as offering clinicians strong and unequivocal support for the application of these methods. However, this less than enthusiastic endorsement should be viewed within the context of studies of the outcome of other marital treatment approaches, none of which have produced an empirically supported mandate that is stronger than that emerging from these studies.

Evaluation of Experimental Designs

Case study designs that specify intervention methods adequately enough to permit replication and that assess therapeutic outcomes with precision are obviously better than no evaluation at all. However, progress in the evaluation of marital behavior therapy requires greater utilization of confirmatory designs. Single-subject and group experimental designs are the obvious choices for this task. Jacobson's (1977) study illustrated the fact that this treatment approach lends itself well to evaluation using both designs.

Single-subject designs fit well within the realm of clinicians' daily service activities and may be the only attempts at experimental validation that full-time clinicians will be prepared to undertake. Such designs have an important place in the empirical evaluation of treatment procedures (see, e.g., Kazdin & Wilson, 1976) that has only begun to be explored with regard to marital behavior therapy. Moreover, detailed discussions of such design are now available (see, e.g., Hersen & Barlow, 1976). These designs do, however, have some important limitations. They naturally involve few subjects, which may set a low ceiling on the generalizability of their results (Hartmann, Roper, & Gelfand, 1977). They are also subject to the "multiple treatment interference" effect described by Campbell and Stanley (1963), an effect in which later procedures are possibly contaminated by those that precede them. For example, in a multiple baseline design format, increased rates of sexual pleasure may be more correctly attributed to the communication that preceded it than to the therapist-mediated feedback-instigation package that was the apparent manipulation. In this situation, the sequence of specific interventions, rather than any one manipulation, may account for most of the variance in outcome. A third problem, particularly in the use of multiple baseline designs, is the possibility that the classes of behaviors that are the targets of intervention may be interdependent rather than independent as the design would require. Therefore, a change in one behavior might necessarily bring about a change in another as well (Gelfand & Hartmann, 1975, p. 94). This may explain the fact that in the studies by Wieman et al. (1974), and by Dixon and Sciara (1977), one of three sets of target behaviors improved before they were the focus of intervention, but after improvements were noted in two other response clusters. In the first of these studies, for example, "sexual behavior" was the third target and was found to improve at approximately the same time as the second target, conversational behavior, improved.

The absence of statistical procedures in evaluating the significance of the changes recorded in these single-subject designs can make their interpretation somewhat subjective and therefore open to challenge. (Potentially useful statistical procedures are now being developed for single-subject designs. See, for example, Kazdin, 1976.)

Because of these and other limitations in single-subject designs (Kazdin, 1973), it is sometimes impractical to use such designs, and therefore necessary to rely on experimental group designs to evaluate treatment effectiveness. A decision to turn to group designs is only the first in a chain of decisions that have to be made, however. First, the design must naturally be adapted to the question that the researcher seeks to answer. Stuart (1971) has suggested that classical no-treatment control groups, when they are feasible, may be useful for answering questions about the absolute utility of a particular experimental method. Similarly, comparison group designs may be better adapted to answering the primary question faced by clinicians, which is, "Which method is better or preferable?" rather than the question, "Should this method, rather than nothing, be used?" which the classical design would answer. In the studies reviewed here, those by Harrell and Guerney (1976) and Jacobson (1977) are illustrations of the use of no-treatment controls, while those of Liberman *et al.* (1976) and Jacobson (1978) illustrate a comparison group approach.

Once a commitment has been made to use either untreated or comparison treatment groups, the next decisions center on means of providing the ethical guarantees of participant rights (e.g., Association for the Advancement of Behavior Therapy, 1977). Researchers who solicit subjects through newspaper ads and who use a carefully chosen consent-granting procedure (Stuart, 1978) find that this can best be handled by telling all clients applying for a clinical service that treatment may require at least a 3-month waiting period. Those feeling intense need for help might then either be referred elsewhere or treated according to the routine program of the agency. Couples willing to accept the waiting period could then be randomly assigned to an immediate intervention track or to a delayed treatment track until the completion of the foretold 3-month period. Because the treatment packages currently under study are time limited, most could be offered within the 3-month period. While this procedure would preclude the collection of followup data on the controls, it would permit a statistical evaluation of the immediate impact of treatment.

If the results of this phase of development are positive—and to date, studies like those of Harrell and Guerney (1976) and Jacobson (1977, 1978) either have not been clearly successful in supporting the value of the behavioral approach or at least have shown the need for further replication—it would be timely to move into stage three, which would make use of comparison group designs. To be acceptable in these comparative studies, each intervention package—be it psychodynamic, Rogerian, Adlerian, gestalt, or any other approach—must have passed a similar test of experimental utility. Should the behavioral approach prove valuable in this context, it would then be advisable to move into the fourth stage—that of component analysis through "knock down" designs. In this stage, an effort would be made to determine which components of the behavioral treatment are necessary and sufficient to produce the desired level of therapeutic gain. Attention could also be paid to the optimal duration of treatment and other service delivery variables. The output at this point would be a program that has been shown to be better than no treatment, superior to alternative methods, and offered in its most efficient format. Moreover, if the research at stages two through four has been carried out with sufficient numbers of subjects and therapists, it would also be possible to determine which groups of subjects are likely to benefit most. For example, Stuart, Tripodi, Jayaratne, and Camburn (1976) showed that lower-class families, those most at risk in juvenile court populations (but not showing more extreme pretest scores on the dependent measures), gained more from family interventions utilizing contracting than did more middle-class families. This is a counterintuitive finding and one that can be quite important in planning services for the families of delinquent youth.

In the same vein, therapist characteristics and biases should be studied in a continuing effort to determine the optimal conditions for service offerings. It would be important, in this regard, to determine whether age and marital status have a bearing upon the effectiveness with which marital behavior therapy can be offered. Also, some evidence has been presented (e.g., Stuart & Lott, 1972) showing that therapists differ in their biases regarding the use of focal technologies. The control of these biases may contribute to improved therapeutic results. As a special illustration of potential influence of such bias, Liberman et al. (1976) asked three therapists as a team to conduct both of the treatments in their experiment, risking the very strong possibility that the therapists' biases would interact with their ability to offer one treatment or the other convincingly and enthusiastically.

Evaluation of Dependent Variables

Even if the validations of behavioral marriage therapy arise from well-designed experimental studies, the results may still be equivocal, misleading, or uninterpretable if the expected changes are not measured adequately. If the measures are biased, unreliable, invalid, insensitive, or too narrowly conceived, specious reports of improvement when deterioration actually occurred or of exacerbation of the problem when marked improvements actually occurred are both very real possibilities.

Review of the outcome measures noted in Table 15.1 shows that thoughts, feelings, and social behavior have all been studied via self-report and direct observation at home, in laboratory, and in clinical situations. Therefore the permutations inherent in the selection of change measures are indeed complex.

One source of bias in outcome measures has been termed "criterion bias" by Meltzoff and Kornreich (1970). This refers to the selection of measures that are "most likely to support the hypothesis" (p. 30). For example, Liberman et al. (1976) evaluated "looks" and "smiles" during sessions of their focal behavior therapy and their comparison condition, although these were targets for behavior change only in the focal group. Change in these nonverbal communications could therefore at best be used as short-range indicators that the focal treatment produced some behavior changes that were hypothesized mediators of the kinds of changes that couples hoped to accomplish when they entered treatment.

An unbiased approach would call for balancing any measures especially relevant to one group with measures particularly appropriate for the targeted changes in the comparison group. In addition, care must be taken in the overall assessment of results not to treat these short-range measures on the same basis as the long-range measures, since the latter are better reflections of the effectiveness of the treatment in producing outcomes anticipated by the clients. That is, simply tabulating the number of positive findings on these measures intermixed with the more valid indices can clearly lead to biased conclusions.

A second measurement problem has been termed "patient response bias" by Meltzoff and Kornreich (1970, p. 30). This refers to the well-recognized tendency of clients to give socially desirable responses that conform to therapist expectations when asked to self-report their therapeutic progress and/or the evaluation of the service that they received. There was particular susceptibility to such a bias in the attempts by Azrin *et al.* (1973) to collect client evaluations of their home behavior, and by Liberman *et al.* (1976) in their solicitation of evaluations of the treatment offered. Another illustration of patient response bias is the possible overstatement by clients of the extent of their marital distress at the start of treatment. Most clinicians have observed that the problems that prompted their clients' request for therapeutic help are not the most extreme crises in their lives. They are, however, times at which clients may have tended to overreact to events that might have been easily taken in stride at other times. This is a potential source of a second measurement artifact: Overreactions by clients seeking treatment may predispose them to greater apparent improvement than is found in control subjects not seeking treatment. Moreover, clients wishing treatment may somewhat overstate their distress in order to increase the likelihood that they will be accepted for therapy or perhaps as a means of seducing their therapists into collusive alliances with the spouse who appears to be suffering the most. All of these conditions contribute to an artifact that resembles regression to the mean (Campbell & Stanley, 1963), and all tend to inflate the magnitude of before–after comparisons. This possibility can be at least partially counteracted by taking baseline measurements for several weeks prior to starting treatment, allowing for the possibility that crisis reactions will dissipate "spontaneously."

"Judge bias" is another source of error in the measurement of therapeutic outcome. In marital behavior therapy studies, this is most likely to be found in observer ratings of interactions between spouses either during treatment, in laboratory exercises, or in home observation.

This is a particular problem if the judges are not naive as to the experimental hypotheses, the identification of clients as experimental or control subjects, or the phase of treatment completed by the client prior to the live or videotaped observation. Use of observational data is one of the strengths of marital behavior therapy research (e.g., Harrell & Guerney, 1976; Jacobson, 1977, 1978; Patterson & Hops, 1972; Patterson et al., 1975). Unfortunately, descriptions of efforts to control for this type of bias are not always complete or reassuring. For example, Patterson and Hops (1972) do report provisions for controlling for observer bias in home observations, but do not mention the precautions taken in the coding of laboratory interaction. In addition, it is important to note that clients may alter their interactions in the presence of observers, and that the attainment of high interjudge reliability ratings in no sense guarantees that the ratings are accurate or unbiased (Hartmann et al., 1977).

Another significant problem is the reliability and validity of self-reported behavior changes that are core dependent variables in all of the studies given in the appendix except for the work of Azrin et al. (1973) and Harrell and Guerney (1976). Unreliable reports may be the consequence of imprecisely defined target behaviors, judgment lapses by the clients who are clearly not at arms' length from the data that they are collecting, and distortions in observations resulting from the fact that each datum point often requires detection of a two-party, interactional event that one person might construe very differently from the other. Most of the studies in the appendix appear to have specified target behaviors adequately. However, only the Oregon group appears to have made an effort to assess the reliability and validity of their data on spouse-reported rates of pleasing and displeasing behaviors. For example, in one of their investigations, Wills, Weiss, and Patterson (1974) asked half of the spouses to increase the rate of their emission of pleasing behavior and assessed changes in the reports of pleases received by the other spouse, concluding that the measure was quite sensitive to such manipulations. It is also important to point out that measures found to be reliable in one context may not be so in another. As mentioned earlier, Liberman et al. (1976) report that their clients found the daily recording of pleasing spouse behavior throughout treatment to be tedious. These authors therefore conclude that this data was unreliable.

Stuart (1979) has suggested that the validity of measures of the effects of behavioral marriage therapy hinges in part, at least, on the way in which both spouses interpret the actions of their mates. An action believed by the therapist to be positive may or may not be positively evaluated by the client, and even if it is positively evaluated, it may not have a salubrious effect upon that person's commitment to the marriage. In no sense, then, is the impact of observable changes in behavior either unidirectional or readily predictable. Wills et al. (1974) found, for example, that wives' ratings of their daily level of marital satisfaction were more influenced by *affectional* pleasures received, whereas husbands' ratings were more influenced by *instrumental* pleasures received. This seems to indicate that certain behaviors were differentially salient for wives' and husbands' marital satisfaction levels.

In general, the reliability and validity of the self-report measures of marital satisfaction used in the studies under review here are acceptable. The Locke–Wallace Marital Adjustment Scale, for example, is reported to have high split-half reliability (Locke & Wallace, 1959). Kimmel and van der Veen (1974) also report that the scale has high test–retest reliability. While Locke and Wallace (1959) also report adequate criterion validity, Funabiki (n.d.) points out that their effort to establish validity falls far short of the guidelines offered by the American Psychological Association (1966) for the establishment of test validity. A recent revision of this scale developed by Spanier (1976) overcomes some of these problems and is our recommendation (see also Stuart, 1979) as an alternative to the Locke–Wallace Scale. Inclusion of a measure such as this scale offers several very important advantages: It is not directly tied to the theory of the treatment being offered and is therefore relatively free of criterion bias; it is in wide use and therefore permits equilibration of the level of marital satisfaction among subjects across many studies; and it serves as a useful introspective reference point against which to evaluate the meaningfulness to clients of the specific behavior changes that are the typical targets of behavioral marriage therapy.

The Oregon group used two additional self-report satisfaction measures in their research. Their Willingness to Change Scale (Weiss *et al.*, 1973) asks spouses to indicate on a seven-point scale how strongly they desire their mates to change in various potential problem areas. Price and Haynes (n.d.) report some concurrent and discriminative validity for this scale, but they indicate that the reliability of this measure has not been checked. The Marital Activities Inventory: Alone, Together, Others (Weiss *et al.*, 1973) measures the frequency with which spouses share activities or pursue them separately. Validity but not reliability data have been reported for this measure as well.

Unfinished as the assessment of the reliability and validity of these instruments may be, the Oregon group should be credited for demonstrating more concern in this area than most other researchers cited in the appendix. For example, no reliability and validity data are reported for the following instruments: the Conjugal Life Questionnaire (Guerney, 1964) used by Wieman *et al.* (1974); the Marital Happiness Scale of Azrin *et al.* (1973), also used by Dixon and Sciara (1977); and the Marital Pre-Counseling Inventory (Stuart & Stuart, 1973) used by Dixon and Sciara (1977), Liberman *et al.* (1976), and Jacobson (1978). Naturally, the failure of these evaluations to appear does not mean that the instruments lack reliability and validity, but their usefulness in research evaluations is questionable until these data are available.

Another dependent measure used in these studies is observational ratings of behavior in laboratory problem-solving or conflict negotiation tasks. Patterson and Hops (1972), Patterson et al. (1975), and Liberman et al. (1976) all used the Marital Interaction Coding System (MICS) developed by the Oregon group (Weiss et al., 1973) to evaluate couples' problem-solving performance in resolving major and minor areas of disagreement or conflict. Adequate interrater reliability (Patterson & Hops, 1972) and criterion agreement of 70% (Weiss et al., 1973) have been reported for this system. Weiss et al. (1973) seem to dismiss the question of establishing the validity of the MICS as premature and indicate their acceptance of its face validity (p. 319). They then seem to suggest more than face validity for the MICS in pointing out that five couples demonstrated change in 10 of the 29 categories between the start and end of treatment, and 5 others made significant changes in 6 code levels. Elsewhere, Patterson et al. (1975) make the puzzling statement that "Weiss et al. (1973) used two a priori groupings of the MICS categories as means of measuring changes following treatment" (p. 299), before stating that subsequent analysis led to identification of those categories that showed large changes following treatment, leading to revision of the original groupings. These revised groupings (facilitating and disrupting behaviors) were then used in a subsequent report of data on what appear to be the same couples included in the earlier (Weiss et al., 1973) report. The impression, perhaps erroneous, is one of revision of the groupings in search of the mix that shows the highest level of change. While Birchler, Weiss, and Vincent (1975) and Vincent, Weiss, and Birchler (1975) both report better evidence for the validity of the MICS, it is clear that the system has yet to pass the stringent test of validity and reliability evaluations.

Jacobson (1977, 1978) and Liberman et al. (1976) both used the MICS in their investigations, with the latter study showing comparatively little change in the observed behaviors. Harrell and Guerney (1976) developed their own coding system, for which reliability and validity data are not reported, and failed to report dramatic improvements through use of their system. At least two explanations of these failures are possible. First, the coding systems may lack sensitivity. A second explanation for some failures to find differences in interaction coded in this way may be that the tasks offered to clients are so unnatural for them that they are unlikely to promote interaction of an intensity that would reflect couples' naturally occurring patterns. As noted earlier, Brehmer (1976) indicated that this is one of the major weaknesses in analogue studies. Laboratory problem-solving interactions may be just as artificial as far as distressed couples are concerned.

A final consideration in evaluating the adequacy of the dependent variable measures relates to their comprehensiveness. Researchers have a broad mix of instruments from which to choose in evaluating their treatment and, given the fact that marriage is an enormously complex interaction, it is essential that many of the available avenues of measurement be used. While it is very costly, and possibly highly reactive, home observation would seem to be an important evaluation tool in this research, but only Patterson and Hops (1972) made use of it—and then only with one couple. While, as Liberman *et al.* (1976) sadly reported, clients can be overwhelmed with measurements, it seems incumbent upon all researchers to include in their assessment armamentarium a measure of marital satisfaction, a measure of the behaviors identified as focal concerns at the start of treatment, a measure of social interaction, a measure of such critical marital interactions as sexual encounters and problem-solving experiences, and measures of such probable serendipities of marital treatment as occupational success, parenting effectiveness and/or self-management and health care behaviors.

Statistical Evaluation

The adequacy of the design of outcome studies is related to progressive attempts to rule out threats to internal validity or, in other words, alternative explanations to that of the treatment manipulation for any effects or outcomes (Campbell & Stanley, 1963; Cook & Campbell, 1976). Another necessary condition for inferring a causal relationship between treatment and effect is that one be able to establish that the treatment and effect covaried. Single-subject designs have typically relied on "visual inspection" of the relationship between intervention and dependent variable data to infer covariation. Most group experiments or studies, however, attempt to meet this condition through the use of statistical tests of significance. In order to justify the assumption of covariation between treatment and effect beyond that due to chance, one must rule out threats to "statistical conclusion validity" (Cook & Campbell, 1976). Statistical validity, in short, is concerned with sources of error variance that may obscure actual differences and with the appropriate use of statistics and statistical tests (Cook & Campbell, 1976).

There are three main threats to statistical validity in the outcome studies of marital behavior therapy listed in the appendix. The first, already discussed in some detail, has to do with the unreliability or undemonstrated reliability of many of the dependent measures. The use of measures of low reliability will increase error variance and thus cause insensitivity to any true changes. This may lead to false negative conclusions about the effect of treatment.

A second threat to statistical validity is also a source of false negative conclusions. When sample size is small, as it is in most of the studies in the appendix, the probability of detecting any actual differences or effects decreases. Small sample size and the consequent reduction in "power" is *not* a problem when one obtains significant results, provided, of course, that the appropriate statistical tests were used.

A third threat to statistical validity, also present in most of the studies in the appendix, could lead to false positive conclusions. When multiple dependent variables are employed, the dependent measures are often correlated. F tests applied to each dependent variable separately are not independent, and it is not known how to calculate the probability that at least one of the F tests will be significant by chance alone (Kerlinger & Pedhazur, 1973, p. 352). Therefore, multivariate procedures are preferable in that they take such lack of independence between dependent variables into account (Kerlinger & Pedhazur, 1973, p. 352) and enable one to assess whether any significant univariate F tests are due to chance (Cook & Campbell, 1976, p. 233). Of the relevant studies in the appendix, only Jacobson (1977, 1978) appeared to use a multivariate test.

Finally, when couples are treated as units, it is likely that there is a dependency between their performance on the dependent measure(s). In such cases, one should consider each couple's score, rather than that of each individual, in the statistical analysis (e.g., see Jacobson, 1977, 1978).

CONCLUSIONS

Behaviorally oriented marriage therapy has been somewhat slower to gain acceptance than have other areas of the human applications of operant technology. Several programs have been described in sufficient detail to permit replication, and the programs differ sufficiently in philosophy and technology to offer replicators a meaningful choice among alternatives. For example, the program developed by the Oregon group (Patterson *et al.*, 1975; Weiss *et al.*, 1973) can be classified as being comparatively a social learning program, whereas Stuart (1969) characterized his program as "operant interpersonal," adding a significant cognitive component to the program in its most recent elaboration (Stuart, 1979). In addition to having a choice of technologies, replicators can also develop a package of measurement procedures ranging from frameworks for coding interaction in clinical, laboratory, and home settings, through scalar means of assessing satisfaction with and commitment to the marriage, to many different methods of collecting data evaluating the success and impact of instigated changes in interactional behavior. Finally, an assortment of clientele is also available: Premarital and marital enrichment services and marital crisis and pre-divorce counseling can be offered to clients recruited through newspaper ads and community groups, such as churches, as well as to the more familiar clientele of marriage and family counseling centers. With a problem as socially significant as marital distress and a range of materials as readily available as those described in this chapter, it is hoped that more investigators will find this area to be of interest and therefore commit themselves to new research efforts aimed at developing more effective treatment packages and validating the usefulness of this evolving social learning technology.

It is our view that the field is now beyond the point at which additional case studies will make an important contribution. We feel that more studies using single-subject and group experimental designs are needed. Single-subject design studies can often serve an important intermediary role in making possible the evaluation of treatment packages and components on a small scale (see, e.g., Kazdin & Wilson, 1978). Classical experimental control group studies are also needed, studies using a sufficiently large number of clients to permit partialing out groups that can be expected to make greater or lesser gains through exposure to the treatment. This is high-budget research if undertaken *de novo*, but because of its significant service output, it can be adapted to the programs of ongoing treatment agencies at a comparatively low cost. To meet the current need of the field, we believe that these research projects should: (a) develop highly explicated training manuals for staff development; (b) take pains to monitor conformity to these manuals of the treatment program as actually delivered by a method such as coding tape-recordings of randomly selected treatment sessions; (c) use heavily triangulated measurement packages that include measurement of change from varied perspectives (Metfessel & Michael, 1967) and multivariate statistical designs; and (d) contain followup data of 2 years or more.

Within this rubric it would be of interest to explore the relative success of several strategies, for example: (a) using married versus unmarried and lay versus professional therapists; (b) offering clients some degree of choice as to the sequence of intervention modules that they receive (Stuart, in press); (c) spacing intervention sessions somewhat more imaginatively than the current weekly ritual and massing of intervention sessions, so that some thought goes into the wisdom of 8-week programs that may serve experimenter rather than client needs; and (d) developing maintenance technologies that differ from those used to promote the focal change in marital distress (Stuart, in press). For example, periodic self-assessments can help couples to identify relationship disturbances before they reach clinical proportions, possibly triggering their self-application of relationship enhancement technologies learned during the final stages of their focal interventions. We believe that such procedures and other related subissues in this field of research represent one of the major domains in which there is an acute need for evaluation and refinement of treatment programs based on social learning theory. Therefore, it is strongly hoped that investments of energy, creativity, and productivity will permit advances in this area in response to social needs, so that marital behavior therapy may achieve the same level as other areas of applied behavior modification research.

REFERENCES

Agras, W. S. Behavior modification in the general hospital psychiatric unit. In H. Leitenberg (Ed.), *Handbook of behavior modification and behavior therapy*. Englewood Cliffs, N.J.: Prentice-Hall, 1976. Pp. 547–565.

American Psychological Association. *Standards for educational and psychological tests and manuals*. Washington, D.C.: APA, 1966.

Association for the Advancement of Behavior Therapy. Ethical issues in behavior therapy practice and research. *Behavior Therapy*, 1977, *8*, 277.

Azrin, N. H., Naster, B. J., & Jones, R. Reciprocity counseling: A rapid learning-based procedure for marital counseling. *Behaviour Research and Therapy*, 1973, *11*, 365–382.

Bailey, K. G., & Sowder, W. T. Audiotape and videotape self-confrontation in psychotherapy. *Psychological Bulletin*, 1970, *74*, 127–137.

Bandura, A. *Social learning theory*. Englewood Cliffs, N.J.: Prentice-Hall, 1977.

Bernstein, D. A., & Paul, G. L. Some comments on therapy analogue research with small animal "phobias." *Journal of Behavior Therapy and Experimental Psychiatry*, 1971, *2*, 225–237.

Birchler, G. R., Weiss, R. L., & Vincent, J. P. Multimethod analysis of social reinforcement exchange between maritally distressed and nondistressed spouse and stranger dyads. *Journal of Personality and Social Psychology*, 1975, *31*, 349–360.

Brehmer, B. Social judgment theory and the analysis of interpersonal conflict. *Psychological Bulletin*, 1976, *83*, 985–1003.

Campbell, D. T., & Stanley, J. C. *Experimental and quasi-experimental designs for research*. Chicago: Rand McNally, 1963.

Caporaso, J. A., & Roos, L. L. (Eds.). *Quasi-experimental approaches: Testing theory and evaluating policy*. Evanston, Ill.: Northwestern University Press, 1973.

Carter, R. D., & Thomas, E. J. A case application of a signaling system (SAM) to the assessment and modification of selected problems of marital communication. *Behavior Therapy*, 1973, *4*, 629–645. (a)

Carter, R. D., & Thomas, E. J. Modification of problematic marital communication using corrective feedback and instruction. *Behavior Therapy*, 1973, *4*, 100–109. (b)

Collins, J. *The effects of the conjugal relationship modification method on marital communication and adjustment*. Unpublished doctoral dissertation, Pennsylvania State University, 1971.

Cook, T. D., & Campbell, D. T. The design and conduct of quasi-experiments and true experiments in field settings. In M. D. Dunnette (Ed.), *Handbook of industrial and organizational research*. Chicago: Rand McNally, 1976. Pp. 225–327.

Danet, B. N. Self-confrontation in psychotherapy reviewed. *American Journal of Psychotherapy*, 1968, *22*, 245–258.

Dixon, D. N., & Sciara, A. D. Effectiveness of group reciprocity counseling with married couples. *Journal of Marriage and Family Counseling*, 1977, *3*, 77–83.

Eisler, R. M., & Hersen, M. Behavioral techniques in family-oriented crisis intervention. *Archives of General Psychiatry*, 1973, *28*, 111–116.

Eisler, R. M., Hersen, M., & Agras, W. S. Effects of videotape and instructional feedback on nonverbal marital interaction: An analog study. *Behavior Therapy*, 1973, *4*, 551–558. (a)

Eisler, R. M., Hersen, M., & Agras, W. S. Videotape: A method for the controlled observation of nonverbal interpersonal behavior. *Behavior Therapy*, 1973, *4*, 420–425. (b)

Eisler, R. M., Miller, P. M., Hersen, M., & Alford, J. Effects of assertive training on marital interaction. *Archives of General Psychiatry*, 1974, *30*, 643–649.

Ellis, A. *The art and science of love.* New York: Bantam Books, 1966.

Farber, B. An index of marital integration. *Sociometry*, 1957, *20*, 117–134.

Funabiki, D. *Marital behavior therapy: Conceptualization, assessment, and treatment.* Unpublished manuscript, State University of New York at Stony Brook, n.d.

Gelfand, D. M., & Hartmann, D. P. *Child behavior analysis and therapy.* New York: Pergamon, 1975.

Greer, S. E., & D'Zurilla, T. J. Behavioral approaches to marital discord and conflict. *Journal of Marriage and Family Counseling*, 1975, *1*, 299–315.

Guerney, B. Filial therapy: Description and rationale. *Journal of Consulting Psychology*, 1964, *28*, 304–310.

Hamerlynck, L. A. (Ed.). *Behavior modification approaches in the management of developmental disabilities.* New York: Brunner/Mazel, in press.

Harrell, J., & Guerney, B. Training married couples in conflict negotiation skills. In D. H. L. Olson (Ed.), *Treating relationships.* Lake Mills, Iowa: Graphic Publishing Co., 1976. Pp. 151–166.

Hartmann, D. P., Roper, B. L., & Gelfand, D. M. An evaluation of alternative modes of child psychotherapy. In B. B. Lahey & A. E. Kazdin (Eds.), *Advances in clinical child psychology* (Vol. 1). New York: Plenum Press, 1977. Pp. 1–46.

Hersen, M., & Barlow, D. H. *Single-case experimental designs: Strategies for studying behavior change.* New York: Pergamon Press, 1976.

Hickok, J. E., & Komechak, M. G. Behavior modification in marital conflict: A case report. *Family Process*, 1974, *13*, 111–119.

Hiller, E. W. Initial complaints as predictors of continuation in psychotherapy. *Journal of Clinical Psychology*, 1959, *15*, 344–345.

Human Development Institute. *Improving communication in marriage.* Atlanta, Ga.: 1967.

Jacobson, N. S. Problem solving and contingency contracting in the treatment of marital discord. *Journal of Consulting and Clinical Psychology*, 1977, *45*, 92–100.

Jacobson, N. S. Specific and nonspecific factors in the effectiveness of a behavioral approach to the treatment of marital discord. *Journal of Consulting and Clinical Psychology*, 1978, *46*, 442–452.

Jacobson, N. S., & Martin, B. Behavioral marriage therapy: Current status. *Psychological Bulletin*, 1976, *83*, 540–556.

Kazdin, A. E. Methodological and assessment considerations in evaluating reinforcement programs in applied settings. *Journal of Applied Behavior Analysis*, 1973, *6*, 517–531.

Kazdin, A. E. Statistical analyses for single-case experimental designs. In M. Hersen & D. H. Barlow (Eds.), *Single-case experimental designs: Strategies for studying behavior change.* New York: Pergamon, 1976. Pp. 265–316.

Kazdin, A. E., & Wilson, G. T. *Evaluation of behavior therapy: Issues, evidence, and research strategies.* Cambridge, Mass.: Ballinger, 1978.

Kerlinger, F. N., & Pedhazur, E. J. *Multiple regression in behavioral research,* New York: Holt, Rinehart, & Winston, 1973.

Kimmel, D., & van der Veen, F. Factors of marital adjustment in Locke's marital adjustment test. *Journal of Marriage and the Family*, 1974, *36*, 57–63.

Lederer, W. J., & Jackson, D. D. *Mirages of marriage.* New York: W. W. Norton, 1968.

Liberman, R. Behavioral approaches to family and couple therapy. *American Journal of Ortopsychiatry*, 1970, *40*, 106–118.

Liberman, R. P., Levine, J., Wheeler, E., Sanders, N., & Wallace, C. J. Marital therapy in groups: A comparative evaluation of behavioral and interactional formats. *Acta Psychiatrica Scandinavica*, 1976, Suppl. 266, 3–34.

Locke, H. J., & Wallace, K. M. Short marital adjustment and prediction tests: Their reliability and validity. *Marriage and Family Living*, 1959, *21*, 251–255.

Locke, H. J., & Williamson, R. C. Marital adjustment: A factor analysis study. *American Sociological Review*, 1958, *23*, 562–569.

Luborsky, L. The patient's personality and psychotherapeutic change. In H. H. Strupp & L. Luborsky (Eds.), *Research in psychotherapy*. Washington, D.C.: American Psychological Association, 1962. Pp. 115–133.

Meltzoff, J., & Kornreich, M. *Research in psychotherapy*. New York: Atherton Press, 1970.

Metfessel, N. S., & Michael, W. B. A paradigm involving multiple criterion measures for the evaluation of the effectiveness of school programs. *Educational and Psychological Measurement*, 1967, *27*, 931–943.

O'Leary, K. D., & O'Leary, S. G. *Classroom management: The successful use of behavior modification*. New York: Pergamon, 1972.

O'Rourke, J. F. Field and laboratory: The decision-making behavior of family groups in two experimental conditions. *Sociometry*, 1963, *26*, 422–435.

Patterson, G. R. *Families: Applications of social learning to family life*. Champaign, Ill.: Research Press, 1971.

Patterson, G. R., & Hops, H. Coercion, a game for two: Intervention techniques for marital conflict. In R. E. Ulrich & P. T. Mountjoy (Eds.), *The experimental analysis of social behavior*. New York: Appleton-Century-Crofts, 1972. Pp. 424–440.

Patterson, G. R., Hops, H., & Weiss, R. L. Interpersonal skills training for couples in early stages of conflict. *Journal of Marriage and the Family*, 1975, *37*, 295–303.

Paul, G. L. Behavior modification research: Design and tactics. In C. M. Franks (Ed.), *Behavior therapy: Appraisal and status*. New York: McGraw-Hill, 1969. Pp. 29–62.

Price, M. G., & Haynes, S. N. *Behavioral conceptualization, assessment and intervention with marital dysfunction*. Unpublished manuscript, Southern Illinois University, n.d.

Schlein, S. *Training dating couples in empathic and open communication: An experimental evaluation of a potential preventative mental health program*. Unpublished doctoral dissertation, Pennsylvania State University, 1971.

Serber, M., & Laws, R. *Tenderness*. A film produced by Behavioral Alternatives, San Luis Obispo, Calif., 1974. Available from Diana Serber-Corenman, Atascadero State Hospital, Atascadero, Calif.

Spanier, G. B. Measuring dyadic adjustment: New scales for assessing the quality of marriage and similar dyads. *Journal of Marriage and the Family*, 1976, *38*, 15–28.

Stahl, J. R., & Leitenberg, H. Behavioral treatment of the chronic mental hospital patient. In H. Leitenberg (Ed.), *Handbook of behavior modification and behavior therapy*. Englewood Cliffs, N.J.: Prentice-Hall, 1976. Pp. 211–241.

Stern, R. S., & Marks, I. M. Contract therapy in obsessive–compulsive neurosis with marital discord. *British Journal of Psychiatry*, 1973, *123*, 681–684.

Stone, A. R., Frank, J. D., Nash, E. H., & Imber, S. D. An intensive five-year follow-up study of treated psychiatric outpatients. *Journal of Nervous and Mental Disease*, 1961, *133*, 410–422.

Strupp, H. H., Wallach, M. S., & Wogan, M. Psychotherapy experience in retrospect: Questionnaire survey of former patients and their therapists. *Psychological Monographs*, 1964, *78* (Whole no. 588).

Stuart, R. B. Operant-interpersonal treatment for marital discord. *Journal of Consulting and Clinical Psychology*, 1969, *33*, 675–682.

Stuart, R. B. Assessment and change of the communicational patterns of juvenile delinquents and their parents. In R. D. Rubin (Ed.), *Advances in behavior therapy*. New York: Academic Press, 1970. Pp. 183–197.

Stuart, R. B. Evaluative research in individual and small group treatment. *Encyclopedia of Social Work*. New York: National Association of Social Workers, 1971. Pp. 576–603.

Stuart, R. B. Behavior modification techniques for the education technologist. In R. Ulrich, T. Stachnick, & J. Mabry (Eds.), *Control of human behavior* (Vol. 3). *Behavior modification in education.* Glenview, Ill.: Scott, Foresman, 1974. Pp. 18–39.

Stuart, R. B. Behavioral remedies for marital ills: A guide to the use of operant-interpersonal techniques. In A. S. Gurman & D. G. Rice (Eds.), *Couples in conflict.* New York: Jason Aronson, 1975. Pp. 241–257.

Stuart, R. B. An operant interpersonal program for couples. In D. H. L. Olson (Ed.), *Treating relationships.* Lake Mills, Iowa: Graphic Publishing Co., 1976. Pp. 119–132.

Stuart, R. B. A behavioral test of informed consent to participate in research. *Behavior Therapy,* 1978, *9,* 73–82.

Stuart, R. B. *Marital and sex therapy: A social learning theory approach.* New York: Guilford Press, 1979.

Stuart, R. B. Are they keeping it off once they take it off? In P. O. Davidson (Ed.), *Advances in behavioral medicine.* New York: Brunner/Mazel, in press.

Stuart, R. B., & Lott, L. Implications of behavioral contracting with delinquents: A cautionary note. *Journal of Behavior Therapy and Experimental Psychiatry,* 1972, *3,* 161–170.

Stuart, R. B., & Stuart, F. *Marital pre-counseling inventory.* Champaign, Ill.: Research Press, 1973.

Stuart, R. B., Tripodi, T., Jayaratne, S., & Camburn, D. An experiment in social engineering in serving the families of delinquents. *Journal of Abnormal Child Psychology,* 1976, *4,* 243–261.

Thomas, E. J., Carter, R. D., Gambrill, E. D., & Butterfield, W. H. A signal system for the assessment and modification of behavior (SAM). *Behavior Therapy,* 1970, *1,* 252–259.

Vincent, J. P., Weiss, R. L., & Birchler, G. R. A behavioral analysis of problem solving in distressed and nondistressed married and stranger dyads. *Behavior Therapy,* 1975, *6,* 475–487.

Weiss, R. L., Hops, H., & Patterson, G. R. A framework for conceptualizing marital conflict: A technology for altering it, some data for evaluating it. In L. A. Hamerlynck, L. C. Handy, & E. J. Mash (Eds.), *Behavior change: Methodology, concepts, and practice.* Champaign, Ill.: Research Press, 1973. Pp. 309–342.

Wieman, R. J., Shoulders, D. I., & Farr, J. H. Reciprocal reinforcement in marital therapy. *Journal of Behavior Therapy and Experimental Psychiatry.* 1974, *5,* 291–295.

Wills, T. A., Weiss, R. L., & Patterson, G. R. A behavioral analysis of the determinants of marital satisfaction. *Journal of Consulting and Clinical Psychology,* 1974, *42,* 802–811.

APPENDIX: REVIEW OF SELECTED OUTCOME STUDIES OF EFFECTIVENESS OF BEHAVIORAL MARITAL TREATMENT

STUART (1969)

Subjects: 4 couples "on the brink of filing for divorce"
Length: 7 sessions in 10 weeks
Format: Conjoint
Design: Case study

Techniques:
1. Couples taught to initiate behavioral change in effort to socialize them into treatment approach.
2. Each spouse asked to request 3 positive, specific behavior changes of other.
3. Couples taught how to make requests effectively.
4. Couples taught to monitor own compliance and that of spouse with therapeutic instigations.
5. Communication skills built through behavioral rehearsal and coaching.
6. Behavioral contracting taught as means of structuring behavior exchange.

Outcomes:
1. Self-reported increase in average daily hours of conversation, frequency of sexual interaction.
2. Improvement in marital satisfaction on inventory adapted from Farber (1957).

Followup:
1. At 24 and 48 weeks, self-reported conversation and sexual behavior changes maintained.
2. Also changes in global rating of marital satisfaction maintained.

PATTERSON AND HOPS (1972)

Subjects: 1 couple with prior training in parenting
Length: 9 sessions in 9 weeks
Format: Conjoint
Design: Case study
Techniques:
1. Weekly reading assignments (Lederer & Jackson, 1968).
2. Evaluation of videotapes of own interaction.
3. Modeling and supervised practice of nonaversive interaction.
4. Training in pinpointing requested behavior changes.
5. Training in *quid pro quo* contracting techniques.

Outcomes:
1. Improvement in 3 classes of problem-solving behaviors in coded laboratory observation.
2. Based on home observation, no change in aversive behavior, but increase in husband–wife interaction time.
3. No changes in self-reported pleases, displeases, or positive thoughts.

Followup:
1. Home observation revealed no change in aversive behavior but maintenance of increase in husband–wife interaction time.

AZRIN, NASTER, AND JONES (1973)

Subjects: 12 couples recruited from college counseling service or through mail solicitation
Length: 14 sessions in 7 weeks
Format: Conjoint
Design: Case study with catharsis counseling followed by reciprocity counseling (replicated A-B design)
Techniques:
1. Catharsis counseling procedure consisted of talk about feelings about marriage and completion of daily marital satisfaction ratings.
2. Reciprocity counseling: (*a*) spouses listed 10 satisfactions given and received at home, with reciprocity discussed in sessions; (*b*) spouses listed other desired interactions; (*c*)

spouses trained to give verbal response to positives received; (d) training in compromise in 3 problem areas, with training in contracting; (e) training in making requests and in adding positive statements to negative messages; (f) training in generalization of contracting skills to new problem areas; (g) couples were asked to read marriage manual (Ellis, 1966) and to discuss their ratings of sexual activities; and (h) daily ratings of marital satisfaction (in 9 problem areas) exchanged and discussed throughout reciprocity counseling.

Outcomes:
1. Self-report marital happiness scale response higher for reciprocity than for catharsis counseling, with 96% of clients reporting greater happiness at end as opposed to beginning of reciprocity counseling.
2. Average happiness ratings were greater on each of 9 areas of scale during last week of reciprocity counseling than during 3 weeks of catharsis counseling.
3. In test of specificity of effect of the procedure, happiness scores were greater in 6 problem areas after direct counseling.
4. In test of generalization, scores were higher in 6 noncounseled problem areas during reciprocity as opposed to during catharsis counseling.
5. None of 12 couples separated or divorced.

Followup:
1. At 1 month, marital happiness scale scores of 88% of couples were higher than at start of reciprocity counseling.
2. At 4 months, all but 1 of the couples remained married and together.

STERN AND MARKS (1973)

Subjects: 1 couple considering separation; wife having "severe obsessional rituals"
Length: Apparently 10 sessions over 5 weeks
Format: Conjoint
Design: Case study
Techniques:
1. Training in how to request and list desired behavior changes.
2. Training in verbal contracts on *quid pro quo* model.

Outcomes:
1. Decrease in wife's rituals, with increase in productivity.
2. Increase in husband's involvement in home improvement and in interaction with wife.
3. Increased frequency of sexual activity.

Followup:
1. At 6 and 12 weeks, wife's rituals remained lower and her productivity higher; husband's home improvement efforts lower, but conversational involvement was sustained.
2. Sexual activity declined, but was higher than at start of treatment.
3. At 1 year, couple separated, but wife's rituals remained under control.

HICKOK AND KOMECHAK (1974)

Subjects: 1 couple considering divorce
Length: 10 weeks
Format: Conjoint and individual, co-therapy
Design: B-A-B design with B = token economy, A = no-token economy
Techniques:
1. Orientation through observation of family interaction and discussion of behavior control.

2. Instigation to cue and emit positive behavior and omit negative responding.
3. Token system exchanged time out of house for physical intimacy or sex.
4. Assertion training for husband, who also received instructions about appropriate sexual behavior.

Outcomes: Self-reported steady increase over all phases in tokens received by wife for sexual interaction and by husband for baby sitting while wife was out of the house.

Followup: At 2 months, wife not leaving house as much and enjoying time with husband more; increased rate of sexual contact maintained, and husband assuming more responsibility for child care.

WIEMAN, SHOULDERS, AND FARR (1974)

Subjects: 1 couple referred by university counseling center
Length: 20 sessions over 24-week period
Format: Conjoint, co-therapy
Design: Multiple baseline design over 3 target behaviors
Techniques:

1. Orientation to principles of reciprocal reinforcement.
2. Selection of 3 target behaviors by each spouse—1 easy, 1 moderate, and 1 difficult—with instructions to exchange behaviors in that sequence.
3. Communication training consisting of "feeling talk" and "emphathetic listening" instruction.
4. Instruction in sexual skills, including mutual pleasuring, sensate focus, and mutual masturbation.

Outcomes:

1. All 3 target behavioral exchanges were successful, based on self-report.
2. Improvement noted on Locke–Williamson Marital Adjustment Scale (Locke & Williamson, 1958) and on Conjugal Life Questionnaire (Guerney, 1964).
3. Spouses reported general improvement in quality of their lives together, with husband reporting abatement of distress due to ulcer problem.
4. Multiple baseline results suggest that intervention accounted for most behavioral changes.

Followup: Informal data at 4 months indicated maintenance of adequate sexual activity, communication change, and rate of exchange of "little" positive behaviors.

PATTERSON, HOPS, AND WEISS (1975)[1]

Subjects: 10 "moderately distressed" couples
Length: Average of 6 sessions
Format: Conjoint, co-therapy
Design: Case study, with couples treated separately as pairs
Techniques:

1. In baseline sessions couples listed pleasurable and displeasurable behaviors and attempted problem-solving negotiation.
2. Couples asked to read Patterson (1971).
3. Spouses trained to recognize pleasing and displeasing behaviors, and to increase rate of pleasing behaviors offered in "love days" procedure.
4. Training in pinpointing and discrimination as means to operationalize expectation.
5. Training in listening, paraphrasing, information gathering, and problem-solving communication.
6. Training in specifying and contracting for behavior changes.

[1]Includes data from Weiss, Hops, and Patterson (1973).

Outcomes:
1. In laboratory problem-solving exercise, facilitative behavior increased and disruptive behaviors decreased.
2. In self-report, husbands and wives both reported increase in pleasing behaviors, while husbands, but not wives, reported decrease in displeasing behaviors.

Followup
1. At 3 to 6 months, for 5 of 10 couples reported by Weiss, Hops, and Patterson (1973), marital satisfaction, as measured by Locke–Wallace Scale (1959), increased.
2. For same couples, desire for change in spouses' behavior decreased, but there was no significant change in amount of time spent together.
3. At 1 to 2 years, 2 of the 7 located couples were divorced and 4 of the 5 remaining couples "seemed to be happier" and reported fewer conflicts.

HARRELL AND GUERNEY (1976)

Subjects: 60 couples recruited from a university community
Length: 8 weekly 2-hour sessions for treatment group; assessment only for no-treatment group
Format: Conjointly in group (3 couples per group)
Design: Experimental, with random assignment to treatment or control group
Techniques:
1. Weekly homework assignments consisting of reading and skill-practice exercises.
2. Training in expressing opinions and feelings and in listening and summarizing partner's message.
3. Partners identify a relationship issue and pinpoint their specific behavioral input or contribution.
4. Partners generate several specific alternative behavioral solutions and *then* evaluate the alternatives.
5. Partners agree to implement, and later renegotiate, a contract (approximately 2 per couple) around the exchange of 1 alternative behavior each.

Outcomes:
1. Treatment group outperformed control group on the following measures:
   a. Adequacy of skills at 2 of the 5 steps in a laboratory conflict negotiation task.
   b. Self-report of adequacy of solutions reached in laboratory conflict negotiation task.
   c. Decrease in negative verbal behaviors (interrupt and "put-down" statements) in laboratory task.
2. Treatment and control group did not differ on the following measures:
   a. Adequacy of skills at 3 of the 5 steps in laboratory conflict negotiation task.
   b. Change on Handling Problems Change Score (Schlein, (1971).
   c. Changes of perceptions of marital satisfaction on Marital Adjustment Scale (Locke & Williamson, 1958), the Family Life Questionnaire—Conjugal (Collins, 1971), the Satisfaction Change Score (Schlein, 1971), and "perceived rate of relationship change" on Relationship Change Scale (Schlein, 1971).
3. Control group outperformed treatment group in that positive behaviors ("agree" and "approve") decreased for treatment group in laboratory task.

Followup: None

LIBERMAN, LEVINE, WHEELER, SANDERS, AND WALLACE (1976)

Subjects: 4 couples in behavioral treatment group, 6 in "interactional" comparison group (all were clients at a community mental health center)
Length: 8 weekly 2-hour sessions; 1 followup session after 1 month

Format: Conjointly in groups

Design: Quasi-experimental due to consecutive rather than random assignment of couples to behavioral versus comparison group

Techniques:

1. Fee deposit returned contingent on attendance.
2. Presentation of therapeutic rationale.
3. Training in discriminating and graphing pleasing behaviors and recording pleases on daily basis throughout treatment.
4. Presentation of "Tenderness" film (Serber & Laws, 1974) depicting physical affection and verbal feedback.
5. For comparison group mainly:
    a. Catharsis, ventilation, sharing of feelings.
    b. Discussion of insight into marital relationship.
6. For behavior therapy group only:
    a. Behavioral rehearsal, modeling, prompting, and feedback to build communication skills.
    b. Behavioral contracting using holistic model.
    c. Massage exercise.
    d. Weekly homework assignments, including assigned reading (Human Development Institute, 1967).

Outcomes:

1. Behavior therapy group complied with more assignments.
2. Behavior therapy and comparison group did not differ on the following measures:
    a. Number of pleasing behaviors given and received.
    b. Number of daily shared activities.
    c. Marital Activities Inventory (Weiss *et al.,* 1973).
    d. Marital Pre-Counseling Inventory (Stuart & Stuart, 1973).
    e. Partners' estimates of own and each others' desires for change (Willingness to Change Questionnaire; Weiss *et al.,* 1973).
    f. Marital Adjustment Test (Locke & Wallace, 1959).
    g. Consumer satisfaction with treatment.
    h. Observations of spouses' touching each other during sessions.
    i. Problem-solving responses, problem description, and positive verbal behavior in laboratory problem-solving sessions as measured by Marital Interaction Coding System (Weiss, *et al.,* 1973).
3. Behavior therapy group outperformed comparison group on following measures:
    a. Increase in congruence or mutual understanding (Willingness to Change Questionnaire; Weiss *et al.,* 1973).
    b. Exchanges of more "looks" and smiles during sessions.
    c. Decrease in negative verbal behaviors (Marital Interaction Coding System; Weiss *et al.,* 1973).
    d. Fewer negative nonverbal responses and more positive nonverbal responses during problem solving (Marital Interaction Coding System; Weiss *et al.,* 1973).

Followup:

1. One couple in each group temporarily separated after treatment termination.
2. At 2 and 6 months, groups did not differ on spouses' estimates of partners' desire for change, with both improved over pretherapy (Willingness to Change Questionnaire; Weiss *et al.,* 1973).
3. At 2 and 6 months, groups did not differ in congruence or mutual understanding (Willingness to Change Questionnaire; Weiss *et al.,* 1973).
4. At 2 and 6 months, groups did not differ on Marital Adjustment Test (Locke & Wallace, 1959), with both improved over pretherapy.

JACOBSON (1977)

Subjects: 10 couples solicited through newspaper ads

Length: Treatment group received pre- and posttherapy assessment interviews and 8 treatment sessions while waiting-list control received only pre- and postassessment sessions

Format: Conjoint

Design: Experimental, with random assignment to treatment or to control group, plus multiple baseline design for 4 or 5 treated couples

Techniques:
1. Signed treatment contract.
2. Each spouse recorded data at home on 2 behaviors of partner for 2-week baseline and during treatment.
3. Reading assignment: Patterson (1971).
4. Instruction, feedback, modeling, and reinforcement with regard to minor and then major problem solving.
5. Nightly problem-solving sessions and behavioral recording as homework.
6. In-session discussion of home data and problem-solving practice.
7. Instruction in holistic behavioral contracts.

Outcomes:
1. In laboratory problem-solving task, experimentals emitted more positive and fewer negative responses.
2. Experimental couples showed greater improvement on Locke–Wallace (1959) than controls.
3. Multiple baseline data suggested contracting effective in promoting specific behavioral changes.

Followup: One year after treatment, Locke–Wallace (1959) scores for experimental couples were marginally higher than at posttest.

DIXON AND SCIARA (1977)

Subjects: 7 couples participating in university extension course on marital improvement

Length: 8 weekly 2-hour sessions

Format: Conjointly in group

Design: Case study, with multiple baseline designs for each couple

Techniques:
1. Spouses listed 10 satisfactions given and received at home and discussed reciprocity.
2. Development of skills in nonjudgmental, behaviorally descriptive communication about daily satisfaction ratings on modified Marriage Happiness Scale (Azrin, Naster, & Jones, 1973).
3. Training in negotiation of behavioral exchanges in areas covered by Marriage Happiness Scale with group sharing and feedback.
4. As maintenance procedure, couples helped to pinpoint which workshop procedures were most effective.

Outcomes:
1. Increase in commitment to and optimism about marriage on Marital Pre-counseling Inventory (Stuart & Stuart, 1973).
2. Improvement in weekly satisfaction ratings on modified Marriage Happiness Scale (Azrin *et al.*, 1973) in areas of affectionate interaction, communication with spouse, and children and/or family interaction.
3. Some support for specificity of effect of treatment procedures as reflected in multiple baseline data from 3 couples.

Followup: None

JACOBSON (1978)

Subjects: 32 "moderately disturbed" couples solicited mainly through advertisements

Length: Initial interview plus 8 weekly 1–1½-hour sessions for treated couples

Format: Conjoint

Design: Experimental, with random assignment to 1 of 3 therapists and 1 of 4 conditions: (*a*) a behavioral program using good faith contracts (GF group); (*b*) a behavioral program using *quid pro quo* contracts (QPQ group); (*c*) a nonspecific treatment condition (NS group); and (*d*) a waiting-list control condition (WL group)

Techniques:

1. Good faith (holistic) group: Treatment techniques duplicated those used in the experimental group in Jacobson (1977).

2. *Quid pro quo* (partitive) group: Treatment techniques identical to those of good faith group except that couples were taught *quid pro quo*, instead of good faith, behavioral contracting.

3. Nonspecific group: Techniques were intended to be roughly equivalent to behavioral treatments on such factors as attention, expectancies, credibility, therapist activity level and directiveness, and rationale for treatment, and to differ from the behavioral treatments in that specific instructions in problem-solving and communication skills and contingency contracting procedures were excluded.

Outcomes:

1. No differences due to therapist or therapist—treatment interaction on the 4 outcome measures.

2. In laboratory problem-solving task, both behavioral groups combined emitted less negative, and more positive, verbal behavior than either the WL or the NS group; considered separately, each behavioral group was superior to each control group on negative and positive verbal behavior with the exception that the GF, but not the QPQ, group outperformed the NS group on a decrease in negative verbal behavior.

3. Both behavioral groups (combined and separately) improved more than either the WL or the NS group on self-reported marital satisfaction (Locke & Wallace, 1959).

4. No differences between the GF and QPQ groups or between the NS and WL groups on positive and negative verbal behavior in laboratory problem-solving tasks or on the MAS (Locke & Wallace, 1959).

5. The 3 treatment groups did not differ from each other and improved more than the WL group on ratings of marital happiness in 12 areas (subscale of Marital Pre-counseling Inventory, Stuart & Stuart, 1973).

Followup: Some average of 1-, 3-, and/or 6-month followup data on the MAS (Locke & Wallace, 1959) indicated that the combined behavioral groups maintained posttest superiority over NS group.

16

Systematic Replication of a Social Learning Approach to Parent Training[1]

MARK R. WEINROTT, BRIAN W. BAUSKE,
AND GERALD R. PATTERSON

BACKGROUND

The Social Learning Project was organized in 1965. Its primary objective was to develop an empirically based, low-cost treatment approach for use with families of aggressive and predelinquent children. Moreover, one aim of the project was to design and implement procedures for evaluating the impact of treatment. This chapter functions as one of several progress reports in that it reviews the earlier work, describes in detail several recent innovations, and indicates the future direction of the project.

From 1965 through 1968 project staff followed a course of single case studies. These served as vehicles for developing the basic treatment and assessment technologies. Guided by the premise that changing the social environment of a disturbed child is paramount, attempts were begun to teach parents to reduce the amount of deviant behavior displayed by their children. The techniques necessary to accomplish this were rather diverse by current standards, owing to the heterogeneity of referral problems and the pioneering stages of treatment development. Reliance on tangible reinforcers was heavy during the initial years, as was the use of contingent

[1]This study was supported by Grants MH 31018 and MH 25548, Center for Studies in Crime and Delinquency, National Institute of Mental Health.

TRENDS IN BEHAVIOR THERAPY

Copyright © 1979 by Academic Press, Inc.
All rights of reproduction in any form reserved.
ISBN 0-12-647450-8

parental attention. To these treatment components were soon added observation training and data collection, use of point systems, parental incentives, time-out, and modeling (Patterson & Brodsky, 1966; Patterson, Jones, Whittier, & Wright, 1965; Patterson, McNeal, Hawkins, & Phelps, 1967). Complementing the intervention procedures was a system for observing and recording behavioral events in the home. A prototype of the multicategory coding system used today generated data for evaluating five consecutive referrals in the first multiple-case outcome study (Patterson, Ray, & Shaw, 1968). In this study, child problems ranged from withdrawal, isolation, and school failure, to tics, hyperactivity, aggression, and setting cars on fire. Prior to the onset of treatment, in-home observations were conducted by highly trained observer/coders. Observations were also scheduled throughout intervention and during followup.

The general treatment plan consisted of having parents read a programmed text designed to teach principles and applications of social learning theory. This was followed by training the parents in observation and data collection. The entire family then engaged in a series of simulated interventions that were described and modeled by the therapist. Most of the training occurred in the home. Interventions were designed to reduce reinforcement for deviant behaviors and increase rewards for prosocial behavior. Family members then practiced these procedures at home. Treatment required an average of 22.8 hours of professional time per family. Four of the five families showed substantial improvement at termination. The fifth was characterized only by high rates of maternal deviant behavior, thereby precluding child improvement on this measure. Followup of 1 to 6 months showed that treatment gains were maintained by three families. The abbreviated followup was a deficiency acknowledged by the investigators, but the preliminary results were indeed encouraging.

A more stringent test of treatment efficacy was soon designed. It would be characterized by: (a) a relatively large number of consecutive referrals; (b) evaluation based on multiple outcome measures; (c) data showing the cost of professional time, both during treatment and for "booster shots" thereafter; and (d) a followup period of 1 year. During the period from January 1968 through June 1972, 27 families were referred to the Social Learning Project by community agencies such as the juvenile court, schools, and mental health clinics. Families were accepted for treatment because at least one boy in each family had been identified as a "conduct problem." Parental descriptions and agency records showed that child management difficulties had existed for years. Families were excluded where either the parents or the target child were severely retarded, acutely psychotic, or clearly brain damaged. Target children ranged in age from 5 to 14 years. The sample contained 8 father-absent families. The majority of families were economically disadvantaged.

Treatment consisted of individual family therapy in which parents were trained to apply skills necessary to reduce rates of deviant behavior and increase rates of prosocial responses. Treatment components included contingent attention, a point incentive system, time-out, and contingency contracting. These are described in Patterson, Reid, Jones, and Conger (1975). Multiple measures of family behavior, attitudes, and personality were obtained prior to, during, and following treatment. The two principal forms of assessment were in-home observations conducted by trained professional observers (Patterson, 1974a) and parent report of preselected noxious behaviors displayed by the referred child (Patterson, 1974b). Results indicated that the independently observed deviant behavior rate showed a significant reduction from baseline to termination and that this improvement persisted through a 1-year followup period. Similarly, parent-reported child coercive behavior also showed a significant decline from baseline to termination. It was concluded that about three out of four families showed considerable improvement. These gains were realized at an average per family cost of 31.4 hours of professional time during formal parent training and 1.9 hours for periodic booster shots during followup.

While these overall findings were clearly indicative, if not conclusive evidence of a persistent treatment effect, there were compelling rationales for systematic replication. The sample was a mixture of high-rate, socially aggressive children and a second subgroup referred for low-rate, rather serious offenses, such as stealing and setting fires. Not only might the two types of children require different forms of treatment, but statistical problems also existed in combining them for group analysis. Eleven of the 27 target children showed deviant behavior rates that were within the range displayed by normal, unreferred children. For these subjects, dependent variables extracted from observation data were simply not appropriate for measuring the impact of treatment.

A second problem was a rather high attrition rate during followup (Kent, 1976). Of the 27 families who were discharged, 11 (41%) were either unwilling to provide data or were impossible to locate 1 year following termination. Unfortunately, families with higher rates of deviant behavior during baseline showed a greater tendency to drop out, although this pattern did not apply to parent-report data. Using the latter measure, it appeared that the more difficult families during baseline continued to provide information.

While the criticism of differential attrition was successfully countered by Reid and Patterson (1976), an important objective of the replication study was to reduce the attrition rate during the posttreatment period.

It was also felt that the method for scoring observation data could be improved. Refinements were also necessary in the manner in which parent-report data were gathered, scored, and analyzed. These changes are detailed later in this chapter.

Another objective of the replication study was to reduce the amount of professional time needed for treatment. As stated earlier, an average of 31 hours of treatment were required on an individual case basis. Two cost-effective procedures were implemented in the present study to reduce costs. First, parents were treated in groups; and second, much of the training occurred by means of videotape. The recordings served the purpose of structuring and pacing each group session and further obviated the need for advanced-level therapists. This leads to another objective of the present study.

The sample of 27 families and the cases that preceded them were treated directly by Jerry Patterson, John Reid, and a few other advanced-level therapists. It was deemed important to replicate the first study using an entirely different group of therapists. To accomplish this, while maintaining contact with the original research team, the Family Center was created. This was a semiautonomous clinical unit that was to serve as a demonstration and replication site for treatment of aggressive children.

To summarize, the objectives of the replication study were to: (a) treat a relatively large number of consecutively referred families; (b) reduce attrition, particularly during followup; (c) develop and implement more sophisticated methods for scoring and analysis of data; (d) reduce the cost of treatment; and (e) conduct treatment using a new group of therapists.

METHOD

Subjects

Subjects were 26 consecutive referrals to the Family Center who fulfilled the following criteria: (a) child, male or female, aged 3 to 12; (b) family resided within a 20-minute drive of the Family Center to accommodate observers and occasional home visits by therapists; (c) neither parent nor child had been previously diagnosed as psychotic, severely retarded, or autistic; (d) primary referral problem was social aggression, either physical, verbal, or both; (e) parents agreed to home observation, telephone interviews, and attendance at therapy sessions; (f) the family had no impending plans for divorce (separation), moving to another community, or placing the child in foster care/residential treatment; (g) the baseline deviant behavior rate for the target child was equal to or exceeded .45 per minute.[2]

Eight subjects dropped out during baseline, or the first few weeks of intervention. The remaining 18 families completed 10 or more weeks of treatment. Of these, 15 target children were boys and 3 were girls. The mean age at intake was 7.4 years. Nine families were intact and 9 had only a single parent.

---

[2]A total deviant behavior rate of .45 per minute is one-half of one standard deviation above the mean rate for normal, unreferred children.

The Family Center

The Family Center opened in 1974 with a staff of seven: a director, two therapists, a school specialist, and three technical coordinators responsible for conducting observations and data collection phone calls. The director and therapists had been trained by Patterson and his colleagues on the Social Learning Project.

Beyond the specific objectives of the replication study, the Family Center sought to develop a client management system that would dovetail with the treatment procedures. The system included a payment schedule based on family income, efficient intake procedures, daily therapist contact for the first 6 weeks of treatment, and parental monetary incentives for cooperation. The Family Center operated independently of the Social Learning Project on a day-by-day basis, although periodic consultation occurred and some administrative ties were maintained.

Treatment

Parents met in groups of three to four families for a 10-week core instructional program. Following this, families were placed on a low-level maintenance schedule to maximize long-term gains and cooperation with the data collection activities during followup. The core program consisted of weekly sessions in which videotaped presentations were complemented by illustrations and consultation provided by a therapist. The videotapes included an array of tasks that required both comprehension and active participation of parents. In addition to the structured group session, the therapist maintained daily telephone contact with the family. Occasionally, home visits were conducted when the parents' data indicated that treatment procedures were not effective. The following sections provide a brief outline of the 10 core instructional sessions. A more detailed description of the program is presented in Fleischman and Conger (1976).

SESSION I: PINPOINTING, OBSERVING, AND RECORDING BEHAVIORS

Parents identify two problem behaviors and two prosocial behaviors and formulate operational definitions of each. Instruction is given in various sampling techniques after which parents practice recording behaviors depicted on videotape. Parents are required to systematically observe their child for 1 hour each day and record the frequency of the problem and prosocial target behaviors. The observation procedure continues through the first 6 weeks of treatment.

SESSION II: POINT INCENTIVE SYSTEM

A simple point system is described and implemented. It includes one problem behavior, one prosocial behavior, and one chore. Parents are taught to use both praise and tangible rewards. Videotapes present many of the do's and don'ts in introducing and managing a point system.

SESSION III: TIME-OUT

Time-out is described in detail. Video vignettes depict correct and incorrect procedures for applying the technique. Parents are instructed to begin using time-out for the most frequently occurring problem behavior for which they have data.

SESSION IV: PROGRAM EVALUATION

To better assess the impact of treatment, participants are taught to graph their data for those behaviors that have been systematically observed during the previous 3 weeks. A parent performance checklist is also administered to determine if parents are adhering to treatment procedures. Examples of checklist items are "hold daily review of point system," "provide reinforcers," "observe and record," "use praise and points following chores." Parents are asked to model these procedures. If doubt arises as to the consistency with which the program is followed, parents may be asked to tape-record specific interchanges among family members (e.g., "selection of reinforcer in advance").

SESSION V: PROGRAM PRESENTATION

This meeting is a semistructured assessment of progress to date with provision for group social reinforcement. Parents describe their program, present data, and identify new behaviors they wish to add to the point system. Depending upon progress, one or more new behaviors may be incorporated. Program review and modification of the point system are routinely conducted during all subsequent group sessions.

SESSION VI: ATTENDING AND IGNORING

Using video vignettes, parents are taught how annoying childish behaviors (e.g., whining, crying, clinging, pouting, repetitive questioning) are inadvertently reinforced through intermittent parental attention. The art of ignoring is espoused as is the use of parental attention for appropriate behavior. Parents with young children (under age 7) and those who appear to be "thick skinned" are encouraged to ignore annoying behaviors. More volatile parents, or those having older children, are asked to attend to positive behaviors, but to use time-out for annoying ones.

SESSION VII: SHAPING

Because children are continually faced with learning new skills (chores, sports activities, self-help), parents are taught to provide instructions that are suited to the child's ability. Illustrative task analyses and presentation styles are depicted. Special emphasis is placed on strategies that prevent teaching sessions from degenerating into arguments.

SESSION VIII: PROBLEM SOLVING

Using a typical problem-solving approach (D'Zurilla & Goldfried, 1971) parents identify a well circumscribed minor problem, pinpoint target behaviors, list possible solutions without regard to their consequences (brainstorming), speculate on the consequences of each alternative, select the most appropriate course of action, and decide how to evaluate its effectiveness. Videotapes depict simulated problem-solving conferences among family members. Emphasis is placed on specific negotiation rules such as "don't dredge up the past."

SESSION IX: CONTINGENCY CONTRACTING

(Contingency contracting is for use with children 10 years and older.) Unlike the previous session, which dealt with well circumscribed problems on a sequential basis, contingency contracting is more appropriate for more pervasive difficulties, such as school adjustment, delinquent activity, and conduct in public or in others' homes. All family members are present at this session. Contingency contracting requires the following steps: (a) reviewing rules of negotiation; (b) stating the child's responsibilities; (c) listing privileges that appeal to the child; (d) drafting a preliminary agreement; (e) reviewing terms of the agreement; (f) finalizing the contingencies; and (g) agreeing upon the length of the contract and agreeing to its subsequent renegotiation upon expiration.

SESSION X: FADING

Parents are given suggestions for gradually eliminating the point system. These include intermittent reinforcement, operating the program during progressively fewer days each week, and removing from the system certain behaviors that are no longer of concern (and not replacing these). Use of time-out, contracting, negotiating, shaping, and contingent attention are to be maintained. Only the structure of the point system is faded.

Following completion of the core program, a successful family will generally enter a phase in which a moderate amount of contact with a therapist is maintained. Such a winding down of treatment normally lasts 6 weeks, with one or two telephone contacts occurring weekly. A family is deemed a tentative success if at the end of the core program there has been: (a) a 50% reduction from baseline levels of targeted deviant behavior using parent-collected frequency data; (b) an absence of serious offenses for 2 months; and (c) more positive family interaction as reported by parents, child, and therapist.

In cases where the family has achieved some gains, but still experiences an occasional relapse, more intensive individual family therapy sessions are held. The content of such sessions varies substantially from family to family, but often involves further negotiation training and careful probing by the therapist as to the application of various treatment components. Occasionally a family will be referred elsewhere.

EVALUATION PROCEDURES

Naturalistic Observation

The Behavior Coding System, BCS (Jones, Reid, & Patterson, 1975; Patterson, Ray, Shaw, & Cobb, 1969; Reid, 1978), is an exhaustive 29-category observation system that provides a sequential record of noxious and prosocial behaviors displayed by family members. These behaviors and their definitions are presented in Table 16.1. The BCS produces a running account of a selected subject's behavior and the reactions of others to that behavior.

Each family member in the replication study served as the observation subject for two 5-minute segments that were preassigned on a random basis. Coded entries were made by observers every 6 seconds. A portable audio pacer generated signals indicating the intervals. Observations were normally conducted just prior to the dinner hour, a time when most parents reported difficulty managing their children.

The BCS yields session scores for each category of behavior and for each family member. These have generally been expressed in terms of rate per minute (Patterson, 1974a). Scores for certain categories have been combined to form composites. For example, combining scores for the 14 deviant behavior categories produces a measure of total deviant behavior (TDB).

Five observations were conducted during baseline. These occurred on consecutive weekdays whenever possible. Additional two-session probes occurred 4, 8, and 12 weeks following the onset of treatment and at termination.[3] Followup probes consisting of two sessions on consecutive days were scheduled 4, 8, and 12 months after termination.

OBSERVER RELIABILITY

Reliability data generated using the BCS have been presented in a number of earlier studies (Patterson, 1974a; Patterson, Cobb, & Ray, 1973; Reid, Hinojosa, & Lorber, 1978). Interval-by-interval observer agreement has consistently been 70 to 80% (over the 29 behavior categories). An intraclass correlation of .96 for the composite TDB was reported by Jones et al. (1975).

Prior to data collection, observers in the replication study were trained to a minimum 70% mean agreement across categories. Thereafter, 13 reliability spot checks were conducted between the three Family Center observers and different observers working on another study for the Social Learning Project. Mean agreement during these sessions was 78.3%.

[3]The termination probe was substituted for 12-week assessment, if the family completed treatment by that time.

TABLE 16.1

Behavior Categories and Definitions for Behavior Coding System

FIRST-ORDER CODE CATEGORIES

First-order verbal behaviors

Command: When a direct, reasonable, and clearly stated request or command is made to another person.

Command negative: A negative command differs from the reasonable command in the manner in which it is delivered. It can be characterized by at least two of the following: (*a*) immediate compliance is demanded; (*b*) aversive consequences are *implicitly* or actually threatened if compliance is not immediate; (*c*) sarcasm or humiliation is directed toward the receiver.

Cry: Whenever a person sobs or cries tears.

Humiliate: When a person makes fun of, shames, or embarrasses another person. The *tone of voice*, as well as the language used, is of prime importance.

Laugh: Whenever a person laughs aloud pleasantly and in an agreeable manner.

Negativism: When a person makes a statement in which the verbal message is neutral, but which is delivered in a tone of voice that conveys an *attitude* of "don't bug me," or "don't bother me."

Whine: When a person uses a slurring, nasal, or high-pitched voice. The content of the statement can be of an approving, disapproving, or neutral quality; the main element is the inflection.

Yell: Whenever a person shouts, yells, or talks loudly. The sound must be *intense enough* that it is unpleasant or potentially aversive if carried on for a sufficient length of time.

First-order nonverbal behaviors

Destructiveness: Those behaviors by which a person destroys, damages, or attempts to damage anything other than a person.

High rate: Any very physically active, repetitive behavior not covered by other categories that, if carried on for a sufficient period of time, would become aversive.

Physical Negative: Whenever a subject physically attacks or attempts to attack another person.

Physical Positive: When a person caresses or communicates by touch with another person in a friendly or affectionate manner.

First-order verbal or nonverbal behaviors

Approval: A clear indication of positive interest or involvement. Approval can be gestural or verbal in nature.

Compliance: When a person does what is asked of him/her or indicates verbally or behaviorally that he/she will.

Disapproval: Whenever a person gives a verbal or gestural criticism of another person's behavior or characteristics.

Dependency: When a person is requesting assistance in doing a task that he/she is obviously capable of doing alone, and it is an imposition on the other person to fulfill the request.

Ignore: An intentional, deliberate nonresponse to an initiated behavior. There is no doubt that the subject has heard but has chosen not to respond.

Indulgence: When, *without being asked*, a person stops what he/she is doing in order to perform a task for another person which that person is fully capable of doing alone.

Noncompliance: When a person does not do what is requested of him/her. Noncompliance can be verbal or nonverbal in nature.

Play: When a person is amusing him/herself, either alone or with other people. Play can be verbal or nonverbal.

Tease: The act of annoying, pestering, mocking, or making fun of another person.

(continued)

TABLE 16.1 (*continued*)

Work: A behavior necessary to the smooth functioning of a household; the work is necessary *for a child* to perform in order to learn behaviors that will help him/her to assume an adult role. A definite service performed for another person.

SECOND-ORDER CODE CATEGORIES

Second-order verbal behaviors

Talk: The exchange of conversation between family members.

Second-order nonverbal behaviors

Attention: When one person listens to or looks at another person. Attending behavior may either be initiated by a person or may be a response to another person's behavior.

Normative: Routine behavior when no other code is applicable.

No response: When a behavior does not require a response, or when a behavior is directed at another person but the person to whom the behavior is directed fails to perceive the behavior.

Receive: When a person receives an object from another person or is touched physically by a person and is passively showing no response to the contact.

Touch: Nonverbal passing of objects of neutral, nonverbal physical contact.

Second-order verbal and nonverbal behaviors

Self-stimulation: A narrow class of behaviors that the individual does to or for him/herself and which cannot be coded by any other codes.

Telephone Interview Report on Social Aggression (TIROSA)

An observation by telephone procedure was designed to: (*a*) measure the daily occurrence or nonoccurrence of behaviors classifiable as socially aggressive; and (*b*) document low-rate events such as stealing, fire setting, bedwetting, and refusing meals. In-home observations are expensive, relatively infrequent, and unlikely to produce data on these low-rate events. Parent report seems appropriate for these behaviors, although the dependability of such data is difficult to ascertain.

The interviewer (not a therapist) begins each TIROSA call with an open-ended question about the positive behaviors displayed by the target child during the previous day. A behavior checklist is then completed. The checklist includes virtually all the problem behaviors reported by parents during intake. These 27 items are shown in Table 16.2. The interviewer does not ask directly about each item. Instead, the checklist is used to record events from a relatively free conversation with the parent. The interchange is kept as natural as possible, but is guided by the interviewer to extract information about deviant behaviors. Subtle prompting about case-specific referral problems is an effective way of eliciting information during the first few calls. Afterward, parents become quite familiar with the format and content of TIROSA, thereby reducing the average time per call to about 7.5 minutes. The interviewer declines to discuss child management strategies and refers any parental requests for advice to the therapist. TIROSA is used solely for data collection and is not to be con-

TABLE 16.2

TIROSA Checklist Items

Arguing, talking back to adult	Negativism
Bedwetting	Noisiness
Competitiveness	Noncomplying
Complaining	Not eating (meals)
Crying	Pants wetting
Defiance	Pouting, sadness
Destructiveness	Running away
Fearfulness	Soiling
Fighting with siblings	Stealing
Fire setting	Teasing
Hitting others (not siblings)	Temper tantrums
Hyperactiveness, running around	Whining
Irritableness	Yelling
Lying	

fused with daily telephone contact between family and therapist. TIROSA calls were conducted daily during baseline, every other day during intervention, and daily for 1 week in each month of followup. It was expected that regular contact during followup would reduce subsequent attrition.

INTERVIEWER AGREEMENT

Jones (1974) reported on a procedure for assessing the reliability of TIROSA data. The resultant measures represent the degree to which different interviewers agree on their interpretation of parental reports. Twelve interviews were conducted, with a second interviewer listening on an extension phone. The second interviewer did not participate in the conversation except to introduce him/herself and obtain the client's consent to listen in. Four individuals served as both regular and second interviewers, with each serving at least twice in both roles. Among the 12 interviews, only 2 were conducted with the same client.

Forty-seven checklist behaviors were recorded over all interviews. Of these, perfect matches by behavior were obtained by the second interviewer for 40 (85%). By summing the entries on the checklist for each interviewer and correlating the pairs of scores over the 12 calls, a rank order correlation coefficient of .98 was obtained. Given the near perfect agreement of the summary score, it was not deemed necessary to monitor reliability of TIROSA on a regular basis.

RESULTS

Observation Data

Rates per minute for each of the 29 code categories were computed for every family during baseline, at termination, and during the most recent followup probe. Of the 18 families that terminated treatment after 10 or more weeks, 14 (78%) provided data at 4 months followup, 11 (61%) at 8 months, and 8 (44%) at 12 months. Four families were either unavailable or unwilling to participate after treatment had ended. The attrition pattern was similar to that observed in the original study (Patterson, 1974a), where 74% of families provided data at 4 months followup, 59% at 8 months, and 41% at 12 months.

Rates for the 14 deviant behaviors were summed to form a composite score labeled Total Deviant Behavior (TDB). The phase means and standard deviations for TDB are shown in Table 16.3. For the families that completed 10 or more weeks of treatment, there was a reduction in the rate of child deviant behavior from .83 per minute during baseline to .36 at termination. The subsample of subjects for whom some followup data were obtained showed a decrease in TDB from .90 during baseline to .31 at termination. Improvement continued through followup as the most recent observation probe for each family yielded a mean TDB score of .23 per minute. This result compares favorably to that of Patterson (1974a). Table 16.3 shows the phase means ($\bar{x}$) and standard deviations (SD) for both the original and replication samples. The 11 children in the original study whose baseline TDB score was within the normal range (less than .45) were excluded.

Two aspects of the comparison are noteworthy. First, in the earlier study, dropouts prior to followup appeared to be more severely handicapped at baseline than those subjects who provided posttreatment data. Differential attrition did not occur in the replication study as those subjects who continued through followup showed a slightly higher mean TDB rate than did drop-outs. Second, the termination and followup means for the original sample were still half a standard deviation above the mean for normal, unreferred children. The termination score of .31 for subjects providing followup data in the replication study was nearly identical to that obtained for a sample of normal children (.28). While the reporting of scores in the form of rates permits a comparison across studies, a more psychometrically sound procedure for scoring observation data has been formulated.

Behavioral observation data are often converted to scores like percentages of total behavior, or rates. In forming composites, scores for individual behavior categories are typically summed to produce a total score. The contribution of each individual behavior score to the composite or total score is determined by the frequency or rate of occurrence. When forming composites in this manner, higher base-rate behaviors are given more weight in the total score than lower base-rate behaviors. Thus, for example, a high base-rate deviant behavior (e.g., whining) weights the composite score more than a low base-rate behavior (e.g., hitting). Since a significant negative correlation of −.41 exists between the perceived aversiveness of

TABLE 16.3
Total Deviant Child Behavior

		Terminated families without followup			Terminated families with followup data (minimum 4 months)			
	N		Baseline	Termination	N		Baseline	Termination	Followup
Original sample (Patterson, 1974a)	16	x̄	1.128	.475	12	x̄	.842	.461	.453
		SD	.924	.283		SD	.618	.319	.454
Replication sample	18	x̄	.826	.361	14	x̄	.900	.307	.232
		SD	.458	.383		SD	.493	.349	.193

the deviant behavior and its base rate (Jones *et al.*, 1975), the simple sum method of forming composites more heavily weights the less noxious behaviors. Since low-rate, and hence more deviant, behaviors seem more clinically relevant in the population of aggressive children, a composite score should reflect this clinically important difference.

Standard scoring of each behavior category before summing scores to form composites solves the problem of varying base rates among different behavior scores. Using the baseline rates for each of the 26 families referred for treatment, the mean and standard deviation were computed for each

TABLE 16.4
Mean Z Scores by Phase for Child Deviant Behavior

Case[a]	Baseline	Termination	Followup	Month of latest followup
2z	.143	−.561	−.428	12
3z	−.142			
4z	.119			
5z	−.171			
6z	.061			
7z	.462			
3y	−.040			
5x	.130	−.700	−.571	12
8x	.449	−.348	−.335	12
1w	−.526	−.498	−.711	12
2w	.115	−.355	−.452	12
5w	−.405	−.484	−.544	12
6w	.001	−.354	.216	12
7w	.343	−.617	−.291	12
2v	.825			
3v	−.199	−.351	−.507	12
6v	.411	−.679	−.588	8
7v	−.152			
8v	−.311	−.596	−.589	4
4u	−.194	−.607	−.711	8
8u	−.295	−.625		
9u	.034	.436	−.534	8
4t	−.042	−.514		
9t	−.264	−.134	−.550	4
2s	−.246	.168		
9s	.064	−.130		
Totals				
x̄	.006	−.386	−.471	
SD	.307	.304	.231	
N	26	18	14	

[a]Missing case numbers (e.g., 1z, 2y) were assigned to families that either: (*a*) dropped out prior to the completion of baseline; or (*b*) received treatment, but failed to fulfill the criterion of a child TDB rate equal to or exceeding .45 per minute.

behavior category. These means and standard deviations, and the rate for a particular observation probe, were used in the standard score formula to generate z scores that are standardized against baseline rates for each behavior. The resultant z scores are then summed across the 14 deviant behavior categories and then divided by 14 to produce a TDB score in which the contribution of each behavior to the total score is equal. The differences in base rates in the raw scores are eliminated by this process of unit weighting. If one wishes to assign other weights that predict the contribution of each response category to socially relevant criterion measures, one should do so after standardizing the scores. However, differential weighting of z scores seldom changes the conclusions one would obtain from unit weighting. Indeed, unweighted z scores and z scores weighted by parental aversiveness ratings correlated .97 in a reanalysis of Patterson's (1974a) earlier data.

Mean z scores by phase are presented in Table 16.4 for the 26 families that completed baseline, the 18 families receiving at least 10 weeks of treatment, and the 14 families who continued providing data during followup. For the latter subgroup, the baseline score of $-.02$ dropped to $-.41$ at termination and continued to decrease through followup ($-.47$).[4] A one-way analysis of variance for repeated measures was performed on these scores using the families for whom followup data were available. A significant main effect for treatment phase was obtained ($F = 12.37$; $df = 2$, 26; $p < .001$). Orthogonal comparisons between the three phase means yielded significant differences between baseline and termination and baseline and the most recent followup ($p < .01$). Therefore, it appears that a powerful treatment effect was found that did not dissipate after therapy was completed. T tests among scores for individual behavior categories showed that rates of disapproval, ignoring, noncompliance, and whining showed significant decreases from baseline to termination. Failure to obtain significance for other behaviors may be attributable, in part, to their relatively low rates during baseline.

TIROSA

A daily summary score was obtained for each subject by simply counting the number of behaviors that were recorded on the checklist section of TIROSA. Table 16.5 shows the mean number of behaviors per day for each of 16 families.[5]

---

[4]The fact that the baseline of $-.02$ was so near zero (the full sample mean) indicates that there was no difference in baseline total deviant behavior scores between drop-outs and those completing treatment.

[5]The TIROSA procedure was not introduced until after one family (2z) had already entered treatment. TIROSA interviews were suspended early in treatment for another family (4t) due to interruption of phone service.

TABLE 16.5
TIROSA Summary Scores

Case	Baseline	Intervention	Followup
5x	6.42	5.29	4.56
8x	6.35	6.44	7.95
1w	5.35	2.15	1.76
2w	4.19	2.38	—
5w	2.81	1.36	1.55
6w	3.32	1.92	.98
7w	10.76	5.49	3.08
3v	3.19	3.32	.79
6v	5.81	4.80	4.31
8v	5.54	2.69	.33
4u	4.05	2.69	1.64
8u	4.44	2.84	1.13
9u	4.97	2.38	1.17
9t	2.09	.43	.04
2s	5.31	.84	.78
9s	2.53	.52	—
$\bar{x}$	4.82	2.85	2.15
SD	2.08	1.81	2.16

The string of data points for each family represents an interrupted time series, the interrupts being equivalent to phase changes.[6] An individual time series analysis was performed separately for each family. The results are presented in Table 16.6. Also included in the table are the lag-1 autocorrelation coefficients for baseline and the entire series. These indicate the amount of serial dependency that exists in the data, that is, the extent to which a TIROSA score on day 1 predicts the score for day 2, that day 2 predicts day 3, and so on. Eleven of the families (69%) showed significant changes in level, trend, or both from baseline to intervention. There was no dissipation of effects during followup for any case.

To maintain the consistency of a group design, it was deemed desirable to aggregate the results across families in such a way that a single summary statistic would represent the presence or absence of a reliable effect. This was accomplished in the following manner. Time series analysis of individual family data includes a transformation that removes

[6]Because the schedule of TIROSA calls varied as a function of phase, data points were not equally spaced. In other words, the time interval between interviews was not consistent over the entire series. This condition is a violation of one assumption underlying interrupted time series analysis. However, the critical criterion for use of this statistical procedure is whether a time series model can be adequately fit to a given data set. Regardless of exigencies in the sampling procedure, a statistical test should be the criterion for determining the suitability of time series analysis with behavioral data. In the present study, the adequacy of model fitting was determined by means of the Box–Jenkins Q statistic (Box & Jenkins, 1970).

TABLE 16.6

Autocorrelations (r) and Time Series t Values

Case	Baseline auto r	Series auto r	Change in level	Change in trend
5x	−.31	.44**	n.s.	n.s.
8x	.17	.38**	n.s.	n.s.
1w	−.31	.37**	n.s.	n.s.
2w	.27	.27	2.88**	n.s.
5w	.05	.14	2.24*	2.81**
6w	.31	.13	2.66**	n.s.
7w	.02	.38**	n.s.	n.s.
3v	.40	−.02	2.06*	2.51*
6v	−.18	.23*	2.99**	2.50*
8v	.17	.06	n.s.	n.s.
4u	.11	−.02	2.10*	n.s.
8u	.02	.25*	n.s.	2.05*
9u	.34*	.10	4.28**	n.s.
9t	.07	.13	4.53**	n.s.
2s	.32	.20	8.21**	n.s.
9s	.41	.28**	7.67**	n.s.

*$p < .05$.
**$p < .01$.

the serial dependency or autocorrelation from the data. The resultant scores, or uncorrelated residuals, are statistically independent of one another. These scores satisfy the assumption of independence necessary to conduct analysis of variance. Using these transformed scores, a phase mean was computed for each family. These means were entered into a one-way analysis of variance for repeated measures. A significant main effect was obtained for phase of treatment ($F = 38.46$; $df = 2, 30$; $p < .001$). Orthogonal comparisons among the three phase means indicated that treatment was successful in reducing parent-reported negative behavior below baseline levels and that the level during followup was also well below that reported in baseline. This is actually a conservative test because the mean for the treatment phase underestimates the degree of improvement attained at termination.

DISCUSSION

The treatment procedures appear to have reduced the output of child deviant behavior. The changes in independently observed and parent-reported noxious behavior persisted through followup. Overall, it seems that about two-thirds to three-quarters of these very troubled families experienced substantial improvement.

Admittedly, a single-group repeated measures experimental design is notoriously weak. Without a comparison group, the potential effects of regression, historical, or maturational variables are confounded with those of treatment outcome. However, there are at least four reasons to conclude that the treatment was in fact responsible for inducing positive change.

First, in an earlier study, 12 consecutive referrals were randomly assigned to either a placebo or social learning treatment group (Walter & Gilmore, 1973). Parents in the experimental group received 4 weeks of training, while those in the placebo group met an equal number of times to discuss audiotapes that they had made concerning their own child-rearing problems. Nonsignificant *increases* in both independently observed and parent-reported child deviant behavior were found for the placebo families. It is of interest that parents in both groups were equally satisfied with their respective treatment approaches. While a 4-week period is quite short, there was not the slightest hint of improvement in the placebo families.

Second, evidence that the social learning techniques produce behavior change can also be found in the serendipitous formation of a multiple-baseline design in the present study. As mentioned earlier, families were treated in groups. However, the Family Center referral rate was sometimes low enough that a family or two was held in baseline for an extended period of time. When a sufficient number of families were available to form a group, then baseline ended. The average length of baseline was 25 days, with a standard deviation of 6.83 days, and a range of 17 to 38 days. Therefore, intervals of varying length preceded the onset of intervention. This constitutes one form of a multiple-baseline design.

Because TIROSA data were collected regularly across phases (regardless of their length), it was possible to examine regression and/or historical effects. The time series analysis tests for changes at or near the point of intervention. If families having a longer baseline began to show improvement prior to intervention (i.e., a decreasing trend in baseline), then it would be more difficult to obtain a significant time series result than if a stable or increasing baseline was evident (Jones, Vaught, & Weinrott, 1977). In the present sample, there was no relationship between the length of baseline and the likelihood of obtaining a significant time series t value. The fact that more families showed improvement shortly after intervention began makes it unlikely that the change was due to some extraneous factor(s).

The third reason for concluding that treatment was directly responsible for the observed improvement is simply the magnitude and quick onset of the effect. Observed deviant behavior plummeted from baseline to termination and showed little instability thereafter. Had the effect been smaller and more variable, then one might argue for an alternative hypothesis. Moreover, had there been a longer period intervening between baseline and the next assessment period, the potential influence of variables other than treatment would be greater. While not presented earlier in this chapter, it was found that a significant reduction in observed deviant behavior was found after only 4 weeks of treatment.

Finally, all target children had a long and consistent history of behavior problems. Some had received other forms of treatment, including medication. It seems unlikely that long-term, documented social aggression would have suddenly been controlled for reasons other than the social learning treatment.

It is significant that the results of the present intervention equal or better those of earlier work on the Social Learning Project. Different therapists were used in the replication study and still the number of therapy hours per family decreased from a mean of 31 (Patterson, 1974a) to 16.15 hours. By using a group format and a sequence of videotapes, the adjusted cost in terms of professional man-hours per family was further reduced to 9.27 hours. This is certainly an acceptable figure and one that should enhance the exportability of this social learning treatment.

While the overall investment of professional time was relatively low, the frequency of parent–therapist contact remained high, particularly during the first 6 weeks of treatment. During this period, daily telephone contact was maintained. It is assumed that routine monitoring of parental performance is desirable if not essential. If doubt arises as to the veridicality of parental reports, the therapist may also speak with the child or ask the family to tape-record certain events (e.g., point review at day's end). A home visit may also be warranted if there is continued doubt as to the parent's ability to manage a program. Basically, the treatment described herein depends upon strict surveillance and immediate feedback. It is seldom considered appropriate to "let things ride" until the next therapy session.

The replication study also represented an opportunity to improve the evaluation methodology. Earlier procedures for scoring and analysis of data were refined to enhance the psychometric properties of scores. A relatively new, albeit simple, manner of forming composite scores from observation data was formulated. This involved unit weighting of each behavior category to be included in a composite (e.g., total deviant behavior).

A telephone interview procedure was also described. Parent-reported deviant behaviors were summarized and analyzed for each family by means of interrupted time series analysis. To aggregate results across families, a transformation was performed that removed the serial dependency in the data and allowed subsequent group analysis to be performed.

While much of the foregoing discussion serves to mollify criticism of results based on a single-group design, it is not intended to discount the importance of a carefully controlled experimental trial. Consequently, the next stage in the evaluation of this social learning treatment consists of random assignment of families to either social learning or traditional therapy conditions in three agency settings. Existing agency personnel are being trained and monitored by the former Family Center staff. With each agency treating 60 families, this study should provide the definitive test of treatment effectiveness and exportability. Multiple outcome measures compatible with those used in earlier studies will provide the basis for evaluation.

ACKNOWLEDGMENTS

The authors would like to express their appreciation to the staff of the Family Center: Bob Conger, Matt Fleischman, Al Levine, John Lloyd, Barry Puett, Val Taylor, and Katie Whalen.

REFERENCES

Box, G. E., & Jenkins, G. M. *Time series analysis forecasting and control.* San Francisco: Holden-Day, 1970.

D'Zurilla, T. J., & Goldfried, M. R. Problem solving and behavior modification. *Journal of Abnormal Psychology,* 1971, *78,* 107–126.

Fleischman, M. J., & Conger, R. E. *T. E. A. C. H. clinical manual: Specific techniques for management of aggressive children.* Unpublished manual, Oregon Social Learning Center, Eugene, Ore., 1976.

Jones, R. R. "Observation" by telephone: An economical behavior sampling technique. *Oregon Research Institute Technical Report,* 1974, *14,* No. 1.

Jones, R. R., Reid, J. B., & Patterson, G. R. Naturalistic observation in clinical assessment. In P. McReynolds (Ed.), *Advances in psychological assessment* (Vol. 3). San Francisco: Jossey-Bass, 1975. Pp. 42–95.

Jones, R. R., Vaught, R. S., & Weinrott, M. Time-series analysis in operant research. *Journal of Applied Behavior Analysis,* 1977, *10,* 151–166.

Kent, R. N. Interventions for boys with conduct problems (Patterson, 1974): A methodological critique. *Journal of Consulting and Clinical Psychology.* 1976, *44,* 292–296.

Patterson, G. R. Interventions for boys with conduct problems: Multiple settings, treatments, and criteria. *Journal of Consulting and Clinical Psychology,* 1974, *42,* 471–481. (a)

Patterson, G. R. Retraining of aggressive boys by their parents: Review of recent literature and follow-up evaluation. In F. Lowy (Ed.), Symposium on the seriously disturbed preschool child, *Canadian Psychiatric Association Journal,* 1974, *19,* 142–161. (b)

Patterson, G. R., & Brodsky, G. A behavior modification programme for a child with multiple problem behaviors. *Journal of Child Psychology and Psychiatry,* 1966, *7,* 277–295.

Patterson, G. R., Cobb, J. A., & Ray, R. S. A social engineering technology for retraining the families of aggressive boys. In H. E. Adams & I. P. Unikel (Eds.), *Issues and trends in behavior therapy.* Springfield, Ill.: Thomas, 1973. Pp. 139–224.

Patterson, G. R., Jones, R. R., Whittier, J., & Wright, M. A. A behavior modification technique for the hyperactive child. *Behaviour Research and Therapy,* 1965, *2,* 217–226.

Patterson, G. R., McNeal, S., Hawkins, N., & Phelps, R. Reprogramming the social environment. *Journal of Child Psychology and Psychiatry,* 1967, *8,* 181–195.

Patterson, G. R., Ray, R. S., & Shaw, D. A. Direct intervention in families of deviant children. *Oregon Research Institute Research Bulletin,* 1968, *8,* No. 9.

Patterson, G. R., Ray, R. S., Shaw, D. A., & Cobb, J. A. *Manual for coding of family interactions*

(NAPS Document No. 01234). New York: Microfiche Publications, 1969. (Available from ASIS National Auxiliary Publications Service, 440 Park Ave. South, New York, N.Y. 10001.)

Patterson, G. R., Reid, J. B., Jones, R. R., & Conger, R. E. *A social learning approach to family intervention* (Vol. 1). *Families with aggressive children.* Eugene, Ore.: Castalia Publishing, 1975.

Reid, J. B. *A social learning approach to family intervention* (Vol. 2). *A manual for coding family interaction,* Eugene, Ore.: Castalia Publishing, 1978.

Reid, J. B., Hinojosa, G., & Lorber, R. *Social learning approach to the outpatient treatment of children who steal.* Manuscript in preparation, 1978.

Reid, J. B., & Patterson, G. R. Follow-up analyses of a behavioral treatment program for boys with conduct problems: A reply to Kent. *Journal of Consulting and Clinical Psychology,* 1976, *44,* 297–302.

Walter, H., & Gilmore, S. Placebo versus social learning effects in parent training procedures designed to alter the behavior of aggressive boys. *Behavior Therapy,* 1973, *4,* 361–377.

17

A Method for Building Complex Academic Repertoires[1]

KATHLEEN KELLY, TEODORO AYLLON,
AND HENRY KANDEL

In analyzing problems of school children, a primary tactic in behavior modification has been to specify target behaviors in topographical terms that easily lend themselves to recording and alteration. Initially, researchers focused their efforts on single-response dimensions, such as regressed crawling (Harris, Johnston, Kelley, & Wolf, 1964), out-of-seat behavior (Barrish, Saunders, & Wolf, 1969), and "inappropriate behavior" in the classroom (Madsen, Becker, & Thomas, 1968). The objective of these interventions was to eliminate some obnoxious or antisocial behavior through the withdrawal of reinforcement for that behavior.

As the methodology developed, a higher complexity of target behaviors was sought by examining their functional properties. Examples of this tactic are studies where academic-related responses, such as study behavior (Hall, Lund, & Jackson, 1968) and attending to academic material (Walker & Buckley, 1968), were brought under the control of reinforcement contingencies. Later, academic performance itself was defined as the target behavior, for example, writing (Miller & Schneider, 1970), mathematics (Lovitt & Esveldt, 1970), and reading (Ayllon & Roberts, 1974). In these and similar studies, a single-response dimension was identified and strength-

---

[1]This chapter is based in part on a dissertation submitted by Kathleen Kelly in partial fulfillment of the Ph.D. degree at Georgia State University.

TRENDS IN BEHAVIOR THERAPY

Copyright © 1979 by Academic Press, Inc.
All rights of reproduction in any form reserved.
ISBN 0-12-647450-8

ened through the use of reinforcement. The dimension of academic responses is complex and still presents methodological problems. Expansion of the procedures to additional academic areas would require that there be a corresponding reinforcement contingency for performance in each academic area. This approach would lead to satiation and therefore loss of the target behavior. On the other hand, to limit the current procedures to one or two academic areas is no viable solution.

An alternative offered by Chadwick and Day (1971) is to increase the complexity of the response definition by treating several academic areas as a single topographical response class: "time at work." Basing the requirement for a unit of reinforcement on this expanded response class, Chadwick and Day (1971) avoided the problem of satiation.

The next step in the growth of applied behavior analysis would be to increase the complexity of the academic responses to be strengthened by going from single to multiple responses. One of the most useful methods for developing complex responses without each component being separately maintained by extrinsic reinforcement is the building of response chains. The general procedure for establishing an operant chain is to strengthen one response (R1) by the immediate presentation of a reinforcer. Then, for the organism to produce the stimulus situation that will allow the performance of R1, it first has to emit R2. Then, R1 can be emitted, after which the reinforcer is made available. Each component of the chain signals the next component and reinforces the previous response. Chains have been useful in building and maintaining complex sequences of behavior with long time delays before any reinforcer is made available.

Technically, chains are characterized by: (a) the linkage of discrete and independent responses into complex sequences; (b) the use of each component to reinforce the previous component and to signal the next component; and (c) a long delay between the initiation of the chain and the actual delivery of the reinforcer. If these characteristics of chaining were to be met for such academic activities as mathematics (math) and reading, a student who did not meet the requirements for math would be prevented from engaging in reading. In practice, this would result in physically restraining the student from going to the reading class! If the student met the requirement for math, he or she would immediately be taken to the reading class to engage in reading. Again, such close adherence to the technical paradigm would result either in chaos for the teacher or in a substantial increase in supportive personnel necessary to transport each child from one classroom to another. Therefore, to use a chaining procedure in an applied setting, one must sacrifice its methodological rigor for social usefulness. On the other hand, it would be questionable whether a procedure that substantially departed from these characteristics could properly be called a chain. These considerations may explain the dearth of applied studies based on chained schedules (Ayllon & Haughton, 1962; Boren & Coleman, 1970; Mahoney, Van Wagoner, & Meyerson, 1971).

A solution to this dilemma may be found by examining the functional characteristics of a chain. Briefly, its functions are to link and maintain independent responses in a specific sequence without increasing reinforcement density. These functional characteristics are potentially beneficial for teaching school children complex repertoires involving several subject matters with minimal dependence on extrinsic reinforcement.

The purpose of the present study was to examine the usefulness of a functional approach to chained schedules of reinforcement in an academic setting. Because previous reports (Keehn, 1967; Mahoney *et al.*, 1971) have indicated that complex behavior can be taught through two conditioning procedures (sometimes referred to as "traditional" and "forward," discussed later in this chapter), it appeared tactically useful to compare these variations of the same functional approach.

METHOD

Subjects

Twenty-one seventh-grade students in an urban middle school participated in the study. This group was one of four homerooms that were assigned to a team of four teachers for morning classes. Of these 21 students, 1 was white and 20 were black. There were 14 boys and 7 girls, with an average age of 12.9 years. The students had an average Iowa Test of Basic Skills composite score of 4.4 grade levels, with a range of 3.0 to 6.5, and an average reading ability of 2.4 grade levels as measured by the Cloze[2] test.

Setting

The program was implemented in an urban, racially mixed school with over 1000 students. The 52-year-old building had recently been converted from a high school to a middle school with grades 6, 7, and 8. All procedures were conducted in the classrooms regularly occupied by the four

---

[2]The Cloze test is a standard procedure for determining a child's instructional level in reading. Passages from readers of predetermined grade levels were selected and every fifth word was omitted. Students who can supply the exact missing word at 40–60% accuracy can comprehend 75% of the material in a conventional passage on that level. This 40% criterion level was used to specify a child's instructional level.

teachers of this teaching team. The standard class period was 38 minutes, and this program was conducted throughout the morning period.

Personnel

The teaching team that agreed to participate in the program consisted of four female teachers with a wide range of experience, from a first-year teacher to one with over 14 years of teaching experience. Two teachers were black and two were white.

The program coordinator was the senior author, who met with each teacher daily throughout the program and weekly with the entire team for group consultation.

Response Definition and Recording

Daily performance was assessed and linked for each child in three subject areas. For some children, the three subject areas included reading, math, and science, while for others they included reading, math, and social studies.[3]

READING

Written workbook exercises comprised the performance assessment for all children in reading. A typical exercise consisted of reading a series of paragraphs and picking out all the words with specified vowel sounds (e.g., the long *a* sound as in "favor"). Completion time for such an exercise was about 12 minutes for the average student. Each child worked at his or her individual level. Workbook exercises were typically preceded by 15 minutes of silent or oral reading in a group. Work was typically scored by the teacher during the last 10 minutes of the 38-minute class.

MATHEMATICS

Individual prescription sheets specified sequentially exactly what material the child was to do. Assignments ranged from 10 to 20 problems in the textbook or ditto sheets accompanying the text material. A student could complete a worksheet in 12 to 15 minutes and often completed two or more in one session. The teacher randomly selected one worksheet from the student's work to grade for that day. Other work was also graded, but

[3]The materials used were *reading:* Gartler, M., & Benditt, M. *The Phoenix reading series* (Levels A and B). Englewood Cliffs, N.J.: Prentice-Hall, 1974; *math:* Dilley, C., Rucker, W., & Johnson, A. *Elementary mathematics series* (Grades 4, 5, and 6). Lexington, Mass.: Heath Publishing, 1972; *social studies:* Naslund, R. *SRA map and globe skills kit.* Chicago: Scientific Research Associates, 1972; *science: Continental press science masters for liquid duplicators.* Elizabeth, Pa.: The Continental Press, 1969.

only one sheet was assessed for the day's score. Scoring took place during the last 10 minutes of class.

SOCIAL STUDIES

Each child worked on his or her own individual level. The work unit was one exercise in the map skills program that could be completed within 20 minutes by an average student. An exercise required 10 to 20 written answers and consisted of locating places or following complex geographical directions on the student map. Work was scored as it was completed, usually during the last 10 minutes of class.

SCIENCE

Science was the only class taught on a group basis. Students performed experiments in small clusters of three or four and often read from their science textbooks. A daily worksheet of five to eight items related to the class experiment or lesson comprised the basis for performance assessment. An average student could complete the sheet in 15 minutes. These were graded by the teacher during the last 10 minutes of class.

Daily performance scores were recorded by each teacher on a 3 × 5 inch card provided daily to each student. Each card was printed with three separate cells corresponding to the three academic areas that were required to earn points. In order for a student to earn points he or she had to perform at 80% or more in each required academic area. This performance level requirement was gradually extended from one academic area to all three areas. The cell for each area under the 80% requirement was outlined in red Magic Marker. Cells not yet in the point system requirement were left unmarked. Thus, the student knew at a glance which areas led to earning points. As the student's work was scored and recorded on the card, each teacher initialed the appropriate cell. Early in the program three children attempted to falsify their scores. This unauthorized "earning" was discovered by comparing the student's card with the teacher's master record. Once it became known that the consequence for cheating was loss of point earnings for 2 days, the students ceased in these attempts. Throughout the study, daily scores were recorded for each student on the material already described. The student was given feedback on daily performance in all academic areas, and the teachers kept records of this performance. The student could discuss his or her performance with the teacher at any time in the program.

Reinforcer Definition

A wide range of backup reinforcers were made available for academic performance using a system of conditioned reinforcers in the form of points. Points could be exchanged for a variety of tangible items and activities (as used by O'Leary, Becker, Evans, & Saudargas, 1969). Backup reinforcers included edibles such as candy, cookies, and gum, as well as toys, records, movie and wrestling passes, and personal care items such as dusting powder, nail polish, and cologne. Points were exchanged for these items each day during a 15-minute period at lunchtime. A storage room was used to display the backup reinforcers that were available at point-exchange period. This motivational procedure is based on the token economy initially developed by Ayllon and Azrin (1968). The effectiveness of this procedure has been amply documented in the educational (O'Leary & Drabman, 1971) and psychiatric literature (Kazdin & Bootzin, 1972).

Procedures

The 21 children were divided into two groups. In the "forward" linking group ($N = 8$), the three academic areas were linked together through a procedure analoguous to the "forward" chaining paradigm (Keehn, 1967; Mahoney *et al.*, 1971). Students initially earned points in the first class of the day, temporally *farthest* away from reinforcement. The next requirement added to the reinforcement contingency for this group was to earn points in the second class of the day. The third class was then added to the reinforcement requirement.

In the "traditional" linking group ($N = 13$), the three academic areas were linked in a manner paralleling traditional chaining procedures. Thus, students initially earned points for meeting a specific academic requirement in the last class of the morning, temporally *closest* to lunchtime. Next, they had to meet a high academic requirment in the preceding class in order to have the opportunity to earn points in their last class. Finally, they had to meet a high academic requirement in all three classes to have the opportunity to earn points in the last class that preceded lunchtime.

The use of two different groups made it possible to explore the area of complex reinforcement schedules in various ways. Therefore, the procedures and results for each group will be presented separately. The procedures for both groups proceeded in three experimental phases or steps.

"FORWARD" GROUP

Step I (science). After baseline measures were taken on students' performance in science for 4 consecutive class days, Step I was initiated. Students were given their point cards with the cell for their first period (science) outlined in red ink, and they were instructed that a score of 80% or higher would give them points to spend in the point-exchange room. Step I continued for 6 school days.

Step II (science + reading). At the beginning of this phase, the students were given their point cards as usual, except that the second cell (reading) was also marked in red. Students were told that they still had to score at least 80% in science to be eligible to earn points in reading. On the first day of Step II, the teacher instructed the class as follows: "I am very pleased with how well you are working in science and want you to keep on working as hard as you are. Since you are doing so much better, we are going to include another subject in our point program. Starting today, you will now earn your points in reading class. In order to earn these points in reading, you will need to continue to have a score in science of 80% or more, and for you this will be easy since you have had so much practice in science. Do you have any questions?"

All questions were answered and the cards were distributed. These instructions introduced each new requirement in the point system. New requirements were added when at least 60% of the students had reached performance criteria of 80% in the academic areas under the reinforcement requirement. Step II continued for 6 school days.

Step III (science + reading + math). This step meant the addition of the third area, math, to the point contingency requirement. Students were told that they were to score at least 80% in science plus 80% in reading to be eligible to earn points in math. Step III continued for 21 school days.

"TRADITIONAL" GROUP

Step I (social studies). Following a 4-day baseline period, during which daily measures were taken on students' performance in social studies, all students received a point card with the cell for their last area (social studies) outlined in red. At the beginning of the class period, procedures for point earning and point exchange were explained to the students and all questions about the system were answered. At the end of the period, all those who had scored 80% or higher were taken to the point-exchange room and allowed to trade their points for items of their choice. Step I was conducted for 6 days.

Step II (social studies + math). Point cards were given out at the beginning of math, which preceded social studies, and the cells for these areas were marked in red. The students were told that in order to continue to earn their points in social studies they would now have to score at least 80% in math as well. Again, all questions were answered until the students indicated they understood the new procedure. Step II was in effect for 6 school days.

Step III (social studies + math + reading). Point cards were given out at the beginning of reading and the cells for reading, math, and social studies were marked. Students were now required to score at 80% or higher in reading *and* math in order to be eligible to earn points in social studies, which also had to be at 80% or higher. Step III lasted for 21 days.

Experimental Design and Evaluation

The dependent variable under observation was the performance of each student in each of the three subject areas. The independent variable was the response-reinforcement contingency described by the response-linking method. Thus, the experimental design selected as the most appropriate for this investigation was the multiple-baseline across-subjects design (Baer, Wolf, & Risley, 1968). Since response linking was applied to all students in the program, a systematic replication across subjects (Sidman, 1960) was made possible and provided further opportunity for the demonstration of experimental effectiveness.

RESULTS

At the completion of this program, 16 of the 21 students were performing at levels of 80% or higher in each of three academic areas. Of the remaining 5 students, all were performing at 80% or above in two of the three academic areas and between 60 and 79% correct in the remaining area. Figures 17.1 and 17.2 show the average daily performance of each group in their three academic areas. It can be seen that both groups responded similarly to the growing requirements for reinforcement.

"Forward" Group

Figure 17.1 shows that the increase in requirements from science to science + reading initially had different effects on student performance in each of the two areas. When students went from performance in science only to science and reading, the group performance in science initially dropped below 70%. By the sixth day of linking science + reading, only one student out of eight performed at less than 80% in Science. Reading rapidly increased to criterion level with no decline in performance after the fifth day in this phase.

When students were required to perform at criterion levels in science + reading + math, all students met the new requirements on the first day with no performance disruption in the other two academic areas.

"Traditional" Group

Figure 17.2 shows the effects of the "traditional" procedure, where the reinforcement starts at the last area, social studies. This is in contrast to the "forward" procedure, where the first area under reinforcement is the first class of the day. Increasing complexity in performance requirements from social studies to social studies + math resulted in an increased performance

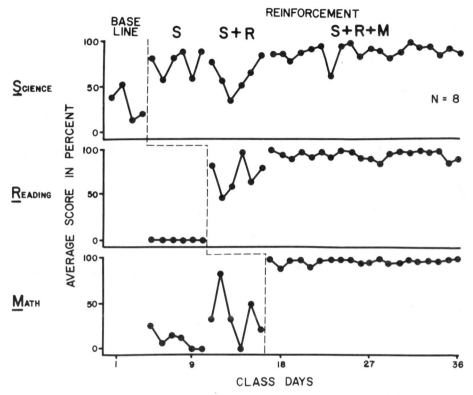

FIGURE 17.1. *In the "forward" group, average daily performance in each academic area is presented in multiple-baseline form. Area to left of dotted line is under baseline conditions, whereas area to right of dotted line designates reinforcement period. First area under reinforcement is Science (S). Linking of academic requirements was made by starting with Science (top of figure) and continuing through Reading (R), plus Math (M) (bottom of figure).*

in math but a slight drop in social studies performance. The same phenomenon was seen in the "forward" group. By the sixth day, however, 10 of the 13 students had reached the 80% criteria. The remaining three students met criteria in nine days. Thereafter, as shown in Figure 17.2, the "traditional" group showed the same consistency in performance as the "forward" group. With few exceptions, students in both groups behaved similarly as requirements changed from step to step.

Collateral Results

Overall changes were also noted in the academic levels of the students between the initiation of the program and the completion of Step III. In reading, students increased an average of 1.0 years in reading level as measured by the Cloze test after 20 days ("traditional" group) or 26 days

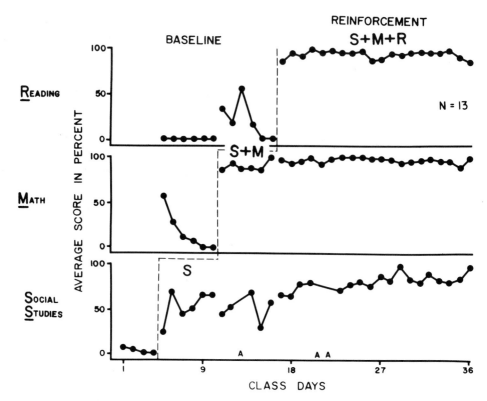

FIGURE 17.2. *In the "traditional" group, average daily performance in each academic area is presented in multiple-baseline form. Area to left of dotted line is under baseline conditions, whereas area to right of dotted line designates reinforcement period. First area under reinforcement is Social Studies (S). Linking of academic requirements was made by starting with Social Studies (bottom of figure) and continuing through Math (M) plus Reading (R) (top of figure). The Social Studies teacher was absent (A) during three days of the program. Data were not collected during that time.*

("forward" group) of reinforcement. They completed an average of 2.0 chapters in math in either 20 days ("forward" group) or 26 days ("traditional" group) of reinforcement. Thus, not only was daily performance high, but students also increased in overall skill level development in both academic areas.

DISCUSSION

The objective of this study was to develop a procedure that would build and maintain a sequence of complex academic behavior in school children. The findings reported here indicate that such a procedure is feasible, highly effective, and academically meaningful.

Three separate academic areas were successively linked, and a high level of performance in each was maintained without the risk of satiation. Throughout the study, reinforcement density remained at a constant level. The number of points a student could earn initially for high performance in *one* academic area was the same number of points he or she could later earn for meeting criteria in all *three* academic areas. The gradual increase of the requirement for reinforcement allowed the student to perform without severe strain on academic responding. By gradually adjusting his performance in each academic area to meet the performance requirement, the student was able, in time, to perform long sequences of academic responding for a comparatively low density of extrinsic reinforcement.

The long delays between performance in the first academic class and actual delivery of reinforcement was bridged by the point system. This bridging was augmented by the use of the red cue, which outlined on the point card the cells of those academic areas that were under reinforcement. The student knew at a glance which areas led to reinforcement and what his or her performance was in those areas already completed for that day. This cue may have served as a reminder to the student that each "red cell" area contributed to the final reinforcement and that high performance was required in each of those areas. Thus, the "red cells" may have prompted the student to "make the grade" in those critical academic areas.

An additional finding was the appearance of emotional behavior, typically in the form of refusals to work and occasionally accompanied by the tearing up of point cards. For example, when the second requirement was added, students became lethargic and refused to work. After 3 days, however, they adjusted to the new requirement and were working once again. This "transitional trauma" was a clear indication that the students recognized that a substantial change had occurred in their environment.

This study showed that there were no functional differences, either in speed of acquisition or in overall effectiveness, between the two procedures for linking the three academic areas. While the "traditional" linking procedure was analogous to the more commonly used chaining technique, it did not prove easier to build, nor was it more efficient than the "forward" linking procedure. Thus, the choice of procedure is best left to the teacher's preference or convenience.[4]

While the data showed dramatic increases in academic performance and while the teachers' reaction to the program was enthusiastic, it seemed important to determine how stressful and academically demanding the program was in the children's own experience. To this end, an anonymous

---

[4]The teachers in this program were so pleased with the performance increases shown by their students that they asked to extend the "traditional" procedure to 16 students known as "low achievers." Within 21 days, 13 of the 16 students in this group were performing at 80% or more in three academic areas. (For details of this study, see Kelly, 1974).

questionnaire was distributed during the final week of the program. The students' responses where overwhelmingly favorable. Without exception, the point system was seen as a positive experience, as indicated in their own comments on the questionnaire: "It's the best thing that ever happened here." "I used to mess around a lot at school but it's more fun to be able to get candy." "When I got points, my work got better." The students also noticed changes in teacher behavior. For example, "They always be fussing at us when we didn't have no points (*sic*) but now they call on us when we raise our hands," one student remarked, pointing out a change he was particularly pleased to see. In retrospect, the students admitted that they initially had reservations about working for points. As one student stated, "Sometimes I didn't think I could do all that work, but I thought about the candy and then I could do it (*sic*)!" In their words, the students indicated that school now held possibilities for recognition and achievement which, for most of these students who were 3 and 4 years below grade level, was a new and meaningful experience.

While this procedure of response linking was technically not a chain, functionally it worked like a chain. Recent work by Azrin (Azrin & Foxx, 1971; Azrin & Nunn, 1973) shows that applied procedures may no longer be easily traced to specific laboratory-based techniques. Applied behavior analysis can take direction from such pioneers as Azrin and his associates in their development of procedures which, while not directly derived from the animal laboratory, do achieve important and meaningful changes in behavior. As Baer *et al.* (1968) point out, applied behavior analysis must focus its efforts upon problems of importance both to society and to the individual. At present, there is great need for methods that will strengthen complex and meaningful academic behaviors in the school (Winett & Winkler, 1972). The procedure presented here represents one attempt to meet this challenge.

ACKNOWLEDGMENTS

Invaluable suggestions in technical interpretation of this manuscript were made by Dr. James M. Johnston and Dr. Kirk Richardson, doctoral committee members. The authors also wish to thank Mr. Elton Powers, Principal, and Dr. Jarvis Barnes of the Atlanta Public Schools for their support throughout this project. Thanks are also due to the teachers, Nell Jernigan, Mary Jones, Caronelle Landiss, and Betty Powell, for their enthusiastic cooperation. Indispensable assistance was provided by Marianne Garber and Al Stoerzinger at various stages in this study.

REFERENCES

Ayllon, T., & Azrin, N. H. *The token economy: A motivational system for therapy and rehabilitation.* New York: Appleton-Century-Crofts, 1968.

Ayllon, T., & Haughton, E. Control of the behavior of schizophrenic patients by food. *Journal of the Experimental Analysis of Behavior*, 1962, 5, 343–352.

Ayllon, T., & Roberts, M. D. Eliminating discipline problems by strengthening academic performance. *Journal of Applied Behavior Analysis*, 1974, 7, 71–76.

Azrin, N. H., & Foxx, R. M. A rapid method of toilet-training the institutionally retarded. *Journal of Applied Behavior Analysis*, 1971, 4, 89–99.

Azrin, N. H., & Nunn, R. G. Habit-reversal: A method of eliminating nervous habits and tics. *Behaviour Research and Therapy*, 1973, 11, 619–628.

Baer, D. M., Wolf, M. M., & Risley, T. R. Some current dimensions of applied behavior analysis. *Journal of Applied Behavior Analysis*, 1968, 1, 91–97.

Barrish, H. H., Saunders, M., & Wolf, M. M. Good behavior game: Effects of individual contingencies for group consequences on disruptive behavior in a classroom. *Journal of Applied Behavior Analysis*, 1969, 2, 119–124.

Boren, J. J., & Coleman, A. D. Some experiments on reinforcement principles within a psychiatric ward for delinquent soldiers. *Journal of Applied Behavior Analysis*, 1970, 3, 29–37.

Chadwick, B. A., & Day, R. C. Systematic reinforcement: Academic performance of under-achieving students. *Journal of Applied Behavior Analysis*, 1971, 4, 311–319.

Hall, R. V., Lund, D., & Jackson, D. Effects of teacher attention on study behavior. *Journal of Applied Behavior Analysis*, 1968, 1, 1–12.

Harris, F. R., Johnston, M. J., Kelley, C. S., & Wolf, M. M. Effects of positive social reinforcement on regressed crawling of a nursery school child. *Journal of Educational Psychology*, 1964, 55, 35–41.

Kazdin, A. E., & Bootzin, R. R. The token economy: An evaluative review. *Journal of Applied Behavior Analysis*, 1972, 5, 343–372.

Keehn, J. D. Is bar-holding with negative reinforcement preparatory or perseverative? *Journal of the Experimental Analysis of Behavior*, 1967, 10, 461–465.

Kelly, K. C. *Effectiveness of two analogues of chained schedules of reinforcement on academic behavior.* Unpublished doctoral dissertation, Georgia State University, 1974.

Lovitt, T. C., & Esveldt, K. A. The relative effects of math performance on single- versus multiple-ratio schedules: A case study. *Journal of Applied Behavior Analysis*, 1970, 3, 261–270.

Madsen, C. H., Jr., Becker, W. C., & Thomas, D. R. Rules, praise, and ignoring: Elements of elementary classroom control. *Journal of Applied Behavior Analysis*, 1968, 1, 139–150.

Mahoney, K., Van Wagoner, R. K., & Meyerson, L. Toilet training of normal and retarded children. *Journal of Applied Behavior Analysis*, 1971, 4, 173–181.

Miller, L. K., & Schneider, R. The use of a token system in project Head Start. *Journal of Applied Behavior Analysis*, 1970, 3, 213–220.

O'Leary, K. D., Becker, W. C., Evans, M. B., & Saudargas, R. A. A token reinforcement program in a public school: A replication and systematic analysis. *Journal of Applied Behavior Analysis*, 1969, 2, 3–13.

O'Leary, K. D., & Drabman, R. Token reinforcement programs in the classroom: A review. *Psychological Bulletin*, 1971, 75, 379–398.

Sidman, M. *Tactics of scientific research.* New York: Basic Books, 1960.

Walker, H. M., & Buckley, N. The use of positive reinforcement in conditioning attending behavior. *Journal of Applied Behavior Analysis*. 1968, 1, 245–252.

Winnett, R. A., & Winkler, R. C. Current behavior modification in the classroom: Be still, be quiet, be docile. *Journal of Applied Behavior Analysis*, 1972, 5, 499–504.

IV

IMPLEMENTING BEHAVIORAL PROGRAMS

18

Social and Political Challenges to the Development of Behavioral Programs in Organizations

ROBERT PAUL LIBERMAN

The boundaries of behavior therapy and behavior modification are expanding geographically as well as intellectually. It was only 20 years ago that behavior therapy was limited to the small working space of Joseph Wolpe in South Africa and to the laboratory at Metropolitan State Hospital outside of Boston, Massachusetts, where Skinner and Lindsley began their pioneering work with psychotic patients. Now, as evidenced by frequent congresses in America and Europe, behavior analysis and therapy has become international, with over 10,000 mental health professionals as members of behavior therapy associations worldwide. In addition, the boundaries of behavior therapy are expanding across topics and intellectual areas as well as across the world. We are moving outward, using behavioral principles to confront health problems such as nutrition, exercise, community mental health, and prevention of heart disease. Learning principles are being employed to improve the quality of the environment, such as reducing the amount of energy resources that people use, encouraging people to ride on buses and trains instead of in private automobiles, and reducing pollution and littering.

We are also moving inward into the areas of self-control, cognitive behavior modification, and cognitive therapy. Clinical researchers such as Mahoney, Beck, Meichenbaum, Bandura, Thoresen, and Kazdin are chasing the psychodynamic demons out of the inner world that used to be

369

Copyright © 1979 by Academic Press, Inc.
All rights of reproduction in any form reserved.
ISBN 0-12-647450-8

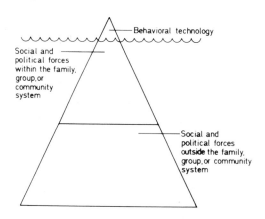

FIGURE 18.1. *Determinants of successful outcome in the development of innovative behavioral programs in organizations.*

inhabited by the id and the superego. They are clarifying how cognitive factors mediate behavior change—factors such as expectations and perceptions, beliefs and attitudes, self-instructions, and self-reinforcement.

Despite this optimism for the future of behavior therapy, we should pay some attention to the problems that we face in applying our knowledge, and to the limitations that hamper or impair our work, and slow our progress. These limiting factors lie primarily outside the domain of behavior therapy. It is often not behavioral technology as such, but rather political and social issues that make or break an innovative program. Organizational challenges face us when we work with families, groups, institutions, and community settings. Moving outward from the one-to-one therapeutic relationship, and away from academic "ivory towers," toward working in the community and in institutions requires us to become aware of the social and political forces in our work settings. As can be seen in Figure 18.1, the small tip of the "iceberg" shows us how little our success is determined by behavioral technology. The rest of the "iceberg" consists of the social and political dynamics inside and outside the family, the group, the organization, and the institutions where we work. The interventions that we carry out in social spheres meet challenges, resistances, and constraints that are not found in the traditional one-to-one relationship. Based on my own experiences, and those of colleagues, I will suggest some partial solutions that might help change agents to develop innovative programs, despite organizational challenges, resistances, and constraints.

DIMENSIONS OF HUMAN SYSTEMS: POWER, AFFECTION, WORK

Initially, we need to gain an understanding of the matrix within which organizational problems exist. The three dimensions of human and social life, outlined in Figure 18.2, describe in global terms most of what we encounter in our work with families, groups, institutions, and communities. As we develop new programs, our actions and efforts take place within this matrix of themes: power, affection, and task orientation. Behavioral principles describe the *process* of our actions: how we acquire, maintain, and modify behavior, thoughts, and feelings. But behavioral approaches do not contribute very much to our understanding of what people want, or how people should behave, or the boundaries and types of behavioral repertoires that define our humanity. The experimental and functional analysis of behavior relates our existence to environmental determinants. But the types of reinforcers that we strive for, the symbolic nature of human beings, the values and goals that we pursue are defined in these three dimensions of the *content* of our experience. The interpersonal themes of power, affection, and task orientation have been found by sociologists to be inherent in small and large social systems. They are reviewed here to alert clinical innovators to their importance as recurring themes in daily interaction with co-workers, patients, and others both inside and outside of institutions and organizations.

Power, the first dimension, contains authority and dominance at one end of the continuum, and dependency and submission on the other end. The dimension of love and affection has cohesion at one end of the continuum with hostility and antagonism at the other end. In the third dimension, task orientation and work, progress, and change move in a forward direction, while reactionary, fantasy, and play behavior move backward on the continuum. These qualitative aspects of our existence are projected onto the clinical and consulting work that we do with families, groups, communities, and organizations. Failure to appreciate these basic qualities of social life may lead to the failure of our demonstration projects and to obstacles in our doing behavioral family and group therapy. Failure to appreciate these dimensions will also make it difficult to transfer effective programs from one place to another.

The dimension of power is involved when we make decisions that affect other people; for example, power means being able to choose the types of patients to participate in a token economy program, or making a decision to use scarce resources in a community center or clinic to run groups rather than individual therapy. Decision making is within the area of power.

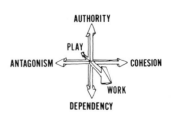

FIGURE 18.2. *Dimensions of human interaction affecting organizational problems and program development.*

The issue of power may also confront us when we are deciding how to organize a behavior therapy unit in a hospital. Eight years ago, when I naively began to establish a Clinical Research Unit, I wanted to have a treatment unit that was totally democratic, where all the nurses and aides as well as psychologists and psychiatrists would have an equal say—one "man," one vote. This turned out to be a goal that did not work. The operational needs within a hospital unit are such that a certain amount of structure and hierarchical authority is necessary to avoid disaster. Nursing staff must have their roles and tasks specified, and someone must supervise and follow-up their completion of tasks as well as coordinate sick leave and vacation time. Strong leadership, as personified in the charge or head nurse, can avert destructive clique formation and competitiveness among staff.

Another example of using power comes from the ways we serve as models for staff, influencing consultees and subordinates through our own demonstrated competence. We can also exploit the modeling capacities of staff people who are "veterans" and who are admired by their peers in the organization. On the continuum of power, the qualities of dominance, decisiveness, managerial skill, leadership, and influence are at one pole, whereas submissiveness, passivity, docility, indecisiveness, and dependency are at the other pole.

Affection is giving support and providing warm interest to other people. This means listening to the complaints of a staff member who has headaches and who needs help in getting symptomatic relief. It means sipping coffee with the manager of a business who has called us in to consult, advise, and improve the morale and the productivity of his workers. It means always assuming that the people who work under us in our organization are doing the best they can, given their backgrounds, their learning histories, their limitations, and the particular situation that they are in. We must have a "shaping" attitude so that we can build on whatever workers bring to our institution, to our community setting, to our family therapy or group therapy. The area of affection also means raising the self-esteem of the people with whom we are working. This can be done by inviting someone who is below us in the hierarchy to co-author an article with us or to assist in giving a presentation. It may mean complimenting a teacher who has done a mediocre job in supervising a student but who, for the first time, has done some systematic observation. The extremes of the dimension of affection are warmth, friendliness, concern, and interest on one side, versus coldness, unfriendliness, distance, and abruptness on the other side.

The third dimension, outlined in Figure 18.2, is the area of work, or getting the job done. Work occurs when we lead a therapy group to help patients overcome their phobias or when we are called in as consultants to help an industry or agency make their supervisors more effective. Task orientation also involves achieving goals. These goals can be to increase the satisfaction of a distressed married couple or to help the nurses in a hospital use positive reinforcement more often. The polar extremes on the work continuum are productivity, achievement, hard work, and accomplishments on one end, versus maintaining the status quo, being disruptive, diversionary, and pessimistic about change at the other end.

SOCIAL AND POLITICAL CHALLENGES FOR THE APPLIED BEHAVIOR ANALYST

What are the problems facing the behavior therapist who wants to use learning principles to deal with significant social problems? Table 18.1 contains a list of eight stages and challenges that are encountered as we attempt to develop new programs or improve existing programs in human services. In this chapter, we will deal with each of these stages and challenges.

Entering an Applied Setting

The first challenge that confronts us socially and politically occurs upon entering a setting, starting a project, or beginning a new job. Whether your work is teaching behavioral psychology at a university where there is student or faculty opposition to your ideas, or whether it is rearranging an institution where things have not changed for many years, you will have to plan your strategy carefully. Many times we slide into a setting without planning in advance. As a pioneer bringing behavior therapy to an alien professional climate, you may only be allowed to work with certain patients or students that no one else wants to deal with. But when we do have a choice, we should make that choice intelligently, so that we do not get "backed into" a situation that punishes and extinguishes our efforts.

Given the constraints noted here, it is important to remember that maximum leverage is available when entering a program or starting a proj-

TABLE 18.1
Stages and challenges in the process of innovating and changing applied social systems

1. Entering an applied setting
2. Demonstrating your competence
3. Setting goals and time frames
4. Maintaining flexibility—a "shaping attitude"
5. Dealing with institutional constraints
6. Coping with sources of conflict
7. Maintaining support from the power structure
8. Maintaining staff performance

ect. We have most of our "credit" and support at this time. Since initial support can be quickly used up, we should seize this opportunity and make as much use of our "credit" and power as we can. For example, if in entering an institution you can get initial support from the administration for some of your operating needs and principles, sustenance for your needs may become institutionalized in a positive fashion. A paradox inherent in institutions is that while certain retrogressive policies continue indefinitely, positive and progressive policies can also continue to survive for a long time. When we began our behavioral program in a state hospital in California I insisted, through many weeks of negotiations with the hospital director, that we must have the power to choose patients and staff. These are two important powers in institutions that can make or break a program. Finally, after my persistently asserting these needs as a precondition of opening a new behavior therapy unit, the director reluctantly agreed. Since 1970 there have been six different directors at the helm, but each has respected that initial agreement and it has been "institutionalized."

The entry process was similarly critical when I was selecting a site to apply behavioral methods in a community mental health center (CMHC). I started my "survey" in San Diego in the south, and finished it in San Francisco in the north, visiting almost every CMHC and speaking with each of the directors before deciding where to start this project. As I talked with them, I tried to assess their personal qualities—their flexibility, openness to new ideas, and rigidity. In determining their willingness to support my somewhat "radical" ideas, I became sensitive to whether they made eye contact, asked probing questions, and seemed interested in what I was saying. These were subtle but important points of initial contact. I also asked for some specific assurances; for example, despite the fact that I held a university appointment, I asked that I be given a part-time job in the CMHC because I realized that it was important to be identified as an "insider" in the mental health center. Thus, when I decided to do my work with the Ventura County Mental Health Department, one element in the agreement I negotiated with the director was a part-time position as a psychiatrist. But even more important than the job assurance was developing a mutually trusting and respectful personal relationship with the director. I arranged to have lunch with him once a month and I brought Kentucky Fried Chicken for our meetings in his office. During those lunch meetings we dealt with my plans and needs, his administrative problems, general issues facing psychiatry, and progress and accomplishments of the program. As we got to know each other, we became genuinely fond of each other, and this affection promoted the changes for which I needed his support. Several years later, after becoming too busy with other projects, I neglected to continue this lunch when a new director was appointed and a working relationship failed to develop. Lack of support from the new director reduced the effectiveness of the established behavioral program.

In addition to forming an entry relationship with the director, it is also necessary to generate support from the line-level clinical staff who will be the mediators of a behavioral program. Within Ventura County there were four separate clinics, each offering comprehensive mental health services to a catchment area of 75,000–100,000 people. Before embarking on the development of behavioral programs, there were several considerations in selecting a particular clinic staff to work with. It was important to find clinicians who were down-to-earth, not stuffed full of psychological theories, who wanted things to happen, and who wanted to change their approaches and try new methods. Advantages to innovation would also accrue if the clinic was relatively autonomous and was located at some distance from the centralized headquarters and the power structure. I finally chose the Oxnard (California) CMHC, which was autonomous and had a pragmatic staff complement of 25 people, small enough for me to develop personal contacts with each clinician as I introduced behavioral innovations. If I had chosen a mental health center with 50 or more staff, it would have been difficult or even impossible to bring about the kinds of changes that I was interested in.

Another illustration of the pitfalls in entering a setting came from our experience disseminating behavioral methods to 40 community mental health centers throughout the United States. Our project received an invitation from one administrative director of a mental health center to provide a workshop to teach his staff how to use behavioral methods. He was very motivated to have us provide training because his center had just been criticized by the State Department of Health for lacking coherence, a consistent treatment philosophy, and effective methods. We were interested in his invitation because it seemed as if we were going to get support from the top. But before we went to give the workshop, we got a telephone call from a psychiatrist in the clinic who confided to us that most of the staff did not want us to come. In fact, only 3 or 4 people out of 50 clinicians really wanted the workshop on behavior therapy. While the director was in favor of our consultation, resistance from the staff at the lower levels would have made it impossible to achieve our training goals. So we did not go there. We went to one of the other 200 mental health centers that desired our training. For most of us in behavior therapy, there are many places to do our work and it is wise to settle on fertile ground.

One example of how to deal with the challenge of the entry or starting-up phase can be seen in the work, carried out by Dr. Thomas Ball at Pacific State Hospital in California, a hospital for developmentally disabled or retarded people, where Dr. Ball set up one of the first token economy projects in 1967. Dr. Ball anticipated that there would be resistance from the hospital staff in establishing a token economy. A series of preliminary meetings with the staff revealed irrational resistance (e.g., giving rewards to retarded people was seen as "bribes"), but also sensible caution and concerns (e.g., the use of tokens might lead to discriminatory and arbitrary fines and repression by inadequately trained staff). These meetings helped Ball to sharpen his own plan, to evaluate his own assumptions, and to develop a carefully thought out position statement. From the resistances articulated by the staff, he wrote a memo and sent it to everyone in the hospital. The memo was titled "Some critical issues regarding the token economy." Thus, he acknowledged the resistance and tried to respond to it in a direct and rational way. For example, one of the concerns of staff regarded charging the patients tokens in exchange for food. Ball described in his memo how easy it would be for the patients to earn tokens, so easy that a patient would hardly ever miss a meal. Since there were concerns that the token economy would serve only the purposes of the staff to make their work easier, the memo emphasized that the token economy was not for the convenience of the staff but for growth and skill building of the residents. There were staff concerns about token economy as a form of mechanistic animal training that denied the integrity of the individual. Ball dealt with these concerns by pointing out how the program was oriented for learning and development—that rather than viewing the retardate as a sick, helpless individual, the token economy focused instead on the positive, intact parts of the person. The memo undercut the opposition to the token economy and led to support from the staff and from the hospital's medical director. An agreement or "contract" was made; in exchange for developing the token economy and offering it to the hospital, Ball would have a choice of patients. He would be able to choose his staff, would have time to train the staff, would be able to control visits by parents, and would have the parents turn over to the staff gifts for patients on the unit so that they could be used as reinforcers. Furthermore, as a psychologist, Ball would be designated director of the program, with full administrative and therapeutic power.

I would like to give more details about the entry process, using as an example the Behavior Analysis and Modification (BAM) Project, which was led by myself, Dr. William DeRisi, Dr. Larry King, and Dr. Timothy Kuehnel. During 1975–1978, the BAM Project disseminated, to 40 other mental health centers, the behavioral procedures that were found to be effective at the Oxnard Mental Health Center during 1971–1975. The behavioral methods that were disseminated include parent training, training in personal effectiveness or social skills, educational workshops, marital therapy, contingency contracting, and behavioral assessment. Each method was packaged as a *module* and was described in an attractive brochure that explained the project. The brochure, which was usually the first contact a professional had with the BAM Project, helped the potential trainee gain a basic understanding of the methods very quickly. Each of the modules were conveniently packaged for easy use by nurses, social workers, psychologists, and psychiatrists working in mental health centers around the country.

After the initial contact in the entry process came the need to gain *administrative and staff support*. New programs will be more readily accepted if they are seen as compatible with the potential users' previously established norms, values, and procedures. Thus, if what you have to offer is seen by your target group as something they can integrate into what they already do, it is more likely to be adopted and used. During early negotiations with mental health centers that expressed interest in the BAM Project, we emphasized that the modules could be used *in addition* to what they already were doing; they did not have to stop what they were doing; the modules simply would add to their skills. We suggested that they could modify our procedures to meet the unique needs of their own center, their own patients, and their own community.

Another step in getting initial support from staff was to *spell* out very carefully the potential *benefits and costs* for their going through the training process. We made it very clear that training required time—2 days, at first, for a workshop and then 2 hours a week of in-service training for 6 weeks. We required the assignment of a liaison person who would have time to write to us, telephone us, help with the transfer of materials from us to the mental health center, and collect evaluation data. As a research project we required that all participating staff take time to fill out a variety of forms so that we could evaluate the impact of our training. In exchange for their time and efforts, they received the BAM training, free of charge, courtesy of a National Institute for Mental Health (NIMH) grant from the United States Government. We also required a written statement of administrative approval and a policy statement expressing positive desire for what we had to offer.

Since some background variables have been shown to relate to the positive reception of new ideas and innovations, we measured these in each CMHC that applied for our program. Of the 600 CMHCs in the United States, 200 have requested BAM training and consultation. Since we were only able to give this training to 40 CMHCs, we evaluated each CMHC that applied for their apparent readiness to adopt innovative methods. The staff of each applicant CMHC indicated whether group decisions were made, whether the morale was high, and whether the CMHC had clear and attainable goals.

Another dimension of importance in the readiness to adopt the BAM Project's innovations was the CMHC's organizational structure. Did staff of the CMHC make decisions about their programmatic priorities, or was there a rigid bureaucratic superstructure that overpowers the staff? The amount of physical and social distance between the members of the organization was also felt to be a very important determinant of innovative change. Was the CMHC a large place that was very impersonal where people only meet in the elevators once a month—or was it a small place where there was a lot of face-to-face contact? A minimum of two-thirds of the staff of the CMHC had to express interest and desire to participate in the initial 2-day workshop before it was scheduled. Questionnaires were used to anticipate resistance to training and to understand the kinds of subgroups and coalitions that had to be dealt with.

Training the staff in each of these 40 mental health centers began with a 2½-day workshop. The first half-day was spent making informal contacts, and getting acquainted with the director of the CMHC, the liaison person for training, and other staff people. Attention was also paid to the task orientation dimension; for example, even before the workshop began, the liaison person was reminded to have the staff clear their calendars for the workshop, complete questionnaires, and arrange for availability of training materials and audio-visual equipment. In starting the training workshop we felt it was important to have the trainers from our project introduced by the center's director. The director's introduction reaffirmed his (or her) support for what we were trying to get across.

We next acquainted the staff with the *rationale for the training*. They were told that we had some useful and practical methods to offer. We explained how the methods were developed in a typical, busy, and service-oriented CMHC in a small city in California. They were told that the methods were tested and evaluated and found to be effective as well as usable by a range of professional and paraprofessional staff. They were also told that the methods and principles could be adapted by them to fit into their already established modes of doing therapy. We tried to give the staff attending the workshop some understanding of the advantages of parent training, contingency contracting, and the other behavioral methods to make it "real" in a clinical sense. Giving the rationale required some personalizing of our contact with the staff—this meant self-disclosure, directness, and enthusiasm. We had to "warm" ourselves up before we went in for the training so that we could communicate enthusiasm to the people at the center.

Another part of the training process was to *dispell stereotypes* of behavior therapy. This meant directly and genuinely responding to people's concerns, acknowledging the hackneyed criticisms of behaviorism, and subtly undercutting the misconceptions that behavior therapy is coercive, manipulative, and mechanistic. We listened to these stereotypes and talked with the people about them without defensiveness or argumentativeness. Most important in dispelling stereotypes was actually demonstrating how the behavioral methods are used. In 2 hours we spontaneously demonstrated, working with real patients from their center, the personal effectiveness or social skills training approach. This, more than anything else, communicated the humanitarian and warmly spontaneous quality of the behavior therapy that we were offering in the training program.

Another element in effective training or dissemination is *accepting hostility* from the people you are trying to train. One illustration of accepting hostility came from a mental health center that was led by a psychologist who was very sympathetic with behavior therapy. But his staff was not, and they did not like his ramming behavioral approaches down their throats. From the staff's point of view, the BAM Project was just another of his attempts to push behavior therapy too hard and too fast. Not realizing this in advance, when we arrived we suddenly found tremendous hostility; people were making sarcastic remarks, they were critical, distracted, and falling asleep, and they were talking to each other instead of listening to what we were saying. At this point we stopped the workshop and had a group meeting to talk about what they were feeling, what was going on, and what their reactions to the workshop were. Then we got the administrative director to obtain his staff's agreement to commit themselves to the training voluntarily rather than to feel that it was being pushed on them from the top. After the air was cleared, we were able to proceed with the workshop.

It is also important in beginning a project or training people to get their *commitment to change*. In the BAM dissemination, the entire staff was given the option to continue or to end the training at the conclusion of the 2-day on-site workshop. In our work with more than 1000 nurses, social workers, and psychologists in centers around the country, over 95% agreed to continue and have committed themselves to go on with the 6 weeks of inservice training that was led by a liaison person in their center. Commitment by staff also meant filling out questionnaires and mailing tape-recordings of therapy sessions to us, which indicated if there was a change in their therapeutic practice after training. The staff commitment included their willingness to make a $10 deposit on the materials they read and the data they were to complete. They got their money back when they sent the materials and data to us.

The last step in the entry phase is the most important. For the BAM dissemination project this was *structuring methods for the center to implement* the behavioral methods after the 2 day on-site workshop. This meant their having very specific dates to continue their training, knowing who was going to lead the training, and deciding how they would transfer their newly learned skills to their clinical practice. Each training module had a different staff person from the CMHC who was responsible for teaching the others in the group. Having the clinical team involved in implementation promoted the adoption of new programs.

Demonstrating Your Competence

The next step for an innovator after the entry phase is *demonstrating his or her competence*. As consultants we can increase our impact by becoming part of the staff that we are trying to influence. Becoming one of the clinicians (if it is in a psychiatric setting) or one of the teachers (if it is in an educational setting) means doing tasks that are difficult, time consuming,

380 ROBERT PAUL LIBERMAN

and tedious. It may mean spending time talking to a noncompliant patient and persuading this patient to take his medication. It may mean working alongside nurses or aides, cleaning the walls where patients have smeared feces. It may mean helping the nurses usher a recalcitrant patient to the time-out room. Initiation into a "fraternity" of clinicians or teachers, with whom we are trying to have impact is a process that involves getting our "feet wet" and our "hands dirty." Inconveniencing ourselves by engaging in odious and repetitive tasks pays handsome dividends later when we begin to ask the staff to change. An example of the initiation process takes place at our Clinical Research Unit every year when the unit's "professionals" (the psychologist, psychiatrist, and director of the program) each spend a rotation working as a nurse on the unit. I take off my suit and tie, put on my jeans, and take commands from the technicians and the nurses. They tell me what to do, because I am not as skilled as they are in dealing with assaultive patients, monitoring eating behaviors, or supervising token economy tasks.

Demonstrating your competence in a community mental health center may mean first treating those difficult patients with whom everyone else has failed. Demonstrate that you can do something for these patients and your effectiveness as a consultant will rise. For example, if you are trying to develop a social skills training program, unless you can demonstrate your own social and therapeutic skills as a trainer, do not expect to influence the clinicians. They will not see you as a relevant model, teacher, or reinforcer unless you first show them that you are effective with patients.

At Pacific State Hospital, before Dr. Ball began his token economy, he spent 3 years personally demonstrating the effectiveness of behavioral methods in simple self-care skills. He taught profoundly retarded patients how to dress, how to brush their teeth, and how to eat. Next, he trained the nursing staff to do the same. Only after demonstrating his success with one-to-one behavior shaping, did he start the larger token economy project.

Setting Goals and Time Frames

Unless clear goals and attainment dates are set, it is very easy to get sidetracked into professional activities that can be achieved more easily and more quickly. When we began our BAM Project we set as goals the completion of three experimental projects in the first year. Halfway through that year we looked at our list of goals and realized that we had only begun one of these experiments. We had done a lot of other professional work, such as showing people around, writing papers, giving lectures, and doing clinical work, all of which were easier and faster to complete than an experiment. Checking our goals enabled us to reorder our priorities and spend more of our time completing the experiments. We now routinely use Goal Attainment Scaling (King, Austin, Liberman, & DeRisi, 1974) as a means of prompting our productivity and evaluating our progress in research and demonstration projects.

Maintaining Flexibility—A "Shaping Attitude"

Maintaining flexibility means having a "shaping attitude," setting small, limited goals and reinforcing approximations to the longer-term vision of how a program might be. Shaping staff behavior is the critical step toward developing more effective treatment programs. To exemplify the use of a "shaping attitude" in flexibly bringing about change in an applied area, I will describe the progress made in introducing record keeping into the Oxnard community mental health center by the BAM Project. The long-term goal was to have the clinical staff keep systematic behavioral records of their patients' progress. Systematic record keeping was viewed by the BAM Project staff as the foundation for a model CMHC based upon behavioral principles.

In considering the reorganization of a community mental health center's record system, helpful guidelines for action came from Alinsky (1972), who achieved considerable success in producing organizational change in political arenas. Alinsky advised the organizer "to recognize the world as it is. We must work with it on its terms if we are to change it to the kind of world we would like it to be. We must see the world, as all political realists have, in terms of what men do and not what they ought to do" (p. 12). Likewise for the behavioral innovator at the Oxnard CMHC, the first step was to recognize the existing methods of record keeping and make a preliminary judgment of "what" and "how much" to measure based on the current practice.

ASSESSING READINESS FOR RECORD KEEPING

Getting a reliable assessment of the Oxnard CMHC staff's recording baseline required asking the right questions and making some careful observations. Clinical line staff tend to be very suspicious of outsiders who show interest in their record keeping. An outsider's interest smacks of an investigation, audit, program evaluation, or, at least, the potential for additional record keeping in the near future. Anyone who has worked closely with busy therapists will appreciate that additional requirements for keeping records are viewed as odious and unreasonable bureaucratic demands.

For the academic researcher, applied settings are a fertile field for sowing ideas and reaping reinforcers, such as publications, grants, and invitations to consult and lecture. On the other hand, the clinician without academic roots, lacking incentives to pinpoint, record, and consequate, is not likely to maintain systematic record keeping, since it entails a response cost beyond ordinary and acceptable practice. Thus, it is very difficult to convince line clinicians of the utility of frequent measurement. As any researcher knows, data collection is laborious and tedious. In contrast with the academic researcher, the clinician's reinforcers are fees or salaries, exchanging interesting clinical anecdotes with colleagues, and the satisfactions emanating from the therapeutic changes and relationships developed with clients. Faced with the demand for service, the clinician must cope and intervene in some way with a wide variety of unselected cases, in contrast to the academic behavior modifier who generally plans strategy in advance, conjures up an experimental design, and selects case material carefully. These distinctions are important to grasp for anyone seriously intent on bringing about lasting changes in a community mental health center and its staff. If the distinctions are ignored, we may encounter a parade of convincing demonstrations of behavior modification that are as fleeting in their impact on the fields of psychology, psychiatry, counseling, and social work as they are elegant in their experimental analysis of behavior (Liberman, 1972; Weiner, 1972). Without the involvement of the line clinical staff in the daily collection of data, actualization of ideal mental health settings in which measurement is a routine part of treatment (Risley, 1972) seems very far off indeed.

A fruitful way of improving record keeping in a community mental health center is to ask three basic questions:

1. What kinds of behaviors can a clinical staff measure?
   a. Which behaviors, if measured, will be of interest to the clinician and helpful to him or her in the therapeutic endeavor?
   b. How much specification, recording, and monitoring can the clinician reasonably be expected to maintain?
   c. How fast a pace should be used to introduce successive increments of specification and recording methods into the various service elements of a community mental health center?
2. What reinforcers, especially natural reinforcers, can be mobilized to start the clinician on the road to measurement and then keep him or her on the road after the novelty wears off and the daily efforts seem increasingly to demand a dogged and plodding commitment to an ideal with questionable payoff?
3. What are the limitations of behavioral measurement when balanced against time, cost, and environmental constraints?

DEVELOPING BEHAVIORAL RECORDS

When I first arrived at the Oxnard Community Mental Health Center, only occasional narrative notes were being written by the staff. These were done primarily at the time of intake and termination or when a crisis occurred, such as a suicide attempt. I took a shaping approach ultimately aimed at developing competence in the Day Hospital and outpatient staff members in carrying out various kinds of recording behavior—event, duration, latency, interval, and time sampling. The first approximation was to have the staff of the Day Treatment Center fill out a simple, one-page patient review form at the time of intake. This form focused the clinician on specifying deficits and excesses of behaviors, setting specific goals, delineating a treatment program to meet the goals, and selecting a measurement system to monitor progress. The staff were urged to substitute this form for more lengthy narrative notes, although they were offered the option of doing both.

After 1 year of using this more specific, problem- and goal-oriented form, the next innovation was a weekly Behavioral Progress Record. All information necessary to a patient's program for the current week was displayed on a single page on a clipboard placed in an accessible location within the nurses' station. The conventional but unwieldy manila folder that previously had served as the patient's clinical chart was relegated to supplementary importance and "buried" in the file cabinet. Weekly goals were set and reviewed by patient, significant others, therapist, and the therapist's supervisor from the BAM Project.

Daily data on the frequency of behavior and the achievement of goals were placed on the Progress Record. The Progress Record cued the staff to set realistic and specific goals for the patients and to make behavioral observations that provided feedback on patients' progress. Concurrently, the BAM Project's training seminars taught recording techniques, and the staff began to use time sampling, event, duration, and latency recording on their weekly Behavioral Progress Records. At the beginning of the BAM Project, no staff members were graphing their patients' behavior. Six months after the project began, a research assistant made an unannounced survey of the clinical charts and found 62% of the patients with behavioral graphs. These graphs were posted on a large bulletin board and, each week, the patient with the most impressive behavioral change was awarded bonus coupons in the Day Treatment Center's token economy.

As time passed, however, and the research staff of the BAM Project began phasing out its frequent, supportive supervision of the Day Treatment team, two phenomena crystalized. The staff decreased its use of graphs to about 10% of the patients, and they specified relatively trivial goals on their weekly Behavioral Progress Records. For example, punctual attendance at the center and earning coupons became overused goals instead of more functional behaviors, such as finding friends and jobs that could be performed in the patient's natural environment outside the clinic. The BAM research staff decided that detailed, daily data on every patient were not necessarily the most valid or reliable indication of clinical progress. Focusing on daily events preoccupied the staff's attention and misguided the staff into working toward attainment of trivial behavioral changes on the site of the Center at the expense of achieving more meaningful goals in the community.

The research and clinical staffs discarded the weekly form for a monthly Behavioral Progress Record, an example of which is depicted in Figure 18.3. The Progress Record required the therapist to specify from one to four goals on a weekly basis and to connect a specific method of intervention with each goal. For example, if the goal was to fill out three job applications in a particular week, the therapist might note "prompt and reinforce" as the method to help the client reach the goal. The new Progress Record allowed for the continued observation of patients' behaviors on a daily basis; for instance, number of greetings initiated or duration of rational speech in 15-minute conversations. Each weekly goal was to be an approximation to the monthly goal. At the end of each week, the therapist checked those goals that were attained. The focus was on functional goals that would enable the patients to learn new behaviors, extending their repertoires to facilitate their reentry into independent, community living.

In the process of evolving a workable recording system, we learned that the pacing of innovations comes out of "the free flow of action and reaction, and requires on the part of the organizer an easy acceptance of apparent disorganization [Alinsky, 1972, p. 165]." This was not easy to grasp or understand since, as academic researchers and behavior modifiers, we were trained in logic, well-formulated designs for action, and structured, ordered experimentation.

Dealing with Institutional Constraints

Most institutional workers are in favor of innovation, but it is usually "innovation without change." There is a basic conflict between innovation and institutions. Institutions basically resist change and instead favor the status quo. "Innovation without change" has undermined the community mental health center program in the United States. Although many innovative ideas have been conceived and put forth, their *implementation* depends, not on science or humanitarianism, but on a broad spectrum of professional and social politics. Innovations, by definition, introduce change; political power structures resist change. Thus, while the cry for innovation has been loud, it has been innovative "talking" that has been encouraged, whereas in fact innovative *action* has been resisted (Graziano, 1975).

In retrospect, the community mental health center's program was vastly oversold and the original goals quickly perverted. Their perversion is, perhaps, due to the unthinking assumption that revolutionary change could be successfully wrought by those professionals and politicians with a vested interest in maintaining the status quo. At any rate, NIMH feebly communicated the original intent of the program to state and local officials; it failed to coordinate the location of the centers with other HEW health and social welfare efforts; it made little attempt to train people for community work; it avoided funding centers outside the narrow confines of the medical model; NIMH did not engage consumers in the planning or opera-

BEHAVIORAL PROGRESS RECORD

NAME___Jane Doe_____   INITIAL VISIT_November 10, 1977_____

LONG-TERM GOALS

Goal:	Avoid washing rituals (totally)	Spent at least 2 hr/day outside	Start a jr. college course	Use relaxation as a coping skill
Expected Date:	12-25-78	12-15-78	2-1-78	12-15-78

SUB-GOALS

Week of 11-17-77	Goal:	Not more than 3 washes per day	Take a walk around block	Get info. from college	Practice relaxation exercises once daily
	Method:	Instructions and reinforcement from husband ⎯ X	Instructions and go with husband ⎯ X	Instructions and phone call reminder from therapist ⎯ X	Tape-recording and instructions ⎯ X
Week of 11-14-77	Goal:	Not more than 2 washes per day	Take a 30-minute walk in neighborhood daily	Register for one course	Practice relaxation twice daily
	Method:	Same as above plus exposure in vivo ⎯ X	Husband to wait at street corner ⎯ X	Praise from husband and therapist ⎯ X	Same ⎯ X
Week of 12-1-77	Goal:	Not more than 1 wash in 3 days	Take a one hour walk to shops each day	Attend class and stay for at least 15 minutes	Practice relaxation in vivo at least 3 times
	Method:	Same ⎯ X	Husband to wait at home ⎯ X	Husband to accompany her to campus ⎯ X	Therapist will cue patient in vivo ⎯ X
Week of 12-8-77	Goal:	No washing this week	Take a 2 hour excursion daily	Attend class for 1 hour alone	Use relaxation in vivo 5 times without prompting
	Method:	Same ⎯ X	Reinforcement from husband and dinner out ⎯ X	Praise and an evening movie with husband ⎯ X	Instructions and anxiety management training ⎯ X

NOTES: Jane has compulsive hand-washing rituals and chronic agoraphobia. Her husband has tended to reinforce these symptoms but can serve as a therapeutic assistant if brought into couple therapy. Marriage needs strengthening by teaching communication skills.

FIGURE 18.3.   *An example of a monthly Behavioral Progress Record.*

tion of centers; and it made only the meagerest evaluation of the program's performance. As a result, community mental health centers tend to be only a renaming of conventional psychiatry, a collection of traditional clinical services that are in most cases not responsive to the needs of large segments of the community.

Working within established agencies and institutions, the innovator will always confront forces and obstacles that prevent change and forward movement on the task dimension. One example of the problem of institutional constraints can be cited from an attempt to establish a token economy system in a training school for delinquent boys (Reppucci & Saunders, 1974). The behavioral psychologists directing the program encountered resistance when they tried to integrate the monetary system of remuneration being used in the school into a new point economy. Constraints against this effort to merge incentives into a single, generalized reinforcement program were manifest from the very top to the very bottom administrative levels. At the top level of administration, the commissioner of the state department in charge of this school was agreeable in theory to the plan. But he pointed out that in practice, any changes in the allocation of money would require approval of the state legislature. Going through the politicians in the state legislature for their approval was an almost impossible task for the behavioral psychologists, who were immersed in the day-to-day efforts of changing a program. At middle management, the head of the school's business office became interested, but he insisted that the business office could not be involved in exchanging points for money. He liked the idea, but he could not do it. At the bottom level, the supervisors of the boys who were giving them their money insisted that their job was to pay the boys for completing work and that they were not there to teach skills or give points. Thus, at every level—at the top, middle, and bottom—there were institutional resistances and constraints that blocked changes in the program.

Another illustration of institutional constraints was given by Tharp and Wetzel (1969) in their work in schools. In one case, they tried to set up a simple incentive program for an underachieving boy that would have allowed him to play football in an after-school athletic program as a daily reinforcer for completing academic work during the day. The principal in the school, the teachers, the football coach, and the parents were all in favor of this behavior therapy approach. Everyone thought it was a good idea, but there was no way for the information about the boy's academic accomplishment to go from the teacher to the football coach. Since no communication channel existed, the school pronounced the plan impossible. Nowhere in the school was there an individual whose normal role included carrying such a message. Both the teacher and the coach would have considered it a violation of their job descriptions to seek out the other. It was necessary in this instance, as in many others, to have a behavior analyst, a special person hired and trained by the consulting psychologists, fill in the interstices in the organization and serve as the communication channel. The behavior analyst either called or came by in the morning to verify the student's criterion performance with the teacher and then delivered the report to the coach.

It should be emphasized that even with the philosophical support of the principal, the organizational structure of the school did not allow for the teacher and coach to regularly and directly communicate about an individual student. This difficulty was entirely independent of the personalities or values of these two mediators; both were reliable, cooperative, and interested professionals. There was simply no time, no moment of spatial proximity, and no channel that would allow for the transmission of information.

The structure of most organizations like schools and hospitals is not designed for allowing an individual to experience the consequences of his or her own behavior. The formal communication patterns within a school district are created for the convenience of the staff and rarely allow for modification to deal with the problems of an individual child. This does not make schools different from other complex organizations, but procedural uniformity—without which large-scale organizations would no doubt go berserk—creates gross, if unintended, absurdity for the individual problem child (Tharp & Wetzel, 1969).

Sometimes, institutional constraints are so rigid that effective and ethical consultation and innovation are not possible. Dr. David Fisher, a behavioral psychologist in the San Francisco area, was invited by the officials of the California State Prison at San Quentin to suggest ways to reduce the high rate of homosexual assaults in the prison. He seriously suggested the implementation of a conjugal visit program, where inmates would have the opportunity to spend private time and entire nights with their wives and girl friends. When the officials rejected this plan but still offered him a position as a consultant on utilizing aversive procedures for homosexuality, Dr. Fisher declined the offer, refusing to compromise his professional and ethical positions.

In a token economy that was established on a coeducational unit in a large mental hospital, the psychiatrist directing the program decided to provide privacy in a bedroom for couples who wished to be alone together to share affection, conversation, or sex. This was a highly valued reinforcer in the token economy with many patients purchasing time for privacy. When news of the private room came to the attention of the hospital administration, the psychiatrist was called up for a meeting and was ordered to stop using the bedroom for this purpose. The intrepid psychiatrist, following the "letter of the law," took out the beds from the room but continued to allow the patients to utilize their private time and space. The room was left furnished with chairs, and the patients were given suggestions from the Kamasutra. Thus, the institutional constraints against patients' privacy and sex were breeched by imaginative programming.

Coping with Sources of Conflict

The innovator, hopeful of change, should be wary of the inevitable conflict between interests, reward systems, and goals that make the process of program development a struggle from which comes compromise. When the sources of conflict are ignored, a promising program may falter and die. For example, an academically based, behavioral child psychologist, Dr. Anthony Graziano, worked with a group of parents to establish a private school for autistic children. He turned to the parents for support after failing to elicit the interest and support of his university or the local mental health agencies. The school was a resounding success, both in the quality of the data reflecting the children's learning and in the satisfaction of the parents. However, Graziano and his graduate students were not content with continuing the status quo but, instead, wanted to innovate further, to make systematic changes in the curriculum and contingencies, and to regularly reevaluate the program and conduct experiments within it. The academic interests and research priorities of the psychologists clashed with the clinical and more conservative aims of the parents, who simply wanted a smooth-functioning, reliable program for their children. Before the conflict in goals was clarified, an irreversible antagonism developed and the psychologists were asked to leave the school (Graziano, 1975).

Another example of conflicting interests comes from the same training school for delinquent youths referred to earlier in the section on institutional constraints. The psychologists who directed the token economy wanted community visits to be awarded to the boys contingent upon their earning sufficient points through prosocial and academic behavior. On the other side, the educators at the school wanted the community excursions open to all, irrespective of point earnings. Here, a conflict surfaced between competing attitudes and values—the psychologists viewing the excursions as potential reinforcers that could motivate the learning of other skills, versus the educators viewing the excursions as educational activities that were inherently valuable (Reppucci & Saunders, 1974).

One of the conflicts that has wracked behavior modification from its early days is the use of aversive stimuli in treatment programs. Behavior modifiers, feeling ethically and professionally competent to use punishment procedures in an effective and humane manner, have justified techniques such as electric shock as being in the best interest of patients whose severely self-destructive or aggressive behavior was life threatening and required rapid intervention and suppression. On the other hand, administrators and politicians have been reluctant to permit the routine use of aversive methods, being concerned about abuse by inadequately trained and supervised personnel and the potential for scandal and exposé. The state of Minnesota temporarily outlawed all behavior modification programs in the late 1960s with the statement that "operant conditioning can be dehumanizing and can at times lead to a total loss of human values. . . . A treatment used in a public facility that is bizarre or cruel or otherwise impossible to explain to the public—even if it gets results—is of nature against the public interest [Lucero & Vail, 1968, p. 233]." Here we see the source of conflict arising from different systems of accountability for the behavior modifier and for the public administrator. The behavior modifier has to justify the methods empirically to a professional and scientific audience, whereas the administrator is held accountable for preventing notoriety and public protest by an audience that includes politicians, the press, and relatives who might be angered by what seems to be cruel treatment.

In the case of aversive procedures, the conflict has had a salutory effect on the entire field. In Minnesota, the behavior modifiers and the administrators met in a series of workshops that led to a set of standards and regulations for operant conditioning programs in the state's hospitals. More recent efforts have led to the development of criteria for competency in the administration of aversive methods with patients; thus, competency-based training and supervision are now possible and personnel can be certified and periodically reevaluated for their proper use of these controversial techniques (Thomas, 1977).

Court decisions that ensure the noncontingent delivery of basic rights and privileges of institutionalized patients (such as meals, personal clothing, privacy, bed, correspondence, telephone) may exert positive influences on the development of new and more effective positive reinforcers. Guaranteeing basic amenities may reduce the importance of deprivation and other aversive conditions as motivators for change. A focus on positive reinforcement control of behavior should force hospitals to introduce new reinforcers beyond those already ensconced. The administrative and legal requirements for informed consent, requiring patients to participate more fully in treatment, planning, and evaluation, is also likely to facilitate the effects of behavior therapy (Kazdin, 1978). These developments, coming out of conflicts between vested interests, may improve institutions and social agencies immeasurably (Wexler, 1973).

The Association for the Advancement of Behavior Therapy (AABT) has promulgated a set of guidelines for ethical practice that offers protection for the public against treatment abuses by clinicians adhering to the guidelines. The guidelines are listed in Table 18.2.

Maintaining Support from the Power Structure

As pointed out in the section on entering a setting, support from the top of the institutional hierarchy is of vital importance to the success of program developers and innovators. This support needs to be cultivated and nurtured indefinitely, and an innovator, program manager, or consultant who takes the boss' support for granted, does so at great peril to the program's survival. In my work at the Oxnard CMHC, I was able to develop and maintain a supportive relationship with the departmental director for 5 years; however, when he resigned and was replaced by another person, I failed to generate support from his successor. The real victim of my overconfidence and negligence in building a supportive tie with the

TABLE 18.2

Guidelines for ethical practice in psychiatric, psychological, counseling, and human service settings[a]

A. Have the goals of treatment been adequately considered?

1. Have the therapist and client agreed on the goals of therapy?
2. Has the client's understanding of the goals been assured by writing out the goals or by having the client restate them in his or her own words?
3. Will serving the client's interests be contrary to the interests of other persons?
4. Will serving the client's immediate interests be contrary to the client's long-term interest?
5. Has the therapist or consultant determined who the client is?
6. Have advisory boards or human rights committees been consulted in the case of pursuing novel treatment goals in an institution?
7. Have the "mediators" of treatment (e.g., nurses, aides, technicians) been involved in the process of goal setting?
8. Do the goals of treatment include plans to restore the client to a less restrictive environment where feasible?
9. Do the goals of treatment include positive, constructive, and functional behavioral elements as contrasted with only suppressing undesirable behavior or instigating behaviors that are of convenience to the therapist or institution?

B. Has the choice of treatment methods been adequately considered?

1. Does the published literature show the procedure to be the best one for that problem?
2. If no literature exists regarding the treatment method, is the method justified as being a standard practice?
3. Has the client been told of alternative procedures that might be preferred by the client on the basis of significant differences in discomfort, treatment time, cost, or degree of demonstrated effectiveness?
4. If a treatment procedure is publicly, legally, or professionally controversial, has formal professional consultation been obtained? Has the reaction of the affected segment of the public been formally ascertained? And have the alternative treatment methods been more closely reexamined and reconsidered?
5. Has the setting in which treatment is to occur been evaluated so that interfering conditions can be corrected and facilitative conditions can be implemented? Does the implementation of the treatment produce a net increase or enrichment of rewards and behavioral options for the client?
6. If a treatment procedure is novel, experimental, or aversive and is being conducted in an institution, have advisory or human rights committees been consulted for their approval?
7. Has the transfer of treatment effects to nontreatment settings been adequately considered?

C. Is the patient's participation voluntary?

1. Has the client freely entered into treatment?
2. If treatment is legally mandated, has a range of treatments and therapists been offered?
3. Is the client's withdrawal from treatment being discouraged by a penalty or financial loss that exceeds actual clinical costs?
4. If the treatment occurs within an institution, has the patient been permitted access to sources of information and advice about the treatment in addition to the treating agents? Has access to relatives and professional consultants of the patient's own choosing been made available to the patient before and during the treatment?

(continued)

TABLE 18.2 (*continued*)

D. *Does the therapist refer the patients to other therapists when necessary?*

1. If the therapist is not qualified to deliver the best treatment, is the client referred to other therapists?
2. If treatment is partially or totally unsuccessful, is the client freely referred to other therapists?
3. If the client is dissatisfied with treatment, is referral freely made?
4. Are institutional resources made available to provide specialized treatment for otherwise refractory clients who require them?

E. *Has the adequacy of treatment been evaluated?*

1. Has a quantitative measure of the problem been obtained?
2. Are measures taken repeatedly during treatment to monitor its efficacy?
3. Have the measures of the client's problem and progress been made available to him or her during treatment?
4. Is there evidence that the program was carried out as planned by the therapist or the "mediators"?
5. Is there evidence of no unintended harmful consequences of the program?

F. *Has the confidentiality of the treatment relationship been protected?*

1. Are records available only to authorized persons?
2. Does the client know who has access to the records, and has he/she agreed?
3. Is written permission obtained from the client before information about treatment is sent to others?

G. *Is the therapist qualified to provide treatment?*

1. Has the therapist had training and/or experience in treating the client's problem?
2. If deficits exist in the therapist's qualifications, has the client been informed?
3. Does the therapist obtain the latest information on treatment methods for the client's problem, such as attending workshops and institutes and reading journals and books?
4. If the therapist is not adequately qualified, is adequate supervision by a qualified therapist provided and the client informed of this relation?
5. If the treatment is administered by "mediators" under the supervision of a therapist or consultant, have the "mediators" been adequately trained to provide treatment?

H. *When another person or an agency is empowered to arrange for therapy, have the personal interests of the subordinated client been sufficiently considered?*

1. Has the subordinated client been informed of the treatment objectives and participated in choice of treatment procedures to the greatest extent possible?
2. Where the subordinated client's abilities are impaired (retardation, psychosis, child), has the client participated in the treatment planning to the extent permitted by his or her abilities?
3. Are the benefits of the superordinate agency or person contrary to the interests of the subordinated client?
4. If the interests of the subordinated and superordinate persons conflict, have attempts been made to reduce the conflict by dealing with both interests?
5. Does the subordinated client have access to an advocate, or ombudsman, and lawyer?
6. In the case of novel, experimental, or aversive treatment, has the client's guardian(s) or human rights advocate been consulted and their permission obtained?

---

[a]These guidelines for ethical treatment were developed by the AABT. Additional guidelines, inserted by Robert P. Liberman and Stephen Flanagan, focus on the special concerns of the institutionalized individual. The guidelines were purposely written in the form of questions to remind therapists about practices or issues that are of central ethical importance and to avoid the coercive tone implicit in guidelines that consist of a series of mandates. The guideline questions were deliberately cast in a general manner that should apply to all psychological, psychiatric, and counseling practices and not specifically to the practice of behavior therapists.

new director was the program at the CMHC. It became increasingly difficult to gain approval for new programs, for innovative use of staff, and for research. The moral of this story is, "Continue to cultivate the roses on the power structure after the first bloom."

Alliances need to be forged with informal as well as formal leaders. In many institutions, the psychiatrist has informal status and power because of traditional attitudes toward medicine and because of his or her prerogatives in prescribing medications, restraints, and determining admissions, transfers, and discharges. Even when a psychologist is in formal control of a program, the psychiatrist can wield much influence among the staff, patients, and relatives. At minimum, an uneasy truce between the psychiatrist and the psychologist is necessary for the latter to move ahead and avoid sabotage of the program. At the Oxnard CMHC, for instance, a psychiatrist who was subtly and sarcastically antagonistic toward behavior therapy wreaked much havoc with the staff's morale until illness led to her resignation.

In some institutions where vertical hierarchies exist within each discipline, the program innovator may not be able to bring about change without having the top figures in nursing, social work, rehabilitation, and medicine all supporting the changes. Needless to say, many times it is impossible, for all practical purposes, to galvanize support across all hierarchies. Organizations with rigid, vertical, hierarchical staffing are inimical to the growth of behavioral programs, which require consistency, coordination, and systematic contingencies of reinforcement by all levels of staff (Liberman, King, & DeRisi, 1976).

There are strategies that can be successful in maintaining support from the power structure. Developing mutually trustful and respectful relationships with the director or chief takes frequent contacts and offers of assistance by the program innovator. These can be genuinely satisfying on a subjective level as well. Having lunch together and inviting the director to parties helps to establish communality and mutual identification. Another strategy involves providing reinforcers to those in power, for example: giving them credit for their support by including their names as co-authors on publications; inviting them to assist in professional presentations; being accessible when licensing teams and other site visitors arrive at the institution to survey its quality; providing positive publicity through articles in the local press; and taking on the management of special problem cases that are embarrassing to the director and the hospital.

As an example of how managing a difficult patient can benefit a hospital director, the staff of the Clinical Research Unit at Camarillo State Hospital agreed to accept a young man with brain damage whose behavioral excesses had made him persona non grata to almost every mental hospital in the state of California. He spit on people and on furniture over 1000 times a day and engaged in a high rate of verbal and physical abuse. He was hyperactive, enuretic, and destructive of the physical environment.

His parents were very influential in the state government and made the lives of top administrators, including the directors of the various hospitals where the young man had been treated, very uncomfortable. Knowing the special behavior modification capabilities of our unit, our hospital director asked us if we would be willing to work with the patient. We agreed and the director offered our services to his boss higher up in the state department of health. The patient came to our unit and, after 2 years of intensive treatment using time-out from reinforcement, positive practice, overcorrection, and token economy, he made substantial improvements in his functioning. The patient is pleased, since he will be able to live in a less restrictive setting, his parents are pleased, the officials in the state department of health are pleased, and our hospital director is pleased. The hospital director is able to take credit for the treatment's effectiveness. The staff of the Clinical Research Unit are pleased not only because the patient has significantly improved, but also because support from the hospital director has been enhanced.

Maintaining Staff Performance

The same types of interventions used successfully in the social learning approach to patients can be employed to maintain the performance of staff members once a behavioral program is in operation. Stimulus control, prompting, modeling, and reinforcement contingencies are all valuable in the maintenance of performance (McGinnis, 1976). Risley and his colleagues (Cataldo & Risley, 1974; Doke & Risley, 1972; LeLaurin & Risley, 1972) have shown in a series of studies how systematic scheduling of staff and displaying cues for staff action improve performance and interaction between staff and residents in a variety of settings. Staff behavior is governed by the instructions and cues embedded in the program structure and schedule. In a study carried out at the Clinical Research Unit at Camarillo State Hospital, it was found that scheduling group activity and therapy sessions increased patient–staff interaction significantly more than a program using individual therapy alone (Olofsson, Wallace, & Liberman, 1978). The use of posted clipboards with treatment memos and data sheets has been found to be an effective cue for staff in both state hospital and community-based day hospitals (Liberman et al., 1976).

Modeling by professional staff and by nursing leaders can have a profound impact upon the efforts of line staff. In one study, the charge nurse of a psychiatric in-patient unit was found to be extremely powerful in maintaining nursing staff involvement with patients during activity groups when she herself was present at the activity and modeled appropriate nurse–patient interaction (Wallace, Davis, Liberman, & Baker, 1973).

Reinforcement contingencies are also important in maintaining staff performance. Salary contingencies have been established in a community mental health center in which clinical staff are paid in proportion to the amount of data collected. While this may be a possible strategy to pursue in private or independent, nonprofit mental health centers where empiricism and behavior modification is highly regarded at the top echelons (Turner & Goodson, 1977), it is not realistic for most existing centers, which are imbedded in inflexible, public agency pay regulations. In fact, tangible reinforcers such as gifts and restaurant dinners have backfired when introduced as bonuses for high levels of staff performance in state hospitals and community mental health centers. Nursing personnel protested that they felt demeaned by the implicit assumption that they needed material incentives to carry out their professional responsibilities. Tangible rewards were an insult to their professional integrity.

When introduced humorously, however, tangible reinforcers can be effective. At one point, the nursing staff on the Clinical Research Unit were dissatisfied with the miniscule amount of time I spent on the unit devoting myself to the clinical care of patients. They confronted me with their concerns and we worked out a contingency contract: I agreed to spend an average of 30 minutes per day on the unit. I had to forfeit 50 cents for each minute below the 30 minutes per day to a fund kept by the charge nurse. If I averaged 30 minutes per day or more, then the charge nurse had to bake me a batch of fudge. This program, which worked, was lightheartedly termed TRUSS—Timetable to Regulate Unit Support from Sawbones (Davis, Williams, & Baker, 1977).

Giving staff members informational feedback on their performance has proven to be effective in enhancing their performance. Panyan, Boozer, and Morris (1970) provided staff members with feedback on the number of training sessions they conducted with retarded residents and found large increases in the percentage of assigned sessions actually conducted. At the Clinical Research Unit at Camarillo State Hospital, a weekly newsletter was published for staff members that gave information on the progress of patients and highlighted the efforts of employees (Patterson, Cooke, & Liberman, 1972). On the same unit, the late-night shift graphs the data from each day's observations and treatment sessions; these graphs are then displayed at twice weekly team meetings to help staff make decisions about changes in patients' programs. Seeing that their data-collection efforts concretely contribute to treatment decisions reinforces staff for the extra efforts required on a behavior modification unit (Liberman, Wallace, Teigen, & Davis, 1974).

Perhaps the most important reinforcement contingencies to maintain staff performance are those that involve the natural consequences of working efficiently and competently; namely, social reward, praise, and spontaneous warmth expressed by the supervisors to the staff. A combination of natural, symbolic, and social reinforcement was used to sustain specification, measurement, and behavioral interventions by the clinical staff of the Oxnard CMHC. While the behavior therapist who enters a community mental health center with hopes of introducing behavioral technology to the clinical staff does not have to sacrifice professional reinforcers, such as publications and scientific meetings, he or she must add to the reinforcement hierarchy the production of competence, recognition, and job satisfaction in the paraprofessional staff.

One source of reinforcers for the CMHC staff was the granting of college credits by local junior colleges and universities. The credits were given to the staff contingent on their completing reading assignments and demonstrating mastery on performance measures for the inservice training. For example, toward the end of the year's training of the day treatment team, staff members obtained college credit if they wrote and verbally presented a synopsis of a clinical case, complete with descriptions of the patient, the methods and interventions used, reliability assessments, results graphed, and discussion of implications for generalization.

The Ventura County Mental Health Department, which administers and supports the Oxnard Mental Health Center, required annual performance reviews and semiannual listings of performance objectives for each staff member. Some of the staff members included the obtaining of college credits and the mastery of a behavioral technique in their personal objectives, thereby further strengthening the reward value of the behavior modification training.

Wherever possible, the staff of the Day Treatment Center were also involved in the receipt of the usual reinforcers for doing research. Staff members have been junior authors on publications of work they have been involved with, they have been consultants to other mental health organizations, and they have conducted tours of the Day Treatment Center for the university and clinical personnel who have heard of the program and have come to visit. Students in psychology, nursing, social work, and residents in psychiatry regularly rotated through the center for training.

The most important natural consequence for maintaining and expanding innovation was the social attention given by the professional consultants, who were viewed as available and effective resource persons. At the Oxnard Mental Health Center, the professionals attended all supervision sessions and case reviews with staff members focusing on the Behavioral Progress Records. Support and encouragement was provided for ingenious, creative interventions with clients, for example, interventions in the homes using relatives as mediators. The staff were praised for setting realistic, functional, and specific goals. The professionals were available for consultation on difficult problems and could be called in by the paraprofessional staff to assist in an intervention or demonstrate a new technique. Professionals from the BAM Project attended staff members' performance reviews and encouraged the staff to set specific objectives for the future that expanded their competence in behavior analysis and modification. For example, some staff members took university-sponsored workshops in sexual counseling, assertion training, interventions with children, and family and couple therapy. Others set performance goals to develop a new workshop for the center or participate in an experimental study with the BAM Project. In short, the innovator's role in a community treatment program should be as a model and reinforcer for the staff performing the direct services. To be effective as a model and reinforcer, he or she must be available, down-to-earth, assertive, and competent as an organizer and clinician.

SUMMARY

Efforts to apply behavioral and learning principles to human problems in hospitals, clinics, schools, and other institutions are limited more by political and social factors than by treatment and educational technology. The consultant or innovator who plans to foster change in a program using behavioral methods should consider the dimensions of power, affection, and task orientation as they relate to the interactions of people within the program and to the connections between the program and its larger social network.

Kurt Lewin once said, "If you want to find out about a system, try to change it." Behavior modifiers have tried to change systems and are only now finding out how they operate. The discovery process has sobered behavior therapists, many of whom began with rosy-hued and optimistic zeal and no realistic appreciation of the limitations and obstacles involved in effecting change. Success in carrying out a programmatic innovation requires stepwise progression through a series of potential obstacles— entering a setting, demonstrating competence, setting goals and time frames, maintaining flexibility, dealing with institutional constraints, coping with sources of conflict, maintaining support from the power structure, and maintaining staff performance. The social value of behavior therapy will ultimately depend not only on its future technological and empirically validated effectiveness, but also on the ability of its proponents to cope with these political and social obstacles to change.

ACKNOWLEDGMENTS

The author acknowledges the vital contributions and ideas of the following colleagues, whose collaboration provided the rich and fruitful experience from which this chapter derives: William J. DeRisi, Larry W. King, Charles J. Wallace, Roger L. Patterson, James Teigen, Robert A. Aitchison, Thad Eckman, Timothy and Julie Kuehnel, Peter N. Alevizos, Edward Callahan, Richard Rawson, Stephen Flanagan, Jeffrey Rosenstein, Francis Lillie, Chris Ferris, Rafael Canton, and Clinton Rust.

REFERENCES

Alinsky, S. *Rules for radicals: A pragmatic primer for realistic radicals.* New York: Vintage Books, 1972.

Cataldo, M., & Risley, T. R. Evaluation of living environments: The MANIFEST description of ward activities. In P. O. Davidson, F. W. Clark, & L. A. Hamerlynck (Eds.), *Evaluation of behavioral programs in community, residential and school settings.* Champaign, Ill.: Research Press, 1974. Pp. 201–222.

Davis, J., Williams, S., & Baker, V. TRUSS: A contingency contract to make sure the unit physician drops by once in a while. *Hospital and Community Psychiatry,* 1977, *28,* 13.

Doke, L. A., & Risley, T. R. The organization of day care environments: Required vs. optional activities. *Journal of Applied Behavior Analysis,* 1972, *5,* 405–420.

Graziano, A. *Child without tomorrow.* Elmsford, N. Y.: Pergamon, 1975.

Kazdin, A. E. Chronic psychiatric patients: Ward-wide reinforcement programs. In M. Hersen & A. Bellack (Eds.), *Behavior therapy in the psychiatric setting.* Baltimore: Williams & Wilkins, 1978. Pp. 91–127.

King, L. W., Austin, N., Liberman, R. P., & DeRisi, W. J. Accountability, like charity, begins at home. *Evaluation,* 1974, *2,* 75–77.

LeLaurin, K., & Risley, T. R. The organization of day care environments: "Zone" vs. "man-to-man" staff assignments. *Journal of Applied Behavior Analysis,* 1972, *5,* 225–232.

Liberman, R. P. Behavioral measurement in clinical settings or how to keep the charts dry in rough seas. In R. Rubin, H. Fensterheim, J. D. Henderson, & L. Ullmann (Eds.), *Advances in behavior therapy* (Vol. 3). New York: Academic Press, 1972. Pp. 65–71.

Liberman, R. P., King, L. W., & DeRisi, W. J. Behavior analysis and therapy in community mental health. In H. Leitenberg (Ed.), *Handbook of behavior modification and behavior therapy.* Englewood Cliffs, N.J.: Prentice-Hall, 1976. Pp. 566–603.

Liberman, R. P., Wallace, C. J., Teigen, J., & Davis, J. Behavioral interventions with psychotics. In K. S. Calhoun, H. E. Adams, & E. M. Mitchell (Eds.), *Innovative treatment methods in psychopathology.* New York: Wiley, 1974. Pp. 323–412.

Lucero, R. J., & Vail, D. J. Public policy and public responsibility. *Hospital and Community Psychiatry,* 1968, *19,* 232–233.

McGinnis, T. Training and maintaining staff behaviors in residential treatment programs. In R. L. Patterson (Ed.), *Maintaining effective token economies.* Springfield, Ill.: Thomas, 1976. Pp. 32–68.

Olofsson, R., Wallace, C. W., & Liberman, R. P. *Evaluating effects of scheduled group activities on a psychiatric unit.* Unpublished manuscript available from the first author, Department of Psychology, University of Uppsala, Box 227, S-75104, Uppsala, Sweden, 1978.

Panyan, M., Boozer, H., & Morris, N. Feedback to attendants as a reinforcer for applying operant techniques. *Journal of Applied Behavior Analysis,* 1970, *3,* 1–4.

Patterson, R., Cooke, C., & Liberman, R. P. Reinforcing the reinforcers: A method of supplying feedback to nursing personnel. *Behavior Therapy,* 1972, *3,* 444–446.

Reppucci, N. D., & Saunders, J. T. Social psychology of behavior modification. *American Psychologist,* 1974, *29,* 649–660.

Risley, T. R. Behavior modification: An experimental–therapeutic endeavor. In R. Rubin, H. Fensterheim, J. D. Henderson, & L. Ullmann (Eds.), *Advances in behavior therapy* (Vol. 3). New York: Academic Press, 1972. Pp. 37–52.

Tharp, R. G., & Wetzel, R. J. *Behavior modification in the natural environment.* New York: Academic Press, 1969.

Thomas, D. R. *Staff competencies required for implementation of aversive and deprivation procedures.* Paper presented at Annual Meeting of the American Psychological Association, San Francisco, August 1977.

Turner, A. J., & Goodson, W. H. Behavioral technology applied to a community mental health center: Administration. *Journal of Community Psychology, 1977, 5,* 209–224.

Wallace, C. J., Davis, J., Liberman, R. P., & Baker, V. Modeling and staff behavior. *Journal of Clinical and Consulting Psychology, 1973, 41,* 422–425

Weiner, H. Comments on Dr. Risley's paper. In R. Rubin, H. Fensterheim, J. D. Henderson, & L. Ullman (Eds.), *Advances in behavior therapy* (Vol. 3). New York: Academic Press, 1972. Pp. 61–64.

Wexler, D. Token and taboo: Behavior modification, token economics and the law. *California Law Review, 1973, 61,* 81–109.

Index